THE RIGHT CHOICE

THE INCREDIBLE FAILURE

OF PUBLIC EDUCATION

AND THE RISING HOPE OF

HOME
SCHOOLING

An Academic, Historical,

Practical, and Legal Perspective

by

Christopher J. Klicka

With Supplementary Chapters by Gregg Harris

NOBLE PUBLISHING ASSOCIATES

GRESHAM, OREGON

NOBLE PUBLISHING ASSOCIATES

Noble Publishing Associates, the publishing arm of Christian Life Workshops, is an association of Christian authors dedicated to serving God and assisting one another in the production, promotion, and distribution of audio, video, and print publications. For instructions on how you may participate in our association, or for information about our complete line of materials write to: NPA, P.O. Box 2250, Gresham, Oregon 97030 or call (503) 667-3942.

ISBN: 0-923463-83-6
Printed in the United States of America.

Dedication

To all home schooling parents who love the Lord and are dying to themselves in order to diligently train their children according to God's law, despite legal or financial hardship or the criticism of others.

Foreword
by D. James Kennedy, Ph.D.

From the earliest days of my ministry, I have borne the conviction that apostasy and anarchy can dominate the life of any nation if the coming generation fails to share the beliefs and ethical values of godly parents. This very day, I am shocked by the realization that, although our Pilgrim Fathers stated in the Mayflower Compact that they would create schools to teach their children the Word of God, it is now unlawful for children in the public schools to read or hear the Word or even to pray publicly to the God of the Bible.

That is why I began a Christian school, deliberately placed under the oversight of the elders of Coral Ridge Presbyterian Church, and with a school board made up of parents who were members of the congregation. In 1971, that was considered a drastic step, but the success of Westminster Academy over the years has placed it in the forefront of Florida's total educational effort.

For the same reason, I welcome this exciting new book by Dr. Klicka, THE RIGHT CHOICE: The Incredible Failure of Public Education and The Rising Hope of Home Schooling—a subject which is considered by many to be as drastic an innovation. You will be convinced by the urgent need for and the invaluable contribution by home schooling as analyzed and prescribed in this scholarly volume.

Let me warn you that the brilliant research which went into the compilation of the facts presented in this book will astound you and shock you. It is difficult for most of us to understand just how insidious and how tireless have been the efforts of secular humanism in the rewriting of curricula and textbooks for the purpose of indoctrinating an entire generation of young people in America's public school systems today.

If you are concerned, and desire authoritative information on what is right about carefully structured Christian home schooling—you will not find a more reliable and enlightening source book than this outstanding work written by the senior counsel for the Home School Legal Defense Association.

Few Americans realize that, from 1620 when the Pilgrims landed until 1837, virtually all education in this country was private and Christian. THE RIGHT CHOICE: The Incredible Failure of Public Education and The Rising Hope of Home Schooling, squarely based on historical principles, brings us to examine the roots that made America great.

Contents

Acknowledgments

My first thanks goes to the Lord who has saved me for all eternity and has brought me to the place where I am today. I praise Him for freely giving me the blessing and privilege of having such a wonderful wife and children and such a tremendous job at the Home School Legal Defense Association.

Special thanks to my wife, Tracy, who supported me throughout this three-year project and encouraged me to complete it. I also thank my children, Bethany, Megan, and Jesse, for helping me realize that children are a gift from God and one of the greatest privileges and responsibilities we have on earth. My daily time with them convinced me that the training of their hearts and minds in the Lord and their education are priorities which demand my time and should not be delegated to those who do not know God.

I want to thank Gregg Harris, my publisher and friend, who made this book possible. His ministry to home schoolers throughout the nation has always been an inspiration to my family and me. His home schooling workshops are helping to fuel the spiritual revival among home schoolers and train them in God's principles.

I also want to thank Matt Arnold, home schooling dad and cartoonist, who provided the illustrations.

I would like to give special thanks to Mike Farris, president of the Home School Legal Defense Association, and Mike Smith, vice-president. I thank both of them for their vision in establishing the Home School Legal Defense Association, their love and godly training of their children, their hearts in desiring to protect families from an ever-encroaching state, and their constant friendship, advice, and encouragement to me over the last seven years.

I thank Ross Tunnell and "Magnificent Graphics" for editing and typesetting my book and changing it to its present form.

Finally, a special word of appreciation goes to John Whitehead of the Rutherford Institute, who got me involved in writing this book, reviewed the original draft in 1990, and encouraged me to have it published.

Preface

Home schooling is an age-old educational method that has experienced a resurgence, beginning in the 1970s in the United States. This resurgence indicates a definite trend away from conventional schooling and standardized educational methods, and a return to the traditional tutorial process involving individualized instruction and apprenticeships. Furthermore, the home schooling movement is representative of a desire of parents to personally teach their own children at home in order to restore the traditional Christian values in education and bring unity to the family. These parents, for the most part, are seeking to train their children in God's principles, so they will grow up to love and obey God.

In short, families who are home schooling are making the "right choice." In many ways home schooling is a moral and spiritual revival where children are being seriously trained in God's Word to not only believe as Christians but to think and live as Christians. Furthermore, home schooling is a return to parent-controlled education with an emphasis on learning the basics and achieving academic excellence. This restoration process is being led by parents willing to take responsibility and to commit themselves to thoroughly educating their children in spite of the sacrifice. This restoration process is succeeding as home schooling is producing skilled and academically talented children with moral fortitude and leadership abilities.

This educational movement, however, has been misunderstood and, in many cases, condemned by the state and public school officials. These officials are convinced that, as representatives of the state, they are guardians of the children and therefore know what is best for the children. As a result, this attempt to restore effective parent-controlled education is meeting intense opposition as home schooling parents are frequently prosecuted under state compulsory attendance and educational neglect laws. This conflict can be narrowed down to one basic issue: to what extent may the state restrict the constitutional right of parents to direct the education of their children? This question is still in the process of being answered, as hundreds of courts and dozens of legislatures debate the subject of home schooling.

I am a home schooling parent and a full-time home schooling attorney. As I have worked to protect home schoolers in the courts and legislatures, I have witnessed first-hand the academic successes and legal struggles of home schoolers. I believe the preservation of the right of parents to teach their children at home is vital to the preservation of freedom, in general, in our country, especially parental and religious freedom. As the moral foundations of our nation are being steadily eroded by textbooks and valueless training which our children are receiving through the public school system, the home school movement is applying biblical principles and absolute truths to each area of academic discipline. Grounding the children in the fundamental truths on which our country was founded is the only way that we, as a nation, will continue to enjoy the liberty that our forefathers secured for us.

In addition, the home schoolers are providing a solution to the educational crisis generated by the incredible failure of the public school system, as the home school children consistently, on the average, academically out-perform their public school counterparts. Home school children are becoming more and more in demand, both in universities and in the work place.

Since home school children will have a strong moral and academic foundation, they will be the leaders of tomorrow who will be able to fill the vacuum being created by the public schools.

The home school families are accomplishing these goals, family by family. Through the growth of the home school movement, families, which provide the backbone of our nation, are being preserved and strengthened.

In the following pages, I expose the modern academic, moral, and philosophical crisis in the public schools and thoroughly explore the solution of home schooling. The chapters include the historical account of home schooling, with a chapter on famous home schoolers of the past. The success of home schooling, the benefits, and the reasons why more and more parents are turning to home schooling will be presented and documented. Also I summarize the biblical principles involved, in order to challenge the readers to make the raising of our children in the Lord a priority and to persuade them that the modern public schools are no place to send our children.

Furthermore, I describe the conflict taking place between home schoolers and the state's attempt to restrict their freedom. Some chapters cover encounters with child welfare investigators, illegal home visits by school officials, the myth of teacher qualifications, and identification of the educational elite who are working to abolish parental rights. I discuss the "pros and cons" of testing requirements, and I identify the rights of home schoolers in the military and the rights of parents home schooling handicapped children.

In addition, I touch on the constitutional defenses and legislative trends involved in preserving the liberty of parents in this crucial area. Parents need to be familiar with their God-given parental rights, as guaranteed in our country. The last few chapters describe some practical tips on how to deal with the media, legislature, and courts. Also an index to home schooling resource organizations is included.

Gregg Harris, a home schooling father and seminar leader, who has dedicated his life to training and encouraging parents in the biblical principles of child instruction and family, has authored chapters 8 and 9 in which he describes the basic steps on how to home school.

I also hope parents will assign this book as required reading for their junior high and high school students. I believe this book will help them appreciate the parent's commitment to home schooling as they consider the advantages of home schooling, its heritage, and the chaos in the public schools. My hope is that our children will want to home school their children and continue from generation to generation. Toward this goal, I have written a special introduction for the home school student.

In conclusion, the future of liberty in our country and the very survival of the family may depend on our commitment to home schooling in both preservation and practice in the coming years. Let us, therefore, make the "right choice" and do all we can to protect this right to teach our children and commit ourselves to training our children in the Lord. A nation and future generations are at stake.

                              Christopher J. Klicka
                              September 8, 1992

Introduction

A n Introduction Specifically for the Home School Student

This book was not written only for parents, but also for home school students. I believe it is vitally important for you, the student at home, to be aware of your heritage as a home schooler and the purpose of home schooling. As you read portions of this book, you will become aware of the extraordinary benefits of home schooling, that many youth will never enjoy.

You will begin to see why your parents have chosen this "different" form of education and have come to appreciate more fully the commitment and sacrifice they have willingly taken upon themselves. When most parents at this time are selfishly seeking their own careers and personal satisfaction, your parents are devoting their time to you. Many other parents send their children to Day Care and then to twelve years at the public school, unaware of the damage they are inflicting on their children emotionally, spiritually, and mentally. By home schooling you, your parents show they care about you and your future.

If you read the first three chapters, you will see what you are "missing" in the public schools. You will see both the blatant problems and the subtle deceptions. God, our Creator and Redeemer, is mocked or ignored in the public schools. Immaturity and selfishness is encouraged. The curriculum teaches that wrong is right, and right is wrong. The academic training in the public schools has brought us shame and is a joke to other industrial nations. By participating in home schooling, you are avoiding wasting a lot of time!

Part Two will show the history and tremendous success of home schooling. You will see renowned scientists, presidents, statesmen, lawyers, businessmen, artists, preachers, educators, and many more men and women from the past who were home schooled. You can take pride in this heritage. I encourage you to study the lives of many of these men and women who lived for the Lord. You will also read about the commands that God has given to your parents to raise you and teach you thoroughly in biblical principles.

As you read the many advantages of home schooling and the consistent academic success of home school students throughout the nation, you will come to realize that home schooling really works. Many home-schooled students have pioneered ahead of you, gaining entrance into colleges and universities throughout the country. This, of course, requires much self-discipline and diligence in your studies now. Without your commitment to learn and your desire to prepare for your future, the benefits of your home schooling will be limited.

The rest of the book will help you see the legal rights and risks of home schooling. You will begin to understand the real legal dangers faced by your parents as they teach you themselves. You will become aware of the forces that are committed to break up your family and take over the minds of the nation's youth. You will see how far we have come in the struggle to restore our rights to be free from excessive governmental intrusions into our families. If you are interested in studying law, you will learn much about the

Constitutional protections of our freedoms and the legal strategies used to preserve our rights.

You are participating in an important historical movement. You make up, in many ways, the hope of the future of our nation. You and hundreds of thousands of home-schooled students around the nation are being grounded in biblical truth and established in academic excellence. You will be able to lead, while many of those in public schools will be floundering. If you take to heart God's principles and love the Lord with all your heart, soul, and mind, you will be wise and you will be blessed. Hopefully, you will begin to develop a vision of where you are going after you leave home and how you can make a difference for the Lord's Kingdom.

Therefore, count yourself privileged to have this opportunity to be home schooled in this day and age. I encourage you to dedicate yourself first to seeking the kingdom of God, and second to disciplining yourself to diligently study and learn. May God bless you as you serve Him!

Christopher J. Klicka

PART
1

THE INCREDIBLE FAILURE
OF PUBLIC EDUCATION

One of the major reasons why people are turning to home schooling is because the state-run public school system has become both academically and morally bankrupt. Since 1963 public schools have virtually been in a "tail spin" with SAT (Scholastic Aptitude Test) scores consistently declining, academic performance dropping, illiteracy increasing, morality slipping, and violence escalating. The educational empire and virtual monopoly of the public school system is starting to crumble. The bankrupt philosophy behind the public school "movers and shakers," both past and present, has led the whole massive system into a moral and academic disaster for millions of students.

Home schooling parents are beginning to say, "We can do a better job ourselves," and they are doing just that! In Part Two it will be shown that the educational restoration process of home schooling is taking place in the midst of a national educational crisis.

These next three chapters will describe the poor condition of the public school system in which nearly 40 million children in the United States are presently being trained.

It is important to note that the academic, moral, and philosophical crisis is clearly affecting all public schools. The following documentation will demonstrate this universal failure of the public schools. It is intellectual dishonesty to believe your local public school is exempt from these destructive influences. The question you must ask yourself is, "How can I prevent my child from becoming one of these statistics?"

CHAPTER 1

THE ACADEMIC CRISIS
IN PUBLIC EDUCATION

"Bill Bennett thinks the schools ought to get five more years to get back to where they were in 1963. 'If they're still bad,' he says, 'maybe we should declare educational bankruptcy, give the people their money and let them educate themselves and start their own schools.'"[1]

"We must do better or perish as the nation we know today."[2]
—Former Secretary of Education Lauro Cavazos.

These two former Secretaries of Education give a startling description of the crisis in education in the public school empire in which nearly forty million children are being taught. A child who attends public school from kindergarten to twelfth grade will spend about fifteen thousand hours there. Since 1963 the public school system has experienced a steady decline in literacy.

Hopefully, these warnings and the alarming statistics below will convince you that sending your children to the modern public school system involves a tremendous risk. Your child could become one of these statistics of failure.

Public Schools Are Failing in 1982

In 1982, the federal government decided the public school system needed a thorough examination. President Reagan formed the National Commission on Excellence in Education which published its findings in the report "A Nation at Risk: The Imperative for Education Reform." The report stated:

> The educational foundations of our society are presently being eroded by a rising tide of mediocrity that threatens our very future as a Nation and a people. . . . If an unfriendly foreign power had attempted to impose on America the mediocre educational performance that exists today, we might well have viewed it as an act of war. As it stands, we have allowed this to happen to ourselves. We have even squandered the gains in student achievement made in the wake of the Sputnik challenge. Moreover, we have dismantled essential support systems which helped make those gains possible. We have, in effect, been committing an act of unthinking, unilateral educational disarmament.[3]

Furthermore, according to the National Commission on Excellence in Education study, public school children in the United States fall short of those in other industrialized countries by nineteen measures of academic achievement. The most significant areas of decline have been in math and reading skills and logic and the ability to draw inferences. One writer commented on the results of the study:

> One of the most shocking findings is that only one-fifth of the seventeen-year-olds in public education can write a persuasive essay; only one-third can solve a mathematical problem requiring several steps; and 13 percent, by the simplest tests of reading, writing and comprehension, are functionally illiterate. [4]

Moreover, the study found that 27 million illiterates were in our nation, most of them churned out by our public school factory. The estimate for functionally illiterate people is at 45 million.

Once the country was alerted, federal and state reforms were begun, and the amount of funds channeled to public education was almost doubled. After over ten years, however, no significant change has occurred. The public school system, both academically and morally, is still failing. In fact, it is destroying America's youth.

After "Reforms" Public Schools Are Still Failing in 1988

On April 26, 1988, Secretary of Education William Bennett released a report assessing America's educational progress since 1983, when the National Commission on Excellence in Education declared the United States to be a "nation at risk." The secretary concluded, "We are still at risk."[5]

This 1988 report discussed results from various statistics gathered from the National Assessment of Educational Progress (NAEP). Concerning writing the report states, "The general picture for all students is still no better than it was in 1974." NAEP's evaluation of its most recent writing assessment is that "performance in writing in our schools is, quite simply, bad."[6]

The results in literature surveys conducted by the NAEP found that children in the public schools knew little about the subject. Less than 50 percent of seventeen-year-olds knew that Byron, Keats, and Wordsworth were poets. Less than 17 percent knew that Tocqueville wrote Democracy in America.[7]

In math, the report documents that American first and fifth graders were found to be lagging badly behind similar groups of students in Japan, Taiwan, and China.[8] Knowledge of history was particularly discouraging according to the "Education for Democracy Project," which was reviewed in Bennett's report. The Project issued this statement, "Many students are unaware of prominent people and seminal ideas and events that have shaped our past and created our present."[9] Bennett's report reviewed the NAEP's 1986 assessment which exposed the glaring lack of historical knowledge by seventeen-year-olds in the public schools. More than two thirds of them did not know when the Civil War occurred while three fourths of them could not say within twenty years when Abraham Lincoln was president.

More than one-fifth of the students could not identify
George Washington as the commander of the colonial
forces during the Revolution. Almost one in three did not
know Lincoln was the author of the Emancipation
Proclamation. And nearly half failed to recognize Patrick
Henry as the man who said "Give me liberty or give me
death." . . . Half the students did not know the meaning of
the Monroe doctrine. . . . Almost 70 percent did not
understand what Jim Crow laws were designed to do.[10]

Ignorance of history will cause disaster for the United States
because the public school children will be condemned to repeat the
mistakes of the past, once they are in positions of authority.

History Rewritten

One reason the public school students are not learning important
history is because the textbook publishers have purposely rewritten
history. The American Federation of Teachers, in a study released
September 13, 1989, found the most important facts missing out of
high school textbooks for public school students. AFT President
Albert Shanker explained that while public school history textbooks
have some good points, "there's a lot that is missing, and what's
missing is important. . . . There is little to convey the ideas, passions,
religious views, and values that would give students a greater sense" of
America's beginnings.[11] Paul Gagan, one of the historians
commissioned to review the textbooks, said the books "fail to make
explicit enough the sacrifices, hard thought, hard work, and high cost
of producing and sustaining democracy in America."[12]

The study criticized the high school textbooks for providing little
to no biographical detail on key leaders. For example, one book
summarizes Abraham Lincoln's and George Washington's lives in
approximately six lines each. Also, the books "contain little about the
impact of religion and religious beliefs in history. Texts rarely discuss
the religious ideas shared in communities and the religious
convictions that motivated many leaders."[13]

Pro-Communist Propaganda

In addition, public school history books are filled with pro-
Communist propaganda. The American Textbook Council reviewed
several current elementary and high school history books and found

quite an inaccurate picture of the Soviet Union (before the fall of communism). The Communist Soviet Union was depicted as providing "all its people with free medical care, free dental care, free day care for small children and free vacations."[14] Furthermore, Russia was described as manufacturing "almost everything, from buses to clothes and from refrigerators to computers." Stalin is shown to be an agricultural hero. Nothing is said of Stalin' s atrocities in murdering millions of peasants and farmers. Nothing is said of the economic crisis in the Soviet Union and the long bread lines resulting from Communist policies.[15]

Numerous Historical Errors in the Textbooks

A further problem that plagues history instruction in the public schools: lack of accurate textbooks. For instance, the Texas Board of Education was in the process of adopting new history textbooks when Mel and Norma Gabler announced they had found 231 "definite, unmistakable, undetected errors of fact."[16] Some of the errors in the public school textbooks included claims that the atomic bomb ended the Korean War (instead of World War II) and that only 53,000 rather than 126,000 Americans were killed in World War I. Also the wrong dates were given for numerous events, including the invention of the telegraph, the first moon walk, the bombing of Pearl Harbor, and the assassination of John F. Kennedy.[17] Each year the Gablers catch hundreds of errors in textbooks designated to be used in the Texas public schools.

Bias against Free-Market Economics

Meanwhile, the schools are consistently producing graduates with little to no understanding or appreciation of America's successful free-market system. Columnist Warren Brookes recounts the conclusion of Milton Friedman:

> I asked Nobelist economist Milton Friedman why most American students still graduate from high schools not only with low performance but with such a socialist perspective. . . . His answer was characteristically clear: "Because they are products of a socialist system. How can you expect such a system to inculcate the values of enterprise and competition, when it is based on monopoly state ownership?"[18]

Friedman is absolutely right. America's public education system is a Socialist system in which the government takes money from those who do not send their children to public school (and who still must pay to educate their children privately) and uses that money to endlessly support a bloated educational monopoly. The public schools hate competition, so how can they teach it?

Even general economic knowledge is sorely lacking. In 1989 the Joint Council on Economic Education administered a basic economics test to 8,205 high school juniors and seniors. Overall, the students only answered 40 percent of the questions correctly on a standard multiple choice test. Only 25 percent demonstrated a clear understanding of inflation, only 34 percent could define profits, and only 39 percent could define the Gross National Product.[19]

Geography Crisis

Geography is not much better. A 1988-89 Gallup Poll, commissioned by the National Geographic Society, found that American students ages eighteen to twenty-four came in last among ten countries tested in geography. Half of the American students did not know the Panama Canal cuts sailing time between New York and San Francisco.[20]

Public Schools Are Still Failing in Reading and Writing in 1990

In January 1990, Secretary of Education Lauro Cavazos released the results of two nationwide tests in reading and writing administered by the NAEP. The Secretary remarked that the reading and writing skills of children in the public school are "dreadfully inadequate," despite a decade of "education reforms."[21] The NAEP report found 58 percent of seventeen-year-olds cannot understand a twelfth grade academic textbook or comprehend many articles in the *Wall Street Journal, Time*, or *Newsweek*. Ninety-five percent of the seventeen-year-olds do not have the reading skills to understand college-level textbooks. Forty-two percent of thirteen-year-olds and 14 percent of seventeen-year-olds cannot read at the eighth grade level, which is about the level of *People* magazine.[22]

Furthermore, in the area of writing, the NAEP test results demonstrated that 85 percent of fourth graders cannot write a well-developed story, and 72 percent of eleventh graders cannot write an adequate, persuasive article. Meanwhile, eighth graders showed a significant, steady decline in the last four years.[23]

Public Schools Are Still Failing Math in 1990 and 1991

Since 1973, national math tests have shown consistently dismal results. The most recent statistics, after years of "reform," were released in the 1990 Nation's Report Card. The results were so poor that Education Secretary Lamar Alexander declared a "math emergency" saying, "None of the states are cutting it. This is an alarm bell that should ring all night in this country."[24] The secretary should have added that this alarm should continue to ring every day and night until Americans wake up.

The math test was given to 126,000 students in grades four, eight, and twelve, and it caused one commentator to remark:

> How bad are eighth graders' math skills? So bad that half are scoring just above the proficiency level expected of fifth-grade students. Even the best students did miserably; at the top-scoring schools, the average was well below grade level. Hardly any students have the background to go beyond simple computation; most of these kids can add but they have serious trouble thinking through simple problems.[25]

Only 14 percent of eighth graders scored at the seventh grade level or above, regardless of whether the students were in a wealthy suburban system or a poor school system.[26]

It seems apparent from these math test results and the many other studies described above that the longer children are in public school, the worse they perform academically. In the Nation's Report Card, for example, 72 percent of fourth graders tested at or above the third grade level, and 11 percent scored at or above the fifth grade level. However, only 46 percent of twelfth graders could perform *seventh grade work* and only 5 percent could do pre-calculus work![27]

This has been documented in many other studies, including one study released on February 11, 1992, concerning the failing public schools in the District of Columbia. The study demonstrated that in reading, children were scoring on the average 52d percentile in the sixth grade, 42d percentile in ninth grade, and 32d percentile in the eleventh grade. Similarly, in math, children in sixth grade scored in the 67th percentile, in the ninth grade the 50th percentile, and in the eleventh grade the 42d percentile.[28] The longer the children are in the public schools, the worse their academic achievements. Does that tell us something about the methods of teaching in the public schools?

On September 30, 1991, the nation's governors released the "National Educational Goals Report" which documented math skills to be even worse. The report found only 15 percent of fourth graders, 18 percent of eighth graders, and 16 percent of twelfth graders reached a "competent" level on a 1990 math survey test.[29]

After a Decade of "Reforms," Public Schools Are Worse

On January 31, 1992, the U.S. Department of Education released a report that showed that the reading skills of nine-year-olds worsened during the 1980's when schools were supposed to be getting better due to massive reforms.[30] The study was based on a review of twenty years of NAEP tests. For example, in 1980, 68 percent of nine-year-olds could summarize the main idea of a passage. By 1990, only 59 percent of nine-year-olds could summarize it.[31] The reading proficiency scale, which measured skills of nine-year-olds, goes from a low of 150 to a high of 350. In 1990, students, on the average, scored only 209, with the 200 level being indicative of "partially developed skill and understanding."[32]

Meanwhile, a study was released in February 1992, which found U.S. students were below the world average in math and science.[33] The survey of 175,000 students worldwide was funded by the Department of Education, the National Science Foundation, and the Carnegie Foundation. In math, American thirteen-year-olds only averaged 55 percent correct answers, while Taiwan and Korea students averaged 73 percent correct, and the Soviet Union averaged 70 percent correct.[34] In science, American thirteen-year-olds scored on the average 67 percent, while Korea and Taiwan scored 78 percent. Some of the other countries that scored above the United States were Slovenia, France, Spain, Hungary, Italy, Israel, Scotland, and Canada. The survey also showed that longer school years and more money spent on education and teachers did not make a measurable difference on student achievement. Hungary, for example, only requires 177 days of instruction, and yet their students scored with the top five countries in both math and science.[35]

According to the 1990 Science Report Card, fewer than half of twelfth grade students could operate at a level of being capable of analyzing scientific procedures and data, and less than 10 percent reached the highest level which is the ability to integrate scientific information.[36]

This pattern is present in nearly all other areas of public education. Public school children are memorizing basic facts: look-say reading, science facts, etc. However, many children cannot think or process those facts into coherent paragraphs. They cannot analyze or integrate the scientific information.

Lack of Competency in Public School Teachers

One of the contributing factors to the academic decline in public schools is the training and competency of teachers. For instance, according to a study released in July 1991 by the Carnegie Commission on Science, Technology, and Government, more than 80 percent of math instructors are deficient in math![37] Also the study found more than two thirds of elementary school science teachers lacking adequate preparation in science.[38]

Rita Kramer documents in her recently released book Ed School Follies: The Miseducation of America's Teachers, that most future teachers who are trained in the nation's teacher colleges primarily receive indoctrination in politics rather than learning.[39] She explains, "Almost nowhere did I find teachers of teachers whose emphasis was on the measurable learning of real knowledge."[40] She spent a year touring fifteen teachers' colleges from Columbia to UCLA. Kramer concludes that America's schools of education are appalling. She found that among teacher-educators today "the goal of schooling is not considered to be instruction, let alone intellectual, but political."

> The aim is not to produce individuals capable of effort and mastery, but to make sure everyone gets a passing grade. The school is to be remade into a republic of feelings—as distinct from a republic of learning—where everyone can feel he deserves an A. . . .
>
> What matters is not to teach any particular subject or skill, not to preserve past accomplishments or stimulate future achievements, but to give everyone that stamp of approval that will make them "feel good about themselves." Self-

esteem has replaced understanding as the goal of education.[41]

Kramer discovered teacher colleges do not teach knowledge but rather four years of methods. As a result, they are "producing for the classrooms of America, experts in methods of teaching with nothing to apply those methods to." She says teachers are no longer being taught to teach reading, writing, history, science, math, or literature—rather they are being trained as counselors, psycho-therapists, social workers, babysitters, and policemen.[42] The "educators" are not educated in knowledge, nor do they love learning, and, as a result, they cannot instill a desire to learn in their students.

She soundly exposes the new emphasis in teacher training on "multiculturalism" and "globalism." She says such teaching is often nothing more than "a thinly disguised rejection of individualistic democratic values and institutions and of the very idea that underneath all our variety of cultural backgrounds, we Americans have been and should continue to become one nation, one culture."[43]

She blames much of the failure of the public schools on those who teach the teachers.

> Next to the media in general and the television in particular, our schools of education are the greatest contributor to the dumbing down of America. They have been transformed into agencies for social change, mandated to achieve equality at all costs, an equality not of opportunity but of outcome. No one can be tested because no one must fail.[44]

Kramer concludes by identifying exactly what the institutions which teach the teachers have become:

> The most prestigious of them are largely concerned with academic reputation within the university setting, competing for funds with the professional schools of law and medicine, and cranking out enormous amounts of research, much of it trivial, with much faculty time and energy writing grant proposals and designing model projects. Little of this helps the classroom teacher.

> The worst of them are certification mills where the minimally qualified instruct the barely literate in parody of learning. Prospective teachers leave, no more prepared to impart knowledge or inspire learning than when they entered.[45]

This poor training of future teachers is apparent in the low standards set by states for teachers to be certified to teach. In fact, fifteen states use exams supplied by the Educational Testing Service in Princeton, New Jersey and set cut-off scores that range from 35 to 55 percent.[46] In Kentucky, the low qualifying score for math certification is 35 percent. Other examples of cut-off scores are 40-45 percent in science, 40 to 55 percent in chemistry, and 40 to 60 percent in physics. These types of low scores would be an F or a D for students who took exams in these subjects. Yet, these same people teach thousands of children throughout the public school system every day.

The students attending teachers' colleges and pursuing education degrees are, on the average, below average on SAT scores. Consistently, these students who are planning to major in education scored below the national average. Such students' average verbal score is 406 (out of a possible 800; national average is 422) and their math score average is 441 (out of a possible 800; national average is 474).[47]

National Endowment for the Humanities Chairman Lynne V. Cheney released a report on November 11, 1991, concerning the failing educational practices in the public schools, including teacher training.[48] Her report concluded that future teachers would be better off spending more time on subject matter and less on "how-to-teach" courses.[49] She identified these failed educational practices as "tyrannical machines" and recommended encouragement of "alternative systems of education" and parents' right to choose.

Public School Teachers Know Something Most Americans Don't

Furthermore, many of these public school teachers send their children to private schools. They know first-hand how bad the public schools have become. For example, the deputy mayor of education of Chicago, Lourdes Monteagudo, says she is sending her eldest daughter to a suburban private academy because the quality of education in Chicago public schools is poor. "I could not support her staying in Chicago until the school system can be reformed because the system is bad."[50]

In fact, a U.S. Department of Education study demonstrates that public school teachers are more likely to send their children to a private school than any other group. The study shows that:

> In Albuquerque, 30 percent of the public school teachers
> send their children to private schools, compared with 14
> percent of the population at large. In Houston and Denver,
> the ratio is 22 to 13; in San Francisco, 28 to 19; in
> Baltimore, 27 to 16; in Los Angeles, 29 to 17; in Atlanta,
> 25 to 14; in Austin, 25 to 13. The cities with the highest
> private school enrollment of public teacher's children were
> New Orleans (50 percent), Washington, D.C. (40 percent),
> and Detroit (35 percent).[51]

Could the public school teachers know something about the
condition of American public schools that the majority of Americans
don't?

The Failure of the Look-Say Method of Reading

Another reason public schools have had difficulty teaching
children to read is because the educational elite have abandoned
time-tested educational techniques and have replaced them with new
and inadequate methods. For instance, the teaching of phonics has
been abandoned almost completely throughout the public school
system. Educational expert Samuel Blumenfeld discovered this
rejection of phonics to be to the detriment of millions of public
school children:

> In the course of researching this book, I made a shocking,
> incredible discovery: that for the last forty years the . . .
> children of America have been taught to read by a method
> (look-say) originally conceived and used in the early 1800s
> to teach the deaf how to read, a (experimental) method
> which has long since been discarded by the teachers of the
> deaf themselves as inadequate and outmoded. The result has
> been widespread reading disability.[52]

The U.S. Department of Education verifies the success of phonics:

> Classroom research shows that, on the average, children
> who are taught phonics get off to a better start in learning
> to read than children who are not taught phonics.[53]

In 1837 Horace Mann developed a reading system based on the
look and say method of memorization for the deaf that was applied in
the Boston schools. Although it was rejected after six years by the
Boston Board of Education, it was adopted later by John Dewey at the
University of Chicago and Arthur Gates at Columbia Teachers'
College. Now the faulty system has become almost universally used
throughout the United States, to the detriment of millions.[54]

The look-say method teaches children to memorize words in context by initially using pictures or clues. According to look-say promoters:

> A child taught this method should be able to recognize 349 words by the end of the first grade; 1,094 by the end of the second; 1,216 by the end of the third grade; and 1,554 by the end of fourth grade.[55]

The phonics method, on the other hand, teaches children how to sound out and blend the letters that make up words in a specific sequence. The child is taught simple words first and works up to the complex words. This method basically gives the child the skill and logic to understand virtually any word in the English language. By the end of fourth grade, a child will generally be able to read and understand at least 24,000 words![56]

Rudolf Flesch, author of *Why Johnnie Still Can't Read*, summarized the difference between the two methods of teaching reading as follows:

> Learning to read is like learning to drive a car. You take lessons and learn the mechanics and the rules of the road. After a few weeks you have learned how to drive, how to stop, how to shift gears, how to park, and how to signal. You have also learned to stop at a red light and understand road signs. When you are ready, you take a road test, and if you pass, you can drive. Phonics-first works the same way. The child learns the mechanics of reading, and when he's through, he can read. Look and say works differently. The child is taught to read before he has learned the mechanics—the sounds of letters. It is like learning to drive by starting your car and driving ahead. . . . And the mechanics of driving? You pick those up as you go along.[57]

In spite of a lack of research supporting the look-say method, the public schools applied and continue to apply the faulty method of reading. Can the public schools be trusted to teach the children in America even in the mechanics of learning?

Nose-dives in Student Test Scores

On August 27, 1991, the latest SAT scores were released by the College Board showing a continued decline. In fact, in the past five years, verbal averages dropped eight points to 422 (out of a possible 800) and math went down to 474 (out of 800) for a total of 896 out of a possible 1600.[58] Even the elite students have not avoided the consequences of lower standards in the public schools. Since 1972 the share of students scoring above 600 on the verbal SAT (on a scale of 200 to 800) has dropped from 11 percent to approximately 7 percent.[59] This is quite a drop from the years 1951 to 1961, when the SAT score total average was 972 out of a possible 1600—76 points higher than the average total score today.[60]

Cost of Public Education Rises While SAT Scores Decline

For the 1991-92 school year, the U.S. Department of Education reported $248.6 billion will go to public elementary and secondary schools. This means that the per-pupil spending in public schools is approximately $6000 per student. Diane Ravitch, assistant secretary for the Office of Educational Research and Improvement stated: "Spending is up and achievement is down."[61] Even the average teacher salary for public school has risen to its highest ever of $34,814. This is for working nine to ten months out of each year.[62]

Therefore, in the last decade, from 1982 to 1992, per-pupil spending has nearly doubled from approximately $3000 per student to just under $6000 per student. However, the SAT scores continue to decline, causing U.S. Education Secretary Lamar Alexander to remark: "We in the 80s went from spending $160 billion to $400 billion [on education on all levels] without much improvement in results."[63] In fact, from kindergarten through the twelfth grade, the United States spends more per student than any other country, except Switzerland.[64] More money is obviously not the answer since spending has doubled but academic results steadily decline. Americans are over-investing in a failing monopoly of public education.

This is further supported by numerous independent studies[65] and by the results of the NAEP math study described above. The study showed that North Dakota ranked the highest on math scores, but was thirty-second in per-pupil spending, while D.C. ranked second to the last on the math scores, but is the highest in per-pupil spending.[66] Research overwhelmingly demonstrates that there is no correlation between spending levels and educational performance.

As a further indictment of the bureaucratic, government-run public school system, only 60 percent of this money even gets to the classroom. At least 40 percent of the money goes to the bureaucracy. According to Albert Shanker, president of the American Federation of Teachers (second largest teachers' union):

> One of the major differences between American schools and all others in the world is that we spend half of our money on bureaucracy, whereas the other schools in the world don't spend more than 20 percent. . . You know, we have about one teacher to every twenty-five kids in the country *but we have one supervisor for every six teachers*.[67]

In California, 40 percent of the $25 billion a year spent on education goes to layers of bureaucracy at state, county, and local levels.[68] Former Secretary of Labor William Brock emphasized that public education is a failing bureaucracy out of control:

> We have public education at the elementary and secondary level that ranks below every industrial competitor we have in the world. . . . Education is the most backward single institution in all the U.S. It is not for lack of money. It's lack of intelligence and will and competence. It is bureaucratic inertia that is unbelievable and inexcusable. Between thirty-eight cents and forty-one cents of our education dollar gets to the classroom. That is an act of irrationality. . . . In the city of New York there are more administrators than there are in all of France. In the state of New York, there are more administrators than there are in all of the European Community, and the E.C. has twelve countries and 320 million people.[69]

The Business World Is Shocked by the Public School Product

Jonathan Kozol, author of *Illiterate America*, estimates that U.S. corporations alone lose $20 billion a year in lost profits, lower productivity, reduced international competitiveness, and increasing remedial training.

David Kearns, chairman of Xerox Corporation, stated, "Public education has put this country at a terrible disadvantage. The American workforce is running out of qualified people." He, too, estimated the tremendous loss the poor performance of public schools will cost American business:

> The American work force is in grave jeopardy. . . . If current demographic and economic trends continue, American business will have to hire a million new workers a year who can't read, write or count. Teaching them how, and absorbing the lost productivity while they are learning will cost industry twenty-five billion dollars a year for as long as it takes. . . . It is a terrible admission, but twenty billion dollars a year for remedial training has become a necessary added cost of doing business.[70]

Gerald Greenwald, vice chairman of Chrysler Corporation expressed his concern with the ill-prepared students coming out of the public schools to work for Chrysler:

> You want to know what Chrysler's most harrowing private nightmare is? Our nightmare will be finding people capable of running that sophisticated plant in the years to come. I'm talking long-term as our current work force retires. We'll have to replace them with the very kids whose performance constitutes that depressing data from Secretary Cavazos. And if they can't read, and if they can't write, and if they can't do simple basic calculations, they're not going to be able to run that billion dollar plant to anywhere near its world class potential. . . .
>
> Did you know that you and I and all the rest of American industry together spend more money each year teaching remedial math to U.S. workers than all the grade schools, high schools, and colleges in this country combined? Chrysler alone is already spending $120 million a year training our workforce, and at least 10 percent of it goes to teach our employees the Three R's that they should have learned in school.[71]

A few other examples include the Metal Fab Corporation of Florida, which estimated that it could save $1.2 million a year if its employees had been properly trained in reading and math. If this were so, the corporation would avoid tremendous waste in misreading blueprints and inaccurately measuring production materials.[72] In 1990, Citicorp Savings Bank of Illinois had to reject 840 of every 1000 applicants because most of them could not fill out the application form.[73] As the result of frequent American worker mistakes on insurance forms, New York Life began sending its insurance forms to Ireland for processing.[74] One study reported in *USA Today,* found: "High school graduates entering the workforce can't read, write, or reason well, say 64 percent of human resource officers for major U.S. companies. This poll of officers of twelve hundred of USA's major companies shows that the educational skills of graduates has declined in the last five years."[75]

A Louis Harris and Associates poll was conducted of employers throughout the country. The results were released in September 1991, demonstrating the low level of preparation for the job market of recently hired high school graduates. Only 33 percent of employers said their recently hired high school graduates were able to read and understand written and oral instructions. Only 25 percent found their high school graduate employees to be capable of doing math functions. Furthermore, only 20 percent of employers found their high school graduate employees to show a sense of dedication to work, and only 19 percent stated that the recent high school graduates were disciplined in their work habits.[76]

In light of the tremendous drain of barely literate public school graduates on American businesses, where will America be in ten years?

The Public School Product Not Ready for College

Colleges are finding that they cannot give many of their students a college education because the students from the public schools are not prepared for college and need remedial training.

For example, a survey of state colleges in New Jersey found that 73 *percent* of all incoming freshman were not proficient in verbal skills, and 69 *percent* were not proficient in the minimal standards of computation.[77] A survey of five thousand college faculty members by the Carnegie Foundation for the Advancement of Teaching found that between 70 and 80 percent of them agreed that there is "widespread lowering of academic standards and grade inflation at their institutions." The faculty members concluded that the majority of students enrolled in their schools are poorly prepared in the basics, reluctant to work hard, and willing to cheat to get good grades.[78]

The Southern Regional Education Board surveyed 826 campuses in fifteen states and discovered that one-third of all freshman need remedial training in reading, writing, or math and are not ready to begin regular college courses.[79] It seems that at least one-third of public high school students are suffering from educational malpractice.

According to another Gallup Poll in 1990, of 696 college seniors, a quarter of them believed Christopher Columbus first landed in America sometime *after* 1500, and over a third of them believed that the Magna Carta was signed by the Pilgrims on the Mayflower. Many of them confused excerpts of the Communist Manifesto with the U.S. Constitution, and over 40 percent could not determine when the Civil War occurred.[80] Al Shanker, president of the American Federation of Teachers, honestly summed up the problems in colleges this way:

> We have huge numbers of kids in colleges and universities who are basically getting their elementary and high school education and calling it a Bachelor of Arts degree.[81]

Even the colleges are having to "dumb down" their standards in order to admit public high school graduates.

Conclusion

Modern public education has been in trouble for thirty years and, instead of getting better, the problems have grown worse. The problems documented above can be personified and summed up in the experience of a recently retired public school teacher.

Edward Rauchut, who for fourteen years was a public high school English teacher, recently quit his job as a teacher in a high school reputed to be one of the best academic schools in the Midwest (Omaha, Nebraska). In a February 1992 "Comment" in *Teacher Magazine*, he related his experience:

> With very few exceptions, I watched for fourteen years as student after student entered and left high school having learned next to nothing during his or her four year term. And the problem is not in someone else's backyard, not in someone else's school district: It's systemic. *My experience has convinced me that if the purpose of the public schools were to prevent children from acquiring an education, they could not do a better job than they are right now, at this very moment, in classrooms all across the nation.*
>
> Ours is an educational system that labels children "learning-disabled" and then calls for more tax dollars to remediate the problem it created. It is an anti-intellectual, morally bankrupt system whose values-clarification classes and bogus drug and sex education programs contribute to the very addictions they sanctimoniously claim to solve. It is a system that crushes our children's intellectual curiosity and then demands that they learn anyway.[82] (emphasis added)

Public schools are failing, and parents need to realize the danger of sending their children to public school. Home schooling is an alternative that is available to parents if they are seriously committed to having their children educated and taught the traditional, biblical values on which this country is founded. If we do not get our children out of the failing public school system, we will lose a generation of children. As parents, we cannot afford to be apathetic or neutral on the issue of public schools. We must act now!

Notes

1. *Detroit News*, Suzanne Fields, 6 October 1989.

2. Education Department's sixth annual report on public schools, 3 May 1989.

3. National Commission on Excellence in Education, "A Nation at Risk: The Imperative for Education Reform (1982), 20. Reprinted in 129 Congressional Record S 6059, S 6060 (daily ed. 5 May 1983).

4. Emmett, "American Education: The Dead End of 80's," *Personal Computing*, August 1983, 96, 97.

5. William Bennett, "American Education; Making It Work," U.S. Department of Education, April 26, 1988, 1.

6. *Ibid.*, 10. The report continues, " Fewer than one-fourth of all seventeen-year-olds tested in 1984 were able to perform at an "adequate" level on writing tasks considered essential to academic study, business, and professional work. Only about 20 percent of them, when asked to write a letter to their principal requesting permission to take a particular schedule of classes, handled this relatively simple assignment satisfactorily. A similarly small percentage performed adequately when asked to write an imaginative passage describing a hypothetical situation and their reactions to it."

7. *Ibid.*, 12.

8. *Ibid.*, 12.

9. *Ibid.*, 13.

10. *Ibid.*, 13.

11. "History Textbooks Don't Portray Democracy Fully, Study Says," *Education Daily*, Vol. 22, No. 178, 14 September 1989, 4. The study was entitled, "Democracy's Half-told Story: What History Textbooks Should Add."

12. *Ibid.*

13. *Ibid.*

14. Suzanne Fields, "Gaps in Their Textbooks," *Washington Times*, 3 May 1990, F1.

15. *Ibid.*

16. Debbie Graves, "More Than 200 Errors Prompt Panel to Fail Books," *Austin American-Statesman*, 8 November 1991, A-9. Also see "Textbook Errors," *Dallas Morning News*, 12 November 1991.

17. *Ibid.*

18. Warren Brookes, "Socialism: A Failure in Public Education" *Washington Times*, 25 September 1989.

19. "Common Measures," *The American School Board Journal*, October 1989, A18.

20. Samallis, "Quick! Name Togo's Capital," *Time*, 6 July 1990, 53. For further description and commentary on the results see "The Phyllis Schlafly Report," Vol 23, No.11, June, 1990, Alton, IL.

21. Carol Innerst, "U.S. School Children's Reading, Writing Skills Inadequate," *Washington Times*, 10 January 1990, A5.

22. *Ibid.*

23. *Ibid.*

24. Pat Wingert and Barbara Kantrowitz, "A Dismal Report Card," *Newsweek*, 17 June 1991, 64.

25. *Ibid.*

26. *Ibid.*, 65.

27. *Ibid.*, 65. Also see *Educational Leadership*, Vol. 47, No. 3, November 1989, 5. Published by Association for Supervision and Curriculum Development, Alexandria, Virginia). This documents that 40 percent of seventh and eighth graders have trouble reading and understanding their textbooks. The article shows that many students, however, do well at age nine but get "lost" during the next four years.

28. Matt Neufeld, "D.C. Schools Fail Two-year Checkup," *Washington Times*, 12 February 1992, B3.

29. James W. Brosnan, "Today's Student 20 Years Behind," *Washington Times*, 1 October 1991, A1.

30. Carol Innerst, "Reading Skills Fell Despite Reforms," *Washington Times*, 1 February 1992, A1.

31. *Ibid.*

32. *Ibid.*, A10.

33. Mary Jordan, "Students Test Below Average," *Washington Post*, 6 February 1992, A1.

34. *Ibid.*, A4.

35. *Ibid.*

36. "The 1990 Science Report Card: NAEP's Assessment of Fourth, Eighth and Twelfth Graders," prepared by the Educational Testing Service for the National Center For Education Statistics, Office of Educational Research and Improvement, U.S. Department of Education, released March 1992.

37. Tim Bovee, "If Johnny Can't Learn, Maybe Teacher Didn't," *Washington Times*, 16 July 1991, A1.

38. *Ibid.*

39. Rita Kramer, Ed School Follies: The Miseducation of America's Teachers (New York: The Free Press, 1991), 211.

40. *Ibid.*, 209.

41. *Ibid.*, 210.

42. *Ibid.*, 212.

43. *Ibid.*, 211.

44. *Ibid.*, 213.

45. *Ibid.*, 220.

46. "Need for Teachers Keeps Passing Scores Low," *Daily Oklahoman and Times*, 14 July 1990.

47. "SAT Scores Decline," *Teacher Magazine*, November/December 1991, 21.

48. Carol Innerst, "Teachers Urged to Focus on Subjects," *Washington Times*, 12 November 1991.

49. *Ibid.*

50. "City Educator Shuns Chicago High School," *Washington Times*, 28 March 1990.

51. William Jasper, "Not My Kids," *New American*, 19 May 1986, 47. The Department of Education study was done under a contract with the American Enterprise Institute and was based on the Census Bureau's data for twenty-two major cities. The researchers were Doyle and Hartle.

52. Samuel Blumenfeld, *The New Illiterates* (Boise, Idaho: Paradigm Co., 1988), 9-10.

53. "Becoming a Nation of Readers," U.S. Department of Education publication, "Becoming a Nation of Readers." 1989.

54. "Illiteracy: An Incurable Disease or Education Malpractice?" an educational research report published by the U.S. Senate Republican Policy Committee, Senator William Armstrong, chairman, 13 September 1989, 5.

55. *Ibid.*, 3-4.

56. *Ibid.*, 4.

57. *Ibid.*, 1.

58. Carol Innerst, "Taxpayers to Invest $414 billion in Schools," *Washington Times*, 29 August 1991, A5.

59. Robert Samuelson, "School Reform Fraud," *Washington Post*, 23 October 1991.

60. David Barton, *America: To Pray or Not to Pray* (Aledo, Tex.: Wallbuilder Press, 1988), 58. Data derived from the College Entrance Exam Board.

61. Carol Innerst, "Taxpayers to Invest," A5.

62. *Ibid.*

63. Lee Mitgang, "Survival, Not Reform, Is Agenda for Nation's Public Schools," *World*, 14 September 1991, 5.

64. Paul Craig Roberts, "U. S. Overinvesting in Education," *Washington Times*, 26 February 1990, D3.

65. For instance, see *American School Board Journal*, June 1991, 12. This article summarizes two recent studies (by Urban Policy Research Institute of Ohio and the Utah Taxpayer's Association) which showed that lower-spending school districts tended to have higher student-achievement scores. Their conclusion was that more spending is not necessarily the answer to each state's educational problems.

66. *Newsweek*, 17 June 1991, 65.

67. Albert Shanker, from the text of a speech he delivered to a conference of teachers and school administrators sponsored by the Gates Foundation in Denver, Colorado, 20-23 September 1989.

68. *The Sacramento Union*, 27 October 1990.

69. *Time*, 23 September 1990.

70. *Milwaukee Journal*, October 1986 and Warren Brookes, "Why An Education President?" *Washington Post*, 25 April 1988, D1; also see David T. Kearns, Dennis Doyle, "Winning The Brain Race," Institute for Contemporary Studies, San Francisco, California, 1988.

71. Gerald Greenwald, vice chairman of Chrysler, was speaking to the National Association of Black Automotive Suppliers, *Detroit News*, 4 May 1989.

72. "Businesses Teaching the Three R's to Employees in Effort to Compete," *Wall Street Journal*, 1 May 1988, 29. For more details on the cost of illiteracy to business see Kerry Knobelsdorff, "Corporations Take Aim at High Cost of Worker Illiteracy," *Christian Science Monitor*, 10 March 1988, 12.

73. Patrick Keleher, Jr., "Business Leadership and Education Reform: The Next Frontier," Heritage Lecture No. 257, 28 April 1990, 1.

74. David Gergen, "Sending Companies to School," *U.S. News and World Report*, 6 November 1989, 112.

75. "Firms Find Grads Lacking in Basic Skills," USA *Today*, 16 July 1990.

76. "Passing School, Flunking Life," chart appeared in *Washington Times*, 3 January 1992, A3.

77. Ronald Nash, *The Closing of the American Heart*, Dallas, Texas (Probe Books, 1990), 46.

78. Carol Innerst, "Students Stumble, Despite Reforms," *Washington Times*, 11 November 1989.

79 "Remedial R's Aid Many Freshman," *Washington Times*, 7 August 1991, A6. Also see "Help Required," *Teacher Magazine*, October 1922, 11, where Virginia's first state wide study of high school students entering college was reported. It found that nearly one in seven freshman in college last year required remedial classes in math, English, or reading. At one Virginia university 79% of the freshman required such remedial courses!

80. The National Endowment for the Humanities commissioned the Gallup Poll of the college students' history and literature knowledge. The test used was designed for seventeen-year-olds by the National Assessment of Educational Progress. The summary of this study appeared in *Washington Times*, 3 April 1990, A1.

81. Albert Shanker, Speech at Gates Foundation conference.

82. Edward Rauchut, "I Quit: A Teacher Refuses to Be Part of a Dysfunctional System," *Teacher Magazine*, February 1992, 26. Rauchut is presently an associate professor at Bellevue College in Nebraska.

FIRST DAY OF SCHOOL...   ...LAST DAY OF SCHOOL.

CHAPTER 2

THE MORAL CRISIS
IN PUBLIC EDUCATION

"*I* am as sure as I am of Christ's reign that a comprehensive and centralized system of national education, separated from religion, as is now commonly proposed, will prove the most appalling enginery for the propagation of anti-Christian and atheistic unbelief, and of anti-social nihilistic ethics, individual, social and political, which this sin rent world has ever seen."[1]

—Dr. A. A. Hodge of Princeton over 100 years ago.

Although the academic crisis documented in the previous chapter is extremely damaging to our children, economy, and nation, the moral crisis in the public schools is far more insidious and far more devastating.

When the moral backbone of a nation is removed, a nation will surely collapse. The public schools have abandoned the absolute moral values and biblical morality on which our country was founded and have replaced them with the religion of humanism, where man is the measure of all things and values are determined by the individual.[2] Therefore, when the bankrupt philosophy of humanism is adopted, and biblical morality is removed in the public schools, only chaos will reign. This chapter will summarize the results of this rejection of absolute moral values beginning with censorship of religion in the curriculum.

Removal from the Public Schools of Virtually All References to Religion

Dr. Paul Vitz conducted a study funded by the National Institute of Education and found an unsettling censorship of nearly all religious events in history textbooks. His study found that in fifth-grade U.S. history textbooks, "the treatment of the past 100 years was so devoid of reference to religion as to give the impression that it ceased to exist in America."[3] After examination of all the most popular public school textbooks for grades one through six, Vitz discovered "religion, traditional family values, and many conservative positions have been reliably excluded from children's textbooks."[4] One of his most disturbing conclusions was that "*none* of the books had a single text reference to a primary religious activity occurring in contemporary American life. . . . For all intents and purposes, religion is excluded from these basic readers."[5]

In his study of eleventh- and twelfth-grade history textbooks, Vitz found:

> For all practical purposes, religion is hardly mentioned as existing in America in the last seventy-five to one hundred years; in particular, none of these books includes any serious coverage of conservative Protestantism in this century. . . . There is not one book that recognizes the continuity of the revival and evangelical movements throughout American history since the Colonial Period. . . . One indication of the biased treatment of religion in American history is the universal tendency to omit from the lists of important historical events almost all dates referring to religion, especially in the last one hundred years.[6]

Vitz also found, after reviewing forty social studies textbooks used in the public schools for grades one through four, that no mention is made even once of "marriage," "wedding," "husband," or "wife." A "family" is commonly defined as "a group of people." Families are routinely depicted without a father, without a mother, or as a couple without children. Marriage is never mentioned as the foundation of the family and yet these books are supposed to be textbooks which introduce the child to an understanding of contemporary American society. There is no doubt, as Vitz explains, that these textbooks clearly foster the notion of family without marriage.[7]

In a conference conducted by the American Family Association in the summer of 1990, Vitz stated that no real change had occurred in the textbooks. He stated, "Although I published my study four years ago, the problem is still there."

Another study was undertaken by Bryce Christensen, associate editor of "Chronicles: A Magazine of American Culture." Christensen found that public school literature books consistently exclude famous works by playwrights, poets, and novelists who wrestle with the meaning of life from a Judeo-Christian standpoint, such as John Bunyan, T. S. Elliot, C. S. Lewis, Walker Percy, John Milton, Flannery O'Connor, and Gerard Manley Hopkins.[8] Instead, stories such as E. E. Cumming's repudiation of the Resurrection in "O Sweet Spontaneous," Ernest Hemingway's nihilism in *The Sun Also Rises*, and Conrad's inaccurate comparison of paganism and Christianity in *Heart of Darkness* are studied by public school children. In addition, literary attacks on biblical beliefs by humanistic writers such as John Steinbeck, Theodore Drieser, and A. E. Housman are frequently taught.[9] Christensen explains that "American high schools offer relatively few Bible-as-literature classes, but they do offer hundreds of literature-as-Bible classes."[10]

Christensen, as a teacher of literature at the secondary and college levels, saw first-hand the consequences of such irreligious and biased literature classes in the public schools. One student wrote in an essay: "I believed in God until my high school teacher helped me become smarter." This child was raised as a believer. Another student informed Christensen that his high school English teacher had taught him that the only standards he had to live by and be accountable to were those of his own making. Another young girl explained that the literature she studied in public high school made her "feel suicidal."[11]

This censorship of the impact of religion in the history and accomplishments of our nation deceives our children by making them think religion is ineffectual and outmoded. This is intellectually dishonest, in light of the many historical documents and contemporary historians that demonstrate the tremendous significant effect biblical Christianity has had on every aspect of our nation. In fact, our legal and governmental systems were founded on biblical principles. The well-known Alexis de Tocqueville wrote in the 1840s of his observations of visiting this country:

> The religious atmosphere of the country was the first thing that struck me on my arrival in the United States. The longer I stayed in the country, the more conscious I became of the important political consequences resulting from this novel situation. . . .

> Religion, which never intervenes directly in the government of American society, should therefore be considered as the first of their political institutions. . . .

> I do not know if all Americans have faith in their religion— for who can read the secrets of the heart? But I am sure that they think it necessary to the maintenance of republican institutions. That is not the view of one class or party among the citizens, but of the whole nation; it is found in all the ranks. . . .

> For the Americans, the ideas of Christianity and liberty are so completely mingled that it is impossible to get them to conceive of the one without the other.[12]

Our children are being lied to every day in the public schools, and this is causing the very fabric of our nation to unravel before our eyes.

In conclusion, this removal of religion and prayer from the public schools was, in effect, the removal of God and His standards. This is by far the most devastating cause of the decline of public schools. David Barton, in his book *America: To Pray or Not to Pray?*, documents the apparent connection between the removal of prayer from the public schools in 1962 by the U.S. Supreme Court in *Engel v. Vitale* and the drastic decline in the public schools. He demonstrates how, beginning in 1962, SAT scores suddenly plummeted and teen pregnancies, teen sexual diseases, teen suicides, violent crimes among youths, teen alcohol and drug abuse, use of pornography among students, and illiteracy rates abruptly increased

200 to 300 percent.[13] His book is based on statistics gathered from the Departments of Education, Justice, Health and Human Services, Labor, and many other sources and studies. Of course, the removal of prayer in 1962 was followed by a long line of court cases that removed nearly every vestige of the Christian religion from the public schools. Barton's research indicates that when God was removed from the public schools, chaos set in. Is this a coincidence or a connection?

Now let us look further at the practical impact which the removal of absolute moral values has had on the youth who have recently "graduated" from the public schools, or who are presently in the public schools.

Violence in the Halls of Education

In 1940 the top discipline offenses, according to educators, were talking, chewing gum, making noise, running in the halls, getting out of turn in line, wearing improper clothing, and not putting paper in wastebaskets. However, by 1982 the top discipline offenses had become rape, robbery, assault, burglary, arson, bombings, and murder. This does not even count the prevalence of extortion, drug abuse, abortion, and sexual diseases.

Throughout the public school system in America violence has become a way of life—something the students just have to get used to. I have talked with hundreds of school officials across the nation who are critical of home schooling because it "shelters" the children from the "real" world. They explain that violence, sex, and negative peer pressure are things children need to confront and deal with so that they will be prepared for the world. It is revolting to hear highly-educated men excuse such violence and immorality. Yet millions of parents fall for such reasoning and continue to put their children at risk by sending them to the public schools.

In 1978 the National Institute of Education released its "Safe Schools" report. Some of its findings were: 1) the risk of violence to teenagers is greater in public schools than elsewhere; 2) over 5,200 secondary school teachers were physically attacked per month, with at least 1,000 of them seriously injured, requiring medical attention; 3) each month 282,000 secondary school students are physically attacked; 4) about 11 percent of secondary school children, 2.4 million, are victims of robbery or theft in a given month; 5) there are about 2,400 acts of arson in schools each month; and 6) more than one-fourth of all schools are subject to vandalism in any given month.[14]

In 1987 the U.S. Bureau of Census undertook the National Crime Survey and found that nearly 184,000 students, teachers, and visitors were *injured* as a result of violent crime in one year.

In May 1991 the National Crime Survey was released by the U.S. Department of Justice's Bureau of Justice Statistics. This study showed that crime on school grounds or in school buildings is becoming more serious. Assaults are much more frequent. Almost three million *violent* crimes and thefts occur on public school campuses annually. This equals approximately sixteen thousand incidents per school day, or one every six seconds.[15]

The National Crime Survey indicated that about sixty-seven students of every thousand teenagers, or 1.9 million are victims of a violent crime, including rape, robbery, assault, and murder each year. Annually, approximately 483,764 of these violent crimes against youth occurred at school or on school property. However, the survey estimated that at least a third of all violent crimes are not reported, making the actual figures much higher.[16] The covering up of crime statistics was exposed by one commentator:

> No one really knows the number of teachers who are victims of violence nationwide. Relatively few districts report campus crime; of those that do, say some sources, under reporting or camouflaging school violence is not uncommon. High crime figures make for bad public relations.[17]

The National Educational Goals Panel released a report in October 1991 and announced:

> Substantial numbers of twelfth graders are victims of violent acts at school. During 1990, 25 percent were threatened and 14 percent were injured without a weapon being used, while 13 percent were threatened and 6 percent were injured with weapons. In addition, 42 percent reported their property stolen and 29 percent reported their property vandalized.

> Nearly one out of five public school teachers reported being verbally abused by students in the previous month. Eight percent reported being physically threatened, while 2 percent reported being physically attacked during the previous year.[18]

Some of the violent crimes involve students robbing other students in order to steal their designer sneakers, sunglasses, and athletic jackets. Students who resist are often beaten and sometimes killed.[19] For example, in Chicago, in the middle of winter, a student was robbed of his $61 sneakers and forced to walk home barefoot. In Detroit a child was shot for his $135 goose-down jacket. The rash of assaults over clothing has prompted many schools to adopt dress codes.

As a result of shootings, some students are wearing bullet-proof vests to school. One former New York policeman, who now sells bullet-proof vests for children, summed it up this way: "The fact that New Yorkers and people throughout the world need protective clothing, especially for children, is a terrible reflection of the collapse of law and order in our society."[20]

In Washington, D.C., drugs and violence were such a problem in one elementary school, that the principal banned regular recess, and the children are only allowed to play outside in a pit enclosed by eight-foot concrete walls, or on a small section of the playground monitored by the police.[21]

Many students drop out of school or become truant in order to avoid becoming victims of continual crime and harassment. Parents often are further frustrated when disruptive children, caught with with weapons or caught victimizing students are simply allowed back into the public school system.[22]

Rape is becoming another common problem among juveniles attending public schools. The FBI documents that one out of every five rapes committed throughout the country is committed by a juvenile.[23] In Montgomery County, Maryland, there were four reported rapes on public school grounds during a five-month period.[24] In the same article, D.C. authorities were alarmed with the growing number of sex crimes committed by juveniles.

After a close look at the immoral teachings in the public schools, as outlined in this chapter, it does not take much imagination to discover the real cause behind the rise in sex crimes on and off public school campuses. For over twenty years, the public schools have been drilling into the heads of forty million students, "If it feels good, do it!" and, "There are no moral absolutes—everything is relative."

The Annie E. Casey Foundation and the Center for the Study of Social Policy issued on March 23, 1992, a report called the "Kids

Count Data Book." This study demonstrates that in the last ten years the chances that a juvenile would violently die as the result of murder, suicide, or accident has increased from sixty-two to sixty-nine deaths per 100,000 children ages fifteen to nineteen. The number of children ages ten to fifteen who were required by juvenile courts to be put in juvenile homes as a result of committing crimes, rose from 142 to 156 per 100,000 youth.[25]

After a study was released of thirty-one city and suburban public schools in Illinois which showed 26.5 percent of the suburban school students were victims of theft and 9.7 percent were assaulted, one official drew the "startling" conclusion:

> There are indications that crime in the schools seems to be affecting the learning process. Students are afraid of being victimized. Teachers are afraid of staying late after school. Those things can only detract from the learning process.[26]

I wonder how long it will take the educational elite to realize that runaway crime, which is encouraged by the public schools' valueless curriculum, may actually detract from the learning process!

In California the most recent data shows that 174,478 crimes took place during the 1988-89 school year, up 5 percent from the previous year. Assaults increased 16 percent to 69,191, and armed assaults rose 25 percent to 1,830. In Philadelphia the number of school crime incidents jumped from 5,861 crimes in 1987 to 7,505 crimes in 1990. In Dade County Public Schools in Florida, assaults rose 9 percent to 1,889.[27]

On August 30, 1992, the FBI released its twenty-five-year study on juvenile violence as part of its annual survey of U.S. crime statistics. The report demonstrates how juvenile crimes have soared "to an unprecedented level" affecting not only "disadvantaged minority youth in urban areas but [is] evident in all races, social classes, and lifestyles" in all parts of the country.[28] The study documents how the white juvenile arrest rate for violent crimes rose 44 percent during the 1980s.[29] Attorney General William Barr, commenting on the alarming rise in juvenile crime, suggested a solution:

> It requires strengthening those basic institutions—the family, schools, religious institutions, and community groups—that are responsible for instilling values and creating law-abiding citizens.[30]

It is apparent from the other statistics described throughout this chapter that the public schools are not only failing to instill values in our nation"s youth, but they are already reaping the results of their self-centered and valueless curriculum by the uncontrolled crime occurring on their own campuses.

Children are not the only ones victimized in the public school; many teachers are becoming crime statistics. In New York City the United Federation of Teachers reported 2790 crimes committed against teachers during the 1989-90 school year. At least one-third of the crimes against teachers were serious violations including assaults, robberies, and sexual offenses.[31]

Teacher Magazine devoted its cover story to violence against public school teachers, dispelling the myth that violence only occurs in the big city schools. It stated: "Every day, thousands of teachers are attacked or threatened in schools. If you think it happens only in New York, Chicago, or Los Angeles, you're wrong."[32] The article documented how violence is prevalent throughout the country's public schools, citing several examples: In Abilene, Texas, a high school student shot a teacher in the head for giving him a low grade; in Florida's Pinellas County, students killed an assistant high school principal and injured another administrator and teacher; in Goddard, Kansas, a fourteen-year-old boy gunned down two teachers and a junior high school principal; in Fort Worth, Texas, a teacher was stabbed to death and a twelve-year-old student confessed to the crime. The writer concluded, "The list is horrifyingly long."[33]

Crime is running rampant on public school campuses and taxpayers are now forced to pay the tremendous costs for high-tech security devices and security guards and dogs. A fifty state check by the Associated Press found the annual security costs of major school systems, including the following: $60 million on security by New York City public schools; $26 million in Los Angeles; $10.3 million in Dade County, Florida; $10.4 million in Philadelphia; and $2.2 million in Boston. Chicago's school system, the nation's third largest, spends $12.5 million a year on security and has 723 security positions. The check of districts in all fifty states found that the cost of security throughout the nation's public schools is in the hundreds of millions of dollars.[34]

Public schools have "sown the wind" by not teaching absolute moral values and are "reaping the whirlwind" as crime escalates while students do "what feels good." Do you want your child to become a "statistical blip" on next year's national crime survey? He has the same chance if you either send him to your local public school or let him loose to roam the streets at night.

Drugs and Alcohol: The Ultimate Insider Trading

Children in the public schools are using drugs and alcohol in record numbers. In fact, drug abuse has become a national crisis. The National Institute on Drug Abuse has found that this nation's high school students have a greater involvement in illegal drugs than those in any other industrialized nation.[35] With the prevailing philosophy of values clarification in the public schools, it is not surprising that children are turning to drugs. Why not? It feels good.

The Texas Commission on Alcohol and Drug Abuse released the results of a state-wide study of drug and alcohol use among secondary school students. According to a sampling of junior high and high school students in thirty-eight school districts in Texas, the most popular substance used is alcohol—76 percent of all secondary students drink. That number jumps to 86.4 percent for high school seniors. Furthermore, 45.7 percent of high school seniors have used marijuana, and 26.3 percent of eighth graders have used inhalants.[36]

In 1988, according to a national study by the National Institute of Drug Abuse, 33.1 percent of high school seniors used marijuana, 7.1 percent used inhalants, 1.2 percent used PCP, 7.9 percent used cocaine, 3.1 percent used crack, .5 percent used heroin, 85.3 percent used alcohol, and 4.7 percent used tranquilizers (not prescribed by a doctor).

Excessive alcohol consumption leads youth to violence and sex, according to Surgeon General Antonio Novello. She drew public attention to the Justice Department statistics which reveal that alcohol consumption is connected with 37 percent of all robberies committed by youth, 27 percent of all murders, 33 percent of all property offenses, and 31 percent of all rapes committed by youth. It also contributes from one-third to two-thirds of all "date rapes."

The surgeon general was also "shocked" by a survey of high school students which found nearly 20 percent of all girls and 40 percent of all boys thought it was "okay to force sex if a girl was drunk."[37]

Over one third of the children in public schools are using drugs. Over 80 percent of public high schoolers drink alcohol. Over 40 percent of high school boys think it is not wrong to force sex on a girl who is drunk. Are these children being taught any worthwhile values in the public school? Is the risk of sending our children to such a school system really worth it?

Sex and the Single Student

Virtually all sex education textbooks used in public schools throughout the country teach that any kind of sex is all right; such as premarital sex, adultery, masturbation, homosexuality, and lesbianism. The basic principle children are taught about sex is "do whatever is comfortable for you."

Mel and Norma Gabler have been reviewing hundreds of public school textbooks for years and report these findings in their book, *What Are They Teaching Our Children.*[38] They found many common but disturbing themes throughout the "health" textbooks used in public schools. One widely used ninth and tenth grade textbook states: "In many societies, premarital intercourse is expected and serves a useful role in the selection of a spouse. In such societies, there are seldom negative and psychological consequences."[39] In another textbook, students are told that "research shows that homosexuals can lead lives that are as full and healthy as those of heterosexuals." The statement is under a picture of two men embracing.[40] Masturbation is also commonly taught as an acceptable sexual option.[41]

Another researcher, Dr. Donald Oppenwal, confirms similar findings in his survey of textbooks. One example which typified the textbooks he reviewed, declared, "Although homosexual acts have been traditionally characterized as deviant or unnatural, there is no evidence that they are any more or less so than heterosexual acts." This same book uses statistics of the frequency of such activity and uses the phrases "experts say" and "most authorities agree" to support homosexuality, masturbation, and premarital intercourse. He found other textbooks that make value-laden statements supporting incest and sadism and masochism.[42]

The Michigan Model, a program being used throughout the state of Michigan, encourages explicit sexual instruction to children starting at age five. One of the exercises requires fifth graders to submit anonymous essays about their sexual experiences. A fifth grade sex education film, "Boy to Man," declares masturbation to be "natural and normal." This film and the film "Girl to Woman," graphically depict male and female genitalia, breast development, and the growth of pubic hair. In other aspects of the program, homosexuality is graphically pictured and described in a favorable light, which is basically nothing more than a form of pornography. The definition of "monogamy" is "one partner at a time."[43] A lawsuit has even been filed against one Michigan school district after seventh through eleventh graders received instruction in "Self-Pleasuring Techniques" that involved techniques in masturbation, and descriptions of sexual fantasies involving group and homosexual acts.[44]

The murder of unborn children is also encouraged in many textbooks. The Gablers document states, "Abortion is discussed as an aspect of birth control in biology and health and homemaking books."[45] Nothing is said in these textbooks of the large amount of research which clearly establishes that life begins at conception and abortion is extermination of a baby's life.

In summary, all teaching of sex in the public school textbooks ignores absolute moral standards. Nearly all forms of sex are acceptable. The children's inhibitions are gradually eroded and their teaching from home and church is soundly and "clinically" rejected.

In addition to the immoral instruction in the textbooks, immoral school policies are also being passed. For instance, the Massachusetts State Board of Education, in October 1991, enacted a policy to encourage local school boards to adopt a condom-distribution policy for high school students.[46] These types of policies are spreading across the public schools in this country, and the effect has been to encourage illicit sexual activity between unwed teens.

Is it healthy for our children to be exposed to such training in the area of sex? Is it fair to them to be forced to learn this sinful and destructive behavior?

Can the Public Schools Teach Moral Values?

The public schools are being run by teachers' unions that annually pass resolutions supporting all types of immorality, including sex before marriage, homosexuality, abortion, and lesbianism. For instance, the National Education Association, the American Federation of Teachers, and the Association for Supervision and Curriculum Development passed resolutions asking school districts to acknowledge the special needs of homosexual students, provide support services to them, and adopt anti-harassment guidelines.[47]

The Maryland State Teachers' Association supported these resolutions and urged similar protection for gays because "when they hide their feelings . . . their emotional and sexual development languishes." The teachers' union simply recognizes homosexuality and bisexuality as the natural result of being human since "our capacity to relate emotionally and physically to other human beings is not limited to the other gender . . . we are diverse sexual creatures."[48] The immoral and deadly lifestyle of homosexuality is readily embraced by the teachers' unions rather than condemned.

These groups promoting immorality in our nation's public schools represent the teachers who are teaching the children! The question comes to mind: Can public school teachers teach moral values in the first place? A quick look at the statistics demonstrates that many teachers are out of touch with traditional Judeo-Christian moral values and even out of touch with the American public.

The majority of public school teachers find nothing wrong with teaching and encouraging sexual immorality. Do you want your children taught by these teachers who hold to the following beliefs?

The Connecticut Mutual Life Insurance Company did a nation-wide survey of thousands of members of the public and of leaders in various fields, such as education, law, business, etc. This report is entitled "The Connecticut Mutual Life Report on American Values in the 80's: The Impact of Belief." Concerning abortion, 65 percent of the general public believed abortion to be wrong while only 26 percent of teachers believed it is wrong. In the area of pre-marital sex, 40 percent of the public believed it is wrong while only 27 percent of the educators found it objectionable. Concerning homosexuality and lesbianism, at least 70 percent of the public opposed it on moral grounds while only 30 percent of the educators opposed it.

Regarding viewing pornographic movies, 68 percent of the public believed it to be morally wrong while 50 percent of the educators found no moral problem with pornography. Seventy-one percent of the public opposed having sex before age sixteen while 54 percent of the educators believed there is nothing wrong with premarital sex. In the area of the mother working, 72 percent of the public believed the mother should not work outside the family while only 46 percent of the educators are morally opposed to mother working.[49]

Teachers Abusing Children

As seen above, a high percentage of public school teachers hold to a moral standard of living that is contrary to God's absolute moral values. As if it is not bad enough that they attempt to convince the students to embrace the same immorality as they themselves hold and the curricula teaches, some of them even practice their immoral beliefs on the students!

For instance, in an issue of *West Education Law Reporter*, a weekly law journal which reports on new education cases, five cases of teacher abuse of students appeared: 1) In Montana a public school teacher was convicted of having sexual intercourse with an eighth-grade girl; 2) in Florida, a public school teacher's aide was convicted of lewd assault upon an eight-year-old autistic school boy; 3) in Wisconsin, parents were suing a local public school for not detecting or preventing a teacher's homosexual assault on their son; 4) in Pennsylvania a public school woodshop teacher hit a student on the head with a chisel; and 5) in Ohio a teacher made a student do twenty-five push-ups naked.[50]

Teacher abuse of students is widespread as illustrated by the following examples. In Chicago, sexual molestation of students by teachers has become a major problem. In one week, four public school teachers were arrested for sexually abusing children in their classes. One of the teachers was photographed performing homosexual acts on two male high school students. He admitted to the police he was trading sex for grades.[51] In Los Angeles, an elementary public school teacher was sentenced to twelve years in prison for sexually molesting four boys that he taught.[52]

In Montana a public high school teacher was convicted of sexually molesting four students and was sentenced to twenty years in prison. The county attorney said he knows that the teacher sexually molested at least forty-five students over the last three decades and others believe the number may be in the hundreds. Many other public school officials knew he was a homosexual and knew of students who repeatedly accused him of sexual molestation. He was a model employee in every other respect, as he donated part of his salary back to the school and volunteered many hours to paint and fix up the school during the summers.[53]

In Cooke County, Illinois, a high school principal was convicted of trading sex for grades with several male and female students over several years. He would even call students out of class and have sex with them in his office. Some students who needed better grades were required to have sex with him in his office two and three times a week.[54] An elementary school teacher in Maine was found unfit to teach after admitting maintaining a sexual relationship with a psychologically disturbed fifteen-year-old high school student.[55] In Oklahoma, an elementary school teacher committed sexual molestation against three fifth-grade boys. The teacher had a history of molestation from previous teaching jobs.[56]

A public school teacher in Oregon was denied renewal of his teaching certificate for sexual misconduct toward his female students in his sixth-grade class which included fondling private parts.[57] In Alaska, a public school music teacher regularly had intercourse in his office with a thirteen-year-old student teacher's aide. She became pregnant and had a miscarriage. Two other students in eighth grade also came forward, claiming he sexually abused them, too. He was convicted of a felony and sentenced to five years of prison.[58] Another public school teacher in Maine was convicted of committing unlawful sexual contact with a fifth-grade student.[59] In North Carolina a student was charged with truancy because she refused to go back to school, where a public school principal had sexually assaulted her. This same principal had resigned from another school after sexually assaulting a student there.[60]

In Fairfax, Virginia, a substitute teacher who had been teaching in the public schools for over two months was actually a convicted murderer who had escaped from prison! The principal in one of the public schools in which the murderer did substitute teaching said the killer was "very organized, very thorough," with "very good rapport with students and staff."[61] I guess you can never know who might be teaching your children in the public school!

Even more frustrating is that, even though these teachers are caught abusing students or discovered to be incompetent teachers, they cannot be easily fired. On March 25, 1992, the *Detroit Free Press* released a report entitled "Shielding Bad Teachers." The report was based on four *Free Press* education writers who interviewed more than 300 people and reviewed 611 cases that went to the Michigan

Teacher Tenure Commission. The findings are disturbing, to say the least.

The report found:

> Michigan's costly, arduous system for firing bad teachers sometimes encourages school districts to simply transfer problems from one school board to another. Or teachers and school boards make secret deals to pay the teacher to go quietly away, running the risk that the teacher could end up in another district.
>
> It's a system designed to protect teachers from arbitrary and vindictive school boards, unions say.
>
> *But no protections are built in for the state's 1.5 million public school students, who can suffer physical, sexual or educational abuse.*[62] (emphasis added)

The report gave many examples of public school teachers who were caught abusing their students, and the school district quietly negotiated a deal which allowed the teacher to transfer to another school district. Also situations were documented in which the school district looked the other way even though evidence continued to mount, in one case for nineteen years, showing that the teacher was making improper sexual advances to students. In 1980 a teacher was found to be sexually fondling students and exposing himself. He appealed, and in 1992 the appeal is still not resolved. It has already cost the Ann Arbor School District $156,437.49 in legal fees. Meanwhile, the teacher has been tried and convicted of murdering his wife with an ax![63]

The report found that a school district spends, on the average, $100,000 or more to fire a teacher, and the process usually takes seven years. As a result, many school districts make secret deals and "pay questionable teachers thousands of dollars and spare them from public exposure of complaints against them."[64] These settlements are rarely disclosed in public. One school board member called it a "conspiracy of silence." Parents are not informed of the abuse of students by teachers, physically or educationally.

Even if bad teachers are caught, many times they work out a deal and merely go teach somewhere else. This is frightening.

This list is only the "tip of the iceberg" of the reported incidences of public school teachers who abuse their students. Also many of these incidences go unreported due to the shame that the children bear or the fear of teacher retaliation. A heavily documented review of many cases of teachers abusing public school students appeared in *West Education Law Reporter*. The survey concluded that the number of cases involving teachers improperly touching students is steadily on the rise. The author of this survey states:

> One can conclude that the problem is far more prevalent than the data reported. There is no way of knowing how many teachers resign each year when their dismissal is threatened for sexual abuse of students.[65]

Knowing the immoral philosophy embraced by many public school teachers today and the immorality which is encouraged in the public school curricula, we should not be at all surprised that so many public school teachers would practice this immorality on the students.

Of course, there are many public school teachers and administrators who would never commit such acts against the students. However, the immorality is still being consistently taught through the curricula. Either way, the children are the ones who suffer as a result of this "anything goes" philosophy. How well do you know the teachers and administrators in your local public school? Could they be practicing the immorality they preach in their public schools?

Sexual Promiscuity Among Teens: Reaping What We Sow

Has this immoral instruction in the public schools had any effect on our youth? The answer is yes, and the effects are devastating.

In 1990 researchers at the Guttmacher Institute in New York and the Urban Institute in Washington analyzed federally funded surveys of teens. This is what they discovered concerning the sexual activity among unwed teens according to age group: 1) among fifteen-year-olds, 33 percent of the boys and 27 percent of the girls were sexually active; 2) among sixteen-year-olds, 50 percent of the boys and 34 percent of the girls have had sex; 3) among seventeen-year-olds, 66 percent of the boys and 50 percent of the girls had engaged in sex; 4) among eighteen-year-olds, 72 percent of boys and 69 percent of girls were sexually experienced; 5) among nineteen-year-olds, 86 percent of boys and 75 percent of girls were sexually active.[66]

For nineteen-year-olds this means that three out of four unmarried women and five out of six unmarried men were sexually experienced!

Many had been having sex for several years with several different partners. No wonder the cases of sexual diseases and AIDS is so high among teenagers.

The survey also showed that many students are under constant intense pressure to join the sexually promiscuous crowd.

The National Center for Health Statistics supports these findings and released comparisons between sexually active teens in 1980 and in 1988. For instance, in 1980, 17 percent of fifteen-year-old girls were sexually experienced, compared with 26 percent in 1988; and in 1980, 36 percent of seventeen-year-old girls were sexually active, compared to 51 percent in 1988.[67]

In some public school systems the statistics are even worse. In D.C., for example, the U.S. Centers for Disease Control reports that 89.5 percent of tenth grade boys and 63.9 percent of tenth grade girls had engaged in intercourse. Of these students, 66.6 percent of the boys and 17.9 percent of the girls had four or more sex partners.[68]

Not surprising, sexual diseases are rampant among teens in D.C. Among fifteen to nineteen-year-olds in 1990, there were 4,135 cases of gonorrhea and 138 cases of syphilis. These diseases can cause birth defects and several other damaging side effects. Based on 11,481 blood samples taken of teens treated in D.C. hospitals, 1 out of 77 teens is infected with AIDS.[69]

In addition, one out of every six babies in the nation in 1981 was born out of wedlock, and among unmarried teens there are three live births for every five abortions.[70] The public schools, which advocate abortion as a form of birth control, are training our children to kill innocent babies.

In conclusion, the public schools' lack of moral instruction and the public school teachers' lack of values are devastating our youth and destroying traditional families. This gradual destruction of our families will inevitably lead to the destruction of our nation.

Humanism: One of the New Religions in Public School

With all the censorship of religion and traditional values from the public schools, a vacuum has been created. This "values vacuum" is being filled by two other value systems: the religion of humanism and the religion of the New Age occultism.

The religion of humanism is quite easy to identify. Humanism simply means that man, rather than God, is the measure of all things.

Humanism does not recognize God or His absolute moral values, but instead asserts that each person can set his own values and control his own destiny. Professor Donald Oppewal, who participated in the study of public school textbooks used throughout the public school system, along with Paul Vitz, summarized the basic tenets of humanism as described in *Humanist Manifesto I* and *Humanist Manifesto II* :

1. Humanism holds to an evolutionary explanation of both human rights and development.

2. Humanism believes that the scientific method is applicable to all areas of human concern and is the only means of determining truth.

3. Humanism affirms cultural relativism, the belief that values are grounded only in a given culture and have no transcultural normativity. [In the words of *Humanist Manifesto II*, third thesis, it says, "We affirm that moral values derive their source from human experience. Ethics is autonomous and situational, needing no theological or ideological sanction."]

4. Humanism affirms an anthropocentric and naturalistic view of life [i.e. there is no supernatural God and man has no soul].

5. Humanism affirms an ethic of individualism, one in which personal values take precedence over community standards for behavior. [*Humanist Manifesto II*, sixth and seventh thesis, advocates any type of sexual behavior between consenting adults, euthanasia, and the right to suicide.]

6. Humanism affirms cultural determinism, the belief that values in a given society are largely determined by environmental circumstances.

7. Humanism believes in the innate goodness and perfectibility of man.[71]

Professor Oppewal then proceeds to demonstrate, through numerous examples of textbooks, how these concepts of humanism pervade public school textbooks.

Of course, as these humanistic concepts completely saturate modern public school textbooks in every subject, God and biblical values have been systematically replaced with the values of humanism.

One example of humanism in the public school textbooks is readily apparent in the widespread teaching of "values clarification." This instruction teaches children that everything is relative, and they alone can determine what is right and wrong for themselves. The Gablers document this type of education throughout public school textbooks in their chapter entitled "Children Adrift." The Gablers state: "The students' 'convictions' are determined on the basis of situation ethics and peer pressure."[72]

The "Problem Solving with People" (PSP) program is a typical example of values clarification taught in the public schools. G. Wes Rowlader, head of a parent group trying to expose this destructive instruction, described PSP as it is used in Michigan:

> Five-to thirteen-year-olds are coerced to use child intuition to solve problems dealing with divorce, death, drugs, etc.— all by voting for the "desired" solution. The teacher, by Model standards, is not to influence a solution. PSP is a decision-making technique for children that determines "right" from a majority vote of peers using feelings to determine solutions. One major problem with PSP—no answer is wrong. This undermines parental authority by implying that all responses are valid.[73]

Also included in this "values clarification" methodology is "death education."[74] Death education teaches death apart from God and ignores the concepts of heaven and hell. Suicide is often discussed and studied as an option that is not necessarily wrong.

Studies are coming out that "death education" may be linked to the runaway suicide rate among teens in America. In 1990, an eight-year-old child in the public schools, committed suicide. He killed himself the day after he was forced to watch a movie about a boy who tries to kill himself.[75] The movie was part of the Michigan Model and was shown in the context of an exploration of feelings, including a list of twenty-five bad feelings that the children are supposed to "get in touch with." Of course, the class is taught "free of values." This boy had an I.Q. of 130, was obedient, and was very active in sports and the arts. He should not even have been thinking of suicide. Dr. William Coulson, who investigated the incident, concluded:

> His parents did not know the movie was shown. The teachers did not prescreen the movie. But I have since looked at the curriculum and been told by the director of the elementary education in that district that the movie was shown as part of a unit on feelings and self-esteem. And I think it's not going to be the last such tragedy that emerges from this model.[76]

In fact, 400,000 adolescents attempt suicide each year. This suicide rate among fifteen- to nineteen-year-olds rose 44 percent from 1970 to 1984, compared to an increase of only 2.6 percent for the nation as a whole.[77]

Another example of humanism is the teaching of evolution. Evolution is a scientific theory which requires the child to develop "blind faith" in science since the formation of the world cannot be observed. Evolution systematically destroys the concept of God and reduces man to an animal. The biblical truth that man is made in the image of God, has worth in Him, and is given by Him unchanging rules by which to live, is replaced with man being nothing more than an expendable animal with no standard to follow. Evolution destroys the values of life and encourages extermination of the unborn. Infamous Communist leaders such as Lenin, Stalin, and Mao Tse Sung, who were responsible for the massacre of millions of their countrymen, were all dedicated evolutionists who believed that men were animals and had no individual worth beyond the "good of the state." With the role of God scientifically explained away by evolution, which is taught as a "fact," children begin to accept the humanistic notion that God is a fable and develop a disrespect for human life.

On the other hand, Scientific Creationism which scientifically exposes evolution as false and defends the truth that this world was created, is forbidden to be taught in public school.[78] The home schooler may be encouraged to know, however, that the Institute of Creation Research has developed scores of heavily documented textbooks and teaching aids for students, that expose the myth of evolution and defend biblical creation.[79]

The teaching of sex education and health courses, which are described earlier in this chapter, directly follow the tenets of humanism by blessing any and all forms of deviant sexual practices. The removal of God and His standards in every subject reflects the humanistic belief that God does not exist and man is autonomous and innately good.

The evidence is overwhelming that the religion of humanism has pervaded the public schools in every subject. Sadly, forty million children in America are captive audiences to these lies.

New Age and Occult Influence

The New Age religion has also seeped into the public schools but it is a little more difficult to identify.

Examples of the New Age practices are Progressive Relaxation, Guided Imagery, Deep Breathing, and Meditation. Progressive Relaxation is the serial relaxation of the major muscles of the body by direction of the teacher, which involves a process of first tensing and then relaxing major muscle groups in a certain order. Often this practice is accompanied by soothing music. I have seen several hypnotists at work, and this technique is always used.

One book utilized as part of the deceptively named "Family Life Education" program, adopted in Virginia, instructs the student:

> Let's take a moment to use our imagination. Relax and get comfortable with both feet on the floor. Let your shoulders relax, and let your arms and hands rest in a comfortable way. Let your head relax. You can let it fall forward a little if that helps you relax. Let your whole body work as if it were in slow motion. Close your eyes, but not tight. Take slow deep breathes. When you let your breath out, you might feel as if you could sink into your chair.[80]

These "mind control" practices are commonly used throughout the public school system.

Guided Imagery involves the use of images communicated to the student by the teacher while the student is in a relaxed state or a hypnotic state. In the program described above in Virginia, a imaginary figure named "Pumsy" is created for the students. This figure is "someone" for the child to go to for comfort, friendship, counsel, etc. In Session 3 and 12 of the curriculum it says:

> You may return to spend time with Friend and Pumsy any time you wish by creating your own Mind Picture whenever you like [Session Twenty-four]. You can come visit your clear pond any time you like. It's as near to you as your own mind, as close to you as your own heart. No one can stop you from going there.[81]

> ... After you have decided what to do with your magic cup, you can start wiggling your fingers, and then when you're ready you can move your arms around a little bit. Next, you can begin to open your eyes and say with me in a clear, strong voice ... 'I am me, and I am enough. I am me, and I am enough. I am me, and I am enough.'[82]

Developing this imaginary person in the student's mind is supposed to build the child's self-esteem. However, it clearly has it roots in the New Age and occult practice of "channeling" and communicating with the spirit world. It also replaces God and leads the children to trust either totally in themselves or develops a dependency on this imaginary person. This can and has led children right into the occult.

A similar program is currently being used in the Michigan public schools, and it is called the "Michigan Model." In this program children are encouraged by their teacher or counselors to picture something in their minds like a clear, blue pond, which is safe and warm. Often the exercise ends after fifty minutes of sitting in a darkened classroom with music tapes playing in the background. Children are then told to open their eyes and repeat: "I can choose how I feel. I can choose how I feel."

The Deep Breathing practice commonly used in public schools encourages students to breathe regularly, being aware of the diaphragm and the lungs. Usually, students are directed to use imagery during these breathing exercises.

Meditation involves repeated exposure of students to words or sounds, directed by the teacher, in order to create a relaxed or altered mental state.

Let me give you two more examples of curricula that apply these New Age techniques. First, the *Impressions* readers are frequently used in the public schools for kindergarten through sixth grades in language arts classes. Harcourt Brace Jovanovich publishes this series through its subsidiary, Holt Rinehart and Winston. It is presently being used in twelve hundred public schools in thirty-four states.[83]

Portions of this series are responsible for thousands of children learning how to create and cast spells to effect change, how to do circle chanting within a witchcraft or magic paradigm, and how to encounter creatures who lust for the flesh of children. One example is the story of "Zini and the Witches" in which Zini discovers the bones and bodies of murdered victims and realizes that his wife is a witch. The chief witch finds out that Zini knows and will only spare him if he brings her the hearts of his mother and sister.[84]

In the *Impressions* curricula children are also forced to read anthologies that describe violent ritual practices, including a poem by

Jack Pretlutsy called "The Sorceress." This poem describes the sorceress casting spells, entering trances, and sending souls to hell, where the demons rejoice with the arrival of each additional soul.[85] Children are also required to role play as witches, and the program applies the symbols, belief systems, and practices of witchcraft and neo-paganism.

Many experts agree that the *Impressions* curricula is saturated with the occult and New Age. Former Wiccan high priest and witch, William Schnoebelen, states that *Impressions* exercises "promote the practices, rituals, and belief systems of witchcraft and neo-paganism." Dr. Carl Raschke, an internationally recognized expert on religion, finds the *Impressions* program to be a "thorough and consistent means of advocacy" and "religious indoctrination" for "witchcraft, Wicca, and neo-paganism."[86] Thomas C. Jensen, an investigator of occult crimes, states *Impressions* teaches rituals and symbols used in Wicca, satanism, and Santeria which is a blend of Catholicism and the Aruba religion.[87]

Children in public schools have been reliably prohibited from learning any kind of aspect of Christianity (except to degrade it), in the name of avoiding the "establishment of religion." However, the empty moral vacuum has been filled to the brim with warped occult practices and the tenets of humanism. If that is not an "establishment of religion," I do not know what is!

Another curricula designed to promote the elusive "self-esteem" of the children is "Developing an Understanding of Self and Others" (DUSO). This program uses forty-two guided imagery exercises. The children are told to lie on their backs or put their heads down on the table while the teacher plays a tape which leads them through various relaxing exercises. The children are introduced to the secret world of "Aquatron" which is inside each of them. Then the children are told to picture "Duso the Dolphin" and "Sophie the Sea Otter," who will help them work through the problems which they may be facing.[88] This is very similar to the other types of programs being used in public schools but are given a different name.

One more example of blatant New Age teaching is in the S.O.A.R. curriculum, which has been used in the Los Angeles public schools among others. One exercise in this program states:

This lesson introduces school children to their psychic workshop and two spirit guides who will help them make decisions. Teacher says, "How would you like a special or custom-built house to go to anytime you want to, with anything you want in it? You could have any person you want come and visit you. It wouldn't matter if he or she was dead or alive, real or imaginary. After today, you will always have this special place and special way of being with anyone you want. Be sure to use them. . . .

"First, you will see your male helper. He is behind the sliding door in your elevator. Use the control panel on the arm of your chair to make the door of your elevator open. . . . Now look at your male helper. . . . He is now real and alive, and he comes into your workshop. This is your male helper. Say 'hello' and ask him his name. Show him around your workshop and tell him how glad you are that he is there with you."[89]

Programs such as these are becoming more and more prevalent throughout the public school system. The *Impressions* program, the Michigan Model, and some of the others, are currently under litigation for violating the establishment clause. Other New Age programs in the public schools have been moderated after concerned citizens have objected. However, the same practices have only appeared elsewhere in the curriculum. The curriculum publishers and creators of the programs, in fact, have developed training seminars for teachers to instruct them on how to counter parental objection to these insidious programs. In spite of minimal public outrage, these types of programs continue to inflict untold damage on our youth.

Conclusion

The public schools are in deep trouble. Since the public school system is responsible for teaching over forty million students in this country, its influence and immoral instruction is being felt throughout our society. The moral crisis in the public schools is acute, and we as a nation are already reaping the consequences in the rise of violence, crime, sexual diseases, divorce, selfishness, various forms of paganism and the occult, and a growing rejection of God's absolute moral standards. In the name of "neutrality," the public schools are steadily and many times subtly assaulting the traditional family and destroying the minds of our youth.

We, as adults, should do all we can to "clean up" the public schools, but can we afford to lose our children in the process? The public schools' curriculum and atmosphere clearly oppose God and His laws. Christians armed with this information can no longer be held guiltless in regard to their children's education. By God's grace, in America, there is an alternative that is working and is allowing children to be raised in the "nurture and admonition of the Lord." That solution is the subject of this book: home schooling.

Notes

1. Archibald A. Hodge, Popular Lectures on Theological Themes (Philadelphia: Presbyterian Board of Publications, 1887), 283-4.

2. Appendix A in this book gives the reader a brief comparison between humanistic education and Christian education, as summarized by scholar and theologian, R. J. Rushdoony.

3. Paul C. Vitz, "Religion and Traditional Values in the Public School Textbooks: An Empirical Study," "Report of NIE Grant: Equity in Values Education: Do the Values Education Aspects of Public School Curricula Deal Fairly with Diverse Belief Systems?" (NIE 6-84-0012; Project No. 2-0099).

4. Ibid.

5. Ibid.

6. Paul Vitz, Censorship: Evidence of Bias in Our Children's Textbooks (Ann Arbor, Mich.: Servant Books, 1986), 56-57.

7. Ibid., 37-38.

8. Ibid.. Appendix B, 122, 123.

9. Ibid., 123.

10. Ibid., 126.

11. Ibid., 122-123.

12. Alexis de Tocqueville, Democracy in America, J. P. Mayer, ed., trans. G. Lawrence (Garden City, NY: Doubleday, 1969), 290-300.

13. David Barton, America: To Pray or Not to Pray (Aledo, Tex.: Wallbuilder Press, 1988).

14. "Safe Schools," a report released in 1978 by the National Center of Education.

15. "Annual Study Shows 3 Million Crimes on School Campuses," National School Safety Center News Service, Pepperdine University, California, October 1991, Dr. Ronald Stephens, Director. This newsletter provides a review of the "National Crime Survey of 1991."

16. Ibid.

17. Denise Foley, "Danger: School Zone," Teacher Magazine, May 1990, 58.

18. "National Goals Report: Building a Nation of Learners," released in October 1991 by the National Educational Goals Panel. Also see excerpts printed in Education Week, 2 October 1991, 18.

19. "Youths Merely Robbed of Clothes Considered Lucky, By Comparison," *Washington Times*, 16 April 1990, A3.

20. Education Week, Vol. X, No. 3, 19 September 1990.

21. "Crime Curtails School Recess," USA Today, 20 February 1990.

22. Carol Innerst, "Pistol-Packing Kids Put School on Alert," *Washington Times*, 23 August 1992, A16.

23. Kristan Metzler, "Two Charged in Girl's Rape—All Age Eleven," *Washington Times*, 21 March 1992, A9.

24. *Ibid.*

25. Spencer Rich, "Report Card on Youth: Downward Trends Dominate," *Washington Post*, 24 March 1992, A17.

26. George Papajon, "School Crime Study Deflates Some Myths," *Chicago Tribune*, 22 March 1991, DuPage Section.

27. "Annual Study Shows 3 Million Crimes on School Campuses," National School Safety Center News Service, Pepperdine University, California, October 1991, Dr. Ronald Stephens, Director.

28. Andrew Glass, "Juvenile Crime Soaring, FBI Reports," *The Sunday Oregonian*, 30 August 1992, A17.

29. *Ibid.*

30. Jerry Seper, "Violent Crime Hits Record Levels, " *Washington Times*, 30 August 1992, A15.

31. *Ibid.*, 7.

32. Denise Foley, "Danger: School Zone," cover page.

33. *Ibid.*, 57-58. In Detroit alone, attacks on public school teachers increased 900 percent in five years. Seventy public school employees were victims of reported physical assaults by students during the 1989-90 school year. See "Attacks on Teachers Skyrocket," *Detroit News*, 20 June 1991, 1A, 12A.

34. "Security Becomes Priority in Schools Across Nation," *Washington Times*, 29 August 1989.

35. "America on Drugs," *U.S. News and World Report*, 28 July 1986, 48.

36. Barbara Linkin, "High Drug Use Found in Schools," *The Daily Texan*, 1 September 1988, results released by the Texas Commission on Alcohol and Drug Abuse.

37. Paul Taylor, "Surgeon General Links Teen Drinking to Crime, Injuries, Unsafe Sex," *Washington Post*, 14 April 1992, A12.

38. Mel and Norma Gabler, *What Are They Teaching Our Children?* (Wheaton, Ill.: Victor Books, 1986). Their latest research can be obtained by contacting them at P.O. Box 7518, Longview, Texas, 75607.

39. *Ibid.*, 66.

40. *Ibid.*, 66-67.

41. *Ibid.*

42. Paul Vitz, Censorship, Appendix A, 108-110. This Appendix reprints the research findings of Dr. Oppenwal, Professor of Education of Calvin College, Grand Rapids, Michigan.

43. G. Wes Rowlader, "Michigan Model," Jackson Citizen Patriot, 24 March 1991, A-14.

44. Action newsletter, published by the Rutherford Institute of Charlottesville, Virginia, June/July 1990, 4.

45. Mel and Norma Gabler, *What Are They Teaching Our Children?*, 69.

46. *Teacher Magazine*, November/December 1991, 21.

47. "Helping Students Understand and Accept Sexual Diversity," MSTA Action Line, February 1992, 8, published by the Maryland State Teachers' Association.

48. *Ibid.*

49"The Connecticut Mutual Life Report on American Values in the 80's: The Impact of Belief," conducted by Research and Forecasts, Inc., New York, 1981, commissioned by Connecticut Mutual Life Insurance Co., 219-225.

50. *West's Education Law Report*, 11 June 1987.

51. William Jasper, *The New American*, 24 March 1986, 36.

52. *Ibid.*

53. "Protected: Town Kept Teacher's Dirty Secret," *The Milwaukee Journal*, 25 November 1990, A10.

54. *People v. Moffat*, 560 N.E. 352 (1990).

55. *Elvin v. City of Waterville*, 573 A2d. 381 (1990).

56. *D.T. v. Independent School District No. 16 of Pawnee County*, 894 F.2d. 1178 (1990).

57. *Reguero v. Teacher Standards Commission*, 789 P.2d. 11 (Or. App. 1990).

58. *Osterback v. State of Alaska*, 789 P.2d. 1037 (Alaska App. 1990).

59. *Martin v. City of Biddeford*, 568 A.2d. 1103 (Me. 1990).

60. *Medlin v. Bass*, 386 S.E.2d 80 (1989).

61. Maria Koklanaris, "Escaped Killer Nabbed Teaching at Fairfax School," *Washington Times*, 16 May 1992.

62. "Shielding Bad Teachers, A Special Three Part Report," *Detroit Free Press*, 15 March 1992, 1A.

63. *Ibid.*, 10A.

64. *Ibid.*

65. Terri Regotti, "Negligent Hiring and Retaining of Sexually Abusive Teachers," 73 ed., *West Education Law Reporter 333*, 21 May 1992.

66. Kim Painter, "Fewer Kids Save Sex for Adulthood," *USA Today*, 5 March 1991, 1D-2D.

67. Barbara Vobejda, "Teen Birthrates Reach Highs Last Seen in 70's," *Washington Post*, 19 January 1992, A3.

68. Amy Goldstein, "D.C. Teens' High Sex Rate Risks Pregnancy, Disease," *Washington Post*, 24 November 1991, A1, A11.

69. *Ibid.*, A11.

70. *Time*, 9 November 1981, 67.

71. Paul Vitz, *Censorship*, 101-104.

72. Mel and Norma Gabler, *What Are They Teaching Our Children?*, 105. See entire chapter, 98-114.

73. G. Wes Rowlader, "Michigan Model," A-14.

74. *Ibid.*, 90.

75. *American Family Association Newsletter*, September 1990, Jackson, Michigan.

76. *Ibid.*

77. *U.S. News and World Report,* Nov. 12, 1984 and Herbert Kohl, "What Teenage Suicide Means," Nation, 9 May, 1987, 603.

78. *Ibid.,* 131-148.

79. Institute of Creation Research, P.O. Box 2667, El Cajon, CA 92021. If you contact them at his address, they will be happy to send you a catalogue of their materials and put your on their newsletter list.

80. Jill Anderson, *Pumsy in Pursuit of Excellence* (Timberline Press, 1987, Eugene, Oregon). These "mind picture" sessions occur in Sessions 3, 6, 9, 12, 15, 18, 21, and 24.

81. *Ibid.,* Session 24 and 3.

82. *Ibid.,* Session 12, 148.

83. Kimberly Parker, "New Age in the Public Schools," *The Teaching Home,* April/May 1991, 77.

84. Ibid

85. *Ibid.,* 79.

86. Journal of the American Family Association, March 1992, Tupelo, MS, 13.

87. "New Age in the Public Schools," The Teaching Home, April/May 1991, 77.

88. *Ibid.*

89. *Ibid.*

CHAPTER 3

THE PHILOSOPHICAL CRISIS
IN PUBLIC EDUCATION

"The public school has become the established church of secular society."[1]

– Ivan Illish

Why do I take time to write a chapter on the modern philosophy behind education? Does the philosophy behind our educational system have any relevance to today's crisis in education? This chapter will show how the philosophy behind public schools has everything to do with why our public school system is in crisis today. I will demonstrate how the philosophical basis of the public schools and the agenda of those who created it have brought us the problems we face today.

For the most part, I will let the "movers and shakers" of the public school movement do the talking. The reader need only compare the philosophy and agenda of these public school advocates to the present condition of the public schools in order to understand the "cause and effect" of their destructive philosophy.

The Christian, especially, needs to take a hard look at this philosophy and determine if it is compatible with God's Word. Chapter 4 discusses at length what the Bible says about parents' responsibility in education. We must ask ourselves: "Can we fulfill these biblically mandated responsibilities and still send our children to public school?"

In order to accurately understand the impact of the public schools' philosophies of education, we need to first define education.

Definition of Education

What is education? In simple terms, education is the transmission of basic skills and values to the next generation. It is inescapably religious, and it cannot be neutral.

So why is education so important? At present, over forty million students are being taught in the public school system. How we educate our youth, therefore, is crucial for the future of our nation.

Furthermore, education, in a general sense, comprises every area of life. This training of our minds ultimately affects all our actions in this life. In fact, the average child spends approximately twelve hundred hours per year in formal education at school. While in kindergarten through twelfth grade, the child spends over seventeen thousand hours in school, which is approximately one-third of all his or her waking hours. God tells us we must redeem the time. Are we doing that in our present educational system?

There is a very valid and often repeated phrase that states "a mind is a terrible thing to waste." The wasting of our children's minds is truly terrible, and the wasting of forty million minds of children in the public school is devastating.

Many of the leaders of the public school system, past and present, recognize the importance of education. They realize how millions of students can be mass-manipulated to conform to one certain pattern. At present, forty million students are being conformed to a clearly humanistic philosophy which has smothered our public school system.

Battle for our Children's Minds

Taking place at this moment is a major battle for our children's minds. This is a philosophical battle which has significant spiritual ramifications. The battle for our children's minds is being waged by those who have a Christian mind-set (requiring the teaching of Scripture as the basis of all knowledge), and the humanists (who believe man is the measure of all things). As I have already stated, education is never neutral. Someone's values will be applied to each and every subject.

Scripture, as we show in chapter 4, claims that all knowledge and wisdom come from God. Therefore, knowledge owes its very existence to God. True knowledge, as a result, cannot be fully understood unless one looks through the lenses of Scripture.

On the other hand, the humanist view of education, as we find in the modern public school system, holds that knowledge exists in its own right. According to the humanists, knowledge can be truly interpreted without reference to God and His constant involvement in all of history. The humanists' goal, as envisioned by many of the founders and present operators of the public school system, is to use education to manipulate and control masses of students. In light of these two battling philosophies, the reader needs to determine for himself which system of philosophy is consistently being taught in the public schools, and which system of philosophy is demanded of all believers to be applied to the education of their children.

In this chapter are several quotes by men of the past and present who have warned us what the public school system will become. You will also find that their warnings have come true. Furthermore, you will read numerous quotes from influential men in the public school community who have clearly revealed their agenda and their desire to eradicate God and His principles from the instruction of our youth. In chapter 5 we find that home schooling and family education was the major form of education for the first one hundred years of our country's existence. I document how this form of education worked, and how it resulted in a moral populace dedicated to building a nation founded on godly principles. This moral and godly foundation forms the basis of the freedoms we enjoy in this country today. In fact, even the literacy rates were close to the 99th percentile *before* compulsory education laws.

Today, we see the direct "cause and effect" of the public school system on our youth and our nation. These statistics are documented in chapters 1 and 2. I encourage you to carefully consider the major philosophical crisis that is presently taking place in our public school system and act now to remove your children from the public school system or encourage others to do so before it is too late.

The Philosophy and Agenda of the Public School Founders and Leaders

State education, as we know it today, did not begin to exist in the United States until the 1840s in Massachusetts.[2] It was not until the early 1900s that state education became widespread.

As a result, by the early 1900s the authority and responsibility of education shifted from the parents to the state. This shift was the beginning of the decaying process of American education. No longer would children be considered sinful and responsible for their behavior but rather "innately good." Education would be manipulated by the elite educational establishment to "save our society." Instead, the "man is the measure of all things" educational philosophy, along with the denial of absolute values, has brought our country into the chaos and crisis occurring today.

Horace Mann, called "the father of public education," led the crusade to establish a public school system throughout the country when he became the first secretary of the newly established Massachusetts Board of Education in 1837. Mann, who was a Unitarian, called himself a Christian and was a "thorough believer in the doctrine of the perfectibility of man."[3] He further believed that children had a "right" to an education, and that right needed to be guaranteed by the state.[4] The education of the child, and not the child himself, was responsible for his action as an adult. He held that "society in its collective capacity, is a real . . . godfather for all *its* children."[5] His goal was to create a nonsectarian school system, and he envisioned that education would bring salvation to society. He wanted to establish "a new religion, with the state as its true church, and education as its Messiah."[6]

Mann stated further:

> What the church has been for medieval man the public school must become for democratic and rational man. God

will be replaced by the concept of the public good. . . . The
common schools . . . shall create a more far-seeing
intelligence and a pure morality than has ever existed
among communities of men.[7]

Horace Mann had a view of education in which the elite must
manipulate and conform the masses in order to create an ideal society.
The state, not the parents, knows what is best for the children. There
is little room left for God in Mann's philosophy of public education.

The second most important man in the modern public school
movement was John Dewey. He was also a signer of the *Humanist
Manifesto* and first president of American Humanist Association. The
major tenets of the *Humanist Manifesto* are listed in chapter 2 of this
book. These tenets, which Dewey affirmed with his signature, flatly
reject God and all absolute values and embrace reason, relativism,
and science as the controlling forces in society. Christian values have
no place in society.

Humanism, as described in the *Humanist Manifesto*, does not
recognize God or His absolute moral values but, instead, asserts that
each person can set his own values and control his own destiny. The
Humanist Manifesto affirms the theory of evolution which teaches that
man has no soul, and reduces man to simply an animal. Since values
are determined by the individual, any type of sexual perversion
between consenting adults, euthanasia, and suicide are all proper. In
fact, the *Humanist Manifesto II*, 6th and 7th thesis, advocates exactly this.

John Dewey, the author of the modern public school system,
signed the *Humanist Manifesto*, consenting to these false principles.
He did not even quietly agree with the humanists. He boldly and
publically signed their "statement of faith." This same man applied
the principles of the *Humanist Manifesto* to America's public school
system.

Dewey believed that man is not a reflection of God, but that
society and education must be "socially planned" by the state. Dewey
stated ". . . all aims and values which are desirable in education are
themselves moral."[8] In other words, humanism is a religion, and its
tenets are the only acceptable source of moral principles. He believed
that these principles of humanism, as outlined in the *Humanist
Manifesto*, must be infused in all public education.

Like Mann, Dewey believed in the "messianic character of
education," a phrase coined by scholar R. J. Rushdoony.[9] For Dewey,

humanism is the religion and the public school teachers are the prophets. Dewey stated:

> I believe all education comes through the stimulation of the child's powers by the demands of the social situations in which he finds himself. . . . Education is the fundamental method of social progress and reform [religion being by-passed]. . . . Every teacher should realize the dignity of his calling; that he is a social servant set apart for the maintenance of proper social order and the securing of the right social growth. . . . In this way the teacher is always the prophet of the true god and the usherer of the true kingdom of god.[10]

This is frightening. But this is exactly what Dewey was working toward. The True God and His absolute moral principles did not fit into Dewey's plans for the public school. Only the religion of humanism would be taught in his school system.

Dewey also emphasized "social unification" as the goal of the public schools in order to promote "state-consciousness."

> The American people is conscious that its schools serve best the cause of religion in serving the cause of social unification; and that under certain conditions schools are more religious in substance and in promise without any of the conventional badges and machinery of religious instruction than they could be in cultivating these forms at the expense of a state-consciousness.[11]

Other humanist leaders recognized and applauded the change that was taking place in the public schools. They knew the humanist agenda was coming to fruition. For example, Paul Blanshard, contributing author of the magazine called *The Humanist*, declared the success of their goals:

> I think that the most important factor moving us toward a secular society has been the educational factor. Our schools may not teach Johnny to read properly, but the fact that Johnny is in school until he is sixteen tends to lead toward the elimination of religious superstition. The average American child now acquires a high school education and this militates against Adam and Eve and all other myths of alleged history. . . . When I was of one the editors of the Nation in the 20's, I wrote an editorial explaining that golf and intelligence were the two primary reasons why men did not attend church, perhaps I would now say golf and a high school diploma.[12]

To Blanshard, Christianity is nothing more than "religious superstition," and the public schools, back in 1976, had already become the most influential vehicles for eradicating belief in Christianity.

John Dunphy, another writer for *The Humanist*, agreed that in the public schools a war is taking place for the minds of our children.

> The classroom must and will become an arena of conflict between the old and the new—the rotting corpse of Christianity, together with all its adjacent evils and misery, and the new faith of humanism.[13]

In the late 1980s Dr. John Goodland wrote a report for the National Education Agency arguing that one of their goals is to re-educate children to turn away from the values of their parents. He said:

> Our goal is behavioral change. The majority of our youth still hold to the values of their parents and if we do not resocialize them to accept change, our society may decay.[14]

The agenda of many public school leaders is to manipulate the masses of students in the American public school system to reject absolute values. This is not just an empty allegation. This agenda is revealed in the public school leaders' own writings.

Another set of convincing quotes are those from many of the professors of schools of education which teach the teachers. For instance, one Harvard professor in 1973 declared war on traditional values, challenging teachers to help make well all the "sick" children who hold to godly values:

> Every child in America entering school at the age of five is mentally ill because he comes to school with certain allegiances toward our founding fathers, toward our elected officials, toward his parents, toward a belief in a supernatural being, toward the sovereignty of this nation as a separate entity. It's up to you teachers to make all of these sick children well by creating the international children of the future.[15]

However, you might challenge this one college professor as being a little extreme. Well, let us review several professors from teachers' colleges, such as Columbia University and Ohio State University, and other influential educators involved in the public school movement.

In fact, scholar R .J. Rushdoony, in his book *The Messianic Character of American Education* thoroughly reviews the writings and teachings of many of these public educators and managers from the middle 1800s until the late 1960s. He sums up the humanistic philosophy of these educators:

> The state is the order of liberty, and the school is the means whereby citizens are prepared for the good life. The state has become the saving institution, and the function of the school has been to proclaim a new gospel of salvation. Education in this era is a messianic and a utopian movement, a facet of the enlightenment hope of regenerating man in terms of the promises of science and that new social order to be achieved in the state.[16]

This messianic and humanistic philosophy is evidenced in the writings of many of these "movers and shakers" in the public schools.

For instance, James G. Carter, who worked along with Horace Mann, to develop state control over schools, believed that as a result of state funding and control "the whole earth will then constitute but one beautiful temple, in which may dwell in peace, all mankind."[17] He also advocated state institutions for educating teachers:

> An institution for this purpose would become by its influence on society, and particularly on the young, an engine to sway the public sentiment, the public morals, and the public religion, more powerful than any other in the possession of government.[18]

Carter, like Mann, saw state education as the "savior" and understood the tremendous power that the enlightened elite could wield, once such a state system was in place throughout the country.

John Swett, who served as the state superintendent of California from 1863 to 1868, helped create the state system of public schools. Swett strongly believed that "the property of the State should be taxed to educate *the children of the State*."[19] [emphasis added]. To make clear his position, Swett declared, "Children arrived at the age of maturity belong, not to the parents, but to the state, to society, to the country."[20] John Swett worked hard to regulate private schools making it a crime for parents to send their children to private schools without the approval of the local school district. Swett was particularly proud of the idea and function of state schools and sincerely believed "no prophets of evil can convince the American people that vice, crime, idleness, poverty, and social discontentment are the results of free public schools."[21]

Chapters 1 and 2 of this book show that what Swett believed state education would cure, it has actually caused: namely vice of every kind, out-of-control crime, and academic decline which contributes to poverty and social unrest. Once state education is divorced from biblical, moral values, and the parents' God-given role is usurped by the state, chaos will result. Faith in the intellectual elite managing the public school system has failed.

Colonel Francis Wayland Parker was called "the father of the progressive educational movement" by John Dewey.[22] Parker was basically an existentialist who believed in the natural divinity of the child.[23] He taught that children gravitated toward good, and that discipline and punishment were harmful for children because they interfered with the child's self-education and his spontaneity.[24] Parker believed that children can be "conditioned" like animals. He stated that salvation of all children could be obtained through state schools.

> We must know that we can save every child. The citizen
> should say in his heart: I await the regeneration of the world
> from the teaching of the common schools of America.[25]

Salvation through education is becoming a familiar refrain, being sung by the public school founders and managers. Parker even went so far as to say, "Every school in the land should be home and heaven for children."[26] Because of his complete faith in public education, he opposed private education and referred to those maintaining private education as practicing "bigotry."[27]

It is clear from many of these leaders in the public school system that they have little room for tolerating private education or the God-given rights of parents.

The educational elite also commonly believe that children can be conditioned, much like Pavlov's dog. William James, Lyman Bryson, and S. L. Pressy held to this view. James, a humanistic psychologist and educator, taught that "habits" would create how a child would believe, rather than the reverse, which is commonly held by Christians.[28]

Bryson, a professor who taught many new teachers over his nearly twenty years at Columbia University, held that "by molding and forming the varied adaptable nature of the young people in any society, education aims to make normal persons out of them."[29] Whose definition of "normal"? As far as Bryson was concerned, and many other past and present public school leaders, it certainly did not include the Christian view of "normal."

S. L. Pressy, professor of educational psychology at Ohio State University taught his future teachers:

> People are what the world has made them. In character, in usefulness, in happiness, they are the product of forces which can be controlled. And the chief agency for such control must be education.[30]

Pressy instilled in his students the understanding that they, as teachers, could mold the children, since the children are just the "product of forces which can be controlled." With proper conditioning, teachers could save our future generations.

Another professor of education at Ohio State University was Boyd Henry Bode. He wrote:

> Authoritarianism places these values in the acceptance of certain habits for the guidance of belief and conduct. Democracy stresses the importance of keeping intelligence free. For the continuous remaking of beliefs . . . intelligence should function as a means of the abundant life and not as a means of the discovery of eternal and immutable truth.[31]

In other words, teaching absolute values restricts true education and is not democratic. Remaking of beliefs is essential to true freedom.

George S. Counts was known for his advocacy of a planned economy and his work to use the public schools to help implement this planned economy which was nothing more than socialism. He had a "messianic" view of education in which state education would usher in the "new order." "Education is identified with the work of the school. As a consequence, the faith in education becomes a faith in school, and the school is looked upon as a worker of miracles. *In fact, the school is the American road to culture.*"[32] Like many of the other public school educators, Counts considered that the teachers were "the spiritual leaders of the masses of people," and that the "teacher is a bearer of culture and a creator of social values."[33]

Counts, like many of the public school leaders discussed above, had a faith in "public education" as being the "salvation" of our nation. Counts and the others eagerly put aside academics in the public schools and replaced it with a social agenda which involved a remaking of our culture and a rejection of our system of traditional values. In 1958 one dean of a teachers' college explained his school's goal: "An educated man is one who is well adjusted and helpful in his community." When asked if such a man could still be considered educated without being able to count his fingers or write his name the dean answered, "Yes."[34] Humanist editor Paul Blanshard, whom I quoted earlier, said that "Johnny" may not be learning to read in the public schools, but his learning the Bible is nothing but superstition. Literacy is secondary to the social agenda. Time has proven this to be true since millions of children graduate from the public schools illiterate, and yet the crime statistics in chapter 2 show the Christian values in our youth have nearly been obliterated.

These "movers and shakers" of the public school system openly admit that their agenda, from the beginning of the public schools, was to manipulate and "condition" the masses of children in order to change their traditional value systems. The goal of literacy and learning basic skills was replaced by a social agenda. This agenda of the public school leaders supports the tenets of the *Humanist Manifesto*, which is clearly a slap in the face of God.

This was recently confirmed by Rita Kramer in *Ed School Follies* who documents how the teacher colleges concentrated on teaching future teachers politics rather than academic knowledge. In chapter 1 I summarize her book in greater detail.

This philosophy pervades the modern public school system. Chapters 1 and 2 demonstrate where this valueless philosophy is taking us.

Former Proponents Verify the Philosophical Failure of the Public Schools

In case you think my conclusions concerning the public school philosophy are somewhat exaggerated, I document below accounts from modern public school leaders who have abandoned the system and are exposing its failures.

For instance, John Taylor Gatto taught for over thirty years in the public school system and was even elected the New York Teacher of the Year in 1989. Gatto independently describes the influence of Horace Mann and others. In his speech while accepting the award, Gatto stated:

> Schools were designed by Horace Mann and by Sears and Harper of the University of Chicago and Thorndyke of Columbia Teacher's College and some other men to be instruments of scientific management of a mass population. Schools are intended to produce through the application of formulae, formulaic human beings whose behavior can be predicted and controlled. . . . The products of schooling are, as I have said, irrelevant . . . useless to others and useless to themselves.[35]

In another example, psychologist W. R. Coulson, who holds two doctorates—one in Philosophy from the University of Notre Dame and the other in Counseling Psychology from the University of California at Berkeley—was even more critical than Gatto. During the 1960s Coulson was an associate of Carl Rogers and Abraham Maslow, gurus to a generation of psychologists and educators and both winners of the "Humanist of the Year Award." It is interesting to note that both Rogers and Maslow finally acknowledge the educational failure of encounter groups, sensitivity training, and values clarification.

In an interview, Coulson remarked:

> American education has experienced a 'meltdown' because it has 'wimped out on substance.' Teachers have 'lost their nerve.' Furthermore, the public schools are highly secularized and seek to 'convert' children to a 'humanistic' ethic. Moreover, the sex and anti-drug education the schools dish out only encourages young people to have sex and use drugs. . . . Coulson believes that we have 'given in' to the 'religion of psychology,' particularly in the area of education, which has become too therapeutic.' He is critical of 'lifestyle' programs which take away from academic achievement. The educational system has in his view fallen into such bogus offerings as 'visualization' and 'relaxation' because today's teachers often can't deliver the academic goods. 'Teachers are not learning to teach,' Coulson says, but instead are becoming 'facilitators.' In that capacity, they 'make students feel good about their disablement.'

> Such trends Coulson sees as proceeding, not just from prominent humanist John Dewey, but from Horace Mann and the fathers of mass education in America. The system, he says, is essential 'unitarianism in the classroom.' What the schools are forking out now is not only religious, Coulson contends, but it is 'religious trash,' and in that judgment he is not alone.[36]

The public schools are "religious," but it is a religion devoid of values. It is a religion of humanism. It has been designed that way since Horace Mann. It has not changed. It has only become worse.

Even the *Harvard Educational Review* recognizes the value-laden nature of modern public schools:

> Parents, social commentators, anthropologists, sociologists, psychologists, and others who have done research on schooling have all understood its value-laden nature. . . . Whatever their values, most parents seem to realize that a good deal of child rearing will take place at school and a great many basic values will be foisted on children there. The school is a social environment in which a child may learn much more than that which is in the formal curriculum.[37]

Another highly reputed educational journal analyzes one of the most destructive and humanistic aspects of the modern public schools' instruction:

> Values clarification appears, at least by default, to hold the view that all values are equally valid. . . . The moral point of view imbedded in values clarification is that of the ethical relativist. In its simplest definition, ethical relativism holds that one person's views are as good as another's; everyone is entitled to his own morality, and when it comes to morality, there is no way of showing one opinion is better than the other. The fundamental objection to ethical relativism is that it can be used to justify virtually any activity in which an individual or society wishes to engage.[38]

The evidence is overwhelming for an indictment to be brought against the leaders of the public school system, past and present, for imposing their devastating agenda on our country's youth.

Unheeded Voices of the Past that Predicted the Results of Secular State Schools

History is a valuable tutor. If we can learn from the mistakes of the past, we can avoid repeating them. Let us briefly review the critique of godly men and other scholars of the past who understood the consequences and warned us about secular, state education. I will let each of them speak for themselves on this issue.

For instance, Archibald Hodge, pastor and theologian nearly one hundred years ago, warned:

I am as sure as I am of the fact of Christ's reign that a comprehensive and centralized system of national education, separated from religion as is now commonly proposed, will prove the most appalling enginery for the propagation of anti-Christian and atheistic unbelief, and of anti-social nihilistic ethics, individual, social, and political, which this sin rent world has ever seen.[39]

Timothy Dwight, president of Yale University from 1795 to 1817, was a man of God. He, too, understood the importance of Christian education:

Education ought everywhere to be religious education . . . parents are bound to employ no instructors who will not instruct their children religiously. To commit our children to the care of irreligious persons is to commit lambs to the superintendency of wolves.[40]

Similarly, Noah Webster echoed this truth:

In my view, the Christian religion is the most important and one of the first things in which all children, under a free government, ought to be instructed. . . . No truth is more evident to my mind than that the Christian religion must be the basis of any government intended to secure the rights and priviledges of a free people.[41]

During the Reformation, Martin Luther warned us:

I am afraid that the schools will prove the very gates of hell, unless they diligently labor in explaining the Holy Scriptures and engraving them in the heart of the youth.[42]

R. L. Dabney, a reformed preacher and writer during the time of the Civil War and following noticed that with the growth of public schools, crime increased. He also made some very prophetic statements in his book *On Secular Education*, describing the inevitable censorship of religion:

But the result of public education is to bring a larger number of children into primary schools, and reduce the illiteracy somewhat—which is a great delight to shallow philanthropists. But the number of youths well educated above the mere rudiments and especially those brought under daily Christian training is diminished.

So, the actual and consistent secularization of education should not be tolerated. But nearly all public men and

> preachers declare that the public schools are the glory of America. They are a finality, and in no event to be surrendered. We have seen that their complete secularization is logically inevitable. Christians must prepare themselves then, for the following results: all prayers, catechisms, and Bibles will ultimately be driven out of the schools."[43]

> . . . But may parents nevertheless neglect or pervert the power? Yes, but does the State never neglect and pervert its powers? With the lessons of history to teach the horrible and almost universal abuses of power in the hands of civil rulers, that question is conclusive. In the case of an unjust or Godless state, the evil would be universal and sweeping. There is no doubt that God has deposited the duty in the safest place [the parents]."[44]

Historian Philip Schaff remarked in 1888:

> It is impossible to draw the precise line between moral and religious education. Absolute indifference of the schools to morals is impossible; it [education] must be either moral or immoral, religious or irreligious. . . . An education that ignores religion altogether would raise a heartless and infidel generation of intellectual animals.[45]

Other leaders of the past saw the advent of public schools as a way for the state to control education nationwide. For example, free-market economist, John Stuart Mill warned:

> A general state education is a *mere contrivance* for *molding people* to be *exactly* like one *another:* and as the mold in which it casts them is that which pleases the predominant power in the government or [the will of] the majority of the existing generation; in proportion as it is efficient and successful, it establishes a *despotism* over the *mind,* leading by natural tendency to one over the body.[46] (emphasis supplied)

Mill had a point that has been proven over and over again. For example, Hitler said, "Let me control the textbooks, and I will control Germany." And he did. Hitler's government also outlawed private education. "Recalcitrant parents were warned that their children would be taken away from them and put in orphanages or other homes unless they enrolled."[47]

These voices may have been from the past, but they ring true today. We would do well to heed their warnings.

The Philosophy and Agenda of the Public Schools Was Fulfilled at the Expense of Our Youth

Who is winning the battle for the minds of our children? It is obvious from reading chapters 1 and 2 and this chapter that the humanists are winning. Here are a few more comments from contemporaries, describing the present condition of the public schools.

A professor at Pepperdine University condemned the public school product when he stated:

> I believe that the decline in education is probably responsible for the widespread use of drugs. To live in the midst of a civilized society with a level of knowledge closer perhaps to that of primitive man than to what a civilized adult requires (which, regrettably, is the intellectual state of many of today's students and graduates) must be a terrifying experience, urgently calling for some kind of relief, and drugs may appear to many to be the solution. . . .

> This is no longer an educational system. Its character has been completely transformed and it now clearly reveals itself to be what for many decades it has been in the process of becoming: namely an agency working for the barbarization of youth.[48]

John Taylor Gatto, mentioned earlier in this book, said he quit teaching because he didn't want to "hurt" kids anymore. In addition, he declared "government schooling . . . kills the family by monopolizing the best times of childhood and by teaching disrespect for home and parents."[49] In an earlier speech on January 31, 1990, in accepting an award from the New York State Senate naming him "New York City Teacher of the Year," Gatto gave more details:

> We live in a time of great school crisis. We rank at the bottom of nineteen industrial nations in reading, writing, and arithmetic. At the very bottom. The world's narcotic economy is based upon our consumption of this commodity: If we didn't buy so many powdered dreams the business would collapse—and schools are an important sales outlet. Our teenage suicide rate is the highest in the world and suicidal kids are rich kids for the most part, not the poor. In Manhattan, 70% of all new marriages last less than five years. So something is wrong for sure. . . . [50]

I don't think that we'll get rid of schools any time soon, certainly not in my lifetime, but if we're going to change what's rapidly becoming a disaster of ignorance we need to realize that the school institution "schools" very well but it does not "educate"—that's inherent in the design of the thing. It's not the fault of bad teachers or too little money spent. It's just impossible for education and schooling ever to be the same thing.[51]

The daily misery around us is, I think, in large measure caused by the fact that, as Paul Goodman put it thirty years ago, we force children to grow up absurd. Any reform in schooling has to deal with its absurdities.

It is absurd and anti-life to be part of a system that compels you to sit in confinement with people of exactly the same age and social class. That system effectively cuts you off from the immense diversity of life and the synergy of variety; indeed it cuts you off from your own past and future, sealing you in a continuous present much the same way television does. . . .

Two institutions at present control our children's lives: television and schooling, in that order; both of these reduce the real world of wisdom, fortitude, temperance, and justice to a never-ending, non-stop abstraction. In centuries past, the time of the child and adolescent would be spent in real work, real charity, real adventures, and the realistic search for mentors who might teach what you really wanted to learn. A great deal of time was spent in community pursuits, practicing affection, meeting and studying every level of the community, learning how to make a home, and dozens of other tasks necessary to become a whole man or a whole woman.[52]

The public schools are in sad shape. In America, by God's grace, we have alternatives to sending children to public school. Please, read the next section of this book about the tremendous academic and moral success of home schooling.

Knowing This, Can We Risk Sending Our Children to Public School?

I will close with three more quotes, which sum up the modern philosophical crisis in the public school.

Author Charles Francis Potter who wrote the book *Humanism: A New Religion,* saw humanism rushing into the public school system.

Education is thus a most powerful ally of humanism, and every public school is a school of humanism. What can the theistic Sunday school, meeting for an hour once a week and teaching only a fraction of the children, do to stem the tide of a five day program of humanistic teaching?[53]

Educational writer Elmer Town, declared:

The public schools have a singular adherence to secular humanism, and defined as a total lifestyle without reference to or need of God . . . the public schools are not neutral, it is anti-Christian. For a Christian to send his children to the public school is just as consistent as sending them to a Unitarian Sunday school: they are learning the opposite of what is taught in the Word of God.[54]

Finally, Robert Thoburn, author and administrator of a large Christian school, tells us about "Satan's big lie."

Obviously the schools are not Christian. Just as obviously they are not neutral. The Scriptures say that the fear of the Lord is the chief part of knowledge; but the schools, by omitting all reference to God, give the pupils the notion that knowledge can be had apart from God. They teach in effect that God has no control of history, that there is no plan of events that God is working out, that God does not foreordain whatsoever come to pass. . . .

The public schools are not, never were, can never be, neutral. Neutrality is impossible.

The big lie of the public schools is that the God of the Bible is irrelevant. The textbooks never mention Him. Everyone assumes that children do not need to know anything about God, God's law, and God's Word in order to become educated people. This is Satan's own lie.[55]

Notes

1. Ivan Illich, *New York Review of Books*, Vol. 13, No. 6, 9 October 1969, 12-15.

2. Samuel I. Blumenfeld, NEA: *Trojan Horse in American Education* (Boise, Idaho: Paradigm Company, 1984), 1.

3. E. I. F. Williams, *Horace Mann, Educational Statesman* (New York: Macmillan, 1937), 205.

4. Rousas J. Rushdoony, *The Messianic Character of Education* (Nutley, N.J.: Craig Press, 1968), 21.

5. *Ibid.*, 24.

6. *Ibid.*, 32.

7. *Ibid.*

8. John Dewey, *Democracy in Education* (New York: MacMillan, 1918), 360.

9. Rousas J. Rushdoony, *The Messianic Character of Education* (Nutley, N.J.: Craig Press, 1968).

10. John Dewey, *My Pedagogic Creed* (Washington D.C.: Progressive Education Association, 1897), 6, 15, 17.

11. John Dewey, *Characters and Events, Popular Essays in Social and Political Philosophy*, Vol. II (New York: Holt, 1929), 515.

12. Paul Blanshard, "Three Cheers for Our Secular State," *The Humanist*, March/April 1976, 17. (A publication of the American Humanist Association which is based in Amhurst, New York.)

13. John Dunphy, *The Humanist*, January/February 1983.

14. Dr. John Goodland in a report written for the National Education Association entitled, "Schooling For the Future." This passage was quoted by Dr. D. James Kennedy in a sermon entitled "A Godly Education," delivered to the Coral Ridge Presbyterian Church in Ft. Lauderdale, Florida.

15. Statements made by a Harvard University Professor at a 1973 teachers' seminar as quoted in *Schooling Choices*, (Portland, Oregon: Multnomah, 1988), 131.

16. Rousas J. Rushdoony, The Messianic Character, 4.

17. James G. Carter, "Letters to the Honorable William Prescott on the Free Schools of New England, with Remarks upon the Principles of Instruction" (Boston: Cummings, Hilliard & Co., 1824), 123.

18. James G. Carter, "Essays upon Popular Education" (Boston: Bowles and Dearborn, 1826), 49-50.

19. John Swett, *History of the Public School System of California* (San Francisco: Bancroft, 1876), 113.

20. *Ibid.*, 115.

21. John Swett, *American Public Schools, History and Pedagogics* (New York: American Book Company, 1900), 168.

22. Rousas J. Rushdoony, *The Messianic Character*, 97. This title was given to Parker in an article in the 9 July 1930 New Republic.

23. Francis Wayland Parker, *Talks on Pedagogics* (New York: John Day, 1937), 18.

24. *Ibid.*, 265-271.

25. *Ibid.*, 328.

26. Ida Cassa Heffron, *Francis Wayland Parker, An Interpretive Biography* (Los Angeles: Deach, 1934), 41.

27. "The School of the Future," *NEA Journal*, 1891, 82-89.

28. William James, *Talks to Teachers on Psychology* (New York: Henry Holt, 1907), 202.

29. Lyman Bryson, *An Outline of Man's Knowledge* (Garden City: Doubleday, 1960), 374.

30. S. L. Pressy, *Psychology and the New Education* (New York: Harper, 1933), 6.

31. Boyd Henry Bode, *Educational Freedom and Democracy* (New York: D. Appleton-Century, 1938), 15.

32. George Counts, *The American Road to Culture* (New York: John Day, 1930), 16.

33. George Counts, *A Call to the Teachers of the Nation* (John Day Pamphlet No. 30, 1933), 19-25.

34. John Keats, *Schools Without Scholars* (Boston: Houghton Mifflen, 1958), 19.

35. John Taylor Gatto, *Dumbing Us Down* (Philadelphia: New Society Publishers, 1992), 26.

36. "Psychologist Unloads on Religious Trash in Nation's Schools," *World*, 27 October 1990, 10. This is based on an interview with Charles Coulson.

37. Stephen Arons, "The Separation of School and State: Pierce Reconsidered," *Harvard Educational Review*, Vol. 46, No. 1 (February 1976), 98.

38. Alan B. Lockwood, "Values Clarification," *Teachers College Record*, Vol. 77, No. 1 (September 1977), 46-47.

39. Archibald A. Hodge, *Popular Lectures on Theological Themes* (Philadelphia: Presbyterian Board of Publications, 1887), 283-4.

40. Timothy Dwight, President of Yale, 1795-1817.

41. Noah Webster, An American Dictionary of the English Language, reprint of the 1828 edition (San Francisco: Foundation for American Christian Education, 1967), 12.

42. Martin Luther, *What Luther Says* Vol I, 449.

43. R. L. Dabney, *On Secular Education*, ed. Douglas Wilson (Ransom Press, 1989), 28.

44. *Ibid.*, 30-3.

45. Philip Schaff, "Progress of Christianity in the United States," *Princeton Review*, Ser. 4, Vol 4 (September 1879), 228

46. John Stuart Mill, *American State Papers: On Liberty*, pub. Benton William (Chicago: Encyclopedia Britannica, Inc., 1972), 318.

47. William Shirer, *Rise and Fall of the Third Reich* (New York, Simon and Schuster, 1960), 255.

48. George Reisman, *The Intellectual Activist*, as quoted in the "Blumenfeld Education Letter," (Boise, Idaho: August 1990), 8.

49. Carol Innerst, "N.Y. Teacher of Year Walks Out on System," *Washington Times*, 22 October 1991, A-1.

50. John Taylor Gatto, *Dumbing Us Down*, 23-24.

51. *Ibid.*, 26.

52. *Ibid.*, 28.

53. Charles Frances Potter, *Humanism: A New Religion* (New York: Simon & Schuster, 1930).

54. Elmer Town, *Have the Public Schools Had It?* (New York: Thomas Nelson, 1974), 101-4.

55. Robert Thoburn, *The Children Trap, Difficult Principles for Education* (Fort Worth, TX: Dominion Press, 1986), 34.

PART

2

THE RISING HOPE
OF HOME SCHOOLING

M any families are turning to home schooling as the solution to the decaying public school system. However, home schooling is not a new idea—it is the restoration of an old and successful idea. It is not only a return to effective, parent-directed education; it is a moral and spiritual reformation.

Part Two will discuss the historical perspective of education in our country, demonstrating that Christian private education and, particularly, home education, was the predominant form of education in our country until the early 1900s. This section will also present the "Home Schooling Hall of Fame," briefly describing the lives of many famous home schoolers of the past. A thorough account of the modern home school movement will show the tremendous academic, economic, social, and spiritual advantages of home schooling. Since much of the home school movement is in the midst of a spiritual revival, the biblical principles will be identified and applied. The lengthy review of Bible verses dealing with education and the parents' responsibilities to train their children in God's ways, leaves little doubt as to whether or not we should send our children to public schools.

In short, home-schooled children are generally both academically literate and biblically literate, preparing them to become leaders of tomorrow. The home education movement is providing a lasting solution to the failing public school system. This academic and moral revival is being achieved independently of the government or any national organization. It is being achieved family by family as more families take seriously their responsibilities before God to train their children.

CHAPTER 4

THE BIBLICAL PRINCIPLES: A SUPPORT FOR HOME SCHOOLING AND AN INDICTMENT OF PUBLIC EDUCATION

"I am afraid that the schools will prove the very gates of hell, unless they diligently labor in explaining the Holy Scriptures and engraving them in the heart of the youth."[1]
—Martin Luther

With a majority of school-aged children attending public schools, education in America has primarily become a function of the state. This public school system is also failing miserably, both academically and morally, as demonstrated in previous chapters. The state, meanwhile, not content to control only public schools, constantly encroaches on the freedoms of private schools and home schools through various case precedents, regulations, and statutes. As a result, many public school authorities have come to believe that they are the guardians of all of the children. In fact, frequently, when I negotiate with public school superintendents, they refer to the children in their school district as "our" children. It is apparent that superintendents sincerely believe they know what is best for "their" children and feel obligated to approve home schools.

Many home schooling parents, however, take offense to this presumption by superintendents. In the tradition of their forefathers, as seen in chapter 5, these parents believe that God, not the state, has given parents the sole authority and responsibility for the education of their children. Approximately 90 percent of the estimated 250,000 home schooling families in the United States are Bible-believing Christians. Therefore, the Word of God is recognized as the source of all truth and the standard by which all things are measured. These parents want their children not only to believe as Christians, but to develop minds so they can think as Christians. They want their children to be biblically literate.

When the United States was formed, the framers of the Constitution and many of the citizens had a biblical mind-set. All of them may not have had a personal relationship with Jesus, but they respected the Bible as defining right and wrong and providing a foundation on which to build the country. As a result, the country prospered. Today, the biblical mind-set has been replaced by a secular mind-set. Public schools are teaching the children to be biblically *illiterate* and to ignore God's absolute moral values. The negative effects are being felt throughout the country, as seen in chapters 1 and 2 of this book. In many ways we have "sown the wind and now reap the whirlwind," as we allow children's minds to be wasted in the public schools, void of godly values and truth. Home schoolers are working to restore that biblical mind-set in their children and trying to fulfill the commands of God concerning the education of their children.

The following is a summary of the biblical principles of education which support Christian home schooling. In these verses the reader will find that God has delegated to the parents *first*, the authority *and* responsibility to teach and raise children.

A close and prayerful study of these verses will demonstrate that sending your children to a public school is *not* a good option. But do not take my word for it. Carefully read the verses yourself and let God speak to your heart.

The Scripture states, to "everyone who has been given much shall much be required" (Luke 12:48). Since we have a free choice in this country to *not* send our children to an ungodly public school, we will, all the more, be responsible.

The Raising of Children Is Delegated to Parents by God

According to the Bible, children belong to God, but the responsibility and authority to raise and educate them is delegated to their parents. For example, in Psalm 127:3-5 it says children are a gift from the Lord to the parents:

> Behold, children are a gift of the Lord; The fruit of the womb is a reward. Like arrows in the hand of a warrior, so are the children of one's youth. How blessed is the man whose quiver is full of them; they shall not be ashamed when they speak with their enemies in the gate.

In Genesis 33:5 Jacob introduces his children to his brother Esau as "the children whom God has graciously given me," and similarly in Isaiah 8:18, the prophet says, "I and the children whom the Lord has given me." (Also see Hebrews 2:13 and Genesis 48:8-9.) Nowhere in Scripture can a reference be found in which God delegates to the state the authority to raise and educate children.

In fact, the only time that God's people were educated by the state was when they were occupied by a heathen nation which left them no alternatives. Some of the more well-known examples are Moses, Joseph, and Daniel. God, nonetheless, has clearly delegated the *responsibility and authority to teach and raise children to the parents first.* Parents can delegate their *authority* to raise and teach their children to someone else (i.e. tutor or church school or private or public school), but they can *never delegate their responsibility to teach their children to anyone else.* In other words, God will always hold parents responsible for the education their children receive. For this reason parents need to be aware of who is teaching their child, what is being taught verbally in class by both the teacher and the peers, and what is being taught in all textbooks and supplemental books and projects. Many home school parents take this responsibility so seriously that they believe they must be the primary teachers of their children.

Children Still Belong to God

Although God has "given" children to parents, children are a "gift of stewardship," which means that parents do not really "own" their children. Parents, therefore, are not free to raise their children any way they want because God gives the parents certain "conditions" that must be met. God still considers the children to be His children. God refers to Jacob's children as "the work of My hands" in Isaiah 29:23. David gave thanks to God for being "fearfully and wonderfully made" while in his mother's womb in Psalm 139:13-14. (Also see God's claim to unborn children whom He has made and called while they are in their mother's womb in Jeremiah 1:5; Psalm 139:13-16; Job 10:8-12; Isaiah 49:1,5; and Luke 1:41,44.)

In Ezekiel 16:20-21 the Lord emphasizes again that the children are His.

> Moreover, you took your sons and daughters whom you had born to Me, and you sacrificed them to idols to be devoured. Were your harlotries so small a matter? You slaughtered My children and offered them up to idols causing them to pass through fire.

God judged these parents severely because they did not meet God's conditions for raising His children. They gave their children up to an idolatrous system which hated God. As a result, home schooling parents, aware of the anti-God curriculum and complete lack of absolute values in the public schools, cannot sacrifice their children to such a system.

The Bible states further that parents must "render to Caesar [the state] the things that are Caesar's, and to God the things that are God's" (Matthew 22:21). In fact, in some of the cases that I have handled, the prosecutor has asked the home school parent on the stand why he is not obeying the law that he be certified, since he says that he believes the Bible, and the Bible commands: "Render to Caesar the things that are Caesar's." Of course, he never finishes the verse. Since the children are not the state's or Caesar's in the first place, but rather God's, parents do not have any obligation to render their children to the public school by enrolling them in public school or complying with excessively restrictive state controls of their children's education and training.

God-Mandated Conditions for Educating Children

Part of the parents' stewardship responsibility in raising children is that certain commands and conditions set by God must be followed in raising and educating His children. For example, concerning children's education, fathers are commanded to "bring them up in the discipline and instruction of the Lord" (Ephesians 6:4).

Furthermore, in Deuteronomy 6:6-9 the Lord, after re-stating His moral law, declares:

> And these words which I am commanding you today, shall be on your heart; and you shall teach them diligently to your sons and shall talk of them when you sit in your house and when you walk by the way and when you lie down and when you rise up. And you shall bind them as a sign on your hand and they shall be as frontals on your forehead. And you shall write them on the doorposts of your house and your gates.

(Also see parallel passages in Deuteronomy 4:9, 11:18-21; Psalm 78:1-11.) In other words, God's commands and truth must be taught to the children by the parents, and they must be taught *diligently*. Children are to be brought up in the "instruction" of the Lord. How can this be achieved if a child spends six to seven hours a day receiving a public education which teaches him to think as a non-Christian?

It is clearly the parents' primary responsibility to teach their children "so that your days and the days of your sons may be multiplied" (Deuteronomy 11:21). These commands to educate our children, of course, cannot be accomplished once a week at Sunday school. It involves a comprehensive approach to education on a *daily* basis. The commands of God should be taught to our children when we sit in our homes, when we rise up, lie down, and when we travel. In other words, *all the time.*

This comprehensive educational program is to be based on God's commands. Two of the goals of godly education, therefore, are that children will put their confidence in the Lord, and that they will keep His commandments.

> For He established a testimony in Jacob, and appointed a law in Israel which He commanded our fathers that they should teach them to their children that the generation to come might know, even the children yet to be born, that they may arise and tell them to their children, that they should put their confidence in God and not forget the works of God, but keep His commandments (Psalm 78:5-7).

Many other verses emphasize that parents have the weighty responsibility of teaching their children what God has done so that the children will not forget (see Exodus 13:8,14; Joshua 4:20-22,24).

Of course, the children also have some responsibility. They must obey the commandments of their parents who, in turn, are obeying God:

> My son, observe the commandments of your father, and do not forsake the teaching of your mother; bind them continually on your heart; tie them around your neck. When you walk about, they will guide you; when you sleep, they will watch over you; and when you awake, they will talk to you. For the commandment is a lamp, and the teaching is light; and reproofs for discipline are the way of life (Proverbs 6:20-23).

Teaching these commands of God comprehensively to our children is "light" to our children and leads them to "the way of life." A side effect of a biblical education, then, can be the salvation of our children's souls for all eternity. Learning God's Law and His principles "tutors" and "leads us to Christ" (Galatians 3:24). If the very souls of our children are at stake, should we risk having them taught thousands of hours of information that is contrary to God's truths and in an atmosphere that denies God's existence?

In addition, our children will receive a tremendous blessing, according to Isaiah 54:13: "And all your [children] will be taught by the Lord; and great will be your children's peace" (NIV). It seems apparent that the "children's peace" will affect the parents by contributing to a peaceful home and minimal rebellion. No wonder so many parents who send their children to the public school for six or more hours a day of ungodly instruction have chaotic homes in which the children regularly challenge the parents' authority and mistreat siblings.

Commands to Train Our Children's Minds

None of us want to waste the minds of our children. Unfortunately, Christians do exactly this when they send their children to the modern public school.

God commands His people in Jeremiah 10:2: "Learn not the way of the heathen" (KJV). The public schools are teaching the children the "way of the heathen," while ignoring God's ways.

Furthermore, David explains that we need to "meditate" on God's Law, day and night (Psalm 1:2). How can our children meditate on

God's Law, when they are never even taught God's Law in the public schools? In fact, Christians are to "take every thought captive to the obedience of Christ" (2 Corinthians 10:5).

This responsibility is immense. Parents must train their children to think God's thoughts after Him. A godly education, therefore, is learning not only to believe as a Christian (for salvation), but to *think* as a Christian. Christian home schooling teaches children to think as Christians. Unfortunately, public schools and some private schools are teaching children who believe as Christians to think as non-Christians. Since Christian parents in the past have neglected their *duty* to follow this comprehensive approach to education, generations of adult Christians now apply ungodly principles in their lives and work places, while simultaneously believing as Christians. In essence, many parents are raising humanistic Christians, many of whom are "lukewarm" and not thinking God's thoughts after Him.

Proverbs 23:7 states, "For as [a man] thinks within himself, so he is." If a child is trained to think as a humanist, he will tend to act and live as a humanist. Moreover, Scripture states, "Everyone, after he has been fully trained, will be like his teacher" (Luke 6:40). This passage continues by describing the blind who lead the blind into the pit. This is why it is so important that parents teach their children to *think* as Christians and that children be taught by godly teachers. Parents must not let their children be conformed to the pattern of this world, but they must be transformed by the renewing of their *minds*, that they may prove what is good, and acceptable, and the perfect will of God (see Romans 12:2). Unfortunately, public schools are working to conform our children's minds to the pattern of this world.

In Matthew 16:23, Peter, thinking like a humanist, told Jesus that He would not have to die. Jesus' response to him was harsh: "Get behind Me, Satan! You are a stumbling block to Me: for you are not setting your *mind* on God's interests, but *man's*." Parents are casting a stumbling block before their children by having them trained to think man's thoughts, instead of God's thoughts, over thirty hours a week.

"Keep seeking the things *above*, where Christ is. . . . Set your *mind* on things above, not on the things that are on earth" (Colossians 3:1-2). The Bible and its principles are things from above—the blueprint that God has given to show us how we are to live. In Matthew 22:37-38, Jesus commanded, " You shall love the Lord your God with all your heart, and with all your soul, and with all your *mind*. This is the great and foremost commandment." How can children love God with their minds when the public school and some private schools train their minds to ignore God's principles and to think as humanists?

Home schooling enables families to properly and comprehensively train their children's minds to think God's thoughts and to develop a biblical mind-set rather than a secular mind-set. However, it is important to make sure you are using a good curriculum and books which are grounded in God's Word. Even a home-schooled child's mind can be wasted if the parents, for instance, just "baptize" humanist textbooks. By this I mean that sometimes parents use humanistic textbooks and merely pray over those books or try to do "damage control." With all the excellent Christian textbooks available and countless Christian books covering every subject, we are without excuse to give our children the most truth we can while they are being educated under our roofs. They will only be stronger and more grounded in God's principles, until truth becomes second nature to them.

In Appendix A, I have reprinted an excellent comparison between a Christian education and a humanistic education so that the reader can determine what types of education his children are receiving, whether at home, private school, or public school.

Negative Socialization

Even though parents are commanded to give their children a biblical education, they must also protect them from "negative socialization." The Scripture warns, "Do not be deceived: Bad company corrupts good morals" (1 Corinthians 15:33). Proverbs 13:20 states, "He who walks with wise men will be wise, but the companion of fools will suffer harm."

The public schools fail miserably in the area of socialization, with the abundance of crime, drugs, immorality, and gang warfare rampant in the school system. Home schooling enables parents to fulfill this responsibility by fostering positive socialization.

Content of True Education

It is clear from the passages above that God delegates to the parents the authority and responsibility for teaching children. God requires us to make certain that His Word and principles are applied in a daily, comprehensive manner to the education and upbringing of our children. Furthermore, He will hold us responsible for how we direct the education of our children. We must be careful not to "cause one of these little ones who believe in Me to stumble" by subjecting them to an ungodly education. Christ explains "it is better for him that a heavy millstone be hung around his neck, and that he be drowned in the depth of the sea" (Matthew 18:6; also see the consequences of disobedience outlined in Deuteronomy 28). Paul further reminds us that if we do wrong, we will "receive the consequences of that wrong . . . and that without partiality" (Colossians 3:25).

Therefore, parents must be careful to provide their children with an education in which the *content* reflects God and is based on His Word. Paul promises,

> All scripture is inspired by God and profitable for teaching, for reproof, for correction, for training in righteousness; that the man of God may be adequate, equipped for every good work (2 Timothy 3:16-17).

"The fear of the Lord is the beginning of knowledge" (Proverbs 1:7; also see Psalm 111:10). "The Lord gives wisdom; from His mouth come knowledge and understanding" (Proverbs 2:6; also see 9:10). In fact, James 1:5 affirms that in Christ are all the treasures of wisdom. Further, in James 3:13-18, it says wisdom which is *not* from above is earthly, natural, and demonic. Wisdom from above (which is found in the heavenly blueprint, the Bible) is "pure, then peaceable, gentle, reasonable, full of mercy and good fruits, unwavering, without hypocrisy." Which form of wisdom is being taught? Public schools and some private schools certainly are not teaching the wisdom from above.

The goal of true education is found in Psalm 119:97-101: To train children in God's laws so they can govern themselves, be wiser than their enemies, have more insight than their teachers, and understand more than the aged. If we train our children this way God will no doubt find us faithful stewards of the children He has placed in our care.

Scripture speaks to every area of life. It is clear that education is inescapably religious. Every subject, as a result, needs to be studied through the lens of God's Word. If parents do this, their children will be equipped for *every* good work and able to apply God's principles to every area of life. Their beliefs will not be separate from their thoughts and actions, as is so often the case with "Christians" today.

Does Sending Our Children to Public School as Missionaries Make it Right?

Many Christian parents rationalize that they are sending their children to public school in order for them to be "missionaries" to the unsaved children. However, there are no biblical examples of children being used as missionaries, but rather adults are always the missionaries. This of course means it is important for adult Christians to become public teachers and administrators, school board members, truant officers, and social workers.

As far as our children are concerned, God commands us, as seen in this chapter, to provide our children with a comprehensive education based on His principles. Sending our children to public school to "save souls" while they receive six or more hours of secular brainwashing does not relieve us of our responsibility before God. Disobeying God by doing something in the name of God does not justify our sin.

For instance, in 1 Samuel 15:1-23, King Saul directly disobeyed God's command to destroy all of the Amalekite animals by sparing the animals and then offering them as sacrifices to the Lord. God rebuked Saul through Samuel, saying,

> Has the Lord as much delight in burnt offerings and sacrifices, as in obeying the voice of the Lord? Behold, to obey is better than sacrifice, and to heed than the fat of rams. For rebellion is as the sin of divination, and insubordination is as iniquity and idolatry (1 Samuel 15:22-23).

Are we trying to make a "sacrifice" to God by sending our children to public school to "save souls" while disobeying God's commands to us concerning raising our children? We must remember to obey is better than sacrifice.

These Biblical Principles Apply to Children in High School

Sometimes families are tempted to educate their children only *until* high school. At that point, they rationalize that their child is ready to be trained in a secular setting or elsewhere. The biblical principles discussed above, however, still apply to high school-aged children. In fact, the high school years are generally the most difficult and formative years for a child. Therefore, consistent, biblical training is more important than ever.

Also the high school years are crucial for the training of the child's mind in God's principles and teaching him how to apply those principles in his life and in the world around him. A high school-aged child is more mature and often ready for learning the weightier matters of God's laws and principles. The four high school years should be the final phase of training the child for adulthood so that he can thoroughly think as a Christian and apply biblical solutions to his future work, family, or college. These years are too valuable to waste and much too risky, considering the peer pressures and subtle humanistic training. God calls our children "arrows" and we need to be sure they are "finished" arrows that are straight, sharp, and sure of their mark. We do not want to shoot into the secular world partially finished arrows that are not fully sharpened and still a little weak. Such "arrows" will often miss their mark and make no impact.

In Appendix D, Elizabeth Smith, a veteran home school mother and teacher, has prepared "15 Reasons to Home School in the High School Years." The reader is encouraged to review and consider these reasons as your children reach high school age.

Home Schooling Is a Biblical Form of Education

As seen above, home schooling has much support from the Word of God. It provides, in fact, the most successful way that parents can fulfill their immense obligations, in providing their children with a comprehensive biblical education and restoring and preserving their families. The goal of home schooling is to raise the children so that each of them will "be diligent to present [himself] approved to God as a workman who does not need to be ashamed, handling accurately the word of truth" (2 Timothy 2:15).

As seen from the verses above, God's truth and His principles are the foundation of all knowledge. Our children must not only be taught to *believe* as Christians but also to *think* as Christians. God's principles must be taught to children in a comprehensive manner on a daily basis. God's truth speaks to every academic discipline. Does modern public education even come close to these commands?

Sending our children to the public school violates nearly every biblical principle described above. It is tantamount to sending our children to be trained by the enemy. No doubt that if Satan had his choice as to which school system he would want us to send our children to, he would choose the public school system. Yet, the vast majority of Christians still send their children to public schools.

As a result, we need to encourage our pastors to start preaching these truths from the pulpit. Until pastors start to take the lead to urge an exodus from the public schools, the minds of many children from Christian families will be wasted and, in some instances, their hearts will be lost. You may want to give a copy of this book, or at least this chapter, to your pastor and encourage him to take a stand on this issue for the sake of our children.

As parents, we cannot escape the responsibility for how our children are trained and educated. God will hold us responsible for the choices we make in regard to our children and to whom we delegate the authority to teach our children.

Home schooling is truly a biblical form of education. It is clear that God is raising up the home school movement in which properly trained children will one day assume leadership. God is blessing the home schooling movement, not because families are home schooling for home schooling's sake, but because the families are faithfully teaching their children to obey and glorify God. May God bless you as you "seek first His kingdom and righteousness" in the education and training of your children, and "all these things shall be added unto you" (Matthew 6:33).

Notes

1 Martin Luther, *What Luther Says*, Vol. I, 449.

CHAPTER 5

THE HISTORY OF HOME SCHOOLING

"All government originates in families, and if neglected there, it will hardly exist in society... The foundation of all free government and of all social order must be laid in families and in the discipline of youth.

... The education of youth, [is] an employment of more consequence than making laws and preaching the gospel, because it lays the foundation on which both the law and gospel rest for success."[1]

Noah Webster

Home schooling is not, by any means, a new phenomenon in our country. It is a time-tested and very successful form of education which has been used since the 1600s. When the public schools were formed and compulsory attendance laws were passed throughout the country in the early 1900s, home schooling almost died out. Not until the 1970s was the modern home school movement born. A glance at the history of "family education" in the home, where many Americans were taught during the first 250 years of their presence on this continent, follows.

Education in Early America Primarily Took Place in the Home

From the founding of this country by the Pilgrims in 1620 and the Puritans in 1630 to the late 1800s, most education took place in homes, with either the parents or a tutor (usually a pastor) providing the instruction.

> Education was mainly a family responsibility in colonial America, and the extent of it was largely left up to the individual. There were no compulsory attendance laws enforced by governments. Most children got at least their early education in the home, where they might be taught to read, write, and figure, but most certainly would be trained in housekeeping . . . and in many of the tasks of making a living.[2]

The colonists were heirs to common law and biblical traditions "stressing the centrality of the household as the primary agency of human association and education."[3] They were "instructed—indeed harangued—by Puritan tracts and sermons proclaiming the correctness and significance" of family education.[4] As a result, individual reading, responsive reading, and community reading were daily activities in the colonial household. After analyzing colonial education, historian Lawrence Cremin concluded the "family was the most important agency of popular education."[5]

The Role of the Bible in Home Education

This principle of home education came from the colonists reading and applying the Bible. The cornerstone of education was their belief that children are a gift and blessing from the Lord to the parents.[6]

Parents were to train their children in the "nurture and admonition of the Lord" and apply biblical principles to every area of life. Education was not a responsibility of the civil government.

In fact, historians agree that the Bible was "the single most important cultural influence in the lives of Anglo-Americans."[7] Alexis de Tocqueville, in his travels throughout the colonies and the frontier, found the Bible to be in nearly every household.[8] Consequently, the most important reason the colonists wanted their children to be literate was so they could read the Bible and thereby learn the principles of living as commanded by God.[9] For that reason, the Bible itself was used as a major textbook in most homes.

> Doubtless, many a colonial youngster learned to read by mastering the letters and syllables phonetically and then hearing Scriptural passages again and again, with the reader pointing to each word until the relationship between the printed and oral passages became manifest.[10]

The Bible was further revered and applied by the textbook writers of that period. The most popular textbooks were *New England Primer* and Noah Webster's books *A Grammatical Institute of the English Language* and *The American Spelling Book*. One hundred million copies of *The American Spelling Book* were sold in early America.[11] All of these books were made up of spiritual rhymes and biblical principles, further evidencing the impact of the Bible on education.[12]

Two-Fold Purpose of Home Education

Home education by the immediate family, or in some instances, the extended family, was two-fold. First, "sustained and systematic instruction" was normally given in order to achieve literacy. Second, vocational education was provided in order to enable the children to learn to be self-sufficient. It is interesting that this is the same two-fold interest that the United States Supreme Court now declares to be the interest of the state.

Literacy education involved daily parental instruction of the children in reading and writing. The reading materials would include the Bible, religious primers, some of the classical writings, history books, and almanacs.

The vocational education included daily household chores which "provided a continuous general apprenticeship in the diverse arts of living."[13] Many times children would work along side their father and mother, learning usually diverse skills. If a child desired a trade or skill other than their parents' skills, he would acquire a formal apprenticeship with another businessman or tradesman. Such apprenticeships were commonplace, whether learning carpentry, iron making, medicine, or law.[14] As a result,

> For many, formal schooling was simply unnecessary. The fine education they received at home and on the farm held them in good stead for the rest of their lives, and was supplemented with Bible reading and almanacs like Franklin's *Poor Richard's*.[15]

The grammar schools that existed were privately run and mere extensions of the home and church. Most children who entered these grammar schools at age eight or nine, however, were already substantially taught at home in reading and writing.[16]

College education was something many of our forefathers did not want or need. Degrees were unimpressive because men were mostly judged by their character and experience. At least nine colleges were quickly established in the middle 1700s, including Yale, Harvard, and Princeton. All of them were founded on Christianity and emphasized biblical and classical studies.[17] The entrance requirements for these colleges were stiff. A freshman in the College of William and Mary in the 1700s had to "be able to read, write, converse, and debate in Greek."[18] The King's College in New York required applicants to translate the first ten chapters of the Gospel of John from Greek into Latin.[19] Yet John Jay entered college at the age of fourteen,[20] John Cotton, Ezekiel Rogers, Reverend Witherspoon, and Jonathan Edwards, at the age of thirteen,[21] and Thomas Jefferson,[22] John Adams, and James Monroe at age sixteen.[23]

Home education provided a complete education for children, making them both literate and self-sufficient, and also prepared those who wanted to proceed to grammar schools and college.

The Founders Never Intended State Education

Thomas Jefferson's beliefs concerning public education and state control reflected our forefathers' fear of such education:

> It is better to tolerate the rare instance of a parent refusing to let his child be educated than to shock the common

feelings and ideas by the forcible asportation and education
of the infant against the will of the father.[24]

State education, as we know it today, did not begin to exist in the
United States until the 1840s in Massachusetts.[25] It was not until the
early 1900s that state education became widespread.

As a result, the authority and responsibility of education shifted,
by the early 1900s, from the parents to the state. This shift, as seen in
Part One of this book, was the beginning of the decaying process of
American education. No longer would children be considered sinful
and responsible for their behavior. Education would be manipulated
by the elite educational establishment to "save our society." Instead,
the "man is the measure of all things" educational philosophy along
with the denial of absolute values, has brought our country into the
chaos and crisis occurring today.

Home Education in Early America Was Successful

As a result of home education and private grammar schools during
the first seventy-five years of our country, the over-all literacy rate was
higher than it is today.[26]

For example, DuPont de Nemours surveyed education in America
in the early 1800s, and discovered a nearly 99 percent literacy rate:

> Most young Americans . . . can read, write, and cipher. Not
> more than four in a thousand are unable to write legibly—
> even neatly—while in Spain, Portugal, and Italy, only a
> sixth of the population can read; in Germany, even in
> France, not more than a third; in Poland, about two men in
> a hundred; and in Russia not one in two hundred. England,
> Holland, and the Protestant Cantons of Switzerland, more
> nearly approach the standard of the United States, because
> in those countries the Bible is read; it is considered a duty to
> read it to the children. . . . In America a great number of
> people read the Bible.[27]

John Adams discovered in 1765 that a "native of America,
especially of New England, who cannot read and write is as rare a
Phenomenon as a Comet."[28] Jacob Duche, the Chaplain of Congress
in 1772, said of his countrymen, "almost every man is a reader."[29]
Similarly, Daniel Webster confirmed that the product of home
education was near-universal literacy, when he stated "a youth of
fifteen, of either sex, who cannot read and write, is very seldom to be

found."[30] An example of the success of home schooling was the ability of the average citizen to read and understand the *Federalist Papers*, which was specifically written for the common man but is rarely comprehended today.

The desire to read resulted in most households building libraries that contained from ten to four thousand volumes, as accumulated by Cotton Mather, a preacher. According to Benjamin Franklin, the American libraries,

> have improved the general conversation of Americans, made the common tradesman and farmers as intelligent as most gentlemen from other countries, and perhaps have contributed in some degree to the stand so generally made throughout the colonies in defense of their privileges.[31]

The home education of many early Americans was supplemented by sermons each Sunday. These sermons were given by pastors who would spend eight to twelve hours in study daily, researching and praying over their weekly sermons.[32]

> Thus, without ever attending a college or seminary, a church-goer in colonial America could gain an intimate knowledge of Bible doctrine, church history, and classical literature.[33]

Home Schooling Has a Proven Track Record

The message is clear. Education at home achieved literacy and self-sufficiency. The colonists understood that the God-given responsibility of training children rests with the parents. The biblical principle that they applied was the principle that the parents had sole control of the process of education. America produced several generations of highly skilled and literate men and women who laid the foundation for a nation dedicated to the biblical principles of freedom, moral law, and self-government. In chapter 7 I will give the reader many accounts of individual success stories of home schoolers in history.

The recent revival of home education, beginning substantially in the 1980s, "is actually the closing of a circle, a return to the philosophy which prevailed in an earlier America."[34]

Notes

1. *Noah Webster's First Edition of an American Dictionary of the English Language*, 12 of Preface by Rosalie J. Slater (San Francisco: Foundation for American Christian Education, 1980).

2. Clarence Carson, *The Colonial Experience* (Wadley, AL: American Textbook Committee, 1987), 124-125.

3. John Barnard and David Burner, editors, *The American Experience in Education*, chapter 1 by Lawrence Cremin, "Education in the Households and Schools of Colonial America" (New York: Franklin Watts, Inc., 1975), 3.

4. *Ibid.*

5. *Ibid.*, 12.

6. See chapter 4 for a summary of the Scripture verses supporting the parents' roles in education which are often quoted throughout the writings of the Puritans and many of the early educators and leaders. Also see Levi Hart, "The Importance of Parental Fidelity in the Education of Children" (Norwich, 1792) and Reverend John Witherspoon, "Letters on Education of Children" (1797), both reprinted in Verna Hall, editor, *Christian History of the American Revolution*, (San Francisco: The Foundation for American Education, 1982), 213-245.

7. Lawrence Cremin, *American Education: The Colonial Experience, 1607-1789* (New York: Harper and Row, 1970), 40.

8. Alexis de Tocqueville, *Democracy in America*, trans. George Lawrence, ed. J.P. Mayer (Garden City, NY: Doubleday and Co., 1969), 290-315.

9. Barnard and Burner, *The American Experience*, 8. Another historian summarized that colonial education's "chief purpose was to support revealed religion." Clinton Rossiter, *Seedtime of the Republic: The Origin of the American Tradition of Political Liberty* (New York: Harcourt, Brace, 1953), 120.

Another reason the colonists encouraged family education was to protect their country from tyranny. "Education is favorable to liberty. Freedom can exist only in the society of knowledge. Without learning, men are incapable of knowing their rights, and where learning is confined to a few people, liberty can be neither equal or universal." Dr. Benjamin Rush, one of the framers of the Constitution, in an essay written in 1786, quoted in Hamilton Abert Long, *The American Ideal of 1776* (Philadelphia: Your Heritage Books, Inc.), xix.

10. *Ibid.*, 8. Also see Pierre Samuel DuPont de Nemours, *National Education in the United States of America* (Newark: University of Delaware Press, 1923), 329-330.

11. Noah Webster, *American Dictionary of the English Language*, preface by Rosalie Slater (San Francisco: Foundation for American Christian Education, 1967), 13.

12. Noah Webster explained the importance of the Bible in education: "The Bible is the chief moral cause of all that is good, and the best corrector of all that is evil, in human society; the best book for regulating the temporal concerns of men, and the only book that can serve as an infallible guide to future felicity." ed. Verna Hall *Christian History*, 21.

Webster further explains his views on education, typifying the philosophy of education prevalent in his time: "In my view, the Christian religion is the most important and one of the first things in which all children . . . ought to be instructed. No truth is more evident to my mind that the Christian religion must be the basis of any government intended to secure the rights and privileges of a free people. . . . When I speak of Christian religion . . . I mean primitive Christianity in its simplicity as taught by Christ and His apostles, consisting in belief in the being, perfection, and moral government of God; in the revelation of His will to men, as their supreme rule of action; in man's accountability to God for his conduct in this life; and in the indispensable obligation of all men to yield entire obedience to God's commands in the moral law and in the Gospel." *American Dictionary of the English Language*, 12.

Also see J. Richard Fugate, *Will Early Education Ruin Your Child?* (Tempe, Ariz.: Alpha Omega Publications, 1990), 58 (or 23 in 2nd Edition, 1992).

13. Barnard and Burner, *The American Experience*, 6.

14. Carson, *The Colonial Experience*, 125 and Barnard and Burner, *The American Experience*, 11-12.

15. Robert A. Peterson, "Education in Colonial America," *The Freeman* (New York: Irvington-on-the-Hudson, 1983), 6. Also see Samuel Eliot Morison, *The Intellectual Life of New England* (Ithaca: Cornell University Press, 1965), 71-72.

16. Peterson, "Education in Colonial America," 5.

17. Carson, *The Colonial Experience*, 124.

18. John Eidsmoe, *Christianity and the Constitution* (Grand Rapids, Mich.: Baker Book House, 1987), 22.

19. *Ibid.*

20. *Ibid.*

21. Fugate, *Will Early Education Ruin Your Child?*, 60-62.

22. Eidsmoe, *Christianity and the Constitution*, 218.

23. *The American Heritage Book of the Presidents* (New York: Dell Publishing, 1967), 62 (also page 160 in II).

24. Saul K. Padover, *Jefferson* (New York: Harcourt-Brace 1942), 369.

25. Samuel Blumenfeld, *NEA: Trojan Horse in American Education*, (Boise, Idaho: Paradigm Company, 1984), 1.

26. Samuel Blumenfeld, *Is Public Education Necessary?* (Old Greenwich, Conn.: Devin Adair, 1981), 27-30 and Rousas John Rushdoony, *The Messianic Character of American Education* (Nutley, N.J.: The Craig Press, 1979), 330.

27. See Nemours, *National Education in the United States of America* (Delaware: University of Delaware Press, 1923), 3-5.

28. Butterfield, ed., *Diary and Autobiography of John Adams* (Cambridge, Mass.: Harvard University Press, 1961).

29. Carl and Jessica Bridenbaugh, *Rebels and Gentlemen* (New York: Oxford University Press, 1982), 99.

30. "Discourse on Education," *The Works of Daniel Webster* (Boston: C.C. Little & J. Brown Co., 1851), 125.

31. Max Farrand, ed. *The Autobiography of Benjamin Franklin*, (Berkley, Calif.: 1949), 86. See Carson, *The Colonial Experience*, 125, for a description of many of the colonial household libraries.

32. Peterson, "Education in Colonial America," 8. For further description of the crucial role of the Calvinistic clergy in educating the people of early America

through their verbal and written sermons, see John Whitehead, *The American Dream* (Westchester, Ill.: Crossway Books, 1987), 35-43 and Eidsmoe, *Christianity and the Constitution*, 17-38.

33. *Ibid.*

34. Beshoner, "Home Education in America: Parental Rights Reasserted" (Kansas City: University of Missouri Law Review 191, 1981), 49.

For instance, in the Plymouth Colony, "most of the heads of families were not only fully competent to teach their own sons and daughters, but found it no severe hardship to give their time to the training of the few whose parents had either died or were needy." See William T. Davis, *History of the Town of Plymouth* (Philadelphia: J.W. Lewis & Co., 1885), 52.

CHAPTER 6

THE ADVANTAGES OF HOME SCHOOLING

"*Education*: comprehends all that series of instruction and discipline which is intended to enlighten the understanding, correct the temper, and form the manners and habits of youth, and fit them for usefulness in their future stations. To give children a good education in manners, arts, and science, is important; to give them a religious education is indispensable; and an immense responsibility rests on parents and guardians who neglect these duties."

-Definition from Noah Webster's *First Edition of an_ American Dictionary of the English Language*, 1828[1]

Sometimes, when people first hear of home schooling, they shudder and express doubt that a child could receive an adequate education at home. This reaction is normal since most Americans were trained in an institutional school and the majority of those attended a public school. I must admit I was initially one of these doubters.

This bias has been nurtured even further by the teacher unions and other pro-public school organizations which propagate myths, such as the necessity of certification of teachers and the claim that the government knows what is best for our children. As a result, many people, at first impression, are quickly ready to dismiss home schooling as a viable option for educating children.

However, once a person can put aside his bias and review the tremendous advantages of home schooling, these advantages speak for themselves. Nearly every week a new study is released which exposes the failing condition of the public school system, in spite of numerous reforms. Studies on home schooling, on the other hand, reveal academic excellence on the part of these students along with possession of a disciplined lifestyle and a moral foundation.

This chapter is intended to provide documentation to convince the doubter, and to give encouragement and "ammunition" to the home schooler, to counter criticism. Home schooling has many advantages, but the most convincing is that it really works.

What is Home Schooling?

Home schooling is exactly what the name implies: a school in the home. The Illinois Supreme Court defined a school as "a place where instruction is imparted to the young."[2] The teachers in a home school are generally the parents, and it is estimated that at least 50 percent of them only have a high school diploma.[3] One element which all the home school parents seem to have in common is a commitment to making the necessary sacrifices to personally provide an education for their children.

As more and more people become aware of the advantages of home schooling, the ranks of home schoolers continue to swell, with estimates ranging as high as one million students presently being home schooled nationwide.[4] The growth of the number of families home schooling from year to year is steady. In fact, in Georgia alone, 5,500 home schoolers registered with the state in 1990-91, which is an 83 percent increase from the previous year when only 3,000 were registered.[5] Approximately 85 to 90 percent of the home schooling families are doing so for religious reasons.[6] In fact, one study of over 2,000 home school families found that 93.8 percent of the fathers and 96.4 percent of the mothers described themselves as being "born again" Christians.[7] These parents believe that God has given them the responsibility and the authority to educate their children.[8] In essence, the modern home school movement is a spiritual revival which has embraced the Puritan and colonial understanding of the centrality of the family in education as described in chapter 5.

The educational establishment initially tried to squelch the home school movement, and the public was generally against it. They claimed that home schooling would hamper a child's growth, and they asserted that parents with merely a high school diploma could never successfully teach their children. By God's grace the home schoolers proved them wrong. Home schooling does work, and the end product is children who academically excel and who readily are accepted into universities.

In this chapter, several advantages of home schooling will be identified in order to demonstrate why home schooling is a solution to today's educational crisis.

Spiritual Life: Home Schooling Teaches What Really Matters

The most important benefit of home schooling is the spiritual aspect. It has been said: "After this life is past, only our life in Christ will last." Since most home schools at present profess a personal relationship with Christ and a belief that the Bible is the inspired Word of God, these families are teaching their children that living for Jesus, in accordance with the Word, is their most important priority. Public schools, on the other hand, ignore God and refuse to acknowledge the fact that everyone needs a Savior or they will eternally perish. Public schools also ignore God's laws and are churning out millions of students who are biblically illiterate.

In home schooling, parents can fulfill the commands in Scripture to teach their children God's truths throughout each day (see chapters 4 and 8 for further discussion). Biblical principles can be applied to each and every subject. Erroneous and humanistic philosophies can be exposed, such as evolution, inaccurate historical revisions, situational ethics, amoral sex education, and New Age influence. The home-schooled child can be consistently and carefully nurtured and trained in the admonition of the Lord so that he develops a strong moral foundation for his life. A comprehensive Christian education can be given to the home-schooled child in response to the biblical commands in Scripture.[9] The parents have the opportunity to concentrate on establishing godly character in their children.

Quality of Life: A Family Who Schools Together Stays Together

The family also benefits from the home school in terms of cohesiveness and increased time spent together. Parents are able to spend hours interacting, teaching, sharing, and nurturing their children. Fathers, no matter what their work hours, can spend much more time with their children because the children's instruction can be adjusted. This time is far above the national average of parents spending approximately seven minutes a day with face-to-face contact with their children, according to a study from Stanford University. The children also do not become segregated from their brothers and sisters by age differences but are able to relate to all age groups.

In my work, I have learned of hundreds of families who were beginning to fragment or whose marriages were dissolving. However, after home schooling, these family relationships were restored and major problems overcome.

In addition, many home school mothers forsake careers and do not work outside the home. This gives the mother enough time to not only thoroughly train her children in academic and spiritual matters, but to spend time with her infant or pre-school children. Home school mothers who stay home to teach their children do not place their infants and toddlers in Day Care. This is a major benefit to her children since children in Day Care are developing various types of negative side effects. Research for the last ten years demonstrates that infants raised in Day Care "are more prone to behavioral problems as young children than their home-reared cousins."[10]

According to Jay Belsky, a child care expert at Penn State's College of Health and Human Development, the research is compelling:

> There was this slow, steady trickle of disconcerting evidence. It looked like kids who were exposed to 20 or more hours a week of nonparental care in their first year of

life . . . seemed to be at elevated risk. They were more likely
to look insecure in their relationships to their mothers, in
particular at the end of their first year of life. [They were
also likely to show] aggression and noncompliance or
disobedience between the ages of 3 and 8. That's it in a
nutshell.[11]

Parents who home school can avoid this "parent trap" of Day Care for
their pre-school children, that is commonly accepted today.

In this fast-moving technological age, time with the family is
harder and harder to come by and there is constant pressure pulling
the family apart. Our time with our children is precious. In fact,
raising children is one of the greatest privileges and responsibilities
God gives us. We never know how long our children will be with us.
This point can best be made by the following excerpt from a letter
which HSLDA received from a home school family in Michigan.
Their thirteen-year-old son collapsed suddenly after getting off a ride
at Disneyland. He had taken a trip to see his grandparents. His
mother writes:

They took him immediately into surgery, but there was
nothing they could do. The aorta wasn't just torn; it was
shredded. God took Jim to be with Him three days before
Jim's fourteenth birthday.

Jim was surrounded with Christian nurses at the hospital.
My mom and dad were allowed to stay in the room with
him. My parents had prayed with him, along with one of his
nurses, even before they knew how serious Jim's condition
was. My mom says that right after the prayer Jim's eyes and
face just glowed and a peace and calm came over Jim which
never left him. God was with Jim every step of the way.

How thankful we are that we have home schooled Jim and
our other two boys for the last six years! We have seen Jim
grow and mature in a way most parents never experience.
We were able to spend many hours a day with him. We
have so many keepsakes and memories.

My brother-in-law, who had gone on many of the
Disneyland rides with Jim said, "Jim had an innocence
about him. You could tell he was untouched by the world."[12]

No doubt every moment counts with our children—especially
concerning the time cultivating their spiritual life. Unlike many
families in our society, home schoolers have the time.

Academic Advantage: Home Schoolers on the Average Above Average

Many studies over the last few years have established the academic excellence of home-schooled children. Not only can home-schooled students compete with children in public school, but they excel, on the average, well above average. The one-on-one tutorial approach to education, which also is centered in the family unit, is a time-tested and winning combination. Below is a brief summary of some of these studies which support the academic success of home schooling.

Independent Evaluations of Home Schooling

Most of the studies discussed below involve tests using the "norm referenced" system of scoring. This simply means the child's achievement is measured against a norm, or set of scores, established by a group of students thought to be typical of the nation as a whole. For example, if home-schooled children in a particular study scored in the 80th percentile, that means that the home-schooled children, on the average, did better than 80 percent of the national sample of the population on whom the test was normed.

In 1982 Dr. Raymond Moore studied several thousand home-schooled children throughout the United States. His research found that these children had been performing, on the average, in the 75th to the 95th percentile on Stanford and Iowa Achievement Tests.[13] Additionally, Dr. Moore did a study of home-schooled children whose parents were being criminally charged for exercising their right to teach their own children. He found that the children scored, on the average, in the 80th percentile.[14]

In 1986 researcher Lauri Scogin surveyed 591 home-schooled children and she discovered that 72.61 percent of the home-schooled children scored one year or more above their grade level in reading, and 49.79 percent scored one year or more above their grade level in math.[15]

In 1988 Dr. Brian Ray, president of the National Home Education Research Institute, reviewed over sixty-five studies concerning home education. He found that home schoolers were performing average or above on testing.[16]

In 1990 the National Home Education Research Institute issued a report entitled "A Nationwide Study of Home Education: Family

Characteristics, Legal Matters, and Student Achievement." This was a study of over 2,163 home schooling families.

The study found the *average* scores of the home school students were at or above the 80th percentile in all categories. This means that the home schoolers scored, on the average, higher than 80 percent of the students in the nation. The home schoolers' national percentile mean was 84 for reading, 80 for language, 81 for math, 84 for science, and 83 for social studies.

The research also revealed there was no positive correlation between state regulation of home schools and the home-schooled students' performance. The study compared home schoolers in three groups of states representing various levels of regulation. Group 1 represented the most restrictive states, such as Michigan; Group 2 represented slightly less restrictive states, including North Dakota; and Group 3 represented unregulated states, such as Texas and California. The Institute concluded:

> No difference was found in the achievement scores of students between the three groups which represent various degrees of state regulation of home education. . . . It was found that students in all three regulation groups scored on the average at or above the 76th percentile in the three areas examined: total reading, total math, and total language. These findings in conjunction with others described in this section, do *not* support the idea that state regulation and compliance on the part of home education families assures successful student achievement.[17]

Furthermore, this same study demonstrated that only 13.9 percent of the mothers (who are the primary teachers), had ever been certified teachers. The study found that there was no difference in the students' total reading, total math, and total language scores based on the teacher certification status of their parents:

> The findings of this study do not support the idea that parents need to be trained and certified teachers in order to assure successful academic achievement of their children.[18]

In 1991 one of the largest compilations of standardized test scores was collected by the Home School Legal Defense Association in cooperation with the Psychological Corporation, which publishes the Stanford Achievement Test.[19] The study involved the administering of the Stanford Achievement Test (8th Edition, Form J) to 5,124 home-schooled students. These students represented all fifty states, and their grades ranged from K-12.

This testing was administered in Spring 1991 under controlled test conditions in accordance with the test publisher's standards. All test administers were screened, trained, and approved pursuant to the publisher's requirements. All tests were machine scored by the Psychological Corporation.

These 5,124 home schoolers' composite scores on the basic battery of tests in reading, math, and language arts ranked 18 to 28 percentile points *above public school averages.* For instance, 692 home-schooled fourth graders averaged in the 77th percentile in reading, the 63rd percentile in math, and the 70th percentile in language arts. Sixth-grade home schoolers, of 505 tested, scored in the 76th percentile in reading, the 65th percentile in math, and the 72nd percentile in language arts.

The home-schooled high schoolers did even better, which goes against the trend in public schools where studies show that the longer a child is in the public schools, the lower he scores on standardized tests (see chapter 1 for more documentation). One hundred and eighteen tenth-grade home school students, as a group, made an average score of the 82nd percentile in reading, the 70th percentile in math, and the 81st percentile in language arts.

The rest of the research below reflects studies of home schoolers residing in certain states. This demonstrates that home schoolers do equally well regardless of their locality.

For example, in South Carolina, the National Center for Home Education did a survey of sixty-five home school students and found that the average scores on the Comprehensive Test of Basic Skills were 30 percentile points higher than national public school averages. In math, 92 percent of the home school students scored above grade level, and 93 percent of the home school students are at or above grade level in reading. These impressive scores are "being achieved in a state where public school SAT scores are next-to-last in national rankings."[20]

In Pennsylvania, 171 home-schooled students took the CTBS Standardized Achievement Test. The tests were all administered in group settings by Pennsylvania certified teachers. The middle reading score was the 89th percentile, and the middle math score was the 72nd percentile. The middle science score was the 87th percentile, and the middle social studies score was the 81st percentile. A survey was conducted of all these home school families who participated in this testing which found that the average student spent only sixteen hours per week in formal schooling (i.e. structured lessons that were preplanned by either the parent or a provider of educational materials).[21]

In North Dakota, Dr. Brian Ray conducted a survey of 205 home schoolers throughout the state. The students scored, on the average, at the following percentiles: the reading score was the 84th percentile, language was the 81st percentile, science was the 87th percentile, social studies was the 86th percentile and math was the 81st percentile.

Further, Dr. Ray found no significant statistical differences in academic achievement between those students taught by parents with less formal education and those students taught by parents with higher formal education.[22]

In West Virginia over four hundred home school students, grades K-12, were tested with the Stanford Achievement test at the end of the 1989-90 school year. The Psychological Corporation scored the children together as one school. The results found that the typical home-schooled students in eight of these grade levels scored in the "somewhat above average" range (61 to 73 average percentile), compared to the performance of students in the same grade from across the country. Two grade levels scored in the "above average" range (80 to 85 average percentile) and three grade levels scored in the "about average" range (54 to 59 average percentile).[23]

In Washington state, a survey of the standardized test results of 3,634 home-schooled students over a period of five years, found that the median cell each year varied from the 64th percentile to the 68th percentile on national norms. The Washington Home School Research Project concluded that "as a group, these home schoolers are doing well."[24]

In Idaho, fifty-four home school students were tested with the Iowa Basic Skills Tests and treated as a separate school district. A comparison based on the overall performance of students in the public schools in Boise with the home-schooled students was performed. The data, based on the averages of each grade tested, demonstrated that in the complete composite home schoolers scored in the 89th percentile, and the Boise public school students scored in the 66th percentile.[25]

A survey of home schoolers in Montana was conducted by the National Home Education Research Institute in 1990. The test results of the Montana home schoolers which were used by the Institute were supplied by the Bob Jones University Testing Service based in South Carolina. The results of the Institute's survey indicated:

> On average, the home education students scored above the national norm in all subject areas on standardized achievement tests. These students scored, on average, at the 72rd percentile in terms of a combination of their reading, language, and math performance. This is well above the national average.[26]

State Department of Education Statistics on Home Schoolers

Several state departments of education or local school districts have also gathered statistics on the academic progress of home-schooled children.

In the spring of 1987, the Tennessee Department of Education found that home-schooled children in second grade, on the average, scored in the 93rd percentile, while their public school counterparts, on the average, scored in the 62nd percentile on the Stanford Achievement test. Children in third grade scored, on the average, in the 90th percentile in reading on another standardized test, and the public school students scored in the 78th percentile. In math the third grade home-schooled children scored, on the average, in the 87th percentile, while their public school counterparts scored in the 80th percentile. In eighth grade the home-schooled students scored, on the average, in the 87th percentile in reading and in 71th percentile in math, while their public school counterparts scored in the 75th percentile in reading and the 69th percentile in math.[27]

Similarly, in 1986, the State Department of Education in Alaska, which had surveyed home-schooled children's test results every other year since 1981, found home-schooled children to be scoring approximately 16 percentage points higher, on the average, than the children of the same grades in conventional schools.[28] In Oregon, the State Department of Education compiled test score statistics for 1,658 home-schooled children in 1988 and found that 51 percent of the children scored above the 71st percentile, and 73 percent scored above the 51st percentile.[29]

In North Carolina, the Division of Non-Public Education compiled test results of 2,144 home school students in grades K-12.

Of the 1,061 home school students taking the California Achievement Test, they scored, on the average, at the 73rd percentile on the total battery of tests: 80th percentile in reading, 72nd percentile in language, and the 71st percentile in math.

The 755 home school students who took the Iowa Basic Skills test scored at the 80th percentile in the total battery of tests: 81st percentile in reading, 77th percentile in language, and 77th percentile in math. The remaining students who took the Stanford, scored, on the average, in the 73rd percentile in the whole battery.[30]

In Arkansas, for the 1987-88 school term, home school children, on the average, scored 75 percent on the Metropolitan Achievement Test 6. They out-scored public school children in every subject (reading, math, language, science, and social studies) and at every grade level. For example, at the tenth-grade level, public school children scored an average of 53rd percentile in social studies, while home school children scored at the 73rd percentile. In science, an area in which home schoolers are often criticized for lack of facilities, the home schoolers scored, on the average, 85th percentile in fourth grade, 73rd percentile in seventh grade, and 65th percent in tenth grade. The public school students, on the other hand, scored much lower in science: 66th percentile in fourth grade, 62nd percentile in seventh, and 53rd percentile in tenth.[31]

According to the Arizona State Department of Education, 1,123 home-schooled children in grades 1 through 9, on the average, scored *above* grade level in reading, language arts, and math, on standardized tests for the 1988-89 school year. Four grades tested were a full grade level ahead.[32]

In Nebraska, out of 259 home-schooled children who returned to public or non-public schools, 134 of them were automatically placed in their grade level according to their age without testing. Of the remaining who were given entrance tests, 33 were above grade level, 43 were at grade level, and 29 were below grade level. Approximately 88 percent of the 259 returning students were at or above grade level after being home schooled for a period of time. This survey is the result of the responses of 429 accredited schools.[33]

Local School District Statistics on Home Schooling

In 1988, thirty home-schooled children in Albuquerque, New Mexico, participated in the state-mandated testing program (Comprehensive Test of Basic Skills) and scored, on the average, in the 83rd percentile for third grade, the 85th percentile for fifth grade, and the 89th percentile for eighth grade. This group of home schoolers scored 20 to 25 percentile points higher than the local public school students scored taking the CTBS in 1987.[34]

In a 1980 study in Los Angeles, home-schooled students were found to be scoring higher on standardized tests than children in the Los Angeles public schools.[35]

In South Carolina the Greenville County School District stated that, "Kids taught at home last year outscored those in public schools on basic skills tests." In that county, fifty-seven out of sixty-one home-schooled students "met or exceeded the state's minimum performance standard on the reading test" of the Comprehensive Test of Basic Skills. The home school students' passing rate was 93.4 percent, while the public school counterparts' passing rate was 83.9 percent. Furthermore, in math, the home-schooled students' passing rate was 87.9 percent compared to the public school students' lower passing rate of 82.1 percent.[36]

In Nevada, according to Washoe County School District's data, home-schooled students scored higher than their public school counterparts in first through seventh grade. All children were tested with the Stanford Achievement test, and home schoolers consistently scored higher in reading, vocabulary, reading comprehension, math concepts, math comprehension, and application.

The most extreme gap between the public school children and the home-schooled children was in the area of vocabulary. For example, fourth graders in public school scored in the 49th percentile, while the home-schooled fourth graders scored in the 80th percentile.[37]

Conclusion of the Studies: Home Schooling Works

These statistics point to one conclusion: home schooling works. Even many of the State Departments of Education, which are generally biased toward the public school system, cannot argue with these facts. Not only does home schooling work, but it works without the myriads of state controls and accreditation standards imposed on the public schools.

Home School Students Accepted into Colleges and Universities

As a result of the excellent academic performance of home schoolers and high SAT scores, children who have been home schooled have had little difficulty being accepted into colleges and universities. Home-schooled students have been accepted into Harvard, Yale, Princeton, and many of the major universities. A list, by no means exhaustive, of over 150 universities and colleges where home-schooled students have been accepted has been compiled by the Home School Legal Defense Association and appears in Appendix B.

One example of the recognition of the academic achievement of home schoolers by institutions of higher learning is a 1990 letter sent to home school leaders in Massachusetts from George A. Schiller, Jr., Director of Admissions at Boston University:

> Boston University welcomes applications from home-schooled students. We believe students educated at home possess the passion for knowledge, the independence, and the self-reliance that enable them to excel in our intellectually challenging programs of study.
>
> Two home-schooled students currently attend Boston University. One is a sophomore in the College of Liberal Arts, the other a freshman in the College of Engineering. Both students are doing very well. Their educational and personal transitions from home schooling to the University are a proven success.

More and more colleges are even adopting specific admission policies for home schools. Generally, the information that these home school admissions policies are requesting is the result of a SAT or an ACT, which records that the child has achieved the basic credit hours for completion of high school (some colleges actually supply the home schooler with the "Academic Credit Report" that can be completed in lieu of transcripts), personal references, and a personal interview.

A recent survey of 755 colleges and universities found that 252 institutions had admitted a total of 835 home school students in the last five years. This does not count home school students who were offered admission but decided to attend a different college. Of the 500 institutions that had not admitted home school students, 87 percent never had any home school applicants, and only 5 percent had a departmental policy refusing to admit home schoolers.[38]

Since the home schooling movement is still "growing up," the number of home school students going into college will only expand each year. However, these pioneering home school students who are being admitted to colleges are proving that home schooling, as a whole, adequately prepares students for college.

Socialization: Home Schoolers Are in the Real World

Academically, the home schoolers have generally excelled, but some critics have continued to challenge them on an apparent "lack of socialization" or "isolation from the world." Often there is a charge that home schoolers are not learning how to live in the "real world." However, a closer look at public school training shows that it is actually those public school children who are not living in the real world.

For instance, public school children are confined to a classroom for at least 180 days each year with little opportunity to be exposed to the workplace or to go on field trips. The children are trapped with a group of children of their own age with little chance to relate to children of other ages or adults. They learn in a vacuum where there are no absolute standards. They are given little to no responsibility, and everything is provided for them. The opportunity to pursue their interests and to apply their unique talents is stifled. Actions by public students rarely have consequences, as discipline is lax and passing from grade to grade is automatic. The students are not really prepared to operate in the home (family) or the workplace, which comprise a major part of the "real world" after graduation.

Home schoolers, on the other hand, do not have the above problems. They are completely prepared for the "real world" of the workplace and the home. They relate regularly with adults and follow their examples rather than the examples of foolish peers. They learn, based on "hands on" experiences and early apprenticeship training. In fact, the only "socialization" or aspect of the "real world" which they miss out on by not attending the public school is unhealthy peer pressure, crime, and immorality. Of course, the average home schooler wisely learns about these things from afar instead of being personally involved in crime or immorality or perhaps being a victim.

Practically, home schoolers generally overcome the potential for "isolation" through heavy involvement in church youth groups, community activities, 4H clubs, music and art lessons, Little League sports participation, YMCA, Scouts, singing groups, activities with neighborhood children, academic contests (spelling bees, orations, creative and research papers), and regular involvement in field trips. In fact, one researcher stated, "The investigator was not prepared for the level of commitment exhibited by the parents in getting the child to various activities. . . . It appeared that these students are. involved in more social activities, whether by design or being with the parent in various situations, than the average middle school-aged child."[39]

In nearly every community throughout the country, local "home school support groups" have been formed in addition to the state-wide home school associations.[40] These local support groups sponsor, in many areas, weekly and monthly activities for the home school students, including physical education classes, special speakers, sports, camping, and trips to museums, industries, farms, parks, historic sites, and hundreds of other activities. Also regular contests are held including spelling bees, science fairs, wood working contests, and geography contests. Home schoolers in many localities have formed home school choirs, bands, sports teams, bowling leagues, educational and activity clubs of every kind, and many types of resource libraries. The state home school associations generally sponsor a major conference where home school children can attend and the older children perform plays, assemble year books, and participate in graduation ceremonies for eighth and twelfth grades. A review of the state home school association and local support group newsletters testify of the great many social activities available. Home school families, as a whole, do not raise their children in social isolation.[41]

In addition, several studies have been done to measure home schoolers' "self-concept," which is the key objective indicator for establishing a child's self-esteem. A child's degree of self-esteem, of course, is one of the best measurements of his ability to successfully interact on a social level. One such study was conducted by John Wesley Taylor, using the Piers-Harris Children's Self-Concept Scale to evaluate 224 home-schooled children. The study found that 50 percent of the children scored above the 90th percentile, and only 10.3 percent scored below the national average.[42]

Another researcher compared private school nine-year-olds with home school nine-year-olds and found no significant differences in the groups in virtually all psycho-social areas. However, in the area of social adjustment, a significant difference was discovered: "private-school subjects appeared to be more concerned with peers than the home-educated group."[43] This is certainly an advantage for home-schooled children who can avoid negative peer influence.

In 1989, Dr. Linda Montgomery studied home school students between the ages of ten and twenty-one and concluded that home-schooled children are not isolated from social activities with other youth. She also concluded that home schooling may nurture leadership at least as well as the conventional schools do.[44]

In 1992, Thomas Smedley prepared a master's thesis for Radford University of Virginia on "The Socialization of Home School Children." Smedley used the Vineland Adaptive Behavior Scales to evaluate the social maturity of twenty home-schooled children and thirteen demographically matched public school children. The communication skills, socialization, and daily living skills were evaluated. These scores were combined into the "Adoptive Behavior Composite" which reflects the general maturity of each subject.

Smedley had this information processed using the statistical program for the social sciences and the results demonstrated that the home-schooled children were *better socialized and more mature* than the children in the public school. The home-schooled children scored in the 84th percentile while the matched sample of public school children only scored in the 27th percentile.

Smedley further found:

> In the public school system, children are socialized horizontally, and temporarily, into conformity with their immediate peers. Home educators seek to socialize their children vertically, toward responsibility, service, and adulthood, with an eye on eternity."[45]

In another 1992 study, Dr. Larry Shyers compared behaviors and social development test scores of two groups of seventy children ages eight to ten. One group was being educated at home while the other group attended public and private schools. He found that the home-schooled children did not lag behind children attending public or private schools in social development.

Dr. Shyers further discovered that the home-schooled children had consistently fewer behavioral problems. The study indicated that home-schooled children behave better because they tend to imitate their parents while conventionally-schooled children model themselves after their peers. Shyers states:

> The results seem to show that a child's social development
> depends *more on adult contact* and less on contact with other
> children as previously thought.[46]

Dr. Brian Ray reviewed the results of four other studies on the
socialization of home schoolers and found:

> Rakestraw, Reynolds, Schemmer, and Wartes have each
> studied aspects of the social activities and emotional
> characteristics of home-schooled children. They found that
> these children are actively involved in many activities
> outside the home with peers, different-aged children, and
> adults. The data from their research suggests that home
> schoolers are not being socially isolated, nor are they
> emotionally maladjusted.[47]

As mentioned earlier, the greatest benefit from home school
socialization is that the child can be protected from the negative
socialization of the public schools associated with peer pressure, such
as rebellious attitudes, immaturity, immorality, drugs, and violent
behavior. This is becoming more of a factor as the crime rate
continues to soar in the public schools, as documented in chapter 2.

Effective Instruction: One-on-One Tutoring

Home-schooled children are being taught with the most effective
method of instruction: the tutorial method. Some of the benefits of
this superior form of education are mentioned below.

For instance, a common difference between public schools and
home schools is the amount of time parents need to spend per week
instructing their children. It is clear that one-to-one instruction or
tutoring by the parents of their child is far more efficient than the
time spent in institutional schools. As a result, the average home
schooler only needs to spend, on the average, two to three hours per
day receiving formal instruction. Furthermore, unlimited learning can
take place beyond formal instruction by spending "time on task" with
various projects and "hands-on" experiences.

Richard Rossmiller of the University of Wisconsin studied
elementary and secondary students throughout the country and
discovered some interesting facts on how much time is wasted each
year in institutional schools. According to his research, the typical
student annually spends 367 hours (more than two hours a day) in
activities such as lunch, recess, attendance-taking, and class
changing, and 66 hours in "process activities" during which teachers

answer questions, distribute material, and discipline students. In addition, the average pupil is absent from the classroom approximately 108 hours annually and loses about 54 hours to inclement weather, employee strikes, and teacher conferences.[48]

This study further documents the differences between the tutorial method (home schooling) and the institutional school. From a legal perspective, home schools should not be required to fulfill institutional schools' hourly requirements without taking into account the inefficient use of time in the classroom.

Other benefits of home schooling include one-on-one instruction in which the parent can develop his child's gifts and overcome the child's weaknesses. This can be done much more accurately and in much less time than in the conventional schools. Gifted children are free to excel and slower students are not left behind.[49]

Also the child can be allowed to focus on what he is most interested in and to excel in his unique talents. The curriculum can be individually geared to the child's needs. Education can be flexible, maximizing the benefits for the child.

In addition, the children can be involved in apprenticeships, and experience much of their education first-hand, instead of only receiving their education through books. Without standardized education as offered in the public schools, the home school can provide unlimited hands-on learning tasks, field trips, and service projects. This practical aspect of learning is often lacking in institutional schools.[50]

Economics: Can the Family Survive on One Income?

Finances are always an important consideration for most families. Many people question whether home schooling is really practical, in light of the high cost of living. Keeping the mother at home to teach the children means the mother will most likely have to give up any job or career she has outside the home. In light of this, is home schooling affordable? A recent study seems to indicate that the average working mother does not really bring home much income, after all the expenses are deducted.

On July 2, 1990, a study was released by the House Democratic Study Group in Washington, D.C.[51] The study revealed that the added income of a working mother was offset by increased work expenses, so that the family's usable income was only marginally increased. Although the average additional income that a working mother brings home is approximately $10,000, the actual *usable* income from a working mother averaged only $1,000 to $,1,500 per year, after the expenses of taxes, transportation, child care, clothes, and meals were deducted. The study estimated that "one-third to one-half of the apparent increase in women's earnings was eaten up by work expenses and taxes."

The original purpose of the study was to determine how much better off families were because the mother worked. It compared two-parent families, factoring in mothers who worked full-time and part-time with the six to seven million mothers who were not employed outside the home. The financial plight of the American family was confirmed by the study, as the average earning of the approximately twenty-five million fathers in two-parent families fell from $31,973 in 1978 to $30,766 in 1988 (measured in constant 1990 dollars).

The average earnings of the working mothers increased because more of them were working and they were working more hours. Combined family income increased from $38,439 to $40,711, a modest gain, given the difficulty and sacrifices families must make to allow a mother to work outside the home.

The 18.1 million working mothers, on the average, make only a marginal increase in usable income from their jobs outside the home. Is the strain and fatigue of an outside job coupled with the small financial gain really worth the cost to their family life and their children's spiritual and mental well-being?

Based on this study, it would seem that home school mothers are not losing that much by forsaking careers for their children's sakes. In fact, many home school mothers start and operate home businesses in which the children can even participate after home school studies are completed. Most importantly, these mothers are placing a priority on the nurturing and discipline of their children, which cannot be measured in dollars and cents.

The "Nationwide Study of Home Education" which involved over two thousand home schooling families found that the average per-pupil expenditure for education is $488.00. Home schooling is very affordable. In addition, by home schooling one child, we save approximately $3,987.00 in tax dollars. Otherwise if we send our child to public school at least $3,987.00 will be spent on that child on the average.[52]

Home Schooling Is Not a Passing Fad

Overall, the success of home schoolers seems to be due to one-to-one instruction, tailoring instruction to the needs and ability of each individual child, more individual responses, and an absence of negative socialization pressure. These advantages, as summarized above, continue to fuel the rapid growth of the home schooling movement.

Notes

1. Noah Webster, *American Dictionary of the English Language* (San Francisco: Foundation for American Christian Education, 1980) reprinted from the original G. & C. Merriam Company, 1828.

2. *People v. Levisen*, 404 Il. 574, 90 N.E.2d 213, (1950). *Black's Law Dictionary* defines the term "school" as "an institution *or place* for instruction or education."

3. In July 1986, Lauri Scogin, B.S., M.A., an independent educational research consultant, did a random survey of three hundred home school families from across the states and found that 45 percent of the parents had a college degree or higher, 50 percent had high school diplomas, and the remainder had below high school. See "Home Schoolers Excel," *The Home School Court Report*, Vol. 3, No.1, January-February, 1987.

   This finding is supported by a recent study of 199 home schoolers conducted by Donald Wynn, Sr., which found that 54 percent of home school parents had college degrees or higher. See "A Study of the Development of Home Schools As an Alternative to Public School Education," as appeared in the *Home School Researcher* (Seattle: Home School Researcher, 1989), Vol. 5 No. 1, 18. (Now located in Salem, Oregon of 1991.)

4. John Naisbett, *Megatrends: Ten New Directions Transforming Our Lives* (New York: Warner Books, 1982), 144 and the Hewitt-Moore Research Foundation study published in "On Home Schooling Figures and Scores," *The Family Report*, Washougal, Wash., Vol.4, No.2, March-April 1986. Also see "Shunning the Schools, More Parents Teach Their Kids at Home," *The Wall Street Journal*, 6 October 1986; "Home School Battle Pits Parents, State," *Houston Chronicle*, 28 December 1986; "Home Schooling," *Pittsburgh Press*, 30 March 1987; and "Home Teaching Rules Rejected," *The State*, Columbia, S.C., 12 February 1987.

5. Laura Wisniewski, "Home Schoolers Learning to Network," *The Atlanta Constitution*, 17 February 1992, A15.

6. This conclusion has been drawn from the applications of over twenty thousand home school families across the nation who have joined the Home School Legal Defense Association since 1985, and from conversations with state home school leaders.

   Also the North Carolina Department of Education released a study for the 1988-89 school term and found that out of 1,385 home schools registered with the state, 1,085 designated themselves as "religious" schools. "North Carolina Home School Enrollment by Ages and Statewide Statistical History" (Raleigh: Division of Non-Public Education, 1 December 1989).

7. Dr. Brian Ray, "A Nationwide Study of Home Education: Family Characteristics, Legal Matters, and Student Achievement," National Home Education Research Institute, Seattle, Washington, 1990. (Now located in Salem, Oregon as of 1991)

8. Many home school authors echo these profound Christian beliefs concerning education, which are commonly held throughout the home school movement. For example, see Blair Adams and Joel Stein, *Wisdom's Children*, (Austin, Tex.: Truth Forum, 1989), 88-130; Gregg Harris, *The Christian Home School* (Brentwood, Tenn.: Wolgemuth & Hyatt, 1988), 61-80; J. Richard Fugate, *Will Early Education Ruin Your Child?* (Tempe, Ariz.: Alpha Omega, 1990), 3-13; Theodore Wade, Jr., *The Home School Manual* (Auburn, Calif.: Gazelle, 1991), 177-186.

9. See Chapter 4 for a detailed review of biblical mandates on education.

10. Daniel Wattenberg, "The Parent Trap," *Insight* magazine, Washington D.C., 2 March 1992, 7.

11. *Ibid.*

12. "What's Worth Fighting For?" *The Home School Court Report*, May-June 1991, Vol. 7, No. 3, 20.

13. Dr. Raymond, Moore "Research and Common Sense: Therapies for Our Home Schools," *Teachers College Record*, Columbia University, Vol. 84, No. 2, 1982, 372.

For further documentation of the academic success of home schooling see N.J. Linden, "An Investigation of Alternative Education: Home Schooling." Ph.D. dissertation, East Texas State University, 1983.

Also see Dr. Brian Ray, "A Comparison of Home Schooling and Conventional Schooling: With a Focus on Learner Outcomes (a paper presented at Oregon State University, 1986). The author concluded, based on reviewing eleven studies which addressed the achievement of home school children, home schoolers were matching, and in many cases, excelling the average school achievement.

14. "Home Schooling: An Idea Whose Time Has Returned," *Human Events*, 15 September 1984.

15. "Home Schoolers Excel," *The Home School Court Report*, Vol. 3, No.1, January-February, 1987.

16. Dr. Brian Ray, *Education and Urban Society*, Vol.21, No.1, November 1988 (Newbury Park, CA), 16-31.

17. Dr. Brian Ray, "A Nationwide Study of Home Education: Family Characteristics, Legal Matters, and Student Achievement" (Seattle, Wash.: National Home Education Research Institute, 1990), 53-54.

18. *Ibid.*, 53.

19. "Home Schoolers Beat National Average on Achievement Tests," *Home School Court Report*, Vol. 7, No. 5, September/October 1991, 18.

20. Statistics compiled by the National Center For Home Education, P.O. Box 125, Paeonian Springs, Virginia 22129, in 1990.

21. "PA Homeschooled Students Score High!" *Pennsylvania Homeschoolers* newsletter, Issue 33, Fall 1990, 1.

22. "ND Research Shows Home Schoolers Do Very Well." *North Dakota Home School Association Newsletter*, Vol. 6, Issue 4, April 1991, 1. The complete study is entitled "Home Education in North Dakota: Family Characteristics and Student Achievement," 1991, National Home Education Research Institute (NHERI) Western Baptist College, 5000 Deer Park Dr. S.E. Salem, Oregon 97301.

23. Psychological Corporation, San Antonio, Texas.

24. Jon Wartes, "Five Years of Home School Testing within Washington State: 1986-1990." This report, concluded in December 1991, is the result of the findings of the Washington Home School Research Project which is conducted by thirteen public school educators and home schoolers. (Available from the Washington Home School Research Project, 16109 NE 169 Pl., Woodinville, Washington 98072.)

25. Res Peters, Idaho Home Educators, Boise, Idaho, 1991.

26. "Study Shows Homeschoolers Ahead in Achievement," *The Grapevine: Montana Home School News*, January 1991, 6. The complete study is entitled "Home Education in Montana: Family Characteristics and Student Achievement," 1991. It was conducted by NHERI (see note 22).

27. Office of the Commissioner, Tennessee Department of Education, *Home School Student Test Results: 1986 and 1987* (Nashville, 1987).

28. *Method: Alaska Perspectives*, Vol. 7, No.1 (Juneau, Alaska Dept. of Education, 1986).

29. "March 1, 1988 Oregon Home School Data Report," *Line Upon Line*, Vol. 11, No. 5 (Beaverton, OR, 1988). The data was compiled from information submitted from the Educational Service District and County Units in Oregon between September 1987 and March 1988.

Office of Policy and Program Development, Oregon Department of Education, Les Marten, *December 1, 1986, Home School Data Report* (Salem: 1986). Showed in 1986 that of 1,121 home schoolers, 76 percent were above the 50 percentile.

30. "North Carolina Home School Nationally Standardized Achievement Test Results 88-89 School Term" (Raleigh: Office of the Governor, Division of Non-Public Education, December 1, 1989).

31. "Standardized Test Results," *Update*, Vol. 7, No. 1 (Little Rock, Arkansas Christian Home Education Association, September 1988). This newsletter reported on test results compiled by the Arkansas Department of Education of 760 home-schooled students.

32. Arizona Department of Education, *Students Taught at Home 1989 Average Grade Equivalents*, compiled by Steve Stephens, State Testing Coordinator, July 1989.

For earlier statistics for Arizona home schoolers' success on standardized tests see article by Patricia Lines, "States Should Help, Not Hinder, Parents' Home Schooling Efforts," *Education Week*, 15 May 1985.

33. "Grade Level Placement of Rule 13 Students Returning to Approved or Accredited Schools," *Dateline: Education*, June 1989.

34. "Albuquerque Home Schoolers Score High," *Teaching Home Magazine* (Portland, Ore.: April/May 1989), 21.

35. Roy Weaver, "Home Tutorials vs. Public Schools in Los Angeles," *Phi Delta Kappan* (December 1980), 254-255.

36. "Home-Taught Students Surpass Public School Peers at Basic Skills," statistics taken from *The Greenville News*, 3 August 1990.

37. "Home Schoolers Beat Public School Students on Test," CHEC Report, Chicago, IL, Summer 1991.

38. "Survey of Colleges Regarding the Admission of Home Schooled Applicants," conducted by Dale Fenton, Associate Director of Admissions, Wheaton College, Wheaton, IL, August 1990.

39. "Socialization Practices of Christian Home School Educators in the State of Virginia," a study of ten Virginia home school families, performed by Dr. Kathie Carwile, appeared in *Home School Researcher*, Vol. 7, No. 1, December 1991.

40. For an extensive list of many of the state home school associations see listing in the back of this book.

41. R. Meighan, "Political Consciousness and Home-Based Education," *Educational Review*, 36 (1984):165-73.

42. Dr. John Wesley Taylor, *Self-Concept in Home Schooling Children* (Ann Arbor, Mich.: University Microfilms International), Order No. DA8624219. This study was done as part of a dissertation at Andrews University. The results of the testing of the 224 home-schooled students was compared to the testing results of 1,183 conventionally schooled children.

43. Dr. Mona Delahooke, "Home Educated Children's Social/Emotional Adjustment and Academic Achievements: A Comparative Study," unpublished doctoral dissertation, California School of Professional Psychology, Los Angeles, 1986, 85.

44. Dr. Linda Montgomery, "The Effect of Home Schooling on Leadership Skills of Home Schooled Students," *Home School Researcher* (5)1, 1989.

45. Thomas C. Smedley, M.S., "Socialization of Home Schooled Children: A Communication Approach," thesis submitted and approved for Master of Science in Corporate and Professional Cummunication, Radford University, Radford, Virginia, May 1992. (Unpublished.)

46. Dr. Larry Shyers, "Comparison of Social Adjustment Between Home and Traditionally Schooled Students," unpublished doctoral dissertation at University of Florida's College of Education, 1992. Dr. Shyers is a psychotherapist who is the Chairman of the Florida Board of Clinical Social Work, Marriage and Family Therapy, and Mental Health Counseling.

47. Dr. Brian Ray, "Review of Home Education Research," *The Teaching Home*, August/September 1989, 49. See Rakestraw, "An Analysis of Home Schooling for Elementary School-Age Children in Alabama," Doctoral dissertation, University of Alabama, Tuscaloosa, AL, 1987; Reynolds, "How Home School Families Operate on a Day-to-Day Basis: Three Case Studies," Unpublished doctoral dissertation, Brigham Young University, Provo, UT., 1985; and Schemmer, "Case Studies of Four Families Engaged in Home Education," unpublished doctoral dissertation, Ball State University, Muncie, IN, 1985.

48. "Home Schoolers Need Less Time," *Home School Court Report*, Vol. 4, No. 2, Spring 1988, 5.

49. See note 8 of this chapter for a list of books which describe the benefits of home schooling.

50. See note 8 for a list of books that describe the benefits of home schooling.

51. *Washington Post*, 2 July 1990.

52. Dr. Brian Ray, "A Nationwide Study of Home Education," National Home Education Research Institute, Seattle, Washington, 1990. (Now located in Salem, Oregon as of 1991: see note 22.)

Wherefore, seeing we also are compassed about with so great a cloud
of witnesses, let us run with patience the race that is set before us.
                                   — Hebrews 12:1

CHAPTER 7

THE HOME SCHOOLING
HALL OF FAME

"It is better to tolerate the rare instance of a parent
refusing to let his child be educated, than to shock the
common feelings and ideas by the forcible asportation
and education of the infant against the will of the
father."[1]   Thomas Jefferson

As seen in chapter 5, family education has established a successful
track record during the history of the United States. Much of this
family-centered education was directed by the parents, and took place
in the home.

Thus far, I have only presented general historical information as
to the excellence of this form of education from both an academic
and a moral perspective. I believe such general information, however,

is hard to fully appreciate without specific examples of individuals positively affected by home schooling.

In this chapter, therefore, I will provide the reader with short descriptions of many renowned leaders, businessmen, statesmen, inventors, scientists, writers, educators, artists, lawyers, and presidents who were successfully home educated for most or all of their childhood education. These true accounts of real men and women from history who were home schooled can serve as an encouragement to both parents and home-schooled children alike.

I encourage you to assign your children further study into the lives of these men and women in order to appreciate their contribution in their various fields. A special emphasis should be placed on the majority of these men and women who relied on the Lord for their strength and wisdom.

Below is a very short list (by no means exhaustive) and descriptions of some of these famous home schoolers who serve as further evidence of the success of parental commitment to home schooling.

Presidents Taught at Home

At least ten presidents were substantially taught through home schooling. For instance, George Washington, often called the "father of our country," received most of his education at home by his father and mother, at least until his father died when George was eleven.[2] His mother carefully and consistently provided him with religious teaching from the Bible.[3] Throughout his remaining childhood, he was taught primarily by family members and experience. He was "a man of hands . . . not without brains, but with hand and brain moving together." This resulted in a basic education in accounting, math, geometry, geography (surveying), and astronomy.[4] Washington later became a brilliant general, businessman, statesman, and the first president of the United States.

Thomas Jefferson was taught to read and write by his father at home.[5]

> The father also set his impressionable boy [Thomas Jefferson] an example of vigorous physical out-of-doors life. Thomas learned to ride, to shoot, to paddle a canoe on the Rivanna, and to hunt deer and turkey. . . .

> Tom did not ride and shoot and canoe only; he also studied diligently. His education consisted of the typical classical curriculum of the period.

> Tom mastered languages, both classical and modern, with great ease. He read Homer in his canoe trips down the Rivanna and Virgil while lying under an oak tree.[6]

Thomas Jefferson later became the third President of the United States and was responsible for drafting the Declaration of Independence.

James Madison was taught to read and write by his mother, and his father taught him his obligations to community service.[7] Primarily his mother and grandmother taught him at home until the age of eleven when he was tutored at home by Reverend Thomas Martin.[8] Of course, he later served as the fourth President of the United States and became a strong protector of religious freedom.

John Quincy Adams was completely home schooled until he was twelve years old. He entered Harvard at the age of fourteen.[9]

> His mother, Abigail Adams, had accepted the responsibility for keeping up the education of her children—especially of her oldest son, John Quincy Adams. . . . First came instruction in the Word of God. So well did his mother commit the Word to young John Quincy's heart that it became for him both compass and anchor in a long life of service.

> From his mother he was also led into the love and inspiration of literature. He learned the poetry of Pope, read the plays of Shakespeare, struggled with Milton, and generally devoured the family library. He listened to his mother's talk of the economic concerns of the war. . . . Duty and service were both ingrained in his parents. He learned much from their example and personal conduct. . . . In addition to his studies in the Bible and his reading in the family library, Abigail Adams directed John Quincy's thoughts towards a knowledge of history.[10]

This godly instruction by his mother and commitment and sacrifice by his parents to personally train their child, helped to produce the integrity and wisdom in John Quincy Adams to enable him to serve as the sixth president of the United States.

Likewise, President Abraham Lincoln received all of his education, except one year, through home instruction.[11] Since his own library was limited, Abraham Lincoln would walk to other households, reading nearly every book within a fifty mile radius. His godly character was instilled in him through his family education, helping him serve as president during the Civil War.

President John Tyler was "tutored at his father's knee."[12] According to several historians, there is no record of him attending school before he enrolled in college at William and Mary at the age of twelve.[13] "Judge John Tyler raised young John to manhood and by all surviving accounts, he did an excellent job of it."[14]

Presidents William Henry Harrison,[15] Theodore Roosevelt,[16] and Franklin Roosevelt were also taught at home. Theodore Roosevelt received an excellent education from his family through home schooling and travel. In fact, as a result, he became one of the few presidents who was endowed "with an encompassing intellectual curiosity and with a real sympathy for and enjoyment of literature and the arts."[17] Franklin D. Roosevelt was taught at home where he received a thorough education and was trained in French and German. At age fourteen, he was enrolled in Groton school and four years later entered Harvard.[18]

President Woodrow Wilson received most of his pre-college instruction through home education.[19] His father, Joseph Wilson, would take young Woodrow on regular field trips to neighboring cities, cotton gins, mills, and factories. Afterward, Joseph Wilson would ask his son questions and have him write down what he saw and learned.[20]

Modern home schooling applies many of the characteristics of home schooling which most of these presidents received: regular field trips, hands-on learning, apprenticeships, development of a love for reading, regular interaction with adults, and emphasis on teaching biblical principles.

Many Delegates of Constitutional Convention Were Taught at Home

At least seventeen of the total delegates to the Constitutional Convention were schooled at home. These men drafted the most significant Constitution in the history of the world to protect and preserve liberty and harness the power of government. Two of the home-schooled delegates, Washington and Madison, whose home schooling experiences are described above, later became presidents of the United States.

Another delegate was Reverend John Witherspoon, Calvinist and Presbyterian pastor, member of the New Jersey Senate, and president of the College of New Jersey (later called Princeton University). He was taught to read by his mother at age four and was eventually able to recite much of the New Testament and Watt's *Psalms and Hymns*.[21] He received much of his teaching at home, with some in grammar school, and he entered the University of Edinburgh at age thirteen. Witherspoon dedicated his life to applying the Word of God to everything he did. He especially focused his attention on training college students in God's principles, and they then used those principles to form our nation.

> Witherspoon was president of the College of New Jersey from 1768 to 1794. In those twenty-six years, 478 young men graduated—about eighteen students per year. Of those 478 graduates, 114 became ministers; 13 were state governors; 3 were U.S. Supreme Court judges; 20 were United States Senators; 33 were U.S. Congressmen; Aaron Burr, Jr. became Vice-President; and James Madison became President.[22]

I'm sure that Mrs. Witherspoon never dreamed that her son, whom she was training at home, would end up training so many leaders of our country.

Delegate Benjamin Franklin, printer, author, inventor, and U.S. minister to France was home schooled. He received all of his schooling at home from his family, except for one year in grammar school and one year with a private tutor when he was between the ages of eight and ten.[23]. He learned the highly skilled trade of printing through apprenticeship and ended up teaching himself science so well that he placed himself on the cutting edge of many new scientific discoveries.

Several of the other delegates were educated entirely at home except for college. Some of these men include William Samuel Johnson, president of Columbia College and a U.S. senator from Connecticut;[24] George Clymer, signer of the Declaration and U.S. representative of Pennsylvania;[25] Charles Pickney, III, governor of South Carolina, U.S. senator and representative;[26] and John Francis Mercer, Maryland delegate and U.S. representative.[27] George Wythe, signer of the Declaration, justice of the Virginia High Court of Chancery, and professor of law, was taught at home by his mother,[28] and William Blount, speaker of the Tennessee Senate and U.S. senator, was instructed at home and in the businesses of his father— real estate and politics.[29] Delegate Richard Dobbs Spaight, governor of North Carolina and a U.S. representative, was orphaned early and educated at home by relatives.[30] John Rutledge, chief justice of the U.S. Supreme Court, was taught by his father until age eleven.[31]

Other delegates were taught at home for much of their early education, such as William Livingston, lawyer and governor of New Jersey;[32] Richard Basset, lawyer, governor of Delaware, and U.S. senator;[33] William Houston, lawyer;[34] and William Few, justice and U.S. senator from Georgia, who only received two years of formal schooling.[35] George Mason, the principal author of the Virginia Declaration of Rights and member of the Virginia Legislature, had some training in grammar schools, but "his most important teacher was his mother, from whom he learned the art of being master of a great plantation and the necessity of personal management, planning, and careful accounts."[36]

Famous Women Who Were Home Schooled

Many renowned women in early America were also successfully taught through home education, such as Abigail Adams,[37] who, in turn, taught her son John Quincy Adams at home; Mercy Warren;[38] Martha Washington,[39] who married a home-schooled husband; and Florence Nightingale.[40] In fact, Nightingale and her sister were instructed by their father, who taught them English grammar, history, philosophy, Latin, French, Greek, German, and Italian. He even taught her to read the Bible from the Greek text.[41] Furthermore, the black author, Phyllis Wheatley, was also primarily educated at home.[42]

Famous Lawyers, Educators, and Preachers Taught at Home

Patrick Henry, orator (the famous speaker for independence— "Give me liberty or give me death!"), framer, lawyer, and governor of Virginia, went to school for a few years but was pulled out at age ten to be home instructed by his father. His father taught him math, Greek, Latin, Bible, and the classics.[43] Patrick Henry was a consistent Christian throughout his life, acquiring his love for the church from his father, and his zeal for the Lord and Calvinist doctrine from his Scottish Presbyterian mother. His mother would have him repeat the sermon text and summarize the sermons he heard on the way home from church.[44] His grandson later explained that Patrick Henry spent one hour each evening in private devotion and prayer. Henry also studied the Bible at length and developed his political beliefs in the necessity of limited government (because of man's sin nature) and in his recognition and desire to preserve God-given rights. He read sermon notes to his family every Sunday night, and afterward his family sang sacred songs while he accompanied with the violin.[45]

John Jay, one of the authors of *The Federalist Papers*, chief justice of the U.S. Supreme Court, and governor of New York, was also taught at home for several years. He was taught by his mother reading, grammar, and Latin, in his early years, and at age eight he was enrolled in grammar school.[46]

John Marshall, soldier, lawyer, diplomat, and also chief justice of the U.S. Supreme Court by age forty-five, was also home schooled. Until he was age fourteen, he was taught by his father and mother entirely in his own home in Fauquier County, Virginia.[47]

> The father worked hard with the son. "My father possessed scarcely any fortune," wrote John Marshall, "and had received a very limited education; but was a man to whom nature had been bountiful, and who assiduously improved her gifts. He superintended my education, and gave me an early taste for history and poetry. At the age of twelve, I had transcribed Pope's *Essay on Man*, with some of his moral essays." Thomas, being a surveyor, had a rudimentary understanding of mathematics and astronomy. He also gradually acquired a library of history and literature. All of this he shared with his son [John Marshall].[48]

Timothy Dwight, grandson of Jonathan Edwards, was entirely taught by his mother at home until he entered Yale at age thirteen. He became born-again at age fifteen and in 1795 became the president of Yale University, which at that time was a school of higher learning dedicated to advancing the cause of Christ.[49]

John and Charles Wesley, renowned preacher during the Great Awakening and missionary/song writer, respectively, were taught at home by their mother, Susanna Wesley. In fact, Susanna taught all of her children at home.

In her "Household School," for six hours a day through twenty years, she taught her children so thoroughly that they became unusually cultured. There was not one of them in whom she did not instill a passion for learning and righteousness.

When her husband, in exasperation, asked her: "Why do you sit there teaching that dull child that lesson over the twentieth time?" she replied calmly: "Had I satisfied myself by mentioning the matter only nineteen times, I should have lost all labor. You see it was the twentieth time that crowned the whole."[50]

Although she was thorough in instructing them in academics, the spiritual welfare of her children mattered most, and she consistently trained her children in the Word in spite of many trials, including the deaths of ten of her nineteen children.[51]

Jonathan Edwards, a Calvinist preacher, theologian, and author, was educated entirely at home by his father.[52] He and his sisters received a superior education from their father.

The course of his education may in this way have been less systematic, indeed, and less conformed to rule, than that ordinarily given in the school. At the same time it was more safe; forming him to softer manners, gentler feelings, and purer affections. In his circumstances, also, it was obviously more comprehensive and universal; and while it brought him acquainted with many things which are not usually communicated until a later period, it also served to unfold the original traits of his mind, and give it that expansion, which is the result of information alone.[53]

Jonathan Edwards went on to become one of the most effective and influential preachers during the Great Awakening.

William Carey was taught by his father.[54] He was instilled with a desire to read everything, and spent much time collecting specimens, as he studied insects and plants.[55] He became a cobbler, scholar, linguist, botanist, and a missionary to India. He is known today as the "father of modern missions."

Dwight L. Moody, famous evangelist, had the equivalent of a fifth grade education with the rest of his learning taking place at home or at work.[56]

American Generals Instructed at Home

In addition to George Washington, General Robert E. Lee, a brilliant southern General, president of Washington and Lee

University in Virginia, and dedicated Christian, was taught at home by his mother.[57]

> At his mother's knee, that divinely appointed school whose instruction no other teacher can impart, and whose lessons when faithfully given are worth all others we receive, he learned his obligations to his maker and his fellow man.[58]
>
> From her he learned to practice self-denial and self-control, as well as the strictest economy in all financial concerns, virtues which he retained throughout his life.[59]
>
> It was from her lips he learned the Bible, from her teaching he drank in the sincere belief in revealed religion which he never lost. It was she who imbued her great son with an ineradicable belief in the efficacy of prayer and in the reality of God's interposition in everyday affairs of the true believer.[60]

Thomas "Stonewall" Jackson, another famous southern General, man of God, and contemporary of Lee, was taught at home by his mother until age seven when he was orphaned.[61] He lived most of his remaining youth working, although he did attend a country school for a time.

Two other successful American generals who were primarily educated at home were George Patton,[62] who grew up in a remote part of Texas, and Douglas MacArthur, who grew up on a succession of army posts.[63] Patton served in World War II, winning many victories against Hitler. General MacArthur served in World War II, leading American soldiers to victory over the Japanese. He also served in the Korean War in which he masterminded the surprise attack which led to the defeat of North Korea.

Renowned Home Schooled Scientists, Businessmen, Authors, and Artists

Booker T. Washington, scientist and founder and president of Tuskegee Normal and Industrial Institute, taught himself to read by using Noah Webster's "blue back speller" and by the constant support and common sense of his mother. By age thirteen he was prepared enough through his self-taught home education to enter an agricultural institute.[64]

Moreover, industrialist Andrew Carnegie[65] and inventor Thomas Edison[66] were schooled primarily through home education.

It is interesting to note that Thomas Edison was expelled from public school at age seven because he was considered "addled" by his public school teacher.[67] He lasted only three months in formal schooling. Over the next three years, his mother taught him the basics at home, and as Edison himself stated, "She instilled in me the love and purpose of learning."[68]

> When he [Edison] was an overly tender 10 years old, his mother introduced him to an elementary book on physical science, and that marked the beginning of his life-long effort to teach himself. He set up his own chemistry laboratory in the basement. Since he was crushed by the overwhelming disadvantage of poverty and had no welfare net to save him, he went to work at the age of 12 and became self-supporting while continuing to educate himself and carry on his own experiments that eventually helped to revolutionize the world.[69]

Famous author Mark Twain,[70] who wrote many American classics including *Huckleberry Finn* and *Tom Sawyer*, was taught primarily at home. Also authors Agatha Christie,[71] who wrote popular mystery novels, and Pearl S. Buck[72] were educated at home, along with George Bernard Shaw.[73] Irving Berlin quit school in second grade and became a self-taught musician.[74]

Photographer Ansel Adams, a "hyperactive" child, was removed from school and taught by his father at home.[75] In his autobiography, Ansel Adams gave tribute to his father's instruction:

> I am certain he established the positive direction of my life that otherwise, given my native hyperactivity, could have been confused and catastrophic. I trace who I am and the direction of my development to those years of growing up in our house on the dunes, propelled especially by an internal spark tenderly kept alive and glowing by my father.[76]

Several renowned artists were taught at home by their parents, including John Singleton Copley and Rembrandt Peale. Copley was taught by his step-father until age thirteen.[77] He then opened up his own painting and engraving shop. He soon became famous for his life-like portraits of contemporary leaders of the colonies during the Constitutional Debate period in the 1700s. Rembrandt Peale received his early education from his father and later dropped out of school at age thirteen to devote himself completely to his art.[78] He painted numerous portraits of well-known contemporaries, such as George Washington, Thomas Jefferson, Andrew Jackson, and Marquis de

Lafayette, many of which are presently on display in Washington D.C.

Newell and Carol Wyeth removed their son Andrew from the public school after only two weeks and instructed him at home.[79] Newell Wyeth reassured his son, "No first rate painter ever came out of college." Andrew Wyeth's father taught him his comprehensive theory of painting and trained him in his studio. Andrew Wyeth went on to become a famous painter who has been given "one-man shows by prestigious museums, including New York's Metropolitan Museum of Art, Washington's National Gallery of Art, and London's Royal Academy of Arts."[80]

Home-Schooled Leaders in Other Countries: Scientists, Authors, Composers, Economists, and Preachers

Some famous foreign men and women who were home schooled were Blaise Pascal, scientist, who invented the calculating machine (forerunner of the computer), discovered the theory of probability and the principle of the vacuum, and helped shape the field of calculus.[81] Author C. S. Lewis was taught by his mother until she died when he was ten. She had already taught him French and Latin, preparing him well for preparatory school which he entered at age thirteen.[82] He became a strong Christian who wrote *Chronicles of Narnia, Screwtape Letters, Mere Christianity*, and many other famous works, both fiction and nonfiction.

Author Charles Dickens was taught reading and writing and Latin from his mother and began working at age twelve.[83] Among some of his more well-know books are *The Christmas Carol*, which extols the godly virtue of charity, and *David Copperfield*.

John Owen was home schooled by his father during his early education and was later transferred to a private academy.[84] He became a respected Puritan pastor, authoring many great works on theology. He also served as chaplain to Oliver Cromwell in England.

Philosopher Charles Louis Montesquieu, who authored "L' Esprit des lois," the famous political treatise which influenced the U.S. Constitution, was educated first at home and then entered the College de Juilly when he was eleven.[85]

William the Silent, Prince of Orange and Protestant leader who founded the Dutch Republic, was taught by his mother at home, along with his sixteen brothers and sisters. His mother was a devout

Lutheran, "practicing a rigid moral code, sincere, generous and simple, her energetic example and spoken precepts molded the characters of all her children."[86]

Artist Claude Monet said, "It was at home that I learned the little that I knew."[87]

John Newton, hymn writer and London preacher, was taught at home by his mother until age seven when she died.[88] Afterward, he was sent to school for approximately three years and then went to sea with his father. His most well-known song which he authored is "Amazing Grace." John Newton recounts his early home instruction:

> The tender mercies of God toward me were manifested in the first moment of my life . I was born, as it were, in His house and dedicated to Him in infancy. My mother . . . was a pious, experienced Christian. . . . I was her only child. . . Almost her whole employment was the care of my education. . . . At not more than three years of age, she herself taught me English. When I was four years old I could read with propriety in any common book. She stored my memory, which was then very retentive, with many valuable pieces, chapters, and portions of Scripture, catechisms, hymns and poems. . . . In my sixth year, I began to learn Latin.[89]

Free-market economist John Stuart Mill was taught entirely at home by his father until age fourteen.[90] He was the eldest of nine children. His father started him in Greek at age three and by eight he had read Herodotus and Plato in the original. At age twelve, he was seriously studying logic.[91]

Many famous composers were taught primarily at home. Wolfgang Amadeus Mozart, born in Vienna, was primarily taught by his father, who historians agree was an excellent teacher.[92] His education began when he was four, and he began his international travel when he was five, causing him to spend nearly half of his time from age five to fifteen on tour. In his travels, Mozart came in touch with every type of music of his day, resulting in a well-rounded cultural and musical education. In fact, his own music became a perfect blend of Italian, German, and French styles. At six, Mozart wrote his first minuet, by nine he wrote his first symphony, at eleven he wrote his first oratorio, and by twelve he composed his first opera.[93]

Composer Anton Bruckner was born in Austria and was one of eleven children. His father was a school teacher and his mother was a singer. By the time he was four years old he displayed a precocious interest in music which his parents encouraged.[94] He learned at home until age eleven and then lived with his grandfather for two years to continue his musical education. When he was fourteen he went to school at a local monastery.[95] Bruckner considered the Lord to be his best friend, and one contemporary stated that he was "perhaps the only great composer of this century [nineteenth] whose entire musical output is determined by his religious faith."[96] Bruckner was extremely well-read in the Bible and always spent time in prayer before composing or teaching.[97] He is known especially for *Te Deum* and composed nine famous symphonies.

Felix Mendelssohn's first teacher was his mother who, among other subjects, taught him music, the tradition of hard work, and self-denial, until he was tutored at age eleven.[98] Mendelssohn became a renowned composer and conductor, an excellent artist in drawing and painting, and an all-around athlete.[99] He is known for his oratorios *Elijah* and *St. Paul*, and many symphonies including the *Reformation Symphony*. He knew his Bible well and worked to the glory of God.[100]

Also composer Francis Poulenc received most of his early education from his mother and father. His mother taught him music, beginning with piano lessons at age five, and his father made sure he completed his academic studies.[101] After his mother taught Francis all that she knew, she had him taught by tutors at least by age fifteen.

Conclusion

These many famous men and women of the past who were taught by their parents at home lends further credence to the effectiveness of this tutorial form of education. The modern home-schooling movement, which blossomed in the 1980s and continues unabated, is confirming the same results, as it begins to produce highly trained and successful graduates. This list of famous home schoolers is just beginning.

Notes

1. Saul Padover, *Jefferson* (Harcourt-Brace, 1942), 369

2. John C. Fitzpatrick, *George Washington Himself* (Indianapolis: Bobbs-Merrill Co., 1885), 19, and also see John Eidsmoe, *Christianity and the Constitution* (Grand Rapids, Mich.: Baker Book House, 1987), 125-127.

3. William Johnson, *George Washington the Christian* (Arlington Heights, Ill.: Christian Liberty Press), 19-22.

4. *The American Heritage Book of the Presidents and Famous Americans*, Vol. 1 (New York: American Heritage Publishing Co., 1967), 11.

5. Saul K. Padover, *Jefferson: A Great American's Life and Ideals* (New York: Mentor Books, 1942), 10-14; Eidsmoe, *Christianity and the Constitution*, 218.

6. *Ibid.*, 11.

7. *The American Heritage Book of the Presidents*, Vol. 2 (New York: Dell Publishing, 1967), 133.

8. *James Madison 1751-1836*, ed. Ian Elliot (Dobbs Ferry, N.Y.: Oceana Pubs., 1969), 1.

9. *Memoirs of John Quincy Adams*, ed. Charles Francis Adams (Philadelphia: J.B. Lippincott, 1874), 7.

10. *The Christian History of the American Revolution*, compiled by Verna Hall, "The Education of John Quincy Adams," Rosalie Slater (San Francisco: Foundation for Christian Education, 1982), 603-604.

11. Benjamin P. Thomas, *Abraham Lincoln: A Biography* (New York: Alfred A. Knopf, 1952), 7, 8, 12; Albert J. Beveridge, *Abraham Lincoln* (New York: Houghton-Mifflin Co., 1928), 63..

12. Robert Seager, III, *And Tyler Too* (Norwalk, Conn.: Easton Press, 1963), 53.

13. *Ibid.*, 50.

14. *Ibid.*, 48.

15. *World Book Encyclopedia* (1986). Harrison received his early education at home and entered Hampden Sidney College at age fourteen.

16. *Encyclopedia Britannica*, Vol. 19 (Chicago, Ill.: William Benton, 1968), 606.

17. *Ibid.*

18. *Ibid.*, 600 and see *F.D.R : His Personal Letters*, ed. Elliott Roosevelt (New York: Duell, Sloan & Pearce, 1947), 5.

19. Ray S. Baker, *Woodrow Wilson: Life and Letters* (Garden City, N.Y.: Doubleday, Page & Co., 1927), 37.

20. Arthur Walworth, *Woodrow Wilson* (Norwalk, Conn.: Easton Press, 1958), 9-10.

21. Martha Lou Lemmon Stohlman, *John Witherspoon: Parson, Politician, Patriot* (Philadelphia: Westminster Press, 1897), 17.

22. Eidsmoe, *Christianity and the Constitution*, 83, and Stohlman, *John Witherspoon*, 172.

23. John Bigelow, *The Life of Benjamin Franklin, Written by Himself* (Philadelphia: J.B. Lippincott, 1957), 99. John Eidsmoe, *Christianity and the Constitution*, 192.

24. M. E. Bradford, *A Worthy Company* (Marlborough, N.H.: Plymouth Rock Foundation, 1982), 30. The footnotes 24 through 36 are taken from Bradford's book. He gives at least eight sources, including a number of biographies for each of the delegates, as supporting his research.

25. *Ibid.*, 97.

26. *Ibid.*, 212.

27. *Ibid.*, 123.

28. *Ibid.*, 176.

29. *Ibid.*, 187.

30. *Ibid.*, 193-94.

31. *Ibid.*, 197.

32. *Ibid.*, 59.

33. *Ibid.*, 110.

34. *Ibid.*, 218.

35. *Ibid.*, 220.

36. *Ibid.*, 155.

37. Charles W. Akers, *Abigail Adams: An American Woman* (Boston: Little, Brown & Co., 1980), 8.

38. Alice Brown, *Mercy Warren* (New York: Charles Scribner's Sons, 1903), 8.

39. Alice Curtis Desmond, *Martha Washington: Our First Lady* (New York: Dodd, Mead & Co., 1963), 7.

40. Mary Lewis Coakley, "The Faith Behind the Famous, Florence Nightingale," *Christian History* (Carol Stream, Ill.: Christianity Today, Inc.), Issue 25, 38 and David Collins, *God's Servant on the Battlefield: Florence Nightingale* (Milford, Mich.: Mott Media, 1985).

41. Edith Deen, *Great Women of the Christian Faith* (Westwood, N.J.: Barbour and Company 1959), 214.

42. G. Herbert Renfro, *Life and Works of Phyllis Wheatley* (Freeport, N.Y.: Books for Libraries Press, 1972), 11-12, and Benjamin Brawley, *The Negro in Literature and Art in the United States* (New York: Duffield & Co., 1939), 17-18.

43. Robert Douthat Meade, *Patrick Henry: Patriot in the Making* (Philadelphia: J.B. Lippincott, 1957), 51. Also see Eidsmoe, *Christianity and the Constitution*, 298-99.

44. Eidsmoe, *Christianity and the Constitution*, 308.

45. Eidsmoe, *Christianity and the Constitution*, 307-315.

46. Eidsmoe, *Christianity and the Constitution*, 165.

47. Leonard Baker, *John Marshall: A Life in Law* (New York: Macmillan Publishing Co., 1974), 13.

48. *Ibid.*, 12-13.

49. *The Christian History of the American Revolution*, compiled by Verna Hall (San Francisco: Foundation for American Christian Education, 1982), 559.

50. Edith Deen, *Great Women*, 143. Also see *Encyclopedia Britannica*, *op. cit.*, Vol. 23, 414.

51. *Ibid.*, 142, 144.

52. *The Works of Jonathan Edwards*, ed. Edward Hickman (Edinburgh, England: Banner of Truth Trust), XVI.

53. *Ibid.*

54. Basil Miller, *Men of Faith: William Carey, Father of Modern Missions* (Minneapolis, Minn.: Bethany House, 1980), 10.

55. *Ibid.*, 8.

56. Virginia Lieson Brereton, "The Popular Educator," which appeared in *Christian History*, ISSN 0891-9666 (Carol Stream, Ill.: Christianity Today, Inc.), Issue 25, 26.

57. William Johnson, *Robert E. Lee: The Christian* (Arlington Heights, Ill.: Christian Liberty Press, 1989), 26-29.

58. *Ibid.*, 27.

59. Emily V. Mason, *Popular Life of General Robert E. Lee* (Baltimore, Md.: J. Murphy and Co., 1874), 22.

60. Viscount Wolseley, *General Lee* (Rochester, N.Y.: George P. Humphrey, 1906), 13.

61. R. L. Dabney, *Life and Campaigns of General T.J. (Stonewall) Jackson* (Harrisonburg, Vir.: Sprinkle Publications, 1977), 10-13.

62. Harry H. Semmes, *Portrait of Patton* (New York: Appleton Century Crofts, 1955), 4-5.

63. I. D. Clayton James, *The Years of MacArthur* (Boston: Houghton Mifflin & Co., 1970), 53. Also see Brian Mitchell, "More Military Families Opting for Home Schools," *Navy Times*, 24 October 1988, 15.

64. Booker T. Washington, *Up From Slavery: An Autobiography* (Boston: Western Islands, 1965), 14-16, 22-23.

65. Burton J. Hendrick, *The Life of Andrew Carnegie* (Garden City, N.Y.: Doubleday, Doran & Co., 1932), 21.

66. Matthew Josephson, *Edison* (New York: McGraw-Hill, 1959), 21.

67. *Ibid.*, 20-23.

68. "Thomas Alva Edison," *The New Encyclopedia Britannica*, Vol. 6, Macropaedia (Chicago: University of Chicago Press, 1983), 308. Also see Gerald M. King, "Home Schooling: Up from Underground," *Reason*, April, 26.

69. Jack Douglas, "Only Freedom of Education Can Solve America's Bureaucratic Crisis of Education," *Policy Analysis*, 17 June 1991, Cato Institute, Washington D.C., 6. Also see Wyn Wachhorst, *Thomas Alva Edison* (Cambridge: MIT Press, 1981), 180-83.

70. DeLancey Ferguson, *Mark Twain: Man and Legend* (New York: Bobbs-Merrill and Co., 1943), 21, 24, 29.

71. Agatha Christie, *Agatha Christie: An Autobiography* (New York: Dodd, Mead & Co., 1977), 19-20.

72. Paul A. Doyle, *Pearl S. Buck* (New York: Twayne Publishers, 1965), 24.

73. Hesketh Pearson, *George Bernard Shaw: A Full Length Portrait* (New York: Harper & Bros., 1942), 11.

74. Michael Friedland, *Irving Berlin* (Stein and Day, 1974).

75. Teresa Amabile, "Personal Glimpses: To His Own Beat," *Reader's Digest*, 1990, 19.

76. *Ibid.*

77. *The Christian History of the American Revolution*, complied by Verna Hall (San Francisco: Foundation for American Christian Education, 1982), 579.

78. *Ibid.*, 584.

79. Richard Meryman, "The Wyeth Family: American Visions," *National Geographic*, Vol. 180, No.1, July 1991, 100.

80. *Ibid.*

81. "Genius with a Heart of Faith," *Glimpses* (Worcester, Pa.: Christian History Institute, 1989), Number 2.

82. Clyde S. Kilby, *The Christian World of C. S. Lewis* (Grand Rapids, Mich.: Eerdmans, 1978), 14.

83. Angus Wilson, *The World of Charles Dickens* (Viking, 1970), 43.

84. *The Works of John Owen*, ed. William Goold, Vol. 1 (Edinburgh, England: Banner of Truth Trust, 1981), XXII.

85. *Encyclopedia Brittanica*, Vol. 15 (Chicago: William Benton, 1968), 785.

86. C. V. Wedgewood, *William the Silent* (New York: Norton and Company, 1968), 10-11.

87. Sheridan Morely, *A Talent to Amuse: Noel Coward* (New York: Doubleday, 1969).

88. John Newton, *Out of the Depths* (Grand Rapids, Mich.: Kregel Publications, 1990), 21-23.

89. *Ibid.*, 21.

90. Michael St. John Packe, *The Life of John Stuart Mill* (London: Secker & Warburg, 1954), 19-20.

91. *John Stuart Mill: Autobiography* (New York: Collier and Son, 1909), 3.

92. Jane Stuart Smith and Betty Carlson, *The Gift of Music* (Westchester, Ill.: Crossway Books, 1987), 55.

93. *Ibid.*, 56.

94. *Ibid.*, 126.

95. *Ibid.*

96. *Ibid.*, 127.

97. *Ibid.*, 130.

98. *Ibid.*, 84-85.

99. *Ibid.*, 86.

100. *Ibid.*, 88.

101. *Ibid.*, 264.

PART
3

THE RIGHT CHOICE:
TEACH THEM AT HOME

More and more parents are becoming serious about the training of their children. They are realizing the public schools are failing their children both morally and academically.

Parents are waking up to the truth that their children are *not* disposable commodities to be blindly turned over to Day Care centers and mass educational systems. Rather, children are gifts from God and the preservation of the family unit is one of our utmost priorities.

The chapters in this section will explain to you how you can start home schooling your own children. You will discover that *any* parent who is willing to sacrifice their time and possibly their career for their children's sakes can succeed at home schooling. Both new and veteran home schoolers will learn much from Gregg Harris' tips on how to apply biblical principles to your children's educations. Without such a biblical foundation your educational program will be incomplete.

God will honor those who honor Him in their commitment to training their children in His ways.

CHAPTER **8**

HOW SHOULD WE THEN TEACH? WALKING IN LIGHT OF GOD'S PRINCIPLES OF EDUCATION

By Gregg Harris

Who among you fears the Lord and obeys the word of his servant? Let him who walks in the dark, who has no light, trust in the name of the Lord and rely on his God. But now, all you who light fires and provide yourselves with flaming torches, go, walk in the light of your fires and of the torches you have set ablaze. This is what you shall receive from my hand: You will lie down in torment (Isaiah 50:10-11).

Your word is a lamp to my feet and a light for my path (Psalm 119:105).

> But if we walk in the light, as he is in the light, we have fellowship with one another, and the blood of Jesus, his Son, purifies us from all sin (1 John 1:7).

> These commandments that I give you today are to be upon your hearts. Impress them on your children. Talk about them when you sit at home and when you walk along the road, when you lie down and when you get up (Deuteronomy 6:6-7).

Chris stated in chapter 4: "The Word of God is the source of all truth and the standard by which all things are measured." To that I heartily agree. But the implications of his statement reach far beyond what is normally attempted by Christians in the church today. Those families who take this statement to heart will find themselves not only living differently from their unbelieving neighbors but also living differently from those fellow Christians who are not so inclined. They will not only keep their children out of the public schools, but they will also establish distinctively different kinds of organizations to support them in providing a different kind of training and instruction for their children—and the difference will be like night and day.

This should be expected. The Bible speaks with absolute authority on every significant area of life. In its own words it serves as the "light for my path." Such illumination is sorely needed. Without God's Word on any matter, we are walking in the dark. If we do not wish to stumble over the things that cause others to fall, we have no choice but to walk in the light. When we commit ourselves to obey God's Word, even in its least controversial instructions, we will see a marked difference in the way we live.

Sociologists have observed that evangelical Christian families today suffer from basically the same problems as their unbelieving counterparts in the same social and economic circumstances. In the Bible-preaching churches, rising divorce rates, increased incidence of drug abuse, premarital sexual activity, teenage pregnancies, and even abortion run neck-and-neck statistically with similar families outside the church. A watching world has the right to ask, "What's the difference?" Why should my neighbor become a Christian if Christians do not fare any better than he does? The answer is painful.

On a practical level, Christians who do not walk obediently in the light of God's Word are not much better off in this world than those who do not believe the Bible. Granted, in eternity, the born-again Christian will be received into heaven while the unbeliever who has rejected Christ will be cast into hell. That brings a wonderful peace which cannot be denied. But in this world, the power of the Holy Spirit to overcome the consequences of the fall of man is very much affected by individual obedience to God's Word. When the Bible says, "Do not commit adultery," and a Christian chooses to ignore God's commandment, the consequences in his broken life and family will be as painful as for the unbeliever who does the same thing. The repentant Christian will be forgiven, but the consequences of his foolishness will still be difficult to bear. It is much better to walk in the light and not stumble at all, than it is to stumble and be forgiven.

The abundant life Christ promised is a life lived in submission to His commandments. We are called to obey Him because our obedience continues to save us from our own foolishness and sin each day. The difference in lifestyles of the obedient Christian and the disobedient non-Christian should be remarkable, not because we are backward and "out of pace" with the world, but because we are walking confidently according to God's wisdom and "setting the pace" for those who have any appreciation for what is right and good. Rather than being out of style, we can actually set the styles. Instead of playing catch up, we can be on the cutting edge of making real progress in all areas of civilization.

Believers and Unbelievers Alike?

Stark contrasts are rare these days. Many home schooling families have confided in me that until they began to teach their children at home, there was not an observable difference between them and their unbelieving neighbors. Obedience in relationship to their children's education was the first really different thing they had ever done. The reaction from friends and family was immediate. Believers and unbelievers *alike* (now there's an interesting situation) were shocked. Walking in the light of God's Word was initially hazardous to their social acceptance.

Now that the fruits of their decision to home school are on display, there is a change afoot. Some of the same people who originally opposed them are now asking for help in getting started home schooling their own children. Walking in the dark, ignoring God's Word on education, and sending their children to the public schools would have been much easier. Now, the salt and light of their personal example are affecting their friends and family members and changing the attitudes of many. That is the way it is with Christians and God's Word. By their fruits you shall know them.

Isn't it ironic? Those who obey God will "shine as lights in the midst of the darkness." Jesus asks, "If the light that is in you (i.e. if what you *think* is light) is actually darkness, how great is that darkness!" There is no greater spiritual darkness than that of self-deception. And there seems to be no greater opposition to God's light than from comfortably religious people. Those who decide to walk in obedience to the counsel of Scripture stand in stark contrast to those who do not. Cain never will like Abel.

That is why I am convinced that home schooling is more than an educational movement. In the Christian community it is a *revival* movement. As Paul discovered, the truth that spawns a true revival will almost always spark a riot at the same time. Those who have a vested interest in keeping things the way they are (the silver idol makers) always oppose what God is doing. It takes real courage to admit you are in the wrong business. Initially, the Christian schools and the Christian curriculum publishers resisted home schoolers. Only a few brave souls extended a hand of support. Today there is much more cooperation. The fruits of the home school revival are just too obvious to be denied.

Revival is always measured in terms of renewed devotion to what it means to be a Christian. That translates into a renewal of zeal for God's Word. Personal evangelism, personal repentance, and personal sanctification all follow. These things are typical of every revival in Church history. The current revival is being expressed as a renewed desire to obey the Bible's truths concerning Christian family life. It's not the first time. The Pilgrims and the Puritans were also concerned with these practical aspects of obeying God's Word. Richard Baxter's *Directory* was full of counsel on Christian family life. Because of that revival movement, England was spared from having a French-style revolution, several Christian colonies were established in North America, and eventually our nation was founded as a Christian republic. Not bad for a handful of Christian families who just wanted to be left alone to worship God and raise their children as they believed the Bible commanded. Home schooling is a revival. What could God have in store for us this time?

Turning the Hearts of Fathers to Their Children

Although there is a segment of the home school community which does not profess Christ and which does not care whether home schooling is biblical or not, the vast majority of home schooling families in America today are Bible-believing Christians. Their reasons for home schooling are an outgrowth of their commitment to serve God faithfully. As Malachi states in the fourth chapter of his prophecy:

> Remember the law of my servant Moses, the decrees and laws I gave him at Horeb for all Israel. See, I will send you the prophet Elijah before that great and dreadful day of the LORD comes. He will turn the hearts of the fathers to their children, and the hearts of the children to their fathers; or else I will come and strike the land with a curse (vv. 4-6).

Many Christian home schooling parents see a partial fulfillment of this passage in the way God has turned the hearts of what were once negligent fathers to the concerns of their children. In response, there is now a growing number of remarkable home school children whose hearts are very much turning toward the concerns of their fathers! My first-born son, Joshua, is among them. At seventeen, he has been home-schooled by his mother and me since he was five. His commitment to serve God with his many talents is a gift from God. Josh and our four other children are not the only ones who have made this commitment. I have met other home schooling teens and their parents who share a vision of the future—a vision which may prove to be the salvation of our nation.

I say this because home school parents and their children are headed for leadership. Under God's direction, they are focusing their households on ministry in the church and in their communities. If anything can stay God's hand of judgment on western democracy in light of our national sins, the home school movement can. Even if God should choose judgment over mercy, these Christian home school families are determined to stand faithful to God through whatever lies ahead. My impression, and the impression of many others, is that they are stable, balanced, courageous Christian families.

Every Christian leader I know who has had direct contact with Christian home schooling families comes away deeply excited about what God is doing. Even Christian school administrators who initially had some reason to keep the home school option out of sight, are now willing to admit that the families in their schools who choose home schooling are usually among the most dedicated Christians they know. That is why so many Christian schools now facilitate home schooling through their administrative offices. They are willing to help parents become more effective teachers of their own children. Testing services, library access, drama, choir, band, sports programs, and other extra-curricular activities are often made available, for a reasonable fee, to home schooling families.

As a group, Christian home schoolers comprise one of the most organized, quickly mobilized, political groups in the country today. They are more likely to be involved in the pro-life movement, more likely to be faithful in prayer and family devotions, more likely to share their faith with others. They are also more likely to become foreign missionaries. In contrast to what is happening in the lives of many Christians sitting right beside them in the church pew, home schooling parents are growing spiritually. They are becoming unpretentious pillars in their local churches and in their communities. They are, in a word, "revived."

Ten years ago I had to choose whether to stay in my ministry as the pastor of a local church or commit myself full time to teaching and encouraging the national home school community. I would not have been able to step down from my pulpit if I did not believe home schooling is a true revival movement. I have done my best to keep it that way. That brings us to an important question: What kind of organizations can best preserve and support the growth of the Christian home school movement? If we are a revival movement, spawned by a renewed commitment to walk in the light of God's Word, how do we keep the holy fire burning?

Meet the Support System

Support groups are to home school families what writers' groups are to aspiring authors. The groups support one another in whatever way the members decide. Because of the rapid growth of home schooling, this support has had to be organized into a support *system* at four basic levels: the state coalition level, state association level, metropolitan association level, and local church or neighborhood level. The differences between these four levels of support are very important. The nature of the support offered at each level directly affects each level's decision whether to accept diversity of faith among its leadership or to require like-mindedness.

State coalitions are normally made up of several state level and metropolitan level home school associations. Coalitions take on major projects, such as lobbying to improve or protect state laws for all home schoolers. This work requires broad-based support and cooperation across the lines that legitimately divide the state associations. Christian, secular, and non-Christian religious groups can and do work well together at this coalition level. Texas is a good example of this. (See chapter 20 for a thorough presentation of the coalitions.) Several organizations can share information to protect the rights of everyone. The Christian Association is usually by far the largest and the strongest. But the smaller non-Christian groups have their state associations, too. This coalition approach works because its goals are narrowly defined and carefully agreed on from the outset. Whenever they are not, the state coalition breaks apart and each state association goes its own way.

The state association level normally coordinates the activities of the metropolitan and local church or neighborhood level support group leaders. These state associations may be Christian or non-Christian. In some states there is more than one Christian group. Christians can have strong differences, and that is all right as long as they are willing to work together for the good of their members. At this level of support the state newsletters are published or co-published with *The Teaching Home*. State home school conferences are held. The main purpose of the state associations is to get the troops (i.e. the home school parents) out for legislative action in response to news of legal or political crisis. The folks at The National Center for Home Education, near Washington, D.C., do a great job of keeping these state association leaders informed of what is lurking in each state legislature's data base. Phone trees then move this information very quickly to the metro and local groups. Most home school parents are prepared to drop everything and go to the state capitol when asked to do so. They make it a "civics field trip" for the whole family.

Metropolitan level support group associations are closer to the local church and neighborhood groups. They host most of the major home school events. Curriculum Fairs are organized at this level and workshops and seminars (such as my own Home Schooling Workshops) are hosted annually. Field trips to the symphony and the zoo may also be coordinated by the metro leadership, if the local or neighborhood groups request it. My home state of Oregon is a good example of strong metropolitan associations in Portland, Eugene, and Medford, linking the local groups to the state association.

Metro groups are becoming fairly sophisticated. Greater numbers make all kinds of things possible. One has a home school marching band. Another hosts a national home school basketball tournament. Many offer high school graduation exercises and even grant scholarships for college. All of this activity is based on the idea that by combining their efforts, local support group leaders and parents can accomplish things that would be difficult or impossible to do by themselves.

It is important to note that most of the activity going on at the state and metro levels can be accomplished with only the home school *leaders* being like-minded in the faith. Non-leadership home school parents, whether Christian or not, are usually free to attend the conferences and fairs as they like, without much regard for religious or philosophical differences. No one tries to check your spiritual I.D. at the door. But you will probably not be asked to speak in the conference unless the leaders know where you are coming from spiritually. Christian groups prefer unabashedly Christian speakers. Non-Christian groups generally prefer non-Christian or nominally Christian speakers who promise not to quote the Bible.

It is only at the local church or neighborhood level of support group activity that individual parents are expected to agree on religious and philosophical issues in order to become members of the support group. Unfortunately, but understandably, this is where some new families get their feelings hurt. They may want to join a group that doesn't want them to join, for one reason or another.

The Need for Distinctively Christian Organizations

Walking in the light makes a difference. Christian parents benefit from the support of their fellow Christians. It helps them fulfill their obligations to their children. Once you get past the legal and technical aspects of teaching children at home, you must respond to your need for spiritual and emotional encouragement. State and metro conferences and curriculum fairs deal with the legal and technical areas very well, without much distinction between Christian and non-Christian parents. But when spiritual and emotional support is needed, the local church or neighborhood support group is where it is normally found. And it is not likely to be provided through an organization that has a mixture of Christian and secular members. Like-mindedness of *membership* becomes important at this point. Walking in the light of God's Word becomes a *group* effort.

At this point I have to point out that like-mindedness is not merely a matter of whether everyone in the group is a professing Christian. Some cults claim to be Christian. Nominal Christians (such as those who claim to be born again, but don't want to make their religious faith a big deal) don't usually feel comfortable with dedicated evangelical Christian parents. When I use the term "mixed group," I'm referring to a group that is not like-minded, and which sees no reason to expect like-mindedness.

Inevitably, in a mixed support group the dedicated Christian home schooler is expected to "tone down" his references to the Lord and to be more "sensitive" to the feelings of others who do not share his faith. The rule seems to be, "Offend God, not man." Prayer during meetings is "offensive" in a mixed group, just as it is in the public schools. Bible references are also out of place. Home school speakers who insist on making the Bible their primary source of authority are not invited to speak in the meetings of a mixed group unless they agree to be "sensitive" (and they don't mean sensitive to the Holy Spirit!). Biblical methods of discipline may be reported by fellow group members to the authorities as "child abuse." As Paul said in 2 Corinthians 6:14-16, "Do not be yoked together with unbelievers. For what do righteousness and wickedness have in common? Or what fellowship can light have with darkness?"

Those are good questions. Yet, some Christians feel obligated to answer, "We are all home schooling." That is true. But our reasons for doing so are very different. Our ultimate goals are different. Like snow lying closely on the ground, but on different sides of a watershed, we will eventually end up in different oceans. Some will go to heaven, others to hell. Faith is a watershed issue.

"That is just the point," some will say. "We have an obligation to let our light shine and lead the unsaved into the kingdom of God." Fine, practice hospitality toward the lost and present the gospel to them. As the host serve them from a position of strength, without compromise. You can be generous with what is yours, because you own it. When you become a co-owner with an unbeliever, it is no longer your decision. Do not become entangled with unbelievers in ways that require your faith to be checked at the door. You are welcome to join the mixed groups and let your light shine there if they will let you. But please do not entice unbelievers into staying in a Christian group by turning down the light.

A brief look at history reveals that Christians are generally naive. As Paul said, "Do not be misled; bad company corrupts good character." Harvard University began as an institution for training Puritan ministers. How did it get so far off track? The mainline Protestant denominations in America were all founded in the light of God's Word. Today most of them are filled with scorners and unbelievers. What went wrong? The answer is that unbelievers were invited to join the leadership teams of these organizations under the plan of winning them to Christ or just being neighborly. "What harm could it do?" Rather than requiring a true like-mindedness in the faith, these once godly institutions attempted to be more tolerant than God Himself. The result has been creeping secularism. When an organization stops being God's, it becomes man's and, ultimately, Satan's.

Now some may ask, "Why make such a big deal about a little support group?" A support group is not a church. Church rules should not apply. I agree that a support group, even if deeply Christian, is not a church. That is why I believe the commandment against having women teaching men does not apply to the home school support groups. Older women are commanded to teach the younger women how to love their husbands and their children. That is what happens most of the time in a good home school support group. No, a support group is not a church. But it is a "whatever." And God tells us . . .

> Commit to the LORD *whatever* you do, and your plans will succeed (Proverbs 16:3).

> So whether you eat or drink or *whatever* you do, do it all for the glory of God (1 Corinthians 10:31).

> And *whatever* you do, whether in word or deed, do it all in the name of the Lord Jesus, giving thanks to God the Father through him (Colossians 3:17).

Whatever you do, work at it with all your heart, as working
for the Lord, not for men (Colossians 3:23).

No matter what else a home school support group may be, it is at
least important enough to be done in a way that will glorify God, in
the name of our Lord Jesus Christ. Why shouldn't a support group
honor God by name? Why shouldn't it have God's glory enthroned as
its ultimate purpose in its founding documents, constitution, and by-
laws? The answer is, because we will be accused of being religious
bigots if we make such a distinction. Discretion has become a hate
crime in America today. Everyone is supposed to act as though all
lifestyles are of equal merit. That is ridiculous! God, we are told,
expresses His anger at the wicked every day. "There is a way that
seems right to a man, but in the end it leads to death" (Proverbs
14:12). The difference between light and darkness is real.

Ten years ago the support groups were small in scale and
influence. Today, in some states the Christian home school
association leaders are consulted directly by the governor of the state
before enacting or vetoing a law that will affect home schoolers. A
few national home school leaders are known by name on Capitol Hill.
A few years from now we may be receiving calls from the president of
the United States. Only God knows where this is headed. So it is not
our place to decide how important what we are doing is going to be.
We have an obligation to our children and one another to build a
foundation under our associations that will stand the tests of time. A
small home meeting today may be the beginning of a powerful
institution tomorrow. History has a way of surprising us.

That is why Martin Luther made his bold declaration, already
quoted several times in this book. "I advise no one to place his child
where the Scriptures do not reign paramount. Every institution which
is not unceasingly occupied with the Word of God must be corrupt."
A home school support group is no more likely to remain faithful to
God than any other institution. It is walking in the light of God's
Word that will make all the difference.

The Need for Unity at the State Level

Christian state and metropolitan home school associations often
require their leaders to sign a statement of faith or some other
document in order to assure a general agreement on basic moral
values, religious faith, and basic educational goals. This is as it should

be. A house divided against itself cannot stand. But a collection of strong state associations can work together in spite of their differences. "A cord of three strands is not quickly broken" (Ecclesiastes 4:12). This implies that three distinct strands can be woven together for greater strength. That is a good description of a state home school coalition. Christian, secular, and other religious groups can pull together for the good of all home school families.

If you prefer another analogy, think of it as a good choir. Many distinct voices singing various parts of the same song are far more impressive than one solo voice, no matter how talented. Christians can serve together as a powerful ally with other non-Christian associations in a state coalition, without becoming entangled with the world or denying Christ. But if anyone tries to change the tune, the choir disbands.

My suggestions are made only with the intent of finding ways for us to work with the diversity that has been in this movement from the beginning. Doctrinally sound, emotionally mature Christian leadership promotes greater unity within the growing Christian home school community. And the Christian home school community works well with the non-Christian groups from a position of strength and generosity. Most Christians are not used to setting the styles in anything. We are accustomed to following the lead of the secular culture and then Christianizing it. This is not like that. In this revival, the Christian who is walking in the light of God's Word has no reason to be coy. We have been given an opportunity to lead by our example. Let the world come, like the Queen of Sheba, and learn from the wisdom God has given to His people. In this area, we are the hosts, not the guests.

The Need for Agreement at the Local Church or Neighborhood Level

As I have said, it is at the local church or neighborhood support group level that the personal beliefs of individual parents become an issue in Christian groups. This is because these local groups are intended to support the personal aspects of home schooling and to provide spiritual as well as practical encouragement and counsel. They normally meet in members' homes or in church fellowship halls. Their children become the closest of friends. Naturally, conscientious parents are very much concerned that everyone in this intimate relationship be like-minded in the faith. It is not unusual for such groups to also serve as growth groups within their local church, under the oversight of a pastor-elder. Do not be offended when people begin asking you some very personal questions about what you believe. They want to know whether to embrace you, try to convert you, or help you find another support group. Please try to see the process from their side.

Today, there are home schooling Christians and home schooling witches. There are home schooling Jews and home schooling neo-Nazis. Home schooling vegetarians don't care for home schooling cattle ranchers. Home schooling Mormons, Scientologists, Jehovah's Witnesses, and Christian Scientists don't get along well. Home schooling New Agers and home schooling Amish are uncomfortable with each other. There are home schooling gays and lesbians. Politically, there are home schooling Libertarians, Conservatives, Liberals, and Communists. Former public school principals and teachers make up one of the largest categories of parents who home school their children. Many hippies and former hippies home school. I know of at least one home schooling superior court justice. If it's diversity you want, the home schooling movement has it! Granted, the numbers in some of these categories are sometimes small, but it only takes a match to start a forest fire.

Some might say, "Aw, what's the big deal? Can't we just all be home schoolers and forget about all our differences?" No, its not that easy. The differences I am talking about have resulted in wars and martyrdom in the not-too-distant past. Our forefathers fought and, in some cases, died because of some of these issues. The differences are ancient and deeply rooted. We have an obligation to our forefathers not to trivialize what they bought with their own blood. Time, law, and general prosperity have buffered or suppressed the overt conflicts. Today, with good fences, we can all be decent neighbors toward one another and vote our conscience in the next election. But without clear boundaries to mark the place where our responsibilities stop and our neighbors' responsibilities start, we will nonetheless have disputes. All it takes is for a child or spouse to announce he has converted to another faith, or channeled his "higher self" (a-la Shirley MacLaine), or discovered his true sexual orientation and otherwise cool heads go ballistic. Again, what fellowship does light have with darkness?

With all this diversity it is not at all inappropriate for church or neighborhood support groups to have some discretion concerning who is invited to join the little group that meets in their own homes or church buildings. They are not being elitist or bigoted—just realistic.

What should Christian groups do? Statements of faith are not a bad idea if it matters to you what others in your group believe. Agreement on certain aspects of child discipline and education are also advisable. If you hope to establish lasting friendships within any group, you should search out a group that shares your general point of view. Never join a group with the idea that you are going to change it. It's supposed to be a *support* group, not a debate team. Its strength is in its *shared* vision.

The problem is, wholesome *discretion*, with its basis in common sense, can easily be mistaken for *discrimination*, with its roots in hatred and bigotry. There *is* a difference, but our emotions easily blur our perception. We are not talking about denying anyone his rights before the law. This is not an employment dispute. Race should have nothing to do with it. Economics should have nothing to do with it. Faith and morality have everything to do with it. Compatibility is the objective.

Not everyone who tells you their group is closed is rejecting you. And even those who inform you that your religious views are incompatible with those of their group are not necessarily doing you a disservice. They are being honest with you and they may be sparing you a lot of grief. Your child or spouse may be the one converted to a new faith. So answer their questions honestly. Ask a few questions of your own. Read the group's literature. Know what you are joining— before you join.

On the other hand, don't fall into the trap of feeling that you have to join one particular group over all the others because it is "the one right group." Assuming a basic agreement in "world view," most local support groups can serve your needs effectively. Just as you are free to patronize any grocery store in town, so you should feel free to participate in any support group that offers you its services at a price you are willing to pay. Be thankful that you have options from which to choose. It hasn't always been this way.

If a really great group happens to be "closed" to new members or has a waiting list, please understand that it may not be "exclusive" any more than you are exclusive when you decide to invite ten people instead of twelve to a dinner party. The size of your dinner table may be the only decisive factor! So it is with some support groups. The home school movement is growing too quickly to do otherwise. You may be the tenth inquirer the group has received that week. Groups that meet in members' homes may not be able to seat more than twenty-five or thirty people, and the quality of the group's activities would suffer if too many children were to participate all at once. Try to imagine things from the inside. The "closed" support group may be like family to one another, with years of experience together. They don't have room for everyone. You are not being personally rejected.

The group you ultimately join may also have to establish a cut-off point and a waiting list. Then you may be on the inside thinking, *Hey, let's not let this group get too big!* Be kind to all the new families, even if you know you disagree with them. "When an alien lives with you in your land, do not mistreat him. The alien living with you must be treated as one of your native-born. Love him as yourself, for you were aliens in Egypt. I am the LORD your God" (Leviticus 19:33-34). Every group should be willing to assist new families in finding or starting new support groups. No one should ever be left out in the cold. And remember, if you have to, you can always share home schooling with a few friends and start a support group of your own. It's not hard to do.

Teaching in the Light of God's Word

If the characteristics that make Christians different from others in the world is our faith in Christ and our obedience to walk in the light of His Word, then our approach to teaching our children will be different from the approaches taken by people who are walking in the dark. Though space does not allow a thorough treatment of all that God's Word has to say about child training and education, I will offer a few examples of what I believe are more biblical approaches. If you are a member of a Christian home school support group, you will have regular opportunities to explore God's Word together. Three biblical keys are found in the words "discipline," "companionship," and "delight." Together they form an educational strategy that has revolutionized the approaches of many home schooling families.

The Importance of Discipline

Child discipline is foundational to successful instruction. A child who has no self-control cannot focus his mind on anything. A child who is hampered by bad habits, irregular routines, and disruptive behavior is his own worst enemy. Someone needs to rescue him from his bondage. He will only be free to learn when he is trained to control himself and his emotions. Cheerfulness and contentment are a discipline. So are courtesy and the ability to work or study.

The contrast between walking in the light and walking in the darkness is seldom more clearly displayed than in the area of child discipline. It is alarming that many parents in the church are confused about discipline when the Bible boldly commands it. The unbelieving world calls virtually all forms of discipline "child abuse." (See chapter 13.) It is not only spanking that is rejected by secular authorities, it is any confrontation with your child in which you use your power and authority over him to win decisively. A stern rebuke may be called "emotional abuse." Warning your child to flee the wrath of God may be called "psychological abuse." In other words, it is believed that if you do not leave your child in the dark to figure out right and wrong on his own, you are an "abusive parent." According to the world's definition, God, the perfect and loving Father in heaven, is an abusive parent. Think about the absurdity of that idea.

The Scriptures command parents to express their love for their children by exercising proper discipline, and that includes spanking them on occasion.

> He who spares the rod hates his son, but he who loves him is careful to discipline him (Proverbs 13:24).

> Folly is bound up in the heart of a child, but the rod of discipline will drive it far from him (Proverbs 22:15).

> Do not withhold discipline from a child; if you punish him with the rod, he will not die. Punish him with the rod and save his soul from death (Proverbs 23:13-14).

Spanking is by no means the only way to discipline a child. Time-out in the corner and denying privileges for disobedience are certainly appropriate for minor offenses. But spanking is one divinely mandated method which must not be ignored. The reference to saving your child's soul from death has more than spiritual salvation in view. God is being literal. The harsh reality in all ages is that whenever an unruly child disregards authority, he is liable to get himself killed by the consequences of his actions. Your child, in the wrong place at the wrong time, running around with the wrong crowd, could become another statistic in the war on drug abuse, AIDs, and drunk driving. It is a sad reality, but it happens. If you cannot or will not train your child to have self-control, he may very well go to an early death.

There are times when a child must be given a spanking in order to impress on him or her the seriousness of the offense. But a spanking is not an act of vengeance or even anger at sin. It is the administration of justice with the objective of restoration. Spanking itself is not the problem, but spanking in anger may be.

Two passages of Scripture put the issue of spanking in a whole new light. The first deals with the ineffectiveness of anger in bringing about righteousness. "My dear brothers, take note of this: Everyone should be quick to listen, slow to speak and slow to become angry, for man's anger does not bring about the righteous life that God desires" (James 1:19-20). The second passage addresses the purpose of all discipline, which is to produce a harvest of righteousness. "No discipline seems pleasant at the time, but painful. Later on, however, it produces a harvest of righteousness and peace for those who have been trained by it" (Hebrews 12:11). Together, these passages make it clear that anger has no legitimate place in the administration of discipline. This is because man's anger is easily generated in one context and attributed to another. A conflict at work may eventuate into a spanking for a little one at home. An argument with your spouse may express itself in over-correcting your children. I call this the Emotional Attribution Syndrome. In reality, angry parents are more likely to be indulging themselves in an emotional outburst. They may call it discipline, but it's not. It's child abuse.

In the administration of a spanking there should always be five steps:

1. Parents should clearly identify the specific offense for which the child is about to receive discipline. If prior instruction has been given on the offending behavior, the child should be reminded of it and shown that what is happening is a predictable consequence of his disregard of or disobedience to what he knew was required of him.

2. The spanking should be administered with a relatively harmless instrument, such as a paddle, which will sting the skin without causing welts or bruising. It should be given on the buttocks or the back of the thighs, not on the other parts of the body.

3. The parent giving the spanking should be looking for remorsefulness and sorrow from the child. The spanking should last long enough to get this response, but no longer.

If the child is unrepentant, it may mean he does not believe he has done anything wrong. In such a case, additional blows will not change his mind and may, instead, create a deep disrespect for his parent's judgment. In any case, the spanking should not last longer than common sense would suggest for a child of his age. Remember that this is just one battle, not the entire war. There will be future occasions to continue correction. Don't be impatient.

4. Following a spanking, there should be ample time to hold your child and let him weep. Affirm your love for him and assure him that he is able to avoid all future spankings if he chooses to.

5. Pray together for God's forgiveness and the strength to turn away from doing what is wrong. Pray for your child, not just about him. And pray for yourself, that God will give you the wisdom and the resolve to be consistent in this important area of responsibility. Try to part on good terms, talking about other things. Be affectionate.

As Christians, we must deal with our anger. But we must not disobey God by discarding a clearly biblical method of child discipline. God loves us. His commandments are for our good and the good of our children. If we, as His children, disobey Him in this, we will feel the hand of God's discipline in our lives.

And you have forgotten that word of encouragement that addresses you as sons: "My son, do not make light of the Lord's discipline, and do not lose heart when he rebukes you, because the Lord disciplines those he loves, and he punishes everyone he accepts as a son." Endure hardship as discipline; God is treating you as sons. For what son is not disciplined by his father? If you are not disciplined (and everyone undergoes discipline), then you are illegitimate children and not true sons (Hebrews 12:5-8).

There is no greater pain in human experience than to have a scornful and disobedient child. On the other hand, there is no greater joy than to know our children are walking in the truth. God has a way of "spanking" parents who disobey His instruction concerning child training. It is called "teenagers." The track record of the modern church is not very good in this area. Typical Christian parents are not walking in God's light any more than their unbelieving neighbors. It should be no surprise to find that today's Christian teens are not likely to be any more godly than their unbelieving friends. The level of pain in the typical Christian family is incredible. Pastoral counselors can't keep up with the demand.

At the same time, God also has a way of honoring those parents who obey Him in the administration of discipline in the home. It is also called, "teenagers." Many home schooling parents are seeing the results of handling this aspect of their responsibilities differently from the world. Home-schooled teens are often more godly than their parents were at their age. They are not on drugs. They are more likely to be virgins when they marry. Many are starting their own businesses while living at home and hiring their friends. Those who are attending college are diligently *studying* when they get there. "Praise the LORD. Blessed is the man who fears the LORD, who finds great delight in his commands. His children will be mighty in the land; the generation of the upright will be blessed" (Psalm 112:1-2). "Wisdom is proved right by all her children" (Luke 7:35). It is a wonderful thing to behold.

You may be thinking, *But it's too late for me. I can't change my children.* That's probably not quite accurate. The truth is you can't change them *quickly.* You can't change them overnight. Child training takes time. Children are not little machines that we just sit down and repair at will. They are young *people.* And that means they need time to grow and develop good habits, self-control, and right attitudes. I believe you can do it. If you get them back into your home, away from the negative peer groups and into better routines, they will improve. Just don't give up.

Schools function like an anesthetic for many parents. They won't endure the discomfort of having to deal with an unruly child and so they send him off to school under the misguided notion that somehow the school will be able to straighten him out. The problems of unruliness and disrespect for parents are seldom solved in school, but the pain is deadened temporarily. The illusion of a happy family is maintained for a little while. But as the undisciplined, disrespectful child grows older in school, his friends begin to offer emotional support to his rebellion. Long-festering problems then erupt into overt alienation, violence, drug abuse, gang involvement, and premarital sexual activity. If your child is a "pain" to you, for God's sake, deal with it while there is still time. As the writer of the Proverbs has said, "Discipline your son, for in that there is hope" (Proverbs 19:18a).

The Power of Companionship

I mentioned getting your children away from negative peer groups. That is because the fundamental principle of education in the Bible is companionship. Who you are *with* has much more effect on what you are than does anything else. Show me who a child admires and wants to be accepted by, and I will show you what that child is going to become. We become like whatever we worship. Children always have their idols. The writer of Proverbs put it succinctly when he wrote, "Those who walk with the wise become wise, but a companion of fools will suffer harm" (Proverbs 13:20).

This proverb has deep implications. First of all, it raises the question of who is walking *with* whom? Contrary to popular opinion, parents do not need to spend more time with their children. Those who try to usually end up at some amusement park. No, children need to spend more time with their parents. Because parents are usually wiser than their children, the parents should decide what to do each day. The children need to spend more time doing whatever their parents are normally doing as wise adults. Work, study, worship, hospitality, political action, evangelism, rest, recreation, and all the other things that make up a good routine should include children. If children are not permitted to be with their parents in these activities, where will they learn them? Certainly not from their peer groups.

Schools, even Christian schools, openly defy this biblical principle. As a true friend of the Christian schools, I feel compelled to administer the "wounds of a friend," wounds which are faithful. If a Christian school were designed from the ground up in obedience to God's Word, it would put at its center the power of companionship. It would not imitate the public school structure as much as it does. Children would spend more time with their parents, with other adults, and with older children. Apprenticeship and age-integration would be the norm, rather than the exception. Children would walk with the wise. Though they include the Bible as part of their school curriculum, most Christian schools do not honor God's Word in the design and management of their schools. Why not take the initiative in this matter and set the pace for school reform? Why not let the world play catch-up? It is all a matter of simply walking in the light.

Age Integration v. Age Segregation

Have you ever wondered why a scout troop or 4-H Club can be so effective in motivating children to learn difficult material, while a "class" on the same topic usually fails? The reason is age-integration. The ratio of children to adults in a scout troop or club is usually much lower. The troop leader is usually an active role model for the children, an inspirational force that commands respect and admiration. If he is not, the troop deteriorates into a gang that merely tolerates the presence of the adult. The odds are also good that the mixture of ages in a successfully run troop or club creates a hierarchy of maturity and skill which ushers younger members into higher levels. Everyone in an age-integrated group wants to grow up, and there is no doubt as to which way is up. Up is what the big kids are doing. Up is why you win badges and awards. Up is what the scout master can do. Wow! But in a classroom, up is seldom so clearly defined. In fact, in a classroom, "up" may really mean "down."

If your child is gifted, and all children are in some way, the other children may not be mature enough to appreciate your child's special talents. He may come to despise the very thing that God intended to make him stand out. More than one child I know has lost interest in his music or art because of the negative response of friends in school. When the child's parents and grandparents, and even older, wiser siblings offered praise and encouragement, the school children responded only with ridicule. Love for what was once important cooled off and died.

The problem is that age-segregated classrooms allow the power of companionship to actually block the desire to learn. A child who is too concerned with pleasing the teacher is likely to be called a "teacher's pet" by the other children and ostracized socially. Children of the same age have no clear criteria for deciding much of anything, but they will try anyway. Popularity will be decided by pooling ignorance with other children. A "youth culture" is created with its own values, social mores, and tastes in clothing and music. The winners of the popularity contest are often the greatest losers. Their social success makes academic success seem unimportant. The gang's acceptance seems more valuable than parental approval. Success, in ways that adults value, often becomes a liability. Understanding your parents is no longer worth the effort. They are out of touch with the real world. Crime is only a word adults use to describe what they can't control. Studying is for the nerds. Sex and drugs are cool. Everybody's doing it.

Sound familiar? Most of us lived through this experience in our youth. Many of us still limp emotionally. Our friends got us into trouble. We wasted a lot of precious time. We had to learn so much the hard way. Today we feel incompetent. We are afraid to make a commitment. Our marriages suffer. As a generation, we are an example of the harm that comes to the companion of fools. Unfortunately, the stakes are higher today than they were when we were in school. The drugs are cheaper and more addictive. The sexually transmitted diseases are more likely to be incurable or deadly. Your child is more likely to ruin his or her life if he or she goes along with the crowd today. The darkness is darker.

Delight-Directed Study

The power of companionship is a double-edged sword which cuts in both directions. Just as surely as bad companions corrupt good character, wise companions make you wise. The Puritans had a saying, "Have good companions or none." The preferred situation is to have good companions.

Our objective, then, is to be good gatekeepers. As I have shown, this is not a matter of choosing better friends, but wiser, usually older, friends. Seek out friends who have good taste, mature values, and the patience to nurture a younger friend's interest in the good things in life. Remember that left to their own devices, all children, including your children, will be foolish. It is only by allowing our children to walk with the wise that we improve their opportunities to become wise.

There is a biblical relationship between the power of companionship and a person's motivation to study. Simply stated, we study what we are delighted in, and we usually catch our delights from our closest companions. This is where the two-edged sword of companionship really cuts to the heart of the matter. Foolish companions will convince a child to "study" foolish delights. Skateboarding and computer games come to mind. Though these activities are an incredible waste of time, children will study them as long as that is what their friends are delighted in. Wiser companions will impart to one another a delight in more worthwhile topics. Literature, science, history, math, gardening, music, wood working, and various sports are all wholesome delights which have enduring value. They are not school subjects in the real world. They are part of life. Proficiency in any of these areas will open doors in the future when the child is no longer a child.

In every case, whether foolish or wise, all true study must be delightful. Once companions settle on an area of mutual interest, they will give themselves to researching it as best they can. They will develop new skills, gather information, and meet regularly to present to one another the results of their efforts. Delight is the flower of companionship, and study is its fruit. Is this biblical? Consider the following:

> But his *delight* is in the law of the LORD and on his law he *meditates* day and night (Psalm 1:2).
>
> Great are the works of the LORD; they are *pondered* by all who *delight* in them (Psalm 111:2).
>
> Praise the LORD. Blessed is the man who fears the LORD, who finds great *delight* in his *commands* (Psalm 112:1).
>
> I *delight* in your decrees; I will *not neglect* your word (Psalm 119:16).
>
> Your statutes are my *delight*; they are my *counselors* (Psalm 119:24).
>
> Direct me in the path of your *commands*, for there I find *delight* (Psalm 119:35).
>
> When *your words* came, I ate them; they were my joy and my heart's *delight*, for I bear your name, O LORD God Almighty (Jeremiah 15:16).
>
> David himself calls him 'Lord.' How then can he be his son?" The large crowd *listened* to him with *delight* (Mark 12:37).
>
> For in my inner being I *delight* in God's *law* (Romans 7:22).

Over and over again we find the word "delight" in relationship to different methods and objects of study. Pondering, meditating, reading, listening—these are words to learn by. There is something very special about this thing the Bible calls delight. Turning to my trusty *1828 Webster's Dictionary* (a reference work published back when Americans still knew the English language), I find that delight is "a high degree of pleasure or satisfaction of mind. Delight is a more permanent pleasure than joy, and not dependent on sudden excitement." That's it! "Delight is a more permanent pleasure . . . of mind!" It has staying power. It will still be there tomorrow and the next day. You can count on a delight. You can even design a child's lesson around it.

Delight-Directed Unit Studies

In education a unit study is a way of organizing a lesson around a particular topic or theme. Many different school subjects are integrated into one unit study, just as many different colors of thread are woven together in a tapestry. Whereas a subject is taught separately from other subjects (e.g. art, history, science), in a unit study these subjects are brought into relationship with one another through the topic. (e.g. the *art* of baseball, the *history* of baseball, the *physics* of baseball). Baseball is the topic. Everything can be studied as it relates to this topic.

I mention this because a child's delight can best be responded to in a unit study. A unit study designed without consideration for the individual child's interests will not be delight-directed. But a unit study designed in response to a child's current delight will harness his interest and get it to pull many other subjects. Whatever wholesome delight he develops through his companionship with older and wiser friends can be pursued as a delight-directed unit study.

I boasted in the Lord earlier that Christians should set the styles rather than merely following them. We should allow the light of God's Word to put us into the position of showing the world the glorious wisdom of God. Delight-directed unit study is an example of this kind of offensive thrust into the darkness of our culture. While secular educators struggle to get children to study, our children will have to be warned not to spend so much time in their books. Delight-directed study is the energy that created the great universities of the past. It may well create new universities in the near future. A Christian Community College could be organized around the principle of apprenticeship, companionship, and delight. Let us show the world the truth of God's inerrant Word. The contrast between our educational system and the world's should be as clear as night and day.

The Path of the Righteous Gets Brighter

"The path of the righteous is like the first gleam of dawn, shining ever brighter till the full light of day" (Proverbs 4:18). So much more could be said about the illumination of God's Word on the process of education. Once we stopped imitating the world, stopped trying to bring the secular school program into our homes, and stopped trying to please those secular parents who only want to home school in the dark, the opportunities to improve education became unlimited. Now, as Christian home school parents, we are setting the pace for true educational reform.

The principles I have presented here are strategic, but they are only the beginning. There are many other biblical concepts that deserve careful attention. Apprenticeships should train God's people in acquiring high levels of skill in the professions. Stewardships should train Christian entrepreneurs in the management of God's material provision. Discipleship (without cultic oppression) should provide for spiritual growth and leadership development in the local church. These biblical relationships are rich with educational potential. But just as with home schooling, their implementation will require men and women to have a balance of courage and humility. The structure of our seminaries, our Bible colleges, our Christian day schools, our Sunday schools, and even our churches should benefit from what we discover. Home schooling provides an excellent laboratory for exploring Christian education. It's not just for the children. All God's children get to be home schooled.

As Christian home schoolers, we are just now beginning to stretch our wings and enjoy the liberty God has given us. It has taken time to shed the blinders and bondage of our experience with conventional school approaches. By coming out from among the "flaming torches" of the mixed multitude in the secular home school associations, the light of God's Word has gotten even brighter. Exciting new insights come as we quietly walk in obedience to what God has shown us. I invite you to join us in this grand adventure. It is not difficult to get started in home schooling. In fact, that is the topic of my next chapter.

CHAPTER 9

HOW TO START
A HOME SCHOOL

By Gregg Harris

Home schooling may seem overwhelming to you at first. How do people ever get started? There are so many different things to think about, and so many decisions to make. Of course, each decision seems to require its own little bit of information. That is where it gets most confusing. Not everyone agrees. Religious convictions, educational philosophies and political ideologies generate great diversity within the home school community. Though most agree that home schooling is great, they don't all agree on why it is so great or how it should be carried out.

In the early years (circa. 1980), there wasn't so much confusion about home schooling. There weren't so many people doing it. The laws in most states were unaccommodating to home schooling, so nearly everyone did it with a "low profile." Only a handful of curriculum publishers would knowingly sell materials to a home schooling family, so choosing curricula was easy—you just took whatever you could get.

There were very few home school support groups to join in 1980, so choosing the "right" group was never discussed. Liberal "unschoolers" and conservative libertarians were all lumped in together with Christian home schoolers by the major media. Even though the differences were just as real as they are today, reporters saw no point in making a distinction. Christian families are now in the majority in the home school community, five to one, and the *media knows* it. But the multiplication of home school leaders, organizations, materials, and options has created an entirely new kind of problem for the beginner—the problem of having to make too many choices.

Nine Steps to Help You Get Started

Over the last ten years of responding to the questions of new home schooling parents (both Christian and non-Christian) in my workshops, I have developed a series of nine steps to guide new families safely into a good start. You may read through this chapter in one sitting, but you will be wise to take each step in its sequential order. The information gained and the decisions made at each point should provide you with a better foundation for making later decisions.

The problem facing the new home schooling family today is "information overload." You probably have more options available than you want or need. Therefore, your approach to getting started should focus on "strategic" decisions. Secondary issues can be considered and decided later. I won't try to dazzle you with a long discussion of educational philosophy, but instead I will explain exactly how to take your children safely and legally out of the public school and get them started in a successful home school program. At one point I will need to discuss the various options and issues that affect your choice of materials. But even then I will try to be concise. I know that you are probably wanting to get started fast.

The nine steps can be taken in relatively short order, if need be. However, it is good if you have the time to ponder each decision for a few days or weeks. It is even better if you have an experienced home schooling friend to talk with throughout this process. Pray for God's wisdom, make your *initial* decisions with confidence in God's answer to your prayer, and go on to the next step. Please don't leave your child in harm's way while you wrestle with abstract or subjective questions. There will be plenty of time for that later—after your child is safely at home. You can always change your mind about those things as you go along.

1. Begin Establishing Consistent Discipline in Your Home

Consistent discipline is one area of focus which should be initiated in your home immediately if it is not already established. When you actually begin teaching your children at home, it will have a direct bearing on your success. If you cannot count on your child to follow your instructions cheerfully, you're going to have trouble making progress in his or her studies. If your child lacks self-control (and most children do), the first step is to focus on establishing better *routines*.

Another aspect of establishing proper discipline in your home is the setting of clear *boundaries* for your child's behavior. We have done this in our home by defining our "house rules." In twenty-one simple statements we help ourselves say the same things to our children, day in and day out, regardless of what kind of mood my wife and I are in. Statements such as, "We do not hurt one another with unkind words or deeds" cover a lot of territory. So does, "We do not create unnecessary work for others." Once these twenty-one house rules are established, discipline has an objective basis, and there is less likelihood that a child will receive correction he doesn't really deserve or fail to receive the discipline he needs.

Don't expect good routines and self-control to appear overnight in your family. You will not spring full-blown into being a perfect home school family unless you already have a track record of being a perfect non-home school family. Your kids will still be your kids. Your marriage will still be your marriage "for better or for worse." By home schooling you will be able to do something constructive for your family life. You will have much more time together, and that is half the solution. Clear communication and consistent discipline comprise the other half. Your family will get better as you consistently apply God's principles to your relationships.

So, begin right now to establish better discipline in your home. Then, while you are moving forward in that important area, take the second step in getting started.

2. Join a Home School Support Group

Support groups are nearly everywhere today. In some communities there are several. The Christian inter-church groups and the individual church-based groups are most numerous. Memberships in these groups can run into hundreds of families. If you are an evangelical, Bible-believing Christian, you will have quite a number to choose from. But there are usually secular groups (unschoolers) and non-Christian religious groups in most metropolitan areas as well. There is no reason for you to have to go it alone.

Home school support groups and associations are to home schooling what writers clubs and writers associations are to aspiring authors. They do whatever they can to support their members in being successful. The reason I advise you to join a support group now, rather than after you have taken your child out of school, is so that you will be surrounded with a multitude of advisors as you take the next seven steps. Some parents join a support group when their child is still in the womb, and I think that's great. Get into the lifestyle as soon as possible, and you will have less to learn when you actually begin formal lessons later on. Don't wait. Join a support group today.

Where will you find them? Call your church office, for there may be a group already meeting in your church. If not, call the larger churches in your area. Many have strong groups that are also open to people from other churches of like belief. Another strategy is to visit your local public library. When a mother arrives with school-age children in tow during regular school hours, bingo! Home schoolers! (Some surveys show that as many as 30 percent of the people who actively use the public libraries today are home schooling families. Ask the librarian if he is aware of any support groups in your community.)

The surest way to make contact with a support group in your state is to write to me at Christian Life Workshops and ask for the address and phone number of the Christian home school association in your state or metropolitan area. Their leaders will have listings of most of the local groups in your area. Don't be surprised if you can see the local group leader's home from your own window! It has happened more than once. There are probably other home schooling families in your neighborhood, right now.

3. Read a Few Good Books

The best way to avoid burning out your home school support group leaders is to read at least one good book on home schooling before you begin asking too many questions. All the major questions (e.g., What about socialization? How do you find enough time? Is it legal? Where do you find curricula?) are answered to some degree in every book on the subject. The book you are reading is no exception. The information you hold in your hands is adequate to get you on a solid foundation if you read it thoughtfully and act on it.

Some people (present company excluded) are just plain lazy. They prefer to have their home school friends and leaders read all the books and then tell them what they say. These inconsiderate folks take up hours on the phone. I know I'm being a bit pointed here, but believe me, your local leaders need more consideration. They want to be helpful. That's why they are there. But they are usually parents, just like you, and their children have to stand by waiting for Mom or Dad to get off the phone. So make it your rule to ask questions only after you have read at least one good book *all the way through*. Then your questions will be much more informed, and the answers you receive will make much more sense to you.

The Selected Resource Guide at the back of this book offers many helpful suggestions. Some of these materials are available from your local libraries and bookstores. If you don't find what you want, suggest that the library or bookstore get involved in carrying more home school literature. Write the publisher of this book he will provide, as a public service, a Suggested Home School Reading List for public libraries and a Suggested Home School Products List for educational bookstores. There are many self-published authors whose materials are not readily available through the major distributors. Your local bookstores and libraries will appreciate your help in tracking down these items. In the mean time, you may order most items by mail direct from the suppliers listed in the Resource Guide.

4. Join Home School Legal Defense Association

Though there are still some serious battles going on in the courts and legislatures of a few regressive states, over the last eight years the laws in over thirty states have been improved to allow for responsible home schooling. The legal battle has shifted to the matter of reducing intrusive state regulations. You can home school in every state, one way or another. Overall, things are looking very good for the growth of home schooling around the world. The idea is getting out that home schooling is legal, and it works. That is due, to a great extent, to the fine work of Home School Legal Defense Association (HSLDA).

HSLDA was founded in 1983 by Michael Farris, a Christian home schooling father who also happened to be an experienced constitutional attorney. Since that time, HSLDA has faithfully served the interests of its member home school families by defending their rights to teach their children at home. Regardless of religious faith (or lack thereof), HSLDA represents parents with remarkable efficiency. Chris Klicka has served as senior council of HSLDA for seven years, and, as you have already seen in prior chapters, he has the conviction and the understanding needed to do his job very well.

Membership in this organization is $100 per year, as of this writing. That is a bargain! Although the odds of any particular family being struck by "legal lightening" are relatively small, thousands of families are "zapped" every year. The resulting expense, not to mention the stress, can be disastrous. At the very least, it poses a serious distraction from teaching your children. At worst, it can mean losing custody of your children to a state bureaucracy. Sad to say, some attorneys will charge huge fees while they try to learn more about home schooling. They may not even try to keep you out of court. Then when you get into court, they may use all the wrong arguments, wasting time and money. Before HSLDA came to the rescue, people have had to sell their homes just to pay lawyers' fees, and then they had to stop home schooling or move to another state when they lost in court. It doesn't have to be that way.

As a member of HSLDA you will have a literal army of home school attorneys devoted to intercepting whatever attack is heading your way—all at no extra charge. Your membership takes care of all your attorney's fees (See chapter 22).

Nine times out of ten a carefully crafted letter to your local school officials will end the matter. Schools don't have the budget to tangle with a home school family that has legal backing. If they persist in their demands, HSLDA will prepare its case and go to work to keep the confrontation from escalating. Unlike some legal professionals, HSLDA has no interest in extending the process. Its only objective is to get the authorities to leave you and all your fellow home schoolers alone. If authorities persist, HSLDA may sue them for violating your civil rights. God has blessed this organization and all of us through it. That is why I add my voice to the national choir of home school leaders who encourage you to join HSLDA and to keep your membership active. These men and women are making history—good history. Help them do their best by keeping your membership in place each year.

5. Select your Approach to Teaching

What, you may wonder, is a teaching approach? I thought I would just sit down with my child, open a text book, and begin to teach. You could do that. It may be just the right thing for you to do. But you ought to know there are different ways of going about it. Some of them are easier to do than others. A few are much less expensive than others. Nearly all can be successful if done with enthusiasm. The important thing to know is that you have several options, and some options are better than others.

The greatest mistake made by new home schoolers is to automatically bring the conventional school's classroom approach into their home. They do this naturally because, to some extent, they have all been students in a classroom. They close their eyes and see in their minds the classroom with its big blackboard, its alphabet cards taped to the wall all the way around the ceiling, its bulletin boards with colorful (and expensive) seasonal displays, and, of course, its big teacher's desk looming over all the little student desks. They see the children sitting there for six or more hours of class time and lots of homework on top of that. To the public school graduate, this seems like common sense. The truth is, it's common nonsense!

Think about it. There is also a school bell in the school. Every time it rings, the children stop in the middle of whatever they are doing (writing a poem, solving a math problem, or painting a picture) and turn to the next assigned task. (And they accuse *us* of not living in the real world! When was the last time you responded in this way to a bell?) If you choose to copy the conventional school's approach, where are you going to draw the line? Why not install a drinking fountain on the wall and build a bathroom with stalls? And don't forget to install metal detectors.

Conventional school buildings, furniture, tools, and hours are industrial-sized because they are designed for managing (and occasionally teaching) large groups of students in a factory-like setting. For your home school this will all be over-kill. The similarity between a public school building and a state prison is frightening. Don't think the students haven't noticed how much of their day is spent in being "detained" instead of being taught. Your home-schooled children are free to study without the inefficiency of a school.

Granted, a small black board will come in handy for showing two or three students at the same time how to diagram a sentence . A bulletin board is a nice place to display student art work. Alphabet cards can be used for a while and then put away. Your kitchen table or counter top will make a fine teacher's desk, and you will only need a third of the time to teach most subjects. Each child should be provided with a study desk for working on assignments without distraction (ideally, in different rooms), and if you need to time an activity, the clock on the wall will do just fine. If you miss the bell, you can always yell "ding" at the proper time.

Remember the biblical story of young David when he was offered the chance to wear King Saul's armor. David was smart enough to recognize that he had better weapons to use against the giant. His slingshot had served him well against a lion and a bear. More important was the fact that God had been his helper in every crisis. So he stuck to what and Who he knew. The rest is history.

New home school moms are seldom so confident. Buying lots of school equipment seems to say to them, "You are a good home school mother. All this stuff proves you are dedicated!" It's Saul's armor—an educational security blanket. Take a lesson from David. Your approach to teaching need not be schoolish. In fact, it can be delightful—for you and your students.

Your approach to teaching should be affected by several factors: your child's style and modality of learning, the number of children you teach at the same time, their grade levels, the level of confidence you have as a teacher, and the amount of money you want to spend on your curriculum. All of these things should be considered as you choose your "five smooth stones" to take into battle.

The Effect of Learning Styles and Modalities on Teaching Approaches

Cathy Duffy explains in her *Christian Home Educator's Curriculum Manuals* what the basic learning styles are and how they can affect your strategies and choices of curriculum for your children. These learning styles are affected by a combination of one's character traits, temperament, and learning modality. The latter may dominate everything else, so I will elaborate on that.

Your modality of learning is the gate through which you prefer to receive your information. The visual, audio, and kinesthetic modalities correspond to the use of the eye, the ear, and the hand in learning. If your child is *visually* oriented, demonstrations will be most effective in presenting difficult material. If he learns best through the *audio* modality, lectures will normally be more effective. If he learns best by the *kinesthetic* modality, he will depend more on his sense of touch. Because most educational programs are primarily audio-visual in nature, we tend to adapt to these modalities over time. Eyes and ears are catered to in our culture.

But some children, and even some adults, are *kinesthetic*. They have to get their hands involved in doing something in order for new information to be meaningful and memorable. (Yes, that is why some children seem to handle everything. They have "smart hands.") In a world that shouts, "Don't touch!" a kinesthetic learner is sentenced to the educational equivalent of blindness and deafness. Beware of discouraging your child's kinesthetic curiosity. Thank God for his ability to learn through his sense of touch.

Before you bury your face in your hands and say, "This is going to be too complicated!" please understand that you do *not* have to cater to your child's preferred modality all the time. In fact, you might be wise to do so only when material is especially difficult for him. As I have said, we live in an audio-visual world. We could all use better dexterity. So no matter what your child's preferred modality, help him over the learning hurdles only as needed. Most of the time you can teach through the modality that is easiest (i.e., the one that makes the most sense) for you. Dr. Walter B. Barbe, Ph.D. and Raymond H. Swassing, Ed.D. have done extensive research in this field, and a *Modality Test Kit* is available. Your local Christian schools may have this test kit and may be willing to administer it for a small fee. Some home school support groups have also purchased the kit and make it available to their members as a service. It is worth your while to identify this important factor.

How Many Children Will You Be Teaching?

If you have only one child, you should have a few more if at all possible. An only child tends to get far too much attention. Larger families, if children are disciplined properly from the start, are easier to home school than small families. The older ones become apprentices in managing the household, and they also assist in the instruction of their younger siblings. Don't be afraid to home school all your children. It may be hard at times, but you will be glad you did it.

However, if you do have three or more students in home schooling at the same time, you will be wise to keep that fact in mind when choosing your curricula. If your materials expect you to put in a full day dealing with every grade level, which grade will get your full attention? The answer is *none*. So choose materials or adapt the materials you choose to work within a reasonable time frame, including both lesson preparation and lesson instruction. The integrated materials, such as Learning Language Arts through Literature, allow several related subjects to be taught as one basic lesson plan. This saves time twice, once in preparation and again in teaching. Both you and your student will be glad you took this route.

My advice is to also choose those materials that encourage students to become independent in their studies. Programmed workbooks, such as those published by Alpha Omega, are of excellent quality, and they emphasize writing essays, doing library (or encyclopedia) research, and giving presentations to the family.

Another source of assistance when you are facing a broad range of grade levels at one time is the correspondence school. This is especially helpful in the upper grades. Christian Liberty Academy has offered an excellent program for many years which is both thorough and flexible. In this way a junior high or high school student can be kept at home, still away from the distractions of a conventional school's social life, and yet receive excellent upper level supervision of his studies in science, math, and other challenging subjects. Correspondence programs are skilled at helping your student to do his or her best in school assignments and still have time for other important interests, such as involvement in a Christian youth ministry, a home or family business, and community sports. The prices are reasonable, in light of all you receive, and the freedom they give you to focus time on the younger students is worth the investment.

A basic caution is in order at this point. No matter how good the quality of the programmed curriculum or the correspondence course, your part as parents must still be played consistently. Stay in touch with each student's work. Read every paper he or she writes, even if it will be graded by someone at the central office. Don't allow workbooks or video tapes to take your place in your child's life. The relationship between you and your child is far more important than any academic subject. The relationship between your child and our Lord Jesus Christ is of still greater importance. Saving time should never become a cloak for your neglect. Use independent study materials with caution.

The Power of Tutoring

No matter what your child's style of learning or how many students you have, in the early grades you will respond by tutoring each child in the basic skills of reading, writing, arithmetic, and presentation skills. That means there will be far more focus on your child's unique needs and interests than would ever be possible in a conventional school. Rather than scatter shot into a crowded classroom of twenty-five to thirty children, you will be taking careful aim at one educational target at a time and hitting that target more often than not. Tutoring is personalized. It is to education what tailoring is to clothing. Everything you use must be adapted to fit. That is why home schooling is so much more efficient and effective than classroom instruction. It takes less time because it wastes less time!

The tools you use in tutoring may include the Bible, school textbooks, the encyclopedia, various handbooks, unit-study guides, field-trips, lectures, demonstrations, and coaching. Whatever you use should be chosen on the basis of your flexible goals and strategies in teaching. These tools are like colors on a palate, and you are the artist. They are like a full pantry of great food, and you are the chef. Don't be afraid to respond to your child's needs creatively. When what you are doing goes against what someone else you know is doing, you are probably doing it right. That is the strength of home schooling and tutoring. It allows for flexibility and diversity.

Though I advise most new home schoolers to start off with one or another of the major lines of curricula and then become more eclectic the following year, I do not mean that anyone should let the curricula be the master. No matter what you choose, it must remain your servant, a resource for your lesson plan. As Ruth Beechick has written, "Bend the book or find another. Make the studies fit the child." In your second year, you will be more confident and ready to mix and match from various publishers, borrow a textbook from a friend for a week just to fill in a gap in your unit study, and then use a field trip to round out a series of lectures. The freedom and flexibility is exhilarating. But flexibility assumes you have something to flex. In other words, you will need a lesson plan of some kind.

Unit Studies v. Text Books

A unit study is a lesson plan that is organized around a common theme or topic. A textbook is a lesson plan that is organized around a specific subject such as science, history, grammar, etc. Which is best? That is a subjective question. I prefer unit studies, but I utilize textbooks as resources and supplements. Others prefer to work the other way around, sticking closely to the textbooks and supplementing with unit studies, as time allows. Conventional schools use textbooks most of the time because unit studies are hard to do with large numbers of students in one classroom. In the process of tutoring, unit studies are much easier to use.

Bob Jones University Press and A Beka Books are the two major Christian school textbook publishers. Both do a very good job. A subcategory of text books includes Alpha Omega Publishing and Accelerated Christian Education (ACE), is comprised of programmed learning materials. These programs, which are very popular with Christian schools, allow students to work with minimal supervision through a series of carefully designed workbooks. Large families appreciate that feature for obvious reasons.

Konos, The Weaver, and Alta Vista are the major publishers of unit study materials at the time of writing. Others are always being developed. Character traits, pets, airplanes, baseball, and various Bible passages have all been used as the basis for fantastic unit studies. The common ground for any unit study is that it integrates many school subjects into a single lesson plan, as each subject relates to the primary theme of the unit. For instance, a unit study on the character trait of "honesty" can draw together history, science, literature, and Bible in a manner that requires much less preparation and teaching time than a separate lesson on each of these school subjects. The result is less stress on the student and teacher alike.

Let me be quick to say the major textbooks are still as popular as ever among those who use unit studies. The only difference is that they are then used primarily as resources rather than strict lesson plans. This growing confidence marks a major development in the home school community. Like the children of Israel, we are finally discarding the approaches we learned in the land of captivity in Egypt and embracing the simple approaches that make better use of home and family structures. The publishers of curriculum realize this and are making great strides in adapting their materials and text books for more flexible use.

Delight Directed Unit Studies

As I explained in my previous chapter, the basis of all true study includes some aspect of *delight*. The question of whether or not a particular unit study is delightful can only be answered by observing the child's personal interests at the time. If the unit study is focused on "honesty," and he is currently excited about "soccer," the unit study is probably not "delight-directed." Unit studies that have been prepared and published by someone who doesn't know your child cannot be as responsive to your child's interests as a home-made unit study. If you want your child to be enthused about his school work, you will need to design the studies in response to his delights.

This is where the many published unit study curricula fall short. They have provided a good plan that is well integrated, but it is still a "shot in the dark" as far as any particular student's delight is concerned. To best use them, you will have to adapt them to your student's interests. Like textbooks, prepared unit studies can be used for information, inspiration, methods, and techniques but their responsiveness to your child's delights will be hit or miss.

A solution to this limitation is found in Valerie Bendt's *How to Design a Unit Study* and Ruth Beechick's *You Can Teach Your Child Successfully*. Both of these books teach you how to create your own unit study lesson plans out of the resources available in your own home and local library. If you do so in response to your child's current interests, your unit studies will also be delight-directed.

When these assignments are based on hobby interests and other delights, your student is more likely to be motivated in his work. The fact that these independent assignments take the place of other school work rather than being assigned in addition to regular school work (e.g. homework), lightens the load on student and teacher alike, without lowering the quality of the education. The fact that this approach will also save you a substantial amount of money is another benefit.

6. Invest In Your Teaching Tools

When I was just a little boy, I tried to fix my bike with a hammer. The chain had come off, and I was determined to get it back on. Upon discovering the damage I had done to my bike, my father told me to always use the right tool for each job. Hammers are fine for some jobs but not for putting chains on bicycles.

The same advice needs to be given to new home schoolers. Certain tools are designed to do certain jobs. Trying to save time or money by getting along without an important tool is not wise. It may cause damage to whatever it is on which you are working. So choose your tools with more than cost saving in mind.

At this point a word to home schooling fathers is in order. If your wife has handed you this book and has said, "Read this!" please understand, Dad, that I am on your side. You are the head of your household, and what you decide to do for your family is your business before God. But as one who has seen quite a few home schooling families get started, I can't help but notice that a double standard exists in the area of investing in good tools. In general, we men can rationalize buying just about any attachment or ratchet set with the statement, "It will save *me* time." We buy tools to save time on tasks that we hardly ever do! Meanwhile, our wives are doing repetitive tasks with inadequate tools. This is bad management. We need to make sure our wives have the equipment they need to do the job we have entrusted to them.

Your wife is going to develop a wish list of materials and tools, and you might be tempted to say, "Honey, do you really need that?" The answer is, "No, she won't need it any more than I needed anything other than a hammer to fix my bike." I'm not advocating wasting money on frills. An investment made in basic tools of the trade in home schooling is a good investment. With that said, let's take a look at what you will want to acquire, new or used, in order to do a great job teaching your children at home.

Select and Order Your Curricula

Today in nearly every major metropolitan area you will find an annual curriculum fair attended by well over one thousand parents and featuring over fifty different exhibitors. Curriculum catalogs will be coming to you in the mail as soon as you put yourself on the mailing list of a few companies. New curriculum abounds. A measure of this incredible growth can be seen in the expansion of the two major curriculum guides. The original *Big Book of Home Schooling* written by Mary Pride in 1987, has grown to a four-volume set. Each volume is as thick as a big city phone book! Cathy Duffy's original *Christian Home Educator's Curriculum Manual* now comes as a two-volume set, one for elementary and one for junior high and high school levels. The question of what to use cannot be answered as easily as it once was.

I have already advised you concerning how your approach to teaching should affect your selection of materials. Learning styles, modalities, number of children, confidence level, and a preference for textbooks or unit studies should be settled for the time being. Having made those decisions, you are now ready to shop for the best prices. The best prices can often be found in the curriculum exhibit halls and curriculum fairs hosted by your local support groups.

These trade shows can seem like a carnival, so "let the buyer beware." Everything looks good when the publisher's representative is standing there explaining the finer points of his material. The wise shopper will bring a shopping list and resist the temptation to buy materials she did not intend to buy. If a company offers a generous return policy, you have more room to maneuver. Don't hesitate to buy an item and then take your time examining it at home. Just be sure to send it back undamaged and on time, if you decide not to use it.

Follow the same approach in dealing with mail order catalogs. If they don't offer a good return policy, shop elsewhere. Be aware that the rush season for curriculum is around July and August. If you order material at this time, your chances of getting it in time for a September school start up are much lower. The bigger companies may be better than the small ones at meeting your deadlines, but even they are faced with occasional back-orders of materials they purchase from other publishers. Plan ahead, and you will not be frustrated waiting for a key item to arrive.

Remember that new information and greater experience will continually affect your feelings about curriculum. The secret is to avoid second guessing every decision every day. Give whatever you decide to use enough time to work. Jumping around from one curricula to another in the same school year is confusing, not only to you as a teacher, but more importantly, to your home school students. So, relax. As Marva Collins, a super teacher in the inner city schools of Chicago once said, "Anything works, if the teacher works." I agree.

What you do with the curriculum you choose is of much more consequence than what you choose to use as your curriculum. You can't really make any disastrous mistakes in curriculum selection because you can always work your way around any weakness in your curriculum. If you don't make good decisions at the outset, don't panic. Just roll up your sleeves and adapt. No matter what you do, there will be challenges.

Also, try to keep your perspective. Sure, it may cost you a little extra money to change your mind. (Maybe even a lot of money.) You will have a stack of materials that you wish you hadn't purchased. But that is a much cheaper way to learn about curriculum then enrolling in a teacher's college. So don't worry too much about making a few wrong choices. You can always sell them in the "used curriculum" room at the next curriculum fair. Chalk the expense up as part of your own education as a home school parent. A Ph.D. in home schooling simply means that your unwanted stack of curriculum is "piled higher and deeper."

Invest in a Good Home Library

Of all the investments you make in your home school, your home library will have the greatest impact, long-range. Every time you say, "Let's go look it up," you will confront the limitations of your home library. No matter how close you live to the local public library, there are going to be times when the following materials will be needed in your home. Begin collecting used reference materials and classic literature in all of the following areas.

Bible study materials, including a study Bible, a Bible encyclopedia, and a Bible concordance. Your pastor may have some excellent used materials he would like to sell to make room for newer editions.

An encyclopedia (preferably, published within the last five years). The more expensive sets (such as Britannica) are not the best deal, in my opinion. If you are buying new, aim at a set that is most useful in the elementary and junior high years (World Book is one good choice). All the encyclopedia sets I have seen make statements about evolution that are simply not true. (Contrary to what you will read there, dinosaurs are no more "ancient" than Adam. The Flood caused many geological formations to develop very quickly. The earth need not be as old as they say.) Supplement your encyclopedia set with volumes on creation science, so that your children will get the whole truth.

A growing library of handbooks on science, home maintenance, auto repair, and more. Reader's Digest offers an excellent line of these, and the older editions are sometimes better than the newer versions. Check your used bookstores for the best prices.

A growing library of "real books." Textbooks, by definition, are not real books. True, they contain predigested snatches of great literature, but real books *are* the great literature. The difference is important. Great novels don't usually fare well in an English literature textbook. The authors of public school textbooks tend to include the most bizarre works of radical authors and then they read all kinds of personal opinions into the plots of every novel. No wonder public school children don't like to read. A well-read home school student can read at least five real books each year. Develop a reading list.*

Most great literature is available in two forms of books—cheap paperback and expensive hardback. The former keep the cost down, but they have very small print and no room for writing notes in the margins. The hardback editions are expensive, but they retain their value as an heirloom to hand down to your children and grandchildren. There is also something to be said for reading a great book several times, perhaps by several people. I prefer to buy fewer books in the hardback version and then treat them as valued friends, always there to inform and entertain. Someday, I hope my grandchildren will read the notes I've written in the margins and the flyleaf and get a sense of what each book has meant to their dear old grandpa.

A growing number of history books. Public school students get only what some liberal professor thinks is pertinent to a child of the "New World Order." For instance, Marilyn Monroe gets more space in some

American history textbooks then George Washington! Fight back. Read a biography on a key person in each period of national and world history each year.* (The list of home school alumni in chapter 7 would make a great place to start.) Read them aloud as a family. You and your family will have a far better sense of what life is really all about. Some of the older history books are full of inspiring stories for all ages. Historians may turn up their academic noses at some of these stories because they were not able to document the events as they happened. But so what? The people who wrote the older history books were often men of openly declared Christian faith. They had no reason to lie. And even when a story is embarrassing to their church, they report it anyway. (You don't see that kind of integrity in the halls of academia today.) Historians such as Charles Coffin did their best to get their stories directly from those who observed events firsthand, and in those cases where a bit of myth slips in, it is fair to say that those "myths" affected the course of our nation's history. That makes them historical in their own right. So read and enjoy the older history books. Follow the old paths.

7. Invest in Your Household Management Tools

Some people avoid establishing good routines, fearing that ruts and rigidity will result. The truth is that most people lack the discipline to follow through with what they know is best. Remember that plans are merely something to flex. Plans that don't bend will simply break.

Planning out a repeating weekly schedule allots enough time to all the important events in a normal day so that plans can flex. A menu planner saves time shopping as well as money on food bills. A loan library system allows you to keep track of what you loan to friends as well as what you borrow. Field trip planners help you get more out of every educational outing. Weekly appointment schedules and housework planners keep you on task without creating extra work.

It is in this process of establishing better household routines that many new home school mothers are overwhelmed. They meet their academic challenge with a plan, but the housework, the meals, and

---

*For a free Suggested Reading List for Literature and History at various grade levels, contact Christian Life Workshops. Write to Reading List, C/O CLW, P.O. Box 2250, Gresham, OR 97080 or call (503) 667-3942

the other obligations of family life are approached with little more than a mental note. The result is inconsistency, missed opportunities, and eventual frustration.

Interestingly, the same parents who balk at purchasing a household organizer do not hesitate to buy a home school planner and record keeper. In practice, the two are inseparable. School work suffers if the household is not organized along the lines of a well-thought-out plan. Housework suffers if school work is not scheduled in reasonable time frames. What is needed is a tool that handles both in an integrated way. That is the logic behind *The Organizer**developed by my wife, Sono. It is her brains in a notebook, a command station right next to the phone where all lines of family communication meet. It is designed to be a complete household management tool that knows you are also home schooling. The result is liberating. Household, time management, and home school record keeping are kept together.

For your sake I beg you to use something—if not *The Organizer*, then something else. But don't try to manage a busy family on the backs of envelopes. Get the right tool. This job is too important to be done empty-handed.

Home Documentation: A School Record Keeper

I have mentioned the need for a home school record keeper. Now it is time to elaborate. Home schooling produces a lot of paper: lesson plans, curriculum selection records, written work, tests, art work, grades, attendance, receipts from extra curricular activities. The question is, where are you going to put it all as it accumulates? The answer may be, on pre-designed forms and reports in a small filing system and a notebook. If you decide to test-drive *The Organizer*,* the the record keeping forms will be included in your three-ring binder. If not, you will need to put together a system that has similar credibility and ease of function. Whatever you do, use something.

If your system is not credible, it will be of questionable value when the time comes to use it. Whether the records are needed to defend your home school in court or to get your child into a college

---

*Information concerning *The Organizer* will be sent free of charge for your consideration. Simply contact Christian Life Workshops, P.O. Box 2250, Gresham, OR 97080 or call (503) 667-3942

someday, you will be glad you kept good records. They will have other important uses in the short term. For one thing, records will give you an objective picture of what has been taught and learned. They will allow you to make decisions about what to do next (next day, next week, next month, and next year). This is crucial to your teaching process. Without some form of record, you will be flying blindly. You will be susceptible to fleeting feelings that you are not making any progress or that you are making more progress than you actually are. Grades on quizzes, tests, and essays give you the feedback you need to resist unfounded feelings, and that by itself is worth all the effort involved in keeping clear records.

There are a few additional records that may not come to mind. These include health records (have your child's eyes and ears checked once in a while), and attendance records. As silly as it might sound, the question of whether your child is *absent* from school is more than a matter of whether he is at home. What if he has the flu? What if she is taking the day off to spend time with visiting relatives? If it is not really a school day, then count your student absent. You'll have far more credibility, not to mention basic honesty, if you show these absences each year. Perfect attendance, like a perfect tax return, raises the suspicion that someone may be cheating. So keep accurate records. You may even "skip school" once in a while when the spring fever overtakes you. That's your decision. Just be sure to mark everyone absent when you do.

8. Equip Your Home for Instruction and Study

The first thing to do in equipping your home for instruction is to purge it of *time wasters*. This includes getting rid of anything that takes precious time and gives little or nothing back. Television is a major time waster. It is not a matter of what is on television, though the programming is usually stupid and offensive, but it is a matter of what doesn't happen in your home when the television is on: the conversations you never have, the books you never read, the projects you never start, and the hospitality you never have time to practice. The decision to get rid of your television is never regretted. Family life improves. Everyone gets so bored that they ultimately go out and do something! Whatever you do, it will be a better use of time than watching television.

I can hear some dads saying, "I only watch news and sports." Well, I have some news for you, sports. The cable channels that cater to you are on the air twenty-four hours a day. When do you turn it off when it is never over? Look at what it does to your children and your family to have instant access to the major media. Wouldn't it be much better to go to more ball games, and subscribe to a good news weekly, than to neglect your kids while watching too many games and too much of "headline" news? The expense in ticket prices and subscription fees is actually a great savings if it brings your life into line with what you say you believe. There are better ways to enjoy an occasional movie.

The Video Player

Take a closer look at your video tape *recorder*. It can be fixed (the same way you "fix" cats and dogs) so that it can't receive any television signals. That makes it merely a video tape *player*. Then you can watch your favorite films, educational science programs, and others by renting them or joining a home school video library in your community. The result is greater control over the content of what you and your children view and better use of time. This is what we have done in our family. We have not had a television in our home (other than a few nights during the 1992 play-offs between the Portland Trailblazers and the Chicago Bulls) in over nineteen years. The results have been wonderful. We have our own "Friday Night at the Movies" with our VCR. Other than that, we read, talk, walk, and live. Take the dare. Get rid of your TV for thirty days and see what an improvement it will make.

Computer Games

While you are in the purging mood, why not evict all the Nintendo and other computer games at the same time? I know your children will probably howl, but they will eventually thank you for rescuing them from childish foolishness. Computer games (other than a few good educational game software), are time bandits. Let your children use their home computer doing more exciting projects. Desktop publish a newsletter. Design a data base for a local company. Do computer research and information brokering. Or just learn how to type. The computer is a great tool, but it is a lousy toy. Guard it carefully. Make it serve your family, or else it will enslave your children. It can be worse than television.

If your children have too many toys and other possessions, consider de-junking the house in preparation for home schooling. Make room for better things. Keep the creative toys (e.g. Lincoln

Logs, Legos, blocks) and box up the non-creative toys (i.e. Monster Robots from the Planet Hell, and that sort of thing). If you can't imagine Christ as a child playing with a particular toy, bag it. Call me old-fashioned, but I *can* see Him playing with tops, marbles, and maybe a yo-yo or two. I *can* see Him riding a bike and swinging on a swing. I *can't* see Him playing with "Masters of the Universe," unless He was pretending to cast the demons out of them. Toys can be either a waste of time or tools of learning. Sometimes it is all in the way you teach your children how to play.

Instructional Furniture

The next phase of equipping your home is to invest in instructional furniture. By that I mean the basics: a small desk for each student, a comfortable desk chair, a good desk lamp, and adequate bookshelves. How many books are adequate? Wall to wall and ceiling to ceiling is a nice place to start. You are going to collect a lot of books. Even if you never read many of them, you will still add to your library every year. It has something to do with the home school mind-set. If the bookshelves are placed against the outside walls of your home, the books will save measurably on winter heating bills.

My next suggestion on instructional equipment may seem like a contradiction to what I said above about television and computers, but it is not. I have advised you on how to control both, and that still stands. It does not, however, change the fact that I believe you will benefit from having a video monitor (not a television!) and a videotape player (or a VCR that is programmed not to receive channels) in your home. The films and video-taped educational programs add tremendously to your home school program. You don't want the major media signals with their commercials. You don't even want National Public Television, with its liberal social agenda. You can get just about everything you want on videotape. The right tape at the right time is powerful.

You should also own a home computer. It doesn't have to be the latest in "bleeding edge" technology. Just a nice, cheap, home computer that handles programs such word processing, simple data bases, accounting software, and spread sheets. If it is a very old computer (four years or more), be sure that all the software you want to use comes with it (just throw away the games) because newer software probably will not run on it. If you can afford a newer computer, start a home business first. Then make your home computer your first major business acquisition. That will make it a tax-deductible expense, when you begin to make a profit on your new business.

Tying up loose ends, a small bulletin board is a good place to display art work. Using magnets on your refrigerator may do even better. A filing drawer or file storage box for school records is important. Get in the habit of keeping records in the right places. Science equipment may be borrowed, but if you come across a good used professional high-powered microscope for under $100, grab it! Then you can loan it out to other families. There is no end to the neat stuff you can collect at really great prices, once you get into the spirit of home schooling. Just make sure you have the room to store it all. All these things come to those who wait—and go to garage sales. Some school districts have great sales as well. Get together with a few other home school families and go shopping on a weekend. It's a lot more fun to share the adventure. That brings us to the final step in getting started.

9. Build the Home School Community in Your Area

I have already described what awaits you in your home school support groups. Now I would like to suggest that you take a step beyond what already exists in your area to develop what could exist, if you take the initiative.

Children respond very well to clubs and troops and other social groups, especially when these groups focus on areas of interest to each child. Most extra-curricular programs are scheduled for the hours after conventional schools let out. It need not be so for you. You and your children can have a science club in the middle of the day. You can have a 4-H Club meeting on a school day morning. If you like, you can have a skating party during regular school hours. The flexibility of home schooling beckons to you. Will you use your new freedom and creativity to design the groups that best serve your children?

Contact a local church that has a gymnasium. These are more common in the major metropolitan areas. Ask if your support group can rent the use of the gym for a weekly physical education day. Basketball, volleyball, and many other sports can be enjoyed in this way.

Pick a local park and announce through the local newsletter and grapevine that a certain weekday morning is Park Day. No need to plan it or organize it. Just show up when you want to. Inevitably, on every nice day there will be a small crowd of home school parents chatting while their children play on the swings and run around the park.

Draw up an annual calendar of major field trips. The local children's symphony should be on there. So should a day at the nearest zoo. If you have a historical pageant in your area, form a caravan to go see it every year. An annual picnic is another popular event. Some groups have an annual campout for a few days at a state park. Others have an annual hike or bike ride. If you want to, you can include a trip to a water park or an amusement park. This may lack major educational value, but it gives your children something extra to mention when their friends in church ask them what it is like to be home schooled.

Home School Co-ops

For those who would like a more formal system of support in home schooling, consider starting a home school cooperative. This is a step above a support group in that it is a contract with other families to share certain responsibilities. We enjoy having a Friday School Co-op with three other families in our neighborhood. My wife teaches Spanish to twelve children in a Spanish Club. She also leads them in her "Fun Physical Fitness Program." A science experiment is prepared and conducted by one of the other dads. Other projects are assigned and provided as desired, and there is always a time of fellowship for everyone. Ours is a small and relatively modest example of a home school co-op. They can be much more involved.

Single parents can share many of the major aspects of managing their households, even to the point of sharing housework, meal preparation, and keeping at least one adult in the home twenty-four hours a day. Job sharing and flexible work schedules make home school co-ops a practical alternative to conventional child care, and they allow single home schooling parents to be successful. If you desire this kind of help, talk to other home schoolers in your local church and support group about it. Take the initiative.

A Final Word of Encouragement

That just about does it. These nine steps have launched many home schooling families into the lifestyle of home schooling. Successful home schooling is a lifestyle. Seasoned home schooling moms accept the fact that they have to grow up as teachers, just as their children have to grow up as students. Experience adds perspective.

Don't freeze up in the face of a decision about teaching approaches or curriculum choices. You'll have plenty of opportunities to re-evaluate your initial decisions. You'll be able to adjust and improve. You may even decide to switch teaching materials altogether. That's okay, provided you make the transitions smoothly enough to keep your children on track.

Making the decision to home school may have come to you in a brilliant burst of light, like the one that knocked Paul off his donkey on the Road to Damascus (and I hope this volume has helped that light dawn on you). Pulling your children out of school may be done very quickly. But getting into the routines of teaching your children at home will involve a little more time.

So, within the time constraints that you face, try to take your time. Your child may need some time to get re-oriented toward the home and away from his peers. She may need to be wooed back into a love for learning. He may need to develop some self-discipline. All of these things take time, and they are worth whatever time they take, even if they don't initially look impressive on school transcripts. Even if you are in a hurry, keep your eye on the true goal—serving God as a family. Don't be so concerned with getting to your destination that you fail to enjoy fellowship with your Maker and with one another along the way.

CHAPTER 10

TO TEST OR NOT TO TEST

WHY ALL THE QUESTIONS?

"The future of American education may be one in which the enterprise of education will be defined entirely by actual learning accomplished and accounted for. Indeed, no education will have taken place unless there is evidence of learning occurred."[1]

—Chester E. Finn, Jr.

One mother told me she has never had her teenage child take a national standardized achievement test, such as the Iowa Basic Skills Test or the Stanford Achievement Test. She believed that such testing artificially and inaccurately measures children. She emphasized that she knows her child's strengths and weaknesses by interacting with him on a daily basis and by giving him her own tests. She believed a child could be eventually tested with questions which would require an answer that would violate his religious beliefs.

However, another home school mother explained that she found standardized testing of her son to be very helpful in measuring her child's abilities and in assuring her that her child was progressing well. She further pointed out that her state law gave her an option of having her child tested with a standardized achievement test or evaluated by a teacher. She much preferred sending in an objective test score rather than his having a subjective evaluation which could be scrutinized and possibly rejected by a public school official.

Who is right? Should home schoolers test their children with a national standardized achievement test? Should home schoolers fight for legislation which would require a portfolio of the child's work to be submitted to the local school district rather than the taking of a standardized achievement test?

I believe this issue of standardized achievement testing has neither a right nor wrong answer. Each family will have to make a personal decision as to the value of testing for its children.

In this chapter, I will briefly summarize some of the benefits and disadvantages of testing so the reader can make up his or her own mind. I will look at testing from two perspectives: a legal perspective and an academic perspective.

Should Standardized Testing Be Legally Mandated?

I believe the state's attempt to "compel" education has caused the academic trouble our youth are in today. Along with this statutory right in each state to force all children into school, the United States Supreme Court created a right to "reasonably regulate" education. As a result, many public school officials will argue that they have the right to know how the home-schooled child is progressing. In states where the law is vague, school officials will often try to add other monitoring requirements in addition to testing, such as home visits, periodic meetings, and regular progress reports. Of course, we object to such excessive intrusion into the privacy of home schoolers.

The best way to dispose of this problem of the state wanting to monitor the progress of the home school student is to repeal the compulsory attendance statutes. Until that happens, however, I believe our goal should be to legislatively limit the interest of the state as far as possible until we return to an "honor system" in all fifty states. For example, in Missouri, Wisconsin, Mississippi, Montana, and Wyoming, home schoolers operate on the "honor system" since they do not have to prove to the state that their children are progressing. In Georgia and Colorado, home schools do have to give their children a standardized achievement test, but they do not have to send the results to the public school.

Furthermore, home schools that operate as private schools throughout the country also are free from testing requirements. In these states, parents have the right to home school with basically no conditions. Home schools are appropriately left "on their honor" and are presumed to be providing their children with an adequate education.

As a result, I believe we should all pursue the goal of preserving this freedom from testing in the states that already enjoy it and work to remove the testing requirement in the remaining states, as strategy and timing dictates. I especially believe we should oppose a nationally-mandated test for all children because there is strong evidence that such a pervasive system of testing could easily be abused to conform the values of the children to something contrary to Christianity. The dangers of national testing and state "assessment" testing are outlined in B. K. Eakman's book, *Educating for a New World Order*, for those interested in further reading on this subject.[2]

However, if you are in a state that requires standardized testing or a progress report or evaluation, you have to make a choice. You could challenge the testing requirement in court or comply with it. So far the courts have unfortunately upheld testing requirements to be constitutional,[3] making it difficult to successfully challenge a testing requirement.

On the other hand, research demonstrates that home schoolers, as a whole, do very well on standardized achievement tests. Therefore, complying with state testing requirements is not usually a problem for home-schooled children. Actually, the public school children are the ones who are often failing these standardized tests! Although required testing is not preferred since it involves government conditions on home schooling and does not accurately depict the child's abilities, it remains the most objective way to show general educational progress. The local school official has no discretion to determine adequacy of the test results and has no choice but to let you continue to home school. Requirements of evaluations, portfolio reviews, or progress reports are much more risky since you are opening yourself up to much greater scrutiny and arbitrary discretion of the public school officials.

Figure 1

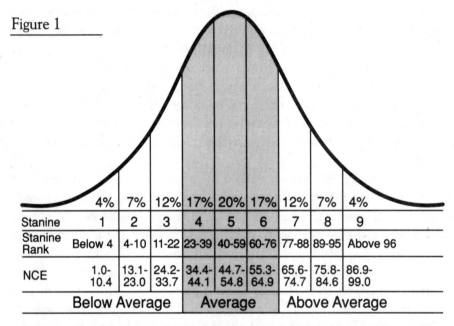

	4%	7%	12%	17%	20%	17%	12%	7%	4%
Stanine	1	2	3	4	5	6	7	8	9
Stanine Rank	Below 4	4-10	11-22	23-39	40-59	60-76	77-88	89-95	Above 96
NCE	1.0-10.4	13.1-23.0	24.2-33.7	34.4-44.1	44.7-54.8	55.3-64.9	65.6-74.7	75.8-84.6	86.9-99.0
	Below Average			Average			Above Average		

A Normal Distribution of Stanines, Percentile Ranks, Normal Curve Equivalents, and Performance Classification.

Regardless of what you believe the limited academic value of standardized testing is, it is the best "objective" way to prove to the school district or the court that your home-schooled child is progressing. The legal advantage of test scores over portfolios or evaluations is that they cannot be subjected to arbitrary interpretation by the school officials or the judges.

Many of the states which have testing requirements have "cut off" percentiles that a home-schooled child must reach in order to continue to home school. In Oregon it is the 15th percentile, and in Colorado it is the 13th percentile. Other states, however, impose a double standard by requiring home schools to score a minimal score which is much higher than the score the public school students must attain. For example, in West Virginia, home schools have to score above the 40th percentile. This is especially ridiculous in light of the fact that 54 percent of the student population fits into the "average" range which is between the 23rd and 76th percentile (see Figure 1). In fact, 27 percent of the "average" students fit into the 23rd to 39th percentile on the bell-shaped curve distribution of the population.

In other words, if a child in a public school scores in the 23rd percentile, he is considered average and no remedial instruction is necessary. On the other hand, home schoolers who score as high as the 39th percentile in West Virginia are considered failures who must be prohibited from being home schooled further. This blatant discrimination against home schoolers is present in a number of other states that require home schoolers to achieve scores above the 23rd percentile. As a result HSLDA has launched its first of many civil rights suits in order to stop this discrimination. The first suit was filed in West Virginia in September 1992.[4]

It is important, at this point, to explain the terminology. "Percentiles" only demonstrate a child's ranking among the whole population of students who took the achievement test when it was standardized. "Percentages," on the other hand, show the number of questions that were answered correctly. "Percentages," therefore, tend to be a more accurate measurement of a child's ability.

In conclusion, home schoolers, on the average, do very well on standardized achievement tests, as seen in chapter 6. They normally score in the 70th to 80th percentile. Yet, I believe our primary goal should be, eventually, to repeal testing requirements and evaluation requirements altogether or to prevent them from being imposed in the first place. In the meantime, however, we need to work step-by-step to improve the testing laws that already exist. The best testing states are those which require testing but do not require the test to be submitted. If that cannot be achieved legislatively and test scores have to be submitted to the public schools, legislation should be crafted which would allow the parents, not the state, to choose which standardized test should be used, who should administer it, and where it should be given (preferably at home). The Psychological Corporation's testing standards encourage its tests to be administered in the child's learning environment since he will perform at his fullest potential. Therefore, home school laws must allow testing to be done at home.

Studies show that testing is not recommended for pre-schoolers and first graders.[5] A low "cut off" of approximately the 15th percentile as a *composite* score should be set in order to be fair in comparison to the public school standards and to take away arbitrary discretion from the local officials. Also options like submitting portfolios and evaluations in lieu of test scores should be included in the law for parents who have children who are poor test-takers or whose children have "special needs."

Do Standardized Achievement Tests Have Any Academic Value?

Much debate is going on today about the value of standardized achievement testing. However, the American Federation of Teachers and other public school advocates are the ones objecting the loudest to standardized testing.[6] I believe their underlying reason for opposing local standardized testing is not to help the students but rather to prevent exposure of the public schools' failure. This means, of course, that we must be cautious in accepting their critique of the value of standardized testing.

Standardized testing has traditionally served two purposes: 1) to contribute to the identification of an individual child's learning problems or gaps in their basic knowledge, and 2) to evaluate the effectiveness of school instructional programs.[7] There are two basic types of scoring systems:

> The first is known as "norm-referenced." Norm-referenced tests measure a child's achievement tests against a norm, or set of scores, established by a group of students thought to be typical of the nation as a whole. The other type of test is known as "criterion-referenced." Criterion-referenced tests measure student achievement against a predetermined standard, or criterion, such as a specific set of eighth-grade reading skills.[8]

Criterion-referenced tests designed by the public school system will many times be a problem for a home schooler because they are often designed to fit the public school's curriculum. There is a danger that the particular test could have value-laden questions that could discriminate against the home-schooled child. Gregory Cizek of the

American College of Testing identifies some of these philosophical difficulties in certain standardized tests, but they are usually "criterion-referenced" tests.[9]

The more popular and safer testing for home schoolers is the norm-referenced testing. The Stanford Achievement and Iowa Basic Skills tests are norm-referenced. These tests tend to have less value-laden questions and are not designed to fit any certain public school curriculum.

As a result, home schoolers' standardized test results can be helpful in determining the child's educational progress, and they can provide an assurance to the home school mother that her teaching is effective. Nonetheless, parents and students need to remember that such test results need to be kept in proper perspective.

When it comes to evaluating a child's progress, the home school parents will know their student's ability and progress much more accurately than the results of a standardized test will demonstrate. Ultimately, your child's performance on your personal tests and his daily studying habits will give you much more valuable and complete information on your child's progress.

Parents must also keep in mind that *low* test scores can signify one of three possibilities: 1) the test scores could be low because the child "choked" on the test and had a bad day, 2) the test results could be low because the test covered subject matter that your home school has not yet covered, or 3) the low test scores may demonstrate that your child is having difficulty mastering the subject matter.[10] Each parent, therefore, must be careful as to how he interprets the results of a standardized test.

One last area that parents must watch out for is how they understand the "grade-equivalent" scores. The first number is the grade level, and the second number is the month of the school year. For instance, "a score of 4.8 means the child is performing at a level roughly equal to that of an average fourth grader in the eighth month of the school year."[11] Testing expert Tom Morganthau states:

> It is perfectly possible for children to make grade-equivalent scores that are wildly out of sync with their actual grade level, which is where the parental misunderstandings begin. Patricia's son, Fred, for example, scored "13.4" in math problem-solving. Taken at face value, that score suggests Fred can do math as well as a college freshman, which is certainly not the case: Fred has never taken algebra,

geometry or calculus, and the test did not cover those subjects. Instead, his grade-equivalent score simply means Fred does eighth-grade math very well.[12]

Provided you keep in mind these potential hazards in interpreting test scores, standardized testing can be one more factor in helping to measure your child's progress.

Furthermore, parents need to be aware that most colleges and graduate schools depend heavily on standardized testing in the form of college entrance tests (the SAT, ACT, or certain graduate level tests). Having children take standardized tests in at least high school may help them become familiar with this type of testing to better prepare them for these standardized entrance exams.

Conclusion: Standardized Testing Must Be Kept in Perspective

As I explained above, home schoolers, on the average, do extremely well on national standardized achievement testing, especially norm-referenced testing. Therefore, these high test scores are particularly effective in demonstrating to judges, public school officials, and the general public that home schooling works. Submitting such test scores to public school officials, as required by some state laws, prevents them from exercising any real discretion over your home school.

Ideally, states should not require any testing or evaluating of home school students but that will take time to change. However, we need to keep in mind that repealing testing might result in a "trade-off," with the legislature or school district attempting to impose certain teacher qualifications or other more intrusive monitoring of home schools in place of testing. We need to be careful in our awareness of the academic problems of standardized testing that we do not "throw the baby out with the bath water" and leave ourselves open to worse regulation of home schooling by the state. I, for one, would much prefer sending in a standardized test score to the school district than submitting to an inspection of my home school by a state official.

Most of these "academic" problems with standardized testing involve how a parent uses the results and how much they rely on them in judging their child's progress. Such test results should be kept in proper perspective and take the "back-seat" to other indicators of progress that only the home school teacher can be aware of and measure.

Ultimately, each family needs to decide what academic and legal value they believe standardized testing will have for their personal situation. The question to test or not to test is yours alone to answer.

Notes

1. R. Rothman, "States Turn to Student Performance as a New Measure of School Quality," *Education Week*, 8 November 1989, 12.

2. B. K. Eakman, *Educating for a New World Order* (Portland, Ore.: Halcyon House, 1991).

3. See *Murphy v. Arkansas*, 852 F.2d 1039 (8th Cir. 1988).

4. *Null v. Jackson County Public Schools*, No. 6:92-0820, U.S. District Court for Southern District of West Virginia, September 1992.

5. Jenny Labalme, "Panel: Prohibit Early Standardized Tests," *Anniston Star*, 23 May 1990, 1A. This article reported on the findings of the National Commission on Testing and Public Policy which recommended banning standardized testing for four and five year olds.

6. "Groups Call for Phase-Out of Standardized Tests," *Education Daily*, Vol. 23, No. 17, 25 January 1990, 1.

7. Tom Morganthau, "A Consumer's Guide to Testing," *Newsweek Special Issue*, Fall/Winter 1990, 66.

8. *Ibid.*, 66.

9. Gregory J. Cizek, "Applying Standardized Testing to Home-Based Education Programs: Reasonable or Customary," *Educational Measurement: Issues and Practice*, Fall 1988, 2-19. Cizek is Program Associate at The American College Testing Program, P.O. Box 168, Iowa City, Iowa 52243.

10. *Ibid.* 66.

11. *Ibid.*

12. *Ibid.*

PART
4

A DESPERATE FOE:
THE ATTACK OF SOCIAL
WORKERS, SCHOOL OFFICIALS,
AND TEACHERS' UNIONS

Home schooling, in the eyes of many public school officials and educational interest groups, such as the National Education Association, is threatening. It is a blatant challenge to their virtual monopolistic control over education in the United States. Additionally, it is a repudiation of their philosophy, which holds that the state and the educational elite know what is best for our children.

While home schooling is in the process of restoring education, it is simultaneously exposing the corruption and failure of the public school system. Home schooling is also embarrassing the public schools since "mere parents," on the average, are performing a better job teaching their children than the public school system. Home schooling is a reassertion of "parental rights," which is considered to be a rebellion by many public school officials and education union leaders who are accustomed to nearly complete control of children.

As seen from the attempts of school officials to teach home school parents "who is boss" through legal intimidation and the resolutions of the education organizations which condemn home schooling, it is apparent that many of them do not approve of home schooling in the least. As long as there is a public school system and compulsory attendance laws, this conflict between home schoolers and the state (and educational unions) will not end.

In this section the reader will be made aware of this conflict in many different areas and the position of the educational elite groups concerning home schooling. Much documentation in this section will show that the law, the Constitution, and the statistics are generally on the side of home schoolers, but the numbers, dollars, and child welfare bureaucracies are on the side of the state and unions. Even so, home schooling, as a minority right, continues to gain greater recognition and protection.

CHAPTER 11

THE ATTACK ON
PARENTAL RIGHTS

" **A** general state education is a *mere contrivance* for *molding people* to be *exactly* like one *another*: and as the mold in which it casts them is that which pleases the predominant power in the government or [the will of] the majority of the existing generation; in proportion as it is efficient and successful, it establishes a *despotism* over the *mind*, leading by natural tendency to one over the body."[1] (emphasis added)

– John Stuart Mill

In spite of the impressive academic record of home schoolers and the numerous benefits of this type of tutorial education, certain groups, usually representing the educational establishment, continue to oppose home schooling in the legislatures. Also, families across the nation are routinely harassed by their local school district or law enforcement officials.

I am convinced that the conflict with home schoolers has nothing to do with education. Home schoolers have consistently proved that it works as documented in chapter 6. In fact, in every single case in which the Home School Legal Defense Association has been involved since its inception in 1983, the children have been proven to be progressing academically, often above average. It is apparent that the real issue involves who has the authority to mandate how the children must be educated. Do the parents or the public schools have this authority?

As a result, home schoolers are on the "front lines" of the battle for liberty in the United States. If they lose, the Christian schools, churches, and families will soon follow suit.

The Clash Between Competing Financial Interests

The main opposition to home schooling is made up of public school officials and teacher's unions. This should be expected since the public school officials and teachers have a financial interest ($3000 to $4000 in tax monies per child for their school district from the state and federal governments) in whether or not home schoolers are allowed to exist. In fact, their jobs may even be on the line. This is a strong financial incentive, especially for small school districts, to disapprove home schools and get the children back in public school. This financial interest, of course, makes it very difficult for the school authorities to remain neutral when determining whether or not a home schooler should be allowed to operate freely. I have had numerous experiences with school officials coming to the door of new home schoolers and telling them that they are causing the school district to lose thousands of dollars in funding since they pulled their children out of school. However, the education of the children is not even mentioned. Chapter 18 discusses many examples of school officials who were worried more about the financial loss to their school district than about children being taught at home. Chapter 18 also provides documentation as to the amount of money each child is worth in state and federal tax dollars, and the constitutional implications.

The Clash Between Educational Philosophies

In addition, there is a philosophical reason for opposition to home schooling. In my experience of talking with hundreds of school officials, I found that many actually believe that they are the "guardians of the children" and, as such, they need sufficient controls over all the children within the boundaries of their school district. They sincerely believe that since they often have had seven years of higher education, they know what type of education is best for the children. They cannot understand how a parent can teach the children. They do not recognize that God has delegated the right to teach children to the parents, not the state.

This combination of both the philosophy of control and the financial and competitive interest makes clear to public school authorities that they must do something about home schooling. Several of the powerful education unions and associations have begun vocalizing their opposition to home schooling in recent years. The following are several examples of the opposition's position reflecting the strong philosophical bias they have against home schooling.

For instance, the National Education Association, a teachers' union, with a budget exceeding $200 million, has consistently opposed home schoolers in the legislatures. Below are excerpts from the 1991-92 resolutions of the NEA:

> C-3. The Association urges its affiliates to seek legislation to ensure that early childhood development programs offered primarily through the public schools be fully funded and available on an equal basis and culminate in mandatory kindergarten with compulsory attendance. . . .
>
> C-40. The National Education Association believes that home schooling programs cannot provide the student with a comprehensive education experience.
>
> The Association believes that, if parental preference home schooling study occurs, students enrolled must meet all state requirements. Instruction should be by persons who are licensed by the appropriate state education licensure agency, and a curriculum approved by the state department of education should be used.
>
> The Association further believes that such programs should be limited to the children of the immediate family, with all expenses being borne by the parents."[2]

If the NEA had its way and every state required parents to be state-certified and have their curriculum approved, at least 90 percent of the home schoolers in the country would be outlawed. On the issue of teacher certification, the NEA ignores the hundreds of studies that have been performed which demonstrate no positive correlation between teacher qualifications and student performance.

According to a July 8, 1988, article by Pat Ordovensky in *USA Today*, this same resolution was overwhelmingly adopted by the 8,400 NEA members attending the convention in 1988. Some of the comments quoted in the *USA Today* article demonstrate just how threatened NEA members feel by home education. The president of the Maryland State Teachers Association, Beverly Correlle, told the reporter that law makers in her state are "caving in to the zealots who push home schooling allowing them to operate with few restrictions." Texas teachers told Pat Ordovensky, "Up to 20 percent of students are being taught at home" in rural Texas.[3]

Annette Cootes of the Texas State Teachers Association declared, "My own personal opinion is that home schooling is a *form of child abuse* because you are isolating children from human interaction. I think home schoolers are doing a great discredit to their children."[4] A quick look at the condition in public schools as documented in Part One of this book will demonstrate that sending children to public school, not teaching them at home, is the real child abuse.

Another national organization is less polite concerning its opposition to home schooling. It would like to see home schooling completely prohibited. The National Association of Elementary School Principals (NAESP) is urging local and state associations to promote legislative changes that will "enforce compulsory school attendance and prohibit at home schooling as a substitute for compulsory school attendance." The NAESP's 1987-88 platform lists eight reasons why home schooling is inferior to the traditional classroom setting. The platform states:

Such schooling:

1. Deprives the child of important social experiences;
2. Isolates students from other social/racial/ethnic groups;
3. Denies students the full range of curriculum experiences and materials;
4. May be provided by non-certified and unqualified persons;
5. Creates an additional burden on administrators whose duties include the enforcement of compulsory school attendance laws;
6. May not permit effective assessment of academic standards of quality;

7. May violate health and safety standards;
8. May not provide the accurate diagnosis of and planning for meeting the needs of children with special talents, learning difficulties, and other conditions requiring atypical educational programs.[5]

It is interesting to note that the worst harassment that home schoolers receive from school districts, in my experience in representing home schoolers, is usually directly from the principal.

Another organization which is diametrically opposed to home schooling is the National Parent Teachers Association. At their 1987 national convention, they passed these resolutions:

> WHEREAS National PTA believes that all children should have access to equal educational opportunities; and
> WHEREAS, the National PTA has consistently supported a quality education for all students; and
> WHEREAS, the number of homeschools and other non-approved schools has increased significantly in the last five years; and
> WHEREAS, there are no uniform standards that home schools and other non-approved schools must meet, such as hours and days of instruction, curriculum, teacher certification, and reporting;
> NOW THEREFORE be it resolved that the National PTA encourages state PTAs to urge state boards of education and/or state legislators to require home and other non-approved schools to meet the same minimum educational standards as *public schools*.

This organization claims to be operating for parents.

Thomas Shannon, executive director of the National School Boards Association, in an interview, calls the home schooling trend "a giant step backward into the seventeenth century." He stated further in the interview:

> We are very concerned that many parents who think they are qualified to teach their youngsters, simply are not. . . . The youngsters are getting shortchanged. . . . Society ultimately has to pay for any mistakes, not to mention the loss of a child who might otherwise have made a maximum contribution.[6]

If he had not said he was talking about home schooling, it would seem apparent that he was describing the failure of the public school system. There is certainly no documentation to support his assertion concerning home schooling.

Bureaucrats in the various state education departments usually are influenced by the teachers' unions. For instance, Wisconsin's state superintendent, Herbert Grover, tried to push for legislation restricting home schoolers. He declared that home schools should be required to "meet all expectations of the public schools. These children are neglected and abused. That is wrong."[7] He also made claims that thousands of home-schooled children were not being educated. However, like many critics of home schoolers, he offered no documentation to back his allegations. HSLDA was able to minimize his attack on home schooling by supplying a special legislative committee whose purpose was to scrutinize home schooling with numerous studies which proved the success of home schooling. The result was that the legislative committee rejected the state superintendent's allegations and recommended no changes to the home school law in Wisconsin.

In conclusion, it is clear the educational elite are protecting their vested interest and ignoring the academic statistics which expose the failure of the public schools and the consistent success of home schoolers.

The Clash Between Parental Rights and State Control

This bias against home schooling by the educational establishment and many school authorities results in numerous legal conflicts across the country each year.

During the 1990-91 school year, nearly two thousand negative legal contacts were handled by HSLDA. These contacts involved various degrees of harassment, ranging from actual or threatened prosecution to the attempted imposition of restrictions in excess of the law.[8]

Misapplication of the law even plagued the thirty-three states that had home school legislation. Single parents or parents with handicapped children received the worst treatment. For example, families were threatened with a termination of their right to home school by school districts trying to impose false notification deadlines, testing or evaluation procedures, curriculum requirements, or in some instances, qualification requirements.

In states where home schools either have to be approved by the school district or operate as private schools, the challenges were more intense. Many members of HSLDA were faced with illegal home visits, curriculum approval, and excessive qualification requirements.

In many of these states the law is somewhat vague, which contributes to the arbitrary treatment of home schools.

As a result, I must daily counsel members as to appropriate action and then, when necessary, intervene on their behalf. This often involves writing lengthy legal letters to the school districts or making numerous phone calls. In 10 percent of the situations where the school districts refuse to back off, the families are charged with educational neglect or criminal truancy.

The reason these home school families are harassed usually is connected to either the school official's philosophical bias and desire to control or the school district's financial interest.

The Battle Is Intensifying

Home education, one of the most important liberties, is protected by the First and Fourteenth Amendments. However, the opposition realizes the danger of this growing movement and is seeking to regulate home schooling out of existence or, at least, into conformity.

This battle has two important fronts remaining: the spiritual battle and the legal battle. The academic battle has already been won with numerous studies documenting the success of home schooling.

As a result, home schoolers must remain committed to prayer for protection and committed to train up the children to think and believe as Christians. Furthermore, parents must remain eternally vigilant in order to fight any legislative attempts to undermine parental liberties. Parents must also have solidarity with home schoolers throughout the nation by supporting ministries such as HSLDA, which is dedicated to defending the rights of all home schoolers.

Notes

1. John Stuart Mill, *American State Papers: On Liberty* (Chicago: Benton William, Publisher, Encyclopedia Britannica, Inc., 1972), 318.

2. "The 1991-92 Resolutions of the National Education Association," *NEA Today*, Vol. 10, No. 1, September 1991, 17-23. The resolutions also stated in G-4. "A teaching license must be recognized as the primary requirement for employment in every public and private school (pre-K to 12)."

3. *USA Today*, 8 July 1988.

4. Ann Zimmerman, "Is Anybody Home?" *Dallas Observer*, 21 November 1991, 20.

5. National Association of Elementary School Principals 1987-88 platform, 3.

6. Mary Esch, "Home Schooling Good or Bad, More Parents Are Willing to Try It," *State Journal Register*, 30 June 1991.

7. *Milwaukee Journal*, 7 June 1990.

8. "The 1990-91 School Year in Review," *The Home School Court Report*, July-August 1991, Vol. 7, No. 4, Home School Legal Defense Association, Paeonian Springs, Virginia. Also see back and future issues of the Home School Court Report for a chronological account of harassment faced by home schoolers around the nation.

CHAPTER 12

THE MYTH OF
TEACHER QUALIFICATIONS

"Some of the worst teachers I've ever seen are highly certified. Look at our public schools. They're full of certified teachers. What kind of magic is that accomplishing? But I can take you to the best teachers I've ever seen, and most of them are uncertified. . . . We don't have evidence at all that what we do in schools of education makes much difference in teacher competence."[1]

Dr. Donald Ericksen, UCLA

Most education officials publicly claim that teachers need special "qualifications" in order to be effective. As a result, public education organizations sometimes target home schoolers with legislation or an interpretation of the law which would require parents to have one of three qualifications: 1) a teacher certification, 2) a college degree, or 3) passage of a "teacher's exam." Although this seems reasonable on the surface, such requirements not only violate the right of parents to teach their children as guaranteed by the First and Fourteenth Amendments, but virtually all academic research documents that there is no positive correlation between teacher qualifications (especially teacher certification requirements) and student performance.

It also seems apparent that Americans in general are seeing through the "smoke screen" of teacher qualifications. On July 23, 1991, the results of a public opinion poll were released by the Washington-based Belden and Russonello public opinion research firm. It found that three out of four Americans disagreed with the notion that teacher certification requirements in public schools assure high-quality teachers. The poll also found that 71 percent do not believe that the lack of teacher certification in private schools means that their teachers are less qualified than public school teachers.[2]

In fact, the National Education Association and some of the other members of the educational establishment are the only ones to defend teacher certification and high qualification standards for home schoolers, in spite of the overwhelming research and popular opinion against the need for such teaching standards. Their vested interest in certified teachers may explain their blindness to the facts.

I have talked with hundreds of school officials who cannot understand how a "mere mother" with a high school diploma could possibly teach her own children. These officials literally take offense that parents would try to teach their children and actually think that they will do as well as teachers in the public school who have at least four years and sometimes seven years of higher education. Unfortunately, critics in the media have also believed this myth and will question the validity of home schooling by asking, "But are the parents qualified?" What is so laughable about this belief in teacher qualifications by public school authorities are the statistics which show the appalling decline in competency among certified public school teachers and the failure of the teacher colleges. Chapter 1 documents many of these statistics.

Since 1983, HSLDA has been battling teacher qualifications for home school parents in the legal arena. I have fought hundreds of school districts which have misapplied the laws in states such as Alabama, Massachusetts, Pennsylvania, Ohio, Michigan, California, and South Carolina. These school districts often used the vagueness of the law to impose college degree or certification requirements on home school parents, which, if successful, would shut down over half of all home schools. As of the printing of this book, the battles have been won in most of these states, either in the courts or in the legislature. Other states such as Iowa, North Dakota, Michigan, Florida, Virginia, Washington, and others have applied more explicit laws requiring home schoolers to be certified teachers. Most of these laws have been finally defeated or repealed, but many families ended up in court in the process. In fact, in North Dakota, for several years virtually every HSLDA family who was discovered by the school district was taken to court for not being certified.

Home schoolers need to remain constantly informed. For example, in 1990, the Kansas School Board Association made an unsuccessful attempt to get House Bill 2392 passed which would have required home schoolers to be certified.[3] Home schoolers, as a result of these continuing attacks by school officials, lobbyists, and the media, need to be familiar with the statistics in this chapter in order to expose the "myth of teacher qualifications" so that no qualifications will be placed on school parents.

This chapter includes several research projects and opinions of professional educators, confirming the absence of a positive correlation between teacher qualifications and student performance. There is also a clear trend in the legislatures and the courts away from enacting or enforcing certification and other teaching standards to restrict home schoolers.

Research and Researchers Which Expose the Myth of Teacher Qualifications

One of the most significant studies in this area was performed by Dr. Eric Hanushek of the University of Rochester, who surveyed the results of 113 *studies* on teacher education and qualifications. Eighty-five percent of the studies found *no positive correlation* between the educational performance of the students and the teacher's educational background. Although 7 percent of the studies did find a positive correlation, 5 percent found a *negative impact*.[4] Those who push for legislation requiring certain teacher qualifications for home schoolers have no research to support the necessity of such standards. The results of these 113 studies are certainly an indictment on proponents of certain teacher standards for home schoolers. Higher teacher qualification does not make better students.

Dr. Sam Peavey, professor emeritus of the School of Education at the University of Louisville, earned advance education degrees from Harvard (Master of Arts) and Columbia (Doctor of Education) and was involved in the preparation of thousands of prospective teachers for state certification. He has served on numerous committees and commissions dealing with the accreditation of schools and colleges. On September 30, 1988, Dr. Peavey testified before the Compulsory Education Study Committee of the Iowa Legislature on the subject of teacher qualifications, citing numerous studies. He stated:

> May I say that I have spent a long career in developing and administering programs for teacher certification. I wish I could tell you that those thousands of certificates contributed significantly to the quality of children's learning, but I cannot. . . . After fifty years of research, we have *found no significant correlation between the requirements for teacher certification and the quality of student achievement.*

Later in his testimony, Dr. Peavey explained that he has found only *one* valid way of identifying a good teacher:

> However, in spite of years of frustration, I am pleased to report to you there has been discovered one valid, legal, honest, professional, common-sense way to identify a good teacher. As far as I know there is only one way, and it is about time for legislators to recognize it and write it into school law. It involves a simple process. Step one is *to stop looking at the teachers and start looking at the students.* Step two is to determine how well students are learning what they are supposed to be learning. The quality of learning provides the only valid measure of the quality of teaching we have yet discovered [emphasis added].

Dr. Peavey concluded his testimony with practical examples of excellent student achievement results by students who were being taught by their parents, most without degrees or certificates. He explained that many studies demonstrate that home-schooled children "commonly score a year or more above their peers in regular schools on standard measures of achievement."[5]

Another expert, Dr. Donald Ericksen, professor of education for the University of California at Los Angeles, stated in a recent interview:

> Some of the worst teachers I've ever seen are highly certified. Look at our public schools. They're full of certified teachers. What kind of magic is that accomplishing? But I can take you to the best teachers I've ever seen, and most of them are uncertified. . . . We *don't have evidence at all that what we do in schools of education makes much difference in teacher competence* [emphasis added].[6]

In a well-known case before the Michigan Supreme Court, concerning a Christian school's challenge to the state's teacher certification requirement, Dr. Ericksen testified as an expert witness on teacher certification. There he explained that extensive research has established that no significant correlation exists between certification (or teacher qualifications) and student learning, and that student testing is a far superior method of determining teacher effectiveness. Dr. Lanier, an expert who testified on the side of the state in favor of teacher certification, admitted under oath that she was unaware of any verifiable evidence establishing any correlation between teacher certification requirements and student learning or teacher competence.[7]

Two education researchers, R. W. Heath and M. A. Nielson surveyed forty two studies of "competency-based" teacher education. Their findings were that no empirical evidence exists to establish a positive relation between those programs and student achievement.[8]

Four other education researchers, L. D. Freeman, R. E. Flodan, R. Howsan, and D. C. Corrigan, did separate studies in the effectiveness of teacher certification requirements. They all concluded that there is no significant relation between teacher certification and teacher performance in the classroom.[9]

The 1990 Science Report Card surveyed almost twenty thousand students in grades four, eight, and twelve. The survey demonstrates that there is no relationship between the science achievement of students and the certification level or advanced degrees of their teachers. For instance, eighth graders taught by teachers who had finished six or more college physics courses had virtually the same proficiency as those teachers who had no courses in physics.[10]

C. Emily Feistritzer, director of the private National Center for Education Information, claimed in a recent interview that she does not know "of a single study that says because a teacher has gone through this or that program, he or she is a better teacher." Supporters of teacher training programs "argue eloquently that teachers need to be grounded in all of these things, but there has yet to be a study that shows that in fact this is the case."[11]

John Chubb, a fellow at the Brookings Institute (a liberal think tank), extensively studied various popular reforms including the push to professionalize teaching, toughen teacher certification standards, and implement more extensive teacher evaluation systems. As a result, he authored a book with Terry Moe, *Politics, Markets, and America's Schools* on the subject of reform of education. Mr. Chubb found "no correlation between student achievement and any of the variables on which school reformers have been concentrating so much time, effort, and money." He continues, "There is little reason to believe" that these actions will improve student achievement and "there is considerable reason to believe they will fail."[12]

Dr. Brian Ray of the National Home Education Research Institute released a report entitled, *A Nationwide Study of Home Education: Family Characteristics, Legal Matters, and Student Achievement.* This was a study of over two thousand home school families in all fifty states. The research revealed that there was no positive correlation between the state regulation of home schools and the home-schooled students' performance. The study compared home schoolers in three groups of states representing various levels of regulation. Group 1 represented the most restrictive states, such as Michigan, which require home schoolers to use certified teachers; Group 2 represented slightly less restrictive states including North Dakota; and Group 3 represented unregulated states, such as Texas and California, which have no teacher qualifications. Dr. Ray concluded:

> *No* difference was found in the achievement scores of students between the three groups which represent various degrees of state regulation of home education. . . . It was found that students in all three regulation groups scored on the average at or above the 76th percentile in the three areas examined: total reading, total math, and total language. These findings in conjunction with others described in this section, do *not* support the idea that state regulation and compliance on the part of home education families assures successful student achievement.[13]

Furthermore, this same study demonstrated that only 13.9 percent of the mothers (who are the primary teachers) had ever been certified teachers. The study found that there was no difference in students' total reading, total math, and total language scores based on the teacher certification status of their parents:

> The findings of this study do *not* support the idea that parents need to be trained and certified teachers to assure successful academic achievement of their children.[14]

Whether the home school parent had a teaching certificate, a college degree, or a high school diploma or less, did not make any difference—all their children scored, on the average, in the 80th percentile.

This study has been confirmed by two other studies of the qualifications of home school parents. Dr. J. F. Jakestraw surveyed the student performance of home schoolers in Alabama and reported:

> This finding suggests that those children in Alabama whose parent-teachers are not certified to teach perform on standardized achievement tests as well as those whose parent-teachers are certified to teach. Therefore, it is concluded that there is no relationship between the certification status of the parent-teacher and the home-schooled children's performance on standardized achievement tests."[15]

Jon Wartes also performed a similar study on home schoolers over three years in the state of Washington and reached the same conclusion.[16]

On the whole, home schoolers' achievements are ranked above average on standardized achievement tests as demonstrated by Dr. Ray's findings in the study cited above and the numerous studies summarized in chapter 6. Dr. Ray and others have found that only 35 percent of teaching mothers have a college degree or higher, and yet their children score no higher on standardized achievement tests than those being taught by mothers without a college degree.

Conclusion of Research

In conclusion, nearly all existing research on teacher qualifications or state regulations demonstrates that they have no significant relation to *student* performance. In fact, teacher qualification requirements have no positive correlation with even *teacher* performance. In the end, as the Coleman Report (U.S. Office of Education, 1964) pointed out, families are the most important factors in determining a student's academic performance.

Statutory Trend Lessening Teacher Qualification Requirements

The trend across the United States is to remove all teacher qualifications standards for home schoolers. The emphasis seems to be on protecting parental rights and, in several states, focusing on student performance through an annual test or portfolio evaluation.

As of September 15, 1992, *thirty-nine* states do *not require* home school parents to have *any* specific qualifications. Home schoolers in these states can home school without proof of any particular educational qualifications. In fact, of the *twelve* states that do have qualification requirements, *five* of them require only a GED or high school diploma. The states in this category are North Carolina, Ohio, Pennsylvania, Georgia, and South Carolina. Of the remaining *six* states, North Dakota and Arizona presently require the passage of a "teacher's test." In Arizona, the test is geared for sixth through eighth graders. New Mexico requires a Bachelor's Degree, but this requirement is routinely waived upon request, leaving a high school diploma as the standard. Tennessee requires a college degree for any parent who is teaching a high school student. Although there is a provision in Tennessee which allows for a waiver, such waivers are routinely denied by the commissioner. West Virginia requires parents to have four years of education beyond their oldest student.

South Carolina used to require a college degree or passage of a teacher's examination. Michael Farris of HSLDA challenged the law and on December 9, 1991, the South Carolina Supreme Court struck down the test, making a high school diploma the only qualification necessary for parents to home school.[17] At the time of this printing, only Michigan requires home school parents to have teaching certificates or use a person with a certificate to teach the children. I presently am handling the case, *DeJonge v. Michigan*, which challenges the constitutionality of that law. The case will soon be heard by the Michigan Supreme Court. Many of the other states formerly had a law like Michigan's, but such teacher qualifications requirements were abandoned.[18]

Major Cases on Teacher Qualifications for Home Schools and Private Schools

Below are summaries of several cases in various states which dealt with the issue of teacher qualifications and found teacher certification requirements or college degree requirements to be excessive or unconstitutional.

In New York, according to its compulsory attendance statute in section 3204, instruction "elsewhere" must be given by a "competent" teacher. The court, in the case *In re Franz*, has interpreted competent to *not* mean certified.[19] Furthermore, home school regulations adopted in June 1988 do not require home school parents to have any qualifications. Home school parents are "competent" as long as they file a notice of intent, quarterly reports of progress, and test results every other year beginning in third grade.

New Jersey law allows *"equivalent* instruction elsewhere than at school."[20] Regarding the interpretation of the word "equivalent," the New Jersey Supreme Court in the *Massa* case stated: ". . . perhaps the New Jersey Legislature intended the word equivalent to mean taught by a certified teacher elsewhere than at school. However, I believe there are teachers today teaching in various schools in New Jersey who are not certified. . . . Had the legislature intended such a requirement, it would have said so."[21]

Ohio law requires home school teachers to be "qualified."[22] State Board of Education regulations define "qualified" as a GED or high school diploma.[23] Prior to these regulations, in *Ohio v. Whisner*, the Ohio Supreme Court struck down Ohio's Minimum Standards which required teacher certification, stating, "Equally difficult to imagine, is a state interest sufficiently substantial to sanction abrogation of appellants' [parents'] liberty to direct the education of their children."[24] The Court also pointed out that the state "*did not* attempt to justify [prove] its interest in enforcing the minimum standards [which included teacher certification requirements] as applied to non-public religious schools."[25]

Michigan is the only state which as of September 1992, still has a statute requiring teacher certification for all schools including home schools. In a three-to-three split of the Michigan Supreme Court, three Justices found:

> Enforcement of the teacher certification requirement, as applied, is not essential to achieve the objective. Unless and until the state can show otherwise, the enforcement of the statutory teacher certification requirement, as applied, would be violative of the First and Fourteenth Amendments.[26]

Unfortunately, since the Michigan Supreme Court split, the earlier erroneous decision by the Court of Appeals, which found teacher certification constitutional, still stands. However, in June 1992 the Michigan Supreme Court agreed to review this precedent by accepting the *DeJonge v. Michigan* case.[27] I have worked on this case since 1985 and it directly challenges the teacher certification requirement.

Indiana presently allows home schools under its law which exempts children from compulsory attendance if they are "provided with instruction *equivalent* to that given in public schools."[28] A federal court in the *Mazenac* case, when trying to interpret the word "equivalent," stated: ". . . it is now doubtful that the requirements of a formally licensed or certified teacher . . . would pass constitutional muster."[29] The Court would not interpret "equivalent instruction" as requiring certified teachers because of the constitutional problems involved.

In Massachusetts, "a child who is otherwise instructed in a *manner approved in advance* by the superintendent . . ." is exempt from attending public school.[30] When establishing guidelines for approving home schools, the Massachusetts Supreme Judicial Court stated, in the *Charles* case, that the superintendents or local public school committees could *not* require the parents to be certified or have college degrees. The Court said: "While we recognize that teachers in public schools must be certified, certification would *not* be appropriately required for parents under a home school proposal. . . . Nor must parents have college or advanced academic degrees."[31] In fact, the home school mother in this case, in whose favor the Court ruled, did not even have a high school diploma.[32]

In Kentucky, home schools operate as private schools. When private schools were required to use certified teachers, even though the statute was unclear, the Kentucky Supreme Court, in the *Rudasill* case, ruled that teacher certification did not apply to private schools and could not be mandated.[33]

In Hawaii, according to its regulations, "parents teaching their children at home shall be deemed *qualified* instructors."[34] In other words, parents are qualified because they are parents. No certain degrees or diplomas are necessary for parents to be able to successfully educate their children.

In South Dakota, a child is allowed to be "otherwise provided with *competent* instruction."[35] The statute further explains that "the individuals [who give instruction] are *not* required to be certified."

In North Dakota, Nebraska, and Iowa, teacher certification requirements were upheld by the courts in the *Shaver, Faith Baptist,* and *Fellowship Baptist* cases.[36] In each of these cases *no* expert testimony or evidence was given to prove teacher certification was necessary or essential for children to be educated. In fact, the state could also not prove, with evidence, that teacher certification was the "least restrictive means" for children to be educated.

Furthermore, the legislatures in all three of these states have *mooted* these cases and vindicated home-schooling parents by repealing the teacher certification requirements. Nebraska and Iowa have created an option in their compulsory attendance statutes to allow parents to home school *without any* qualifications. North Dakota allows parents to pass a "teacher test" in order to opt out of teacher certification.[37]

Conclusion

Educational research does not indicate any positive correlation between teacher qualifications and student performance. Many courts have found teacher qualification requirements on home schoolers to be too excessive or not appropriate. The trend in state legislatures across the country indicates an abandonment of teacher qualification requirements for home school teachers. In fact, Americans, in general, are realizing that the necessity of teacher qualifications is a myth. The teachers' unions and other members of the educational establishment make up the small minority still lobbying for teacher certification in order to protect their disintegrating monopoly on education.

Notes

1. "The ABC's of Reform: Give Parents a Choice," *Insight*, 24 September 1990, 13.

2. Carol Innerst, "Parents Prefer Private Schools," *Washington Times*, 24 July 1991, A3.

3. "Worst Home School Bill in the Nation Introduced in Kansas," *Home School Court Report*, March/April 1991, 5. Also "Kansas Teacher Certification Bill Shelved," *Home School Court Report*, May/June 1991, 6.

4. Dr. Eric Hanushek, "The Impact of Differential Expenditures on School Performance," *Educational Researcher*, May 1990.

5. Dr. Sam Peavey, testimony at a hearing before the Compulsory Education Study Committee of the Iowa Legislature, 30 September 1988. Dr. Peavey made similar statements in an interview with *Insight* , 24 September 1990, 13.

6. "The ABC's of Reform: Give Parents a Choice," *Insight* , 24 September 1990, 13.

7. *Sheridan Road Baptist Church v. Department of Ed.*, 396 N.W. 2d 373, 419 fn. 64 (1986).

8. "The Research Basis for Performance-Based Teacher Education," *Review of Educational Research*, 44, 1974, 463-484.

9. See W. R. Hazard, L.D. Freeman *Legal Issues in Teacher Preparation and Certification*, ERIC, Washington, D.C. 1977; R. E. Flodan, "Analogy and Credentialing," *Action in Teacher Education*, Spring/Summer 1979; R. Howsam and D. C. Corrigan, *Educating a Profession* (Washington D.C., American Association of Colleges for Teacher Education, 1976).

10. "The 1990 Science Report Card: NAESP's Assessment of Fourth, Eighth, and Twelfth Graders," prepared by the Educational Testing Service for the National Center for Education Statistics, Office of Education Research and Improvement, U.S. Department of Education released March 1992.

11. "The ABC's of Reform: Give Parents a Choice," *Insight*, 24 September 1990, 13.

12. *Ibid.*, 17. See John Chubb and Terry Moe, *Politics, Markets, and American Schools* (Washington, D.C.:Brookings Institution, 1990), 202-205.

13. Dr. Brian Ray, "A Nationwide Study of Home Education: Family Characteristics, Legal Matters, and Student Achievement" (Seattle: National Home Education Research Institute, 1990), 53-54.

14. *Ibid.*, 53.

15. Dr. J. F. Jakestraw, "An Analysis of Home Schooling for Elementary School-age Children in Alabama," Doctoral dissertation at the University of Alabama, 1987.

16. Jon Wartes, "Washington Home School Research Project," Woodinville, Washington, 1987-1989.

17. "Home Schoolers Win EEE Case," *Home School Court Report*, January/February 1992, 1; *Lawrence v. South Carolina Board of Education*, 412 S.E.-2d 394 (1991).

18. See, e.g., Florida, F.S.A.§ 232.02 (4) (1982), and Florida Admin.Reg.6A-1.951 (1974); New Mexico, N.M.S.A.§ 22-10-3 (1981); Virginia, Virginia Code § 22.1-254 (1980); Washington, R.C.W.§ 28A.27.010 (1980); Iowa Code Ann. section 299.1 (1988); North Dakota Century Code section 15-34.1-04 (1987).

19. *In re Franz*, 55 A 2d 424, 427 (1977).

20. New Jersey Statutes Annotated § 18A:38-25.

21. *State v. Massa*, 231 A.2d 252, 256 (1967).

22. Ohio Rev. Code Ann. § 3321.04(A)(2).

23. See Ohio State Board of Education Administrative Code Chapter 3301-34.

24. *Ohio v. Whisner*, 47 Ohio St.2d 181, at 214 (1976), 351 N.E. 2d 750.

25. *Ibid.*, at 217.

26. *Sheridan Road Baptist Church v. Dept. of Ed.*, 396 N.W.2d 373, 421 (1986).

27. "Michigan High Court Accepts DeJonge Case," *The Home School Court Report*, Vol. 8, No. 1, July/August 1992, 1.

28. Ann. Ind. Code § 20-8.1-3-34.

29. *Mazenac* v. *North Judson-San Pierre School Corporation*, 614 F.Supp. 1152, 1160 (1985).

30. Ann. Law of Mass. ch. 76, §1.

31. *Care and Protection of Charles*, 504 N.E.2d 592, 602 (Mass. 1987).

32. *Ibid.*, 504 N.E.2d at 594, ftn. 2.

33. *Kentucky State Board* v. *Rudasill*, 589 S.W.2d 877, 884 (1977).

34. Dept. of Ed. Regs. 4140.2(D)(2).

35. S.D. Cod. Laws Ann. §13-27-3.

36. See *North Dakota* v. *Shaver* 294 N.W. 2d 883 (1980), *Nebraska* v. *Faith Baptist Church*, 301 N.W. 2d 571 (1981), and *Fellowship Baptist Church* v. *Benton*, 815 F.2d 485 (1987).

37. See Revised Stat. of Nebraska §79-1701(3); N.D. Century Code §15-34.1-03; and Iowa H.F. 455(1991).

CHAPTER 13

FIGHTING DIRTY:
INCREASE IN CHILD
WELFARE INVESTIGATIONS

"In too many cases, Child Protective Services cannot
distinguish real abuse from fabrication, abuse from neglect,
and neglect from poverty or cultural differences."[1]
-San Diego County Grand Jury

You are at home diligently teaching your children when you hear
an unwanted knock at the door. You hope it is just a salesman but you
know deep inside it is probably a public school official. You offer a
prayer, answer the door, and instead of only a truant officer, you find a
child welfare agent. The agent accuses you of child neglect and
demands entry into your home and insists on being allowed to

interrogate your children alone. When you refuse, the agent threatens to get a court order. But you are innocent! What should you do?

This scenario may sound dramatic, but this is exactly the type of contacts more and more home schoolers are receiving throughout the country. I have handled thousands of legal conflicts in the last seven years between home schoolers and the state, and this year there have been more child welfare and social service investigations than all of the previous years combined. I used to talk to a child welfare agent every other month, but now I talk to at least two agents every week.

Why is there such an increase in child welfare contacts? It seems apparent that some school districts are starting to play "hardball" with home schoolers. They see the child welfare and social service agencies as a "back door" way of closing down home schools. In several instances, I have tracked down referrals to child welfare agencies to the local principal or truant officer.

I believe another reason that more home schoolers are referred to social service is because of the availability of "child abuse hotlines" throughout the country. Although these "hotlines" can be used for a good purpose, they can also be used to harass home schoolers. Nasty neighbors who resent the fact that a particular family is home schooling can make an anonymous call to a "hotline" and fabricate some story about child abuse going on at the home of the home schooler. In most states, the child welfare worker has an obligation under law to investigate all referrals, even if based on an anonymous tip, within twenty-four or forty-eight hours. As a result, home schoolers are being subjected to some very intimidating confrontations with child welfare agents.

Of course, what makes child welfare and social service agents so intimidating is that, unlike truant officers, they are known to routinely take children from their parents.

In every instance so far of fabricated abuse or neglect, we have been successful, by God's grace, to resolve the investigations favorably by counseling the family or intervening directly with the child welfare agent. In fact, in HSLDA's entire history since 1983, we have never had any children taken from the home over home schooling, nor have any families ever had to stop home schooling.

Although we have been successful thus far, the intensity of contacts by social service agents is increasing. The harassment is continuing. In this chapter I will summarize some of the confrontations that innocent home schoolers have had with social workers in which I was involved, review the statistics that show the child welfare system is abusing the children, and offer some practical suggestions on how to handle visits by social workers.

Are Any States Safe from These Investigations?

I have found that home schoolers from both favorable and unfavorable states toward home schooling have experienced child welfare investigations. For example, in Georgia, normally a favorable state, one family who was following their religious convictions concerning home educating, was harassed by the local truant officer. After a while the truant officer decided to turn them over to a social worker for educational neglect. A group of families in another county was intimidated by a social worker who attempted to circumvent the home school law and impose illegal requirements on them. Another HSLDA member in Georgia was a single parent who lived in subsidized housing. Since she was poor, the social worker assumed she could not home school her children and even threatened to take the children.

In Colorado, a family was investigated by a social worker under somewhat bizarre circumstances. In the middle of the night, the family heard someone trying to break into their house. They called the police who came into the house to inspect the door to which forced entry was attempted. Instead of writing much of a report on the attempted burglary, the police officer started asking questions concerning the children. After he left he contacted a social worker to investigate the family for child abuse. The allegations were that clothes were seen lying around the house, dishes from the night before were still in the sink, and there was a strange odor in the house. With four children it was true that there were some clothes lying around, and the family had figured that they were too tired that night and, as a result, would do dishes in the morning. As for the odor, it was the middle of winter and the family had just had an Italian dinner that night. Sure sounds like major child abuse to me! I assume we all are child abusers if this constitutes child abuse.

In Virginia, a family was turned over to the child welfare even though they were operating under a religious exemption as allowed by statute. The child welfare agent tried to intimidate the family in order to meet with the children privately. I refused on behalf of the family, and I was able to convince a superior to convince the agent to close the case. In Oklahoma, a child welfare agent came to the door as the result of a neighbor turning the home school family over for child abuse because they were home schooling.

In Indiana and Illinois, home schoolers were reported to child welfare by neighbors who fabricated stories about child abuse. In Michigan, child welfare and social service agents are more plentiful than virtually any other state. On numerous occasions, home schoolers have been turned in to child welfare by their school officials who have been frustrated because they cannot prosecute them under the truancy laws.

In Kansas, the law requires that any child who is reported as "not in attendance at school" is automatically turned over to the local social service agency for possible educational neglect. Superintendents who do not recognize children in non-accredited schools which operate in the home as being in attendance at school, routinely turn them over to the social services for an investigation.

HSLDA has helped members in virtually every state who have been contacted by child welfare agents. Every one of these situations described above was linked to home schooling and served as a "back door" way of harassing home schoolers. Also every one of these situations was resolved without giving in to the social workers' frequent demands to enter the house or interview the children.

Fabricated Allegations against Home Schoolers

Nearly every type of allegation has been raised against home schoolers. Usually it is a combination of things. For example, a common allegation is neglect of education and an untidy house. Sometimes there are accusations that the children were seen regularly playing outside during school hours or seen playing outside at dusk. Many times there is an accusation of the children having "worn out" clothes. In some instances, spanking has been one of the allegations. Let me give you several true stories that serve as examples of various fabricated allegations against home schoolers that I have represented.

A home school father in Michigan was seen picking up his two-year-old child by her arm and taking her into the house while she was crying and was reported for child abuse. I set up a meeting with the social worker and counseled the family on what they should say. I told them to explain their religious convictions concerning raising their children from a "positive standpoint," avoiding Bible verses which spoke about the "rod." Instead, I told them to explain their beliefs emphasizing verses such as Matthew 18:6 which states that if you harm or offend a child, it is better that a millstone be tied around your neck and you are thrown into the deepest part of the ocean. In other words, their religious convictions demand that they do not do anything that will harm their children. When the family began presenting these religious beliefs to the agent, he became visibly uncomfortable and suddenly announced that he would close the case. He then abruptly left. This, by the way, is a valuable lesson to remember concerning what type of information about your religious beliefs you should share with a social worker.

Can We Be Investigated for Spanking?

The answer to that question is *yes!* However, there are ways to reduce the risk. Let me give you some actual examples.

In Colorado, a home schooler was reported after spanking a child in public. Someone had followed them to their car and wrote down the license plate. Based on this situation and many others, I recommend as a safety precaution that you never spank your children in public, no matter what the circumstance. Wait to discipline them at home, or you may find yourself the object of a full-scale investigation.

In Fairfax county, a pastor gave a seminar on child discipline which included spanking. A parishioner told that she had to discipline her child while a neighbor was visiting. She spanked the child in another room and then explained to the neighbor a little of what she learned from the pastor. The neighbor, who was against spanking, reported the pastor to the child welfare agency for "bruising their children and for twenty minute spanking sessions." The social worker who then initiated the investigation told me she thought she might have a religious cult on her hands that abuses children. I expressed my disbelief to the social worker that she was seriously investigating what an anonymous source claimed she heard from a person who heard it from another person. That is thrice removed hearsay! I told her that her evidence was very flimsy, and I set the parameters for a meeting.

In preparation for the meeting, I told the home schooling pastor and his wife not to recount any specific incidents of spanking, since the social worker had nothing on the family that would stand up in court. I told them that they should emphasize the positive verses such as Matthew 18:6. Since the social worker had no evidence, the only evidence she could acquire would be from what information she could gather from the pastor and his wife. Since the parents carefully avoided all specific examples and spoke in general terms, the social worker had to close the case.

Spanking has always been a biblical form of punishment and very successful, when properly and consistently applied to acts of disobedience (e.g. Proverbs 22:15, 23:13-14, and 29:15). It traditionally has been the best form of discipline when administered in love and followed by forgiveness.

Fortunately, no state has completely outlawed spanking, although various state adoption agencies require parents to not spank their adopted children. However, there has been a push by so-called "child rights advocates" to pass legislation to outlaw spanking. For instance, in 1992, H.R. 1522 was introduced in the U.S. House of Representatives to prohibit corporal punishment or infliction of "bodily pain upon a child as a form of punishment" for any organization or entity that receives federal funding. As of the printing of this book, this bill is still pending. If such a bill would pass, it would send a message across the states that spanking is wrong and should be regulated.

However, some state policies consider "excessive spanking" as abusive. The difference between normal spanking and excessive spanking is left to the discretion of each social worker. As a result, many social workers strongly disapprove of spanking entirely and will manipulate it into an incident requiring a full-scale investigation.

One HSLDA family had just moved to Alabama two weeks earlier and had not yet met anyone in their neighborhood. However, the Department of Human Resources agent received an "anonymous tip" that the children had "bruises" and demanded a strip search! When I refused to allow a strip search, the agent became upset and stammered, "No one else ever refused a strip search before!" She also implied that the family had something to hide. I had the family get a statement from their personal physician who verified that the children were fine, and the situation was resolved. In Kansas, another HSLDA family with similar allegations acquired their personal doctor's statement that everything was fine, but the social worker's supervisor rejected it. The supervisor threatened to get a warrant. We called his bluff and the situation was resolved, based on the family doctor's statement.

The comment of the social worker in Alabama above is a common response I hear from social workers frequently concerning their other demands. They are personally offended that we would refuse to let them into the home or interview the children. Many of them insinuate that the family must be guilty even though they have nothing but an anonymous tip.

Of all the child welfare workers who have threatened HSLDA members that they will obtain a search warrant or a court order to take the children, we have yet to see one actually come back with a search warrant. These social workers are so used to getting whatever they want from the families, that our choice to stand on the families' privacy and Fourth Amendment rights shocks them.

False Day-Care Center Allegations

Some home school families are turned over to the social service department for running "Day Care centers." For instance, in Florida, a social worker (HRS) watched a home school family's home, based on an anonymous tip that the family was running an illegal and unlicensed Day Care center. It turned out that all six children going in and out of the home were members of the same family! I guess this social worker did not know that home school families tend to have more than the national average of 1.8 children!

In Alabama, a home school mother was turned in to a social worker for running an unlicensed Day Care center because she started taking care of one infant, five days a week. She was threatened with a felony and the social worker wanted to come into the home. I discovered, as usual, that the social worker was stretching the truth, since running an unlicensed Day Care center was not a felony. However, in Alabama, anyone taking care of a child more than four hours a day and who is not a relative, must get a license! In order to avoid further investigation, the family chose to no longer watch the infant.

The False Allegation of "Lack of Supervision"

"Lack of supervision" or "children outside during school hours" is one of the most common allegations which accompanies educational neglect allegations against home schoolers. In Michigan, some particularly nasty neighbors looking for an excuse to get a home school family in trouble saw one of the children run outside one night. The neighbors called the child welfare agency and reported the incident as "lack of supervision." The social worker wanted to come into the home and talk with the children. We refused and explained that the child had only run out for a moment in order to get the cat that had escaped out the door.

Another Michigan home school family was reported by an anonymous tipster who claimed the children were not supervised, the children did not attend school, the boys ran around barefoot, an old rusty car was in their yard, the boys slept in the attic, and one boy liked to kill mice (can you believe that anyone would want to kill mice?). I talked with the child welfare agent who said she would prosecute the family for neglect and get a search warrant. She also wanted a special study done on the child who killed mice because she thought he might have a psychological problem. We were able to prove to the social worker that the children were being legally home-schooled, there was no rusty car in the yard (except their own functional, slightly rusty car parked in the driveway), and the children did not sleep in the attic. As far as lack of supervision, I told the agent the charge was false, and the children have the right to play in their own yard. In regard to killing mice coming from a nearby swamp, we had no apologies but wondered at the competence of the agent. As a result, the case was closed.

One home school family had recently moved to Florida. Within weeks, they were visited by a truant officer who questioned the legality of their schooling. The truant officer left and reported them to the Health and Human Services Department. A few days later, an HHS agent appeared at the door and demanded to interview the children within twenty-four hours or he would send for the police. The allegations were that "the children were home during school hours and the children were sometimes left alone." I explained the legality of their home schooling and denied the "lack of supervision" charge (the family only had one car and the father took it to work leaving the mother at home). I then called his bluff and refused to have the children interviewed. After talking with the parents, we allowed him to come by the door and only see the children from a distance. He ended up closing the case, since he had no evidence but an anonymous tip.

One really outlandish investigation of a home school family who was legally home schooling occurred in New Jersey. In the first visit, the agent from the Division of Youth and Family Services accused the mother of kidnapping some of her children because she had so many children. The mother produced birth certificates to prove that all the children were hers. The following year, another agent came by and said someone called and reported that the "children were seen outside during school hours." She demanded to enter the house, but the mother, under my instruction, refused. The agent then said she would be back with the police. She never came back that day, indicating that she was only bluffing. I called her and proved that the family was legally home schooling and the case was closed.

In California, a single mother was contacted by a social worker with allegations that "the children were not in school, the mother was incapacitated, and the caretaker was absent." I talked with the social worker and she admitted the allegations were based solely on an anonymous tip. However, she insisted on talking with the children separately. When I objected, she said that she would get a police officer, and that she did not need a warrant. We held our ground and she settled for a meeting with the mother and a witness only. The situation was resolved.

One mother in Michigan was visited about a month after her husband died, and the social worker alleged "the children were not in school and the house was a mess." I called the social worker, explained the legality of home schooling, and convinced her to close the case. In Kansas, an SRS worker contacted a home school family and demanded entrance to the home. She alleged children were "locked in basement and deprived of food." After the SRS agent, when asked, admitted that the allegations were made by their former maid, we were able to convince her that the allegations were fabricated by the maid as retaliation for being dismissed for doing lousy work. The social worker dropped the case.

Know Your Doctor!

It is important at this point to give you a warning about doctors. Doctors, like many other professionals, are duty-bound in nearly all states to turn in parents they suspect of child abuse. I have handled several situations in which doctors have reported home schoolers to the child welfare agency, either because they did not approve of home schooling or because the child had a bruise somewhere or a dislocated joint. Of course, children commonly get bumps and bruises, but that is not abuse.

The best way to avoid this potential problem is to know your doctors. If your doctor knows and trusts you, he will properly interpret bumps and bruises for what they are and use his discretion to *not* report you to the social service agency. Also use wisdom concerning each injury on whether it is necessary to bring the child to the doctor in the first place. If your child has a bruise that could be deemed suspicious by the doctor, wait another day or so to bring your child in.

I was helping my two-year-old child up the stairs, and her shoulder came out of the socket. I thought of taking her to the doctor but remembered a week earlier when I helped a home school father whose doctor reported him to child welfare agency because he had brought his daughter in for the same reason. I was especially concerned because we were in an HMO program and did not know which doctor would be assigned to help us. As a result, we opted on taking our daughter instead to our chiropractor with whom we were good friends. He quickly popped the shoulder back in and totally understood that it could happen to anybody.

A common allegation raised during flu season, along with educational neglect, is "lingering colds." This is another form of so-called abuse, of which I'm sure we would all be found "guilty." It is such a shame that our tax dollars have to pay for social workers who waste their time on such flimsy allegations. In all of these instances, the investigations were closed after we proved to the social workers that the children had visited a doctor recently.

Another allegation involving "health issues" which I will describe is the "thin child" accusation. For example, in Wisconsin, a home school family was reported by an anonymous tipster. I secured a copy of the report by the social worker which said:

> The caller was concerned because the children were all thin and thought that removal of food was possibly a form of discipline. The caller thought this discipline may have been a practice of the parents' religion which was thought to have been *Born Again*. The caller thought that these parents give a lot of money to the church and spend little money on groceries. The caller's last, somewhat passing concern, was that [the mother] home schools her children.

As usual, the anonymous tip was a complete fabrication. It is apparent from the report that the caller was biased against both the fact that the family was home schooling and that they were Christians. This is a common thread that I see often as I represent home schoolers facing social worker allegations.

Other Outlandish Allegations

A single mother in a low-income apartment in California was reported to the social service agency for a "child not in attendance at school" and a "messy house." The social worker came to her door and demanded entry. When she refused and asked for him to put his questions in writing, he left. Within the hour, however, he was back with a police officer who also demanded entry in order to "see if house was sanitary, child was fed, whether there was food in the house, and to ask the child a few questions." He also wanted to see proof of an education taking place.

The mother handed the phone out the door to the policeman and I told him he had no right to go into the home without a warrant, and he agreed. Over a forty-five-minute period, I kept talking to him and then to the mother to see if the situation could be settled. Meanwhile, the mother and daughter picked up around the house while I talked with the officer. I finally convinced the police officer to agree to not question their home schooling, talk with their daughter, or let the social worker do any searching in the home. Based on my assurances, he promised to only go in the house for one or two minutes and not to scrutinize it very closely. As a result, the family let the police officer in, and he was in and out in a few moments finding everything to be fine.

One of the most ridiculous allegations against a home school family that I ever heard was from a child welfare agent in Michigan who received an anonymous tip that the "mother was seen selling all her children's shoes and coats at a rummage sale." I asked the agent if he was serious, and he said it was his job to investigate all allegations. The mother obviously had only sold clothing that would no longer fit the children. The case was resolved after I let the agent stop by and see that the family did have coats and shoes for their children.

The last allegation I will mention is another example of how outlandish anonymous tipsters can become. A family in Texas was investigated by a social worker based on the following allegations: 1) children were not in attendance at school; 2) children were unsupervised and running around the neighborhood; 3) children were dirty and abused; and 4) the house may be used for drug trafficking, since people were seen frequently coming in and out of the house. The social worker demanded to interview the children (a six and seven-year-old) or she would be forced to seek a court order.

The social worker knew nothing about home schooling, and I was able to convince her to not pursue it any further. Concerning the other allegations, the mother was able to convince the social worker that they were false. The children had recess during the day but were always supervised and mostly played in their fenced yard. Occasionally, the boys would catch frogs in a nearby ditch and get a little muddy—hardly abnormal for little boys. The mother was a curriculum supplier and had people occasionally come by to pick up curriculum. So much for being a drug pusher! The mother stood firm and would not let her children be interviewed separately, in spite of threats by the social worker to obtain a court order. Finally, the social worker, having no evidence, closed the case.

How Social Workers Bluff and Intimidate Parents

When I talk to most lawyers, they seem to be afraid of social workers. Many have told me that if a social worker initiates an investigation against a family, that family needs to cooperate fully with those demands. However, I could not and still cannot stomach having the families voluntarily waive their constitutional rights. This is still America. Besides, I have heard of too many situations in which families outside of HSLDA let the social worker come into the house or talk to the children, and the social worker ended up gathering additional information which was interpreted as abuse. The results of some of these situations were the removal of the children from the home.

Bluffing and intimidation are common tactics of social workers. Time and time again, I have been faced with threats by social workers who say that the law gives them the authority to come into the home or requires them to be allowed to interview children. However, not one has been able to show me such a law. Most child abuse laws allow them to interview children *if* they obtain a court order, which usually can *only* be obtained *if* they have "good cause shown" or some sort of "probable cause." An anonymous tip, which is usually the only "evidence" a social worker has on a home school family, is neither adequate nor reliable. As a result, virtually all courts will not grant a warrant to enter the house or remove children. No social workers have shown me that they have the right, by their own authority, to enter a home against the parent's wishes.

Of course, if your child is in a public school or away from your home, social workers in most states have the authority to interview those children or remove them without parental consent. In those cases, parents are not notified of anything until the child is already placed in a juvenile home or a foster home. This is obviously another important advantage that home schoolers have over the child who is sent to the public schools.

Another way social workers routinely gain entry into families' homes is to intimidate or persuade the family to "voluntarily" allow them entrance. If they convince you to give them permission to enter, they then can claim that you waived your constitutional rights. We recommend to members of HSLDA that they never let social workers in who are investigating allegations against their family, *unless* they have a warrant signed by a judge. Then the families are instructed to immediately call HSLDA, and I or one of our other staff lawyers will call the social worker.

Many social workers will bring a police officer with them in order to intimidate families into cooperating and allowing them entry into the house. However, these police officers also have no authority to come into the home without a warrant. When I challenge social workers as to why they resorted to using these "strong armed" tactics, they give me all types of excuses. For example, one social worker brought a police officer to the home of an Alabama home schooler to convince her to stop home schooling. When I confronted the social worker, she said she brought the officer along for "protection" since the allegation described the home school mom as a "big woman." In Kansas, an SRS agent tried to gain entry to a home by bringing along a police officer. When I challenged her, she claimed she had only gotten a ride from the police because she was not familiar with the area.

Another problem I have discovered is that many social workers with whom I have dealt, have never even heard of the right of privacy and the Fourth Amendment right to freedom from unreasonable searches and seizures. Many do not understand what due process is or that a person is considered innocent until proven guilty. When, on these constitutional grounds, I challenge them in their assertion that they have the right to enter the home or interview the children, they try to deny that such rights even exist.

In Kansas, for instance, I dealt with a Social Rehabilitative Service's agent who insisted she had the right to come into the home school family's home. After I refused, she checked with her superior who admitted that she had no authority to enter the home. The SRS agent then explained that no one had ever refused her entry before.

How Social Worker Contacts Can Often Be Resolved

Below is the average scenario and recommended steps to follow which we explain to members of HSLDA. Each time an HSLDA family is contacted by a child welfare agent, they are first instructed to find out what the agent wants. At this time, we recommend that our members obtain the agent's business card.

The agent will frequently try intimidation to obtain entry. For example, the agent will say: "I have received allegations of child abuse and educational neglect. I need to come into your house right away and talk to your children. I am sure we can clear this all up today." If you refuse entry, the agent will sometimes threaten to obtain a court order. In our experience, it is usually a bluff, but, this is not always the case. Then the family will call HSLDA, and an attorney will either talk directly to the social worker outside the door, or if the agent has left, he will call him at his office. We have found that immediately opening the lines of communication will often slow things down and help prevent some of the horror stories which have involved removal of children.

When I receive calls from HSLDA members, I respond by calling the agent, finding out the allegations, and explaining the legalities of the family's home school. If I cannot resolve it over the phone (which I can normally do about 30 percent of the time), I will set the parameters for a meeting with the family. Although I will not allow the child to meet with the child welfare agent, on certain occasions the parents will meet with the agent according to the limitations I set up beforehand. In a few instances, I let the agent "see" the children from a distance but not talk to them. You never can be certain what the most intelligent of children might say or how the social worker could manipulate your child's words against you. It is just not worth the risk.

If a meeting is held, I spend a long time preparing the parents. I recommend that the children be sent over to a friend or relative's house. I always instruct the families to deny the specific allegation, speak in generalities, and keep the social worker on the subject. For example, if the allegation is about a messy house, do not answer questions about child discipline. Or if the agent asks, "Did you spank your child ten times with a belt buckle?" do not reply, "No, I only spanked him six times with a spoon." The social workers love these kind of responses because they did not have evidence to begin with and were "fishing." And now you have admitted to spanking your children with an instrument. You and I know that spanking is not wrong or illegal, but to some social workers it only affirms their suspicions and can be a factor to be used against you. Instead, your response should simply be, "No, that is absolutely false," and you should go on to explain your religious belief from Matthew 18:6, which prohibits you from ever harming your children. As the Bible states, we need to be wise as serpents and gentle as doves.

The reason we encourage members of HSLDA to not allow their children to be interviewed by social service agents are simply these: 1) parents do not have to let their children be interviewed unless there is an official warrant; 2) such interviews put the children through unnecessary and sometimes damaging trauma; and 3) many social service agents will not limit themselves to only asking about the specific allegations. For example, a family in Texas agreed to have their children interviewed about a simple allegation of "lack of supervision." Although the social worker agreed to limit her questions to only the supervision issue, she asked the children questions such as: "Do you like being home schooled?" "Do you get spankings?" "How often? Do your parents touch you in your private parts?" "How do they do it?"

These types of questions are completely offensive and they demonstrate that some social workers are on a "fishing expedition" to get home schoolers into trouble. The best protection parents have is to not let the social workers talk to the children.

More often than not, the child welfare agents are relying much more on intimidation rather than any substantial evidence. Nearly every single child abuse investigation of HSLDA families has been resolved without going to court, with every allegation being false or extremely exaggerated.

I should mention that you should carefully teach your children, especially rebellious ones, of the consequences of turning their parents in to the social services department. I have counseled several families over the years who had a rebellious teenager run away and make up allegations against their parents, simply to get attention. However, in every situation, once the teenager found out the tremendous amount of trouble he caused his brothers, sisters, and parents, and saw the conditions he was kept in at the juvenile or foster home, he regretted ever going to the social service department. Therefore, try to prevent such sad scenarios by teaching your children some of the stories above and some of the horrendous statistics below.

Warning: Every Child Abuse Case Is Different and the Information in This Chapter Is Not Intended to Be Legal Advice

Although this information and these stories are true, each social worker is different and each set of circumstances needs to be personally analyzed. I recommend membership with HSLDA or hiring separate legal counsel.

For example, some situations, due to "home-town" justice, have become quite severe. In California, the social workers and the police were so intent on interrogating a home-schooled child separately at the police station that they threatened our local counsel with "obstruction of justice," since he insisted on being present with the child. By God's grace, the child never did have to be interviewed.

In Alabama, HSLDA represented a home school family in the *Richards* case before the Alabama Court of Appeals. This involved a low-income home school mother who was contacted by a social worker over some allegations of child abuse and educational neglect. Under my counsel, the family refused to allow the social worker to come into the home or interrogate the children. In order to muscle this family, charges of child neglect were brought, based on no evidence whatsoever, but only on an anonymous tipster who admitted she did not have personal knowledge of the family's situation. Nevertheless, a hearing was held on whether an anonymous tip was enough to require the social worker to enter the home and interrogate the children. Following "home-town justice," the lower court agreed that it was and ordered the family, under contempt of court, to allow the social worker into the home and to interrogate the children.

Attorney Michael Farris of HSLDA appealed the decision to the Alabama Court of Appeals on the basis that the Fourth Amendment to the Constitution requires government officials to have "probable cause" (some kind of reliable evidence) in order to obtain entry into individuals' homes. He also requested a stay to stop the enforcement of the search warrant. On March 10, 1992, the Court of Appeals granted that stay which protected the family from additional harassment until the Court of Appeals ruled on the merits of the case.[2]

On August 28, 1992, the Alabama Court of Civil Appeals reversed the lower court decision and ruled:

> We suggest, however, that the power of the courts to permit invasions of the privacy protected by our federal and state constitutions, is not to be exercised except upon a showing of reasonable or probable cause to believe that a crime is being or is about to be committed or a valid regulation is being or is about to be violated. . . .
>
> The "cause shown" [in this case] was unsworn hearsay and could, at best, present a mere suspicion. A mere suspicion is not sufficient to rise to reasonable or probable cause.[3]

In short, this case clearly concludes that an anonymous tip is not sufficient for a social worker or court to order the parents to submit to a home visit or interrogation of their children. To our knowledge, this is the first appellate court case that significantly curtails the powers of the social service agents.

Therefore, I recommend you secure legal counsel if you ever find yourself being investigated by a social worker, or call HSLDA if you previously joined as a member.

Social Workers Themselves Expose the Abuse in the Child Welfare Agencies

Occasionally, I will talk with social workers who are fed up with the system and who willingly expose all its problems. When I called one social worker in Chicago who was investigating a home school family, we resolved the false allegation over the phone and then she proceeded to tell me the following information.

Well over 50 percent of all referrals to her child welfare agency are "unfounded." Unfortunately, she complained, many of the cases are deemed unfounded after families are broken apart and children are put in foster homes. She explained that many hospitals and health centers are in the "business" of "always" finding child abuse. She said they will conclude child abuse even if you bring them a salamander!

Expressing her concern about the new training of recently hired social workers, she said that younger social workers are encouraged to go on "fishing expeditions." In the old days, social workers tried to prove a reported family was innocent and considered the family innocent until proven guilty. Now the "system" operates on the principle that a family is "guilty" . . . period.

After seeing so many families broken up, so many careers destroyed, and so many children harmed by the system, she now refers to the child welfare system as "the child abuse industry." She said she was due to retire in the next year. Her frankness on the abuse of the system is particularly sobering and it confirmed my assumptions that I had developed in dealing with numerous social workers around the country.

I have had several other conversations with social workers from various states who have developed the same opinion of their work. For instance, a social worker with whom I resolved a fabricated allegation concerning a home schooler, confessed that 90 percent of all the cases of alleged child abuse she handled turned out to be "unfounded." She explained that she spent most of her time "spinning her wheels." She felt the number of false allegations coming into her office was on the rise.

In Alabama and Florida, I met two recently resigned social workers who were now home schooling their children. Both admitted intimidation was a routine procedure they were taught and always used to get their way. Their goal, in fact, was to get into the house and talk with the children, no matter what the allegation. They would regularly demand entry and act as if they had the right to come in on their own authority. If the parent still was not fooled into voluntarily allowing them in, they would threaten to get a policeman. One ex-social worker told me, "If I ever had a social worker come to my door who acted like I did, I would be scared stiff and probably comply with their demands!" She also said that no judges she knew would ever sign a search warrant or issue an order to take a child based on only an anonymous tip. Both of these social workers admitted 60 percent to 70 percent of their cases were "unfounded."

I will relate one more conversation I had with a social services worker in Michigan who is also a home school father and a member of the local school board. He said that he had been working as a social worker for years, and he has seen much change. He said that social workers have become much more aggressive and eager to go on "fishing expeditions." He agreed with the description of the system that I learned from the other social workers. He said that many social workers use intimidation and deception.

I asked him how long "unsubstantiated" claims stay on the record, and he said sometimes five years and sometimes longer. He said a family whose case was rendered unfounded had a right to have their records "expunged" or erased. However, he warned me not to trust social workers to expunge records, because they usually will not. He recommended going to their office and personally watching the file being destroyed.

I asked him if the individual being investigated has a right to request a copy of their file or to see their file. He affirmed they could do this, but social workers will often refuse on the grounds that the information in the file is "confidential." At that point, he said, the social worker is bluffing. If a person just evokes the "Freedom of Information Act," the social worker is required by law to show him the records in the case file.

However, social workers still have tricks to prevent you from seeing the file they might have on you concerning an "unfounded" allegation. One home school family in Indiana was investigated by a social worker because the mother was home schooling and her children were supposedly left "unattended." After some negotiation, the case was closed. I asked for the records to be expunged and for the mother to get a copy. The mother went down to the social service office to get a copy of the file and to watch the file be destroyed, and the social worker claimed she could not find the file! It is a shame that the social workers are free to damage people's reputations and to keep on file unfounded claims.

As discussed earlier, one of the key problems contributing to the abuse of the child welfare system is the "child abuse hotlines," which can be used anonymously. In effect, the falsely accused person never has a right to face his accuser but still has to suffer through a full-scale investigation by the social service agency, which could result in his children being taken away. You would think this only happens in Communist countries such as China or North Korea!

Legislation needs to be introduced throughout the country to require all tipsters who call hotlines to identify themselves. Also a heavy criminal penalty or fine needs to be enacted which would be imposed on any tipsters who fabricate allegations. Possible language could be: "No allegations received on child abuse hotlines or in any other manner can be investigated by the child welfare agency unless the source of the allegations is identified and proven reliable. If such allegations are deemed false, the informant shall be subject to charges of fraud and a fine or jail sentence shall be imposed by a court of law."

Such a bill would significantly stop the endless flow of calls to child welfare agencies which are made out of malicious intent (between 50 percent to 90 percent of all the allegations). This would save endless hours of "wild goose chases" by social workers so that they could investigate *real* child abusers instead of innocent families.

Another alternate provision to have enacted in your state would be a provision that would clearly state: "An anonymous tip is not sufficient evidence by which a judge may grant an order to remove children from the home or to grant a search warrant." Such safeguards are badly needed throughout the country.

Studies and Statistics Prove the Widespread Abuse Within the Child Welfare System

Some individuals have criticized me for being too "black and white" on this issue, and maybe a little "hyper." My response is that my experience, keeping social workers away from the children of home schoolers and out of their houses, is nothing compared to the horror stories that happen regularly to others outside membership with HSLDA. The statistics, studies, and books exposing this "child abuse industry," are quite numerous.

For example, the San Diego County Grand Jury issued a fifty-six page report based on a seven month investigation and interviews with more than 250 social workers, therapists, attorneys, judges, doctors, and families.[4] The discovery was shocking.

The Grand Jury found San Diego's child protection system to be "out of control, with few checks and little balance." The Grand Jury found that the system has developed a mind-set that child abuse is rampant and its structure and operation are "biased toward proving allegations instead of finding the truth." The jury declared:

> The burden of proof, contrary to every other area of our judicial system, is on the alleged perpetrator to prove his innocence. . . .
>
> [Social workers rarely try] to find information favorable or evidence exculpatory to the parents. Instead [they] appear to undertake investigations with a bias toward finding facts to support detention or removal and report only that information that justifies detention.[5]

Constitutional rights are ignored and the family has virtually no protection. The Grand Jury reported, "In too many cases, Child Protection Services cannot distinguish real abuse from fabrication, abuse from neglect, and neglect from poverty or cultural differences."[6]

Furthermore, the Grand Jury heard testimony that 20 to 60 percent of the children in the system do not even belong there! After reviewing 300 child abuse cases, the Grand Jury concluded that 250 of the cases need corrective action or reopening.[7] This is a lot of innocent families, as high as 60 percent, whose children should never have been removed from their parents in the first place.

The Grand Jury found that "some social workers routinely lie even when under oath in court." Also numerous times social workers will disobey or ignore court orders.[8]

The jury also discovered that every aspect of the system is in the business of confirming "child abuse," even if it is not there. The county counsel, judges, therapists, and hospitals all work together against the parents:

> County counsel, which represents Child Protection Services in court hearings, "has not been screening cases adequately." In fact, the jury said, screening deputies are pressured "to file petitions on cases which are questionable."
>
> The Juvenile Court system, which should be the ultimate check in the system, "is not fulfilling its role." The jury found that the court does not appear "to offer an even playing field in which the judicial officer serves as a neutral arbiter of the facts."[9]
>
> Rarely, the jury said, does a judge demand a "high standard of performance" from the Social Services staff. The judges "are viewed and appear to view themselves as pro-child which translates to pro-DSS," it said.[10]
>
> Therapists reported that "as long as they are in agreement with the social worker, their reports are given great weight.

> On the other hand, if they disagree with the social worker, their recommendations may not even appear in the report to the court" the Grand Jury said.[11]

> The report also charged that the Center for Child Protection (CCP) at Children's Hospital, which examines most of the local children suspected of being abused, has lost its objectivity. "A highly respected (appellate court) jurist testified that this lack of objectivity within the CCP has poisoned the stream. He felt that much of the bias and even zealotry found in the child dependency system could be traced back to training conferences and meetings at the behest of the Center for Child Protection."

> The jury also found that "patently erroneous testimony" by center physicians "played a significant role" in several cases in which children were removed from their homes.[12]

This is a travesty. The child welfare system has turned into a system which literally abuses children. In San Diego, like many other communities, once your children are taken, justice can rarely be found in the system.

I might make mention of a nonprofit organization called the Victims of Child Abuse Legislation (VOCAL) which was started by parents who unjustly had their children removed from their homes over false allegations. It is developing chapters throughout the country for the purpose of promoting legislation which would reform the child welfare system to prevent the widespread abuse such as is happening in San Diego.[13] You may want to consider supporting their efforts and request their newsletter.

The statistics of the abuse of children by the child welfare system go on virtually endlessly. Putting children in foster care is becoming routine, even though the studies show that the children would be better off at home, especially when so many of the allegations turn out to be false.

> Professionals estimate that 35 to 70 percent of children who end up in foster care should not be there and can be severely damaged psychologically by the experience. "Research over the past 40 years says that if you remove the child from the home, you traumatize the child more than he is already hurt," says Charles P. Gershenson, former chief of research and evaluation of the Children's Bureau of the U.S. Department of Health and Human Services.[14]

Still increasing numbers of children are routinely being removed from homes with little to no evidence of wrong doing. A report from the National Commission on Family Foster Care documents that there are presently 340,000 children being raised outside the homes of their natural parents, up from 225,000 in 1985.[15]

There are approximately 2.4 million *reports* of child abuse each year. Experts conclude that at least 1 million of those reports are erroneous or did not involve risks that could lead to foster placement.[16]

In one county alone—Cobb County, Georgia—I discovered that in 1991, the local Child Protection Services received 4,196 reports of child abuse. Of that total of reported cases only 879 were confirmed. I learned of this information while I was arguing with a child welfare worker who was investigating a home school family. The worker would not understand why we would not allow her into the home or speak with the children. I told her the family was innocent and was being harassed due to false allegations. After she told me the Cobb County statistics, I told her she had just proven my point.

In New Hampshire, the Department of Child and Youth Services (DCYS) data shows that in 1991 there were 6,434 abuse reports. Believe it or not, 5,524 of those reports turned out to be *false!* This means that 86.2 percent of all child abuse reports were false. The statistics over the last eight years show that the number of founded cases is dropping and yet the number of false child abuse reports is rising. In 1984, 54 percent of the child abuse reports turned out to be false. There were 3,855 abuse reports of which 1,814 were founded and 2,041 were false. In 1990, 86 percent of the child abuse reports were found to be false. There were a shocking 5,616 abuse reports, with only 709 which were proven to be founded or legitimate abuse allegations, and 4,907 turned out to be false child abuse reports![17] The system is out of control. Many thousands of innocent families are being abused by the system.

In 1985, a comprehensive study on the abuse of the child welfare system was done by Dr. Douglas Besharov of the American Enterprise Institute for Public Policy Research. His study was published as an article in the *Harvard Journal of Law and Public Policy.* He concludes:

> Much of the present high level of intervention is unwarranted and some is demonstrably harmful to the children and families involved. More than sixty-five percent of all reports of suspected child maltreatment—

involving over 750,000 children per year—turn out to be
"unfounded." . . . The present level of overreporting is
unreasonably high and is growing rapidly. There has been a
steady increase in the number and percentage of
"unfounded" reports since 1976, when approximately only
thirty-five percent of reports were "unfounded.".[18]

Since Besharov's study, the situation has only worsened with
record numbers of families falsely reported for child abuse.

Two important books have been published in the last few years
which confirm much of the reports above and provide important
documentation of the frequent abuses of the modern child welfare
system: *Wounded Innocents* by Richard Wexler (1990)[19] and *The Child
Abuse Industry* by Mary Pride (1989).[20] If I had read these books *before*
I played "hardball" with social workers, I would have been paralyzed
with fear. The thousands of true accounts of the breaking up of
innocent families and the mental, emotional, and physical abuse of
innocent children by the child welfare system will make it difficult to
believe that this really happens in America. However, we must wake
up to the fact that this does happen in America, and we need to do
something about it.

The Child Abuse Industry begins by documenting that over one
million families annually are falsely accused of child abuse. These, of
course, are only the ones who had the money and knowledge to fight
back. Mary Pride shows how many laws are written so vaguely that
virtually anyone could be found guilty of child abuse and many times
are. She documents that every state has set up "hotlines" to take calls
from anonymous tipsters. These same laws protect malicious callers
from lawsuits or prosecution. She demonstrates with case after case
that families accused of child abuse are routinely denied the right to
due process or a fair trial. She shows that social workers regularly
ignore families' constitutional rights and take children from public
schools and come into your home, if you will let them.[21]

In the other well-documented book, *Wounded Innocents*, Wexler
warns:

The war against child abuse has become a war against
children. Every year, we let hundreds of children die, force
thousands more to live with strangers, and throw a million
innocent families into chaos. We call this "child
protection."[22]

That is quite an indictment! He demonstrates that the hotlines have become a "potent tool for harassment." He shows how untrained, inexperienced, and sometimes incompetent social workers are allowed to label parents as "child abusers" and remove the children entirely on their own authority. He states, through the child abuse laws, "We have effectively repealed the Fourth Amendment, which protects both parents and children against unreasonable searches and seizures." He shows that the child welfare system often denies due process to the "accused" child abusers.[23]

When dealing with the question "What is neglect?," Wexler answers: "Anything a child saver [social worker] wants it to be." He gives scores of examples of outlandish allegations that innocent families are confronted with and which result in removal of their children.

Wexler shoots holes in the child welfare system's claims that two million children are abused each year and that is why they must be so aggressive. In actuality, that number represents only the *reported* cases. Over half of the reported cases are false. In fact, in 1987 there were 1,306,800 *false* child abuse reports. Sexual maltreatment, which is commonly argued for the need to increase the power of social workers, only makes up 15.7 percent of all reports! Minor physical injury constitutes only 13.9 percent and severe physical injury only constitutes 2.6 percent.[24]

> This means for every 100 reports alleging child abuse:
> -at least fifty-eight are false
> -twenty-one are mostly poverty cases
> -six are sexual abuse
> -four are minor physical abuse
> -four are unspecified physical abuse
> -three are emotional maltreatment
> -three are "other maltreatment"
> -one is major physical abuse.[25]

After he shows that the "child abuse panic" is a myth and an excuse to give unconstitutional powers to the social service agencies, he documents the terrible abuse children receive in foster homes and juvenile homes. The true accounts and statistics are sobering and shocking. In Kansas City, a study was done showing that 57 percent of children in foster care to have been placed in "high risk of abuse or neglect" situations."[26]

I could go on with the statistics, but I recommend that you read the two books mentioned above for further proof of the abusive child welfare system. Something needs to be done to protect innocent families from this system which is out of control.

This Is Spiritual Warfare

It is clear that home schoolers are under attack: but it is more than a physical attack, it is a spiritual attack.[27] The Scriptures tell us: "Put on the full armor of God that you may be able to stand firm against the schemes of the devil. For our struggle is not against flesh and blood, but against the rulers, against the powers, against the world forces of this darkness, against the spiritual forces of wickedness in the heavenly places" (Ephesians 6:11-12).

The home schooling movement is primarily a Christian revival taking place through education of our youth. Satan has a good thing going in the public school system since the courts have censored God and His principles and values from the public schools. But home schooling, as far as Satan is concerned, is out of control. There is no uniform way to censor all God's truth out of the home school textbooks or forbid the home school parents from comprehensively applying God's principles to each and every subject they teach to their children. The home school children are going to be the leaders of tomorrow who not only *believe* as Christians but *think* as Christians and are fully equipped to communicate God's truths in every area of life.

Furthermore, home schooling is strengthening the Christian family. That is also something Satan has been trying to undermine throughout our country. As a result, this attack should be expected. Home schoolers have been making great gains legislatively and have been prospering academically and growing spiritually. Now Satan is lashing back.

Let us remember, "The weapons of our warfare are not of the flesh, but divinely powerful for the destruction of fortresses. We are destroying speculations and every lofty thing raised up against the knowledge of God, and we are taking every thought captive to the obedience of Christ" (2 Corinthians 10:4-5). As we teach our children, let us take *every* thought captive to the obedience to Jesus Christ so our children will make a difference for God in this world. As we face conflict and harassment from the state authorities, let us count it a privilege to suffer persecution for Christ's sake as we are faithful to God's call. Pray that this spiritual battle with its physical consequences may be won.

I have written this chapter, not to create fear, but to make you aware of a real and growing problem, so that you will be motivated to pray for God's protection for home schoolers and work for legislative change to end the abuse of the social welfare system. An actual example of a family who was overly fearful was a home school family I talked to in Michigan. Since the family was afraid that someone would turn them in to the authorities, they followed a routine every week. Every Sunday evening they would pack one of their cars with empty suitcases, load the children in the car, and the mother would drive the car away to an appointed spot a few blocks away. Then, under the cover of darkness, the mother and children would sneak back into the house and remain there all week without leaving. The father, of course, would still go back and forth to work. The mother covered all the windows with thick black cloth so no light could be seen in the house in the evening before the father would come home. Then every Friday afternoon, the children and mother would sneak back to their car and drive back to their home and unload the car as if they were just coming back from being on a trip all week. This family apparently did this one whole school year out of fear.

This was certainly an extreme reaction, but it illustrates an important lesson: We should not live in fear. Instead, we need to put our trust in the Lord and act wisely. In 1 Peter 3:13-14, it says:

> And who is there to harm you if you prove zealous for what is good? But even if you should suffer for the sake of righteousness, you are blessed. And do not fear their intimidation, and do not be troubled.

God will honor those who honor Him.

Notes

1. *Families in Crisis: Report #2*, a 56 page report by the 1991-92 San Diego County Grand Jury, after 7 months of investigation of the Child Protective Services.

2. *The Home School Court Report*, Vol. 8, No. 2, March/April 1992, 1.

3. *H. R. v. Department of Human Resources*, No. 2910279, Alabama Court of Civil Appeals, 28 August 1992, 6. In February, 1993, the Alabama Supreme Court upheld the Court of Appeals decision by refusing to reconsider the case on appeal.

4. Okerblom and Wilkens, "Child Protection System Ripped," *The San Diego Union Tribune*, 7 February 1992, A-1 and A-19. This article summarizes "Families in Crisis: Report #2," A report by the 1991-92 San Diego County Grand Jury.

5. *Ibid.*

6. *Ibid.*

7. *Ibid.*

8. *Ibid.*

9. *Ibid.*

10. Abrahamson, "Child Protection System in S.D. Scored by Grand Jury," *The Los Angeles Times*, 7 February 1992, p. A-1 and A-28 through A-29. This article summarizes *Families in Crisis: Report #2*, A report by the 1991-92 San Diego County Grand Jury.

11. *Ibid.*

12. Okerblom and Wilkens, *San Diego Union Tribune*, 7 February 1992, A-19. This article summarizes the Grand Jury's report.

13. Victims of Child Abuse Legislation, P.O. Box 7653 Vallejo, California 94590.

14. Daniel Kagan, "Saving Families Fosters Hope For America's Troubled Youth," *Insight*, 29 April 1991, 16.

15. *Ibid.*

16. *Ibid.*

17. "Is DCYS Running Out of Abusers?" *Christian Home Schooling News*, Vol. 2, No. 4, April/May 1992, Manchester, New Hampshire, 3.

18. Douglas Besharov, "Doing Something About Child Abuse: The Need to Narrow the Grounds for State Intervention," *Harvard Journal of Law and Public Policy*, Vol. 8, 1985, 556.

19. Richard Wexler, *Wounded Innocents: The Real Victims of the War Against Child Abuse* (Buffalo, NY: Prometheus Books, 1990).

20. Mary Pride, *The Child Abuse Industry* (Westchester, Ill: Crossway Books, 1989).

21. *Ibid.*, 13-14. The rest of the book describes hundreds of actual incidences of abuse of children by social workers.

22. Wexler, *Wounded Innocents*, 14.

23. *Ibid.*, 15.

24. *Ibid.*, 86-88.

25. *Ibid.*, 87.

26. *Ibid.*, 198.

27. For an insightful, though fictional analysis of the spiritual battle taking place for our children, I recommend reading *Piercing the Darkness* by Frank Peretti, available through Great Christian Books, 1-302-999-8317.

Q: WHICH SITUATION HAS NEVER RESULTED IN A CHILD ABUSE INVESTIGATION?

1 KIDS (GASP!) LEARNING AT HOME.

2 KIDS PLAYING (OH MY!) IN THE YARD.

3 DISHES (MY GOODNESS!) IN THE SINK.

4 PUBLIC SCHOOL-BASED HEALTH CLINIC.

A: **4** (!)

CHAPTER 14

OPEN FOR INSPECTION:
THE ILLEGALITY OF HOME VISITS

"It is our view that both the Fourth Amendment and also the constitutionally derived right to privacy and autonomy which the U.S. Supreme Court has recognized, protect individuals from unwanted and warrantless visits to the home by agents of the state."[1]

A frequent problem home schoolers face throughout the country is that in which certain school districts unilaterally impose a "home visit" requirement on home schoolers. Home schoolers who refuse to allow home visits are "disapproved" and often charged with criminal truancy. Usually under a home visit requirement, a school official can visit a home school at anytime, observe instruction in the home, inspect facilities, and demand certain changes.

Nearly all of these school districts which have home visit requirements are in states where the education statutes *do not mandate* home visits. In other words, the various state legislatures have never delegated this authority to school districts in the first place. In fact, the last state in the entire country, South Dakota, which still authorized school districts, by statute, to conduct home visits, finally repealed this burdensome requirement in 1993.

The teacher unions, however, are regularly lobbying for heavier restrictions on home schoolers, including home visits. For instance, in the Spring of 1991, L.D. 888 was introduced in the Maine Legislature, which would have required home schoolers to submit to monthly home visits in order to "ensure that a level of academic instruction comparable to in-school instruction is being provided." The bill would have also given the state authority during these "inspections" to "determine whether the equivalent home instruction program should be continued, altered, or terminated." I testified at the legislative hearing along with many home schoolers resulting in the bill being killed in committee.

The purpose of this chapter, therefore, is to demonstrate that home visits of home schoolers should not be practiced or legislated in any state because they are inherently *unconstitutional* for four basic reasons.

Home Visits Violate the Fourth Amendment and the Right to Privacy

First of all, home visits are a violation of the home school families' *right to privacy* and their right to be free from warrantless searches and seizures as guaranteed by the *Fourth Amendment*.

On August 7, 1986, in *Kindstedt v. East Greenwich School Committee*,[2] the practice of home visits was struck down, setting precedent for the entire state. This case involved the Kindstedt family who was "disapproved" by the local school board solely because they refused to "bow the knee" and submit to home visits. I talked with the authorities on their behalf, showing them that the family was providing an excellent education and that such mandated home visits were unconstitutional. The school board refused to budge, so we appealed the case to the commissioner of education who held a formal hearing and wrote an extensive written opinion in favor of the family. The Commissioner held,

> "It is our view that both the Fourth Amendment and also the constitutionally derived right to privacy and autonomy which the U.S. Supreme Court has recognized, protect individuals from unwanted and warrantless visits to the home by agents of the state."[3]

Furthermore, he stated,

> "In view of the legal and constitutional considerations, we are unable to perceive any rationale whereby a home visitation requirement would be justifiable under circumstances such as these."[4]

It is clear from this decision that home visitation cannot be mandated by public school officials over parental objection. The privacy of the parents, family and home is at stake. Such privacy of the parents was protected in the United States Supreme Court in *Griswold v. Connecticut*.[5]

A school official can only inspect a home schooler's home if the family voluntarily allows them to come in or if the state official has a warrant or court order signed by a judge. Any home school family who does not want to voluntarily participate in home visits cannot be required to do so without violating their Fourth Amendment and privacy rights.

It is a fundamental principle of due process that if a government official comes into one's home for the purpose of making a determination of whether or not a criminal law is being complied with, then such an intrusion into the home is a search within the meaning of the Fourth Amendment. Since violation of the compulsory attendance law is a crime, a home visit by a public school official to determine compliance with the law is a violation of the home schooler's Fourth Amendment rights.

A home visit by a public school official to inspect a home school is equal to a "warrantless search" since it invades the privacy of the home. The U.S. Supreme Court stated: "Except in such special circumstances, we have consistently held that the entry into a home to conduct a search or make an arrest is unreasonable under the Fourth Amendment unless done pursuant to a warrant."[6] It seems apparent that home visits are unconstitutional.

Many school district officials expect their "requirement" for home visits to be complied with readily and without question. If a family will not agree to such an invasion of privacy, the school officials often wrongly assume that the home schooler is trying to hide something. The school officials believe that such a visit is an "inconsequential" request. However, the framers of the Constitution secured, for all citizens, protection from these types of arbitrary state intrusions. The U.S. Supreme Court makes clear their intent:

> Though the proceeding in question is divested of many of the aggravating incidents of actual search and seizure, yet, as before said, it contains their substance and essence, and effects their substantial purpose. It may be that it is the obnoxious thing in its mildest and least repulsive form; but illegitimate and unconstitutional practices get their first footing in that way, namely, by silent approaches and slight deviations from legal modes of procedure. This can only be obviated by adhering to the rules that constitutional provisions for the security of person and property should be liberally construed. A closed and literal construction deprives them of half their efficacy, and leads to gradual depreciation of the right, as if it consisted more in sound than in substance.[7]

Home schoolers are constitutionally justified to refuse warrantless searches such as home visits. There is neither statutory or constitutional authorization for parents to open their houses to public school officials.

Home Visits Violate the Fifth Amendment Right to Due Process

During the last several years, two states, New York and Pennsylvania, engaged in home visits of home schools even though such a requirement was not specifically mandated by law. In both states the practice of home visits was abruptly discontinued by case precedent and subsequent legislation.

In New York, two county court decisions, *In the Matter of Dixon*[8] and *In the Matter of Standish*,[9] both held home visits to be unconstitutional. In *Dixon*, the court held:

> This Court firmly believes that the insistence of the Hannibal Central School District authorities to effect the desired on-site inspection was arbitrary, unreasonable, unwarranted, and violative of the Respondents' [home

school parents] due process rights guaranteed under the Fifth Amendment of the Constitution of the U.S. The school district cannot expect to put itself in the position of conducting the inspection and then turning around and impartially or objectively determining whether the program subject to that inspection meets the required criteria for valid home instruction.[10]

Regarding protection from self-incrimination, the court explained:

The Respondents, further, cannot reasonably be put in a situation where they in effect are being forced to give evidence that might be used against them at a future date.[11]

The court concluded that the home visit requirement is both "unconstitutional" and "unenforceable." This reasoning of the decision was confirmed in *In the Matter of Standish.*

In order to cure the vagueness in the New York compulsory attendance law, the State Education Department issued "Regulations of the Commissioner of Education" for home schooling. The regulations give the local school boards no authority to conduct home visits (unless a home school is on probation), thereby ending the practice of routine home visits in the state of New York.

In Pennsylvania, at least one quarter of the 501 school districts were mandating home visits although not required by law. The HSLDA, as a result, sued eleven school districts for violating the civil and constitutional rights of the home schoolers. The federal court ruled in favor of the home schoolers in *Jeffery v. O'Donnell*[12] and declared the law "unconstitutional for vagueness." The legislature subsequently passed §13-1327.1 in 1988 which clearly ended the practice of home visits.

It is important to add that certain school districts in South Carolina also sought to impose home visits on home schoolers even though not mandated in the law. On February 27, 1989, the attorney general said that such a practice of mandatory home visits was prohibited by the intent of law:

Because the amendments do not expressly provide for an on-site visit and because the only reference to the site is the "description" of the place of instruction, a reasonable reading of the whole statute (*Sutherland Statutory Construction*, Volume 2A, sec. K6.05) indicates that the legislature's intent was not to authorize blanket requirements for on-site visits.[13]

In conclusion, where home visits are not clearly mandated by law, local school district policies that have tried to impose such requirements are routinely found to be arbitrary, unreasonable, unwarranted, a violation of the Fifth Amendment, not the intent of the legislature, unconstitutional, and, in several instances, based on unconstitutionally vague laws.

Home Visits Violate Establishment of Religion Clause

The home visitation requirement also violates the First Amendment prohibition of establishment of religion. Approximately 85-90 percent of home schoolers are operating home schools based on their religious convictions. In effect, these families are operating religious schools in their homes.

In *Aguilar v. Felton*,[14] the U.S. Supreme Court held that the establishment clause bars the use of federal funds to send public school teachers and other professionals into religious schools to carry on instruction *or* to provide clinical and guidance services. The Court further ruled that use of state and federal aid to assist religious schools violated the establishment clause by creating an *excessive entanglement* of church and state, since the aid was provided in a pervasively sectarian environment.

In addition, the aid, which was in the form of public school teachers and professionals, required an ongoing public inspection in order to insure the absence of a religious message. This inspection would require pervasive state presence in the religious schools who utilized the advice of these public school teachers. Justice Powell went so far as to say that such guidance by public school teachers in religious schools constituted direct state subsidy to those schools.

The Court specifically condemned the fact that "agents of the state must visit and inspect the religious school regularly."[15] It also found unconstitutional that religious schools "must endure the ongoing presence of state personnel whose primary purpose is to monitor teachers and students."[16]

Most local home visit provisions give the local public school system the right to come into the religious home school, review their religious instructional materials, discuss the families' religious instructional program, and observe the actual instruction. This service is provided with the use of state and federal money. Since many home schools are pervasively religious schools engaged in pervasively religious instruction, such home visits and their subsequent cost to the state constitute *excessive entanglement with the religious home schools*.

In the sensitive area of First Amendment religious freedoms, *the burden is on the school district* to show that implementation of home visits will not ultimately infringe upon and entangle it in the affairs of a religion to an extent which the Constitution will not allow.[17]

Furthermore, the home visits are not an end in themselves, but they are part of a regulatory scheme likely to lead to official efforts to alter the operations of that religious home school. In some instances, the home visit results are used to close down the home school. Such entanglement by the school district is excessive and severely condemned by the U.S. Court.

Home Visits Are Not the Least Restrictive Means

The requirement of home visits effectively denies a majority of parents their *fundamental* rights to teach their own children which is guaranteed by the U.S. Constitution.

First, the Fourteenth Amendment guarantees all citizens the right to liberty. The U.S. Supreme Court in a long line of cases has interpreted this right of liberty to include the concept of parental liberty. The Fourteenth Amendment right is described in detail in chapter 17. This fundamental right of parents to teach their children is guaranteed because they are parents, *not* because they have been specifically "approved" by a local school official during a home visit.

Secondly, the First Amendment guarantees all citizens and families the right to freely exercise their religious beliefs. At least 85 to 90 percent of all home schoolers believe they must home school in order to be faithful to their religious convictions. These families believe they have been called by God to personally teach their own children, applying God's Word to every subject. They believe they cannot delegate this authority to either a public or private school because they would be violating God's command.

All home schoolers who are home schooling for religious reasons, therefore, are prohibited from exercising their First Amendment rights by the requirement of home visit. Their religious convictions will not allow them to be visited in their home by a public school official.

All of the above First Amendment claims demand the application of the well-known *compelling interest test* established by the U.S. Supreme Court, as discussed in chapter 17 of this book. This test demands that the state prove, with evidence, that home visits are *necessary* for children to be educated and, secondly, that home visits are the "least restrictive means" for the state to protect its interest in education.

Not a single study exists that proves home visits are necessary for children to be educated. Hundreds of thousands of parents are doing just fine without them. Secondly, only one state out of fifty mandates home visits by statute, and many of those states, such as Wisconsin, Montana, Wyoming, Missouri, and Mississippi, have no monitoring requirements of any kind. Home visits, therefore, are hardly the least restrictive means of regulating education.

Conclusion

Mandatory home visits are clearly unconstitutional for many reasons. However, if the school official has a warrant signed by a judge that allows him to come into the home, the home schoolers have no choice but to allow him entrance. This, of course, is very rare, since very few school officials or child welfare workers will have warrants. Since its inception in 1983, the HSLDA has never had one of its 28,000-member families faced with an official warrant to search their home as a result of home schooling. However, there have been hundreds of threats each year.

Furthermore, a home schooler can *voluntarily* allow a school official into the house, but such visits are risky and can cause untold trouble for the family. The public school official may see something in the home schooler's house or in the curriculum which he does not like, and another battle begins. In fact, I know of cases, not involving HSLDA members, where home schoolers voluntarily let the official into their homes. In these instances, the official found something else objectionable, though minor, and referred them to the local child welfare agency. The children were taken out of the home for months. If the official had never been allowed entrance into the home, he would have nothing on the family and would have closed the case. Most of the time, officials are operating on anonymous tips, which in most jurisdictions can never form a basis for a warrant.

The best policy, therefore, is to avoid home visits altogether and keep school officials out of homes of home schoolers. It is also important to fight any legislation that would impose such a requirement. In chapter 13, I provide more information on home visits being conducted by social workers and the importance of keeping social workers who are on "fishing expeditions" out of your home.

Notes

1. *Kindstedt v. East Greenwich School Committee*, slip. op. (Rhode Island Commissioner of Education, 7 August 1986), 5, fnt. 12.

2. *Kindstedt v. East Greenwich School Committee*, slip.op. (Rhode Island Commissioner of Education, 7 August 1986).

3. *Ibid.*, 5, fnt. 12.

4. *Ibid.*, 7.

5. 381 U.S. 479 (1965).

6. *Steagald v. United States*, 451 U.S. 204, 211 (1981).

7. *Boyd v. United States*, 116 U.S. 616, 635 (1886).

8. *In the Matter of Dixon*, slip. op., No. N-37-86, Family Court of Oswego County, Nov. 21, 1988.

9. *In the Matter of Standish*, slip. op., No. N-125-86, Oswego County, Dec. 23, 1988

10. *Dixon, supra*, slip op., 5.

11. *Dixon*, 5.

12. 702 F.Supp. 516 (M.D. PA 1988). See Chapter 18 for more details about the *Jeffery* case.

13. South Carolina Opinion of the Attorney General, 27 February 1989, 2.

14. 87 L.Ed.2d.290 (1985).

15. 4735 U.S., 413.

16. *Ibid.*

17. *Surinach*, 604 F.2d 73, 75-76 (1st Cir. 1979). See also *Committee for Public Instruction*, 444 U.S., 646.

CHAPTER 15

AMALEKITE TACTICS?
PICKING ON THE HANDICAPPED

"While these regulations [of the federal Education of the Handicapped Act] define the nonpublic school child's right to participate in public agency services, they do not expand or limit a state's authority to regulate or otherwise set standards for the education of children residing in the state whose parents choose to enroll them in nonpublic educational programs."[1]
– U.S. Department of Education

When Israel left Egypt, the Amalekites attacked Israel. However, they would rarely attack armed forces or the main group of the

Israelites. Instead they would pick off the stragglers, who were often made up of the sick or weak.

Some public school authorities, unfortunately, seem to have adopted the tactics of the Amalekites when they are dealing with handicapped children who are being home schooled. When they find it difficult to pick on home schoolers with average or above average students, they turn to harassing the handicapped or special needs home school children. Going after handicapped children that are home schooled is somewhat easier since it is harder for the family to prove educational progress. It is also easier to intimidate the families into thinking they are not qualified. Of course, the incentive is greater also, since special needs children are worth nearly twice as much in state and federal tax dollars which will be sent to the local school district.

As a result, oftentimes, home school families with children with special needs or handicaps are harassed and restricted more than other home school families. In fact, in several states such as Arkansas, anyone can home school a child, *unless* that child is designated as needing special education services. In Arkansas, the special needs child can only be home schooled if the parent has a valid special education teaching certificate.[2] As a result of this discriminatory treatment, many home schoolers with special needs children begin to think they have less parental rights than everyone else. Constitutionally, this could not be further from the truth.

Parents with special needs children are protected by the same Constitution as all other parents. Therefore, they too have the protection of the First and Fourteenth Amendments.

One HSLDA home school family in Colorado had their child in special needs classes in the public school. After awhile, their child basically stagnated, as the classroom atmosphere became unbearable. They decided that they could do a better job themselves so they notified the school district that they were going to home school. Although it was legal to home school in the state, the local school district would not disenroll the child. The district felt the child's IEP recommendation could not be fulfilled by a mere mother. It called the family nearly every week, trying to pressure them back in for more meetings and more conferences with the public school's specialists. The mother could barely stand the intimidation and began to doubt herself. I was called and was able to convince the school district to retreat.

In Illinois, a family disenrolled their child from all special needs programs except speech therapy. Over and over again the school district tried to pressure the family to come into various meetings in which the child would be evaluated and recommendations given. The school district believed the parents were not qualified. Finally, the school district initiated a due process proceeding, pursuant to the Education of the Handicapped Act (EHA), since they believed the family was still under the jurisdiction of that act because the child was still receiving speech therapy. The family followed my advice and withdrew their child from speech therapy and provided a written statement to the school district breaking all ties. After further negotiation, the family was finally left alone.

In Indiana, a couple who educated nine adopted handicapped children was harassed repeatedly by school officials. Scores of other families were home schooling in the area, but this family was singled out because all the children had special needs. The school district was losing a lot of money.

The personal experiences I have had with defending handicapped children who are harassed only because they are home schooling, could go on and on. In every instance, the situations were resolved, and in every instance, the parents were able to do a better job because they cared about their children and best understood their special needs.

Below is a short summary of the legal rights and conflicts of parents who home school children with special needs.

The Improper Application of the EHA to Private Home Schools

A common adage, that government controls nearly always follow government money, often rings true with home schoolers who receive public school services for their special needs children. Many times the controls are not immediately visible but they usually surface as soon as the parents begin to disagree with the public school authorities' "recommendations" for new therapy or a different educational approach.

At the very least, home schoolers who receive public school services for their special needs children, place themselves under the jurisdiction of the federal EHA and local state regulations which implement that act. The reader can see this actually being applied in the example of the family from Indiana and the family from

Pennsylvania discussed below. The EHA funding is given to each state, based on the number of special needs children and on how closely the state follows the EHA regulations. As a result, each state has passed some form of regulations to implement the EHA requirements.

However, special needs home schoolers who want to discontinue public services or, in some instances, those who never asked for the service to begin with, are faced with an attempt by some state officials, superintendents, and principals to require special needs home schoolers to comply with the EHA anyway. This action by school districts is, of course, improper because the EHA was established to make public school services available to all children on a *voluntary* basis.

Parents who do not want the free special needs services, therefore, are not under the jurisdiction of the EHA and should not have to abide by the federal EHA regulations, or the state's regulations which implement the EHA rules.

The purpose and intent of the EHA , described in 20 USCS §1400(c), is:

> . . . To assure that all handicapped children have *available* to them . . . a free appropriate public education which emphasizes special education and related services designed to meet their unique needs, to assure that the rights of handicapped children and their parents or guardians are protected, to assist states and localities to provide for the education of all handicapped children, and to assess and assure the effectiveness of efforts to educate handicapped children.

Throughout the entire act, the purpose of making *available* a free appropriate education to handicapped children, is the central theme. The act defines a "free appropriate public education" as:

> Special education and related services which (A) have been provided at public expense, under public supervision and direction, and without charge, (B) meet the standards of the state educational agency, (C) include an appropriate preschool, elementary, or secondary school education in the state involved, and (D) are provided in conformity with the individualized education program required under section 614(a)(5) [20 USCS §1414(a)(5)].[3]

The intent of the act, therefore, is to provide statutory guidelines for local public schools to make available a free public education to the handicapped. The act is *not* a compulsory attendance statute for handicapped children. Section 1412(2)(B) only allows states to receive federal money for special education services *if* "a free appropriate public education is available for all handicapped children between the ages of three and eighteen." Most states have compulsory ages set between ages six and sixteen. If the EHA were a federal mandate compelling all handicapped children between the ages of three and eighteen to receive special education services, it would be in direct conflict with every compulsory attendance statute in the country.

It is clearly apparent, therefore, that parents who do *not* want to take advantage of a free public education for their handicapped child, are not mandated to do so. Such a mandate would also violate the parents' fundamental right to direct the education of their children, as guaranteed under *Pierce v. Society of Sisters*.[4] In the *Pierce* case, the U.S. Supreme Court declared parents have the right to choose a *private* educational program for their children, and, as a result, the Court struck down an Oregon law that mandated only public school attendance. Parents of special needs children are not required to use any public educational services. To privately educate their special needs child is the parents' choice. By doing so, they avoid the state's controls pursuant to the EHA.

Example of Misapplication of the Law to Home Schooling the Handicapped.

In Pennsylvania, the Ehmann family withdrew their handicapped child, George, from the public schools in order to instruct him privately, and voluntarily discontinued all state and federal assistance. As a result, they no longer remained under the jurisdiction of the EHA and were no longer subject to the due process procedures of 20 U.S.C. §1415. Nonetheless, the Philadelphia school district alleged that the Ehmanns were still under the jurisdiction of the federal EHA and initiated a hearing under the due process procedures of the EHA to force the family to follow the "recommendations" of the public school special needs experts. The public school, of course, wanted the child to stay in a public school special needs class. The family, as is their right, unilaterally withdrew their child from the special needs program and completely home schooled him privately.

The assistant general counsel of the Philadelphia Board of Education asserted the Ehmanns are *"precluded"* from removing their child from the public school placement and teaching him privately. The counsel stated,

> It is our belief that the Ehmanns by their refusal to comply with federal laws and procedures enacted for the protection of handicapped children, are in violation of Pennsylvania's Compulsory Attendance Laws.

This school district was attempting to make it mandatory that a special needs child comply with federal controls, even though all ties to the public school had been severed.

I filed a brief with the independent hearing officer who was assigned to hear the case pursuant to the due process procedures of the EHA[5] and requested the hearing officer dismiss the case, since he and the EHA had no jurisdiction.

I argued that the purpose and the intent of the EHA is not to *compel* all handicapped children to utilize federally funded special education services, but rather to make available a "free and appropriate" education to those who *choose* to take advantage of such federal services. The Ehmanns are *not* enrolling their child in the public school, so the superintendent has no authority to impose federal public school standards. Furthermore, the superintendent has no legal authority to initiate federal due process procedures pursuant to the EHA because those due process procedures *only* apply to children enrolled in *public* school programs for the handicapped children, not children being *privately* home schooled, such as the Ehmanns. The only consequence for the Ehmanns in withdrawing their child from the special needs program in order to home school him is that they forfeit all federal and state aid.[6] I also presented the following position of the U.S. Department of Education.

The U.S. Department of Education Supports Special Needs Home Schoolers

The U.S. Department of Education has confirmed that the EHA has no jurisdiction over home schools and private schools. In a letter of June 24, 1988, to Mike Farris of HSLDA, Charles O'Malley, the executive assistant for Private Education stated:

> There is nothing in the EHA statute or regulations that indicates that the free and appropriate public education requirement applicable to participating states was intended to interfere with the right of parents to educate their

children at home or in a private school in accordance with their State's provisions for these alternatives.[7]

Furthermore, the letter explains that the EHA was not intended to regulate schools or families who choose not to participate in public agency services. O'Malley emphasizes that the rights of nonpublic school children and the limited obligations of public agencies for those children are defined in the EHA regulations.[8] However, O'Malley adds:

> While these regulations define the nonpublic school child's right to participate in public agency services, they do not expand or limit a State's authority to regulate or otherwise set standards for the education of children residing in the State whose parents choose to enroll them in nonpublic educational programs.[9]

In other words, the EHA standards for an appropriate education do *not* apply and were not *intended* to apply to handicapped children in home schools and private schools who do not participate in public agency services.

Ehmann Decision in Favor of Parents' Rights

The independent hearing officer refused to grant my motion to dismiss, and ruled against the family and in favor of the public school's definition of an "appropriate" education for this special needs child.

I appealed to the secretary of education of Pennsylvania, Thomas K. Gilhool, and he ruled in favor of the Ehmanns, granting the motion to dismiss on June 9, 1989.[10] He ordered that the hearing officer's findings of fact and conclusions of law be rejected and vacated.[11] He also ordered the school district and the family to proceed under the Pennsylvania compulsory attendance act, not the federal EHA procedures.[12]

Conclusion

Home schooling special needs children takes a tremendous effort on behalf of parents. HSLDA receives regular reports of the consistent success that these parents are achieving, oftentimes far beyond the progress the special needs child made in the public school. In fact, many learning disabilities or handicaps are conquered in the home setting. Thomas Edison, as explained in chapter 7, was labeled "addled" by the public school and lasted only three months. It was through home instruction that he thrived. One of the major reasons for success seems to be the fact that parents know their children best and, therefore, can best meet the needs of their handicapped child.

In order to avoid taking the risk of being subject to objectionable federal and state controls, experience dictates that home schooling children with special needs should be done completely in the private realm. Although some home school families have had no conflict from the school district which provided them with special needs services, the family is taking a risk. HSLDA has even had families turned over to the social services for investigation, since they refused to follow the public school's recommendation regarding the type of educational help the handicapped child should have.

If an HSLDA family withdraws their child from a public special needs educational program, we advise them to avoid signing any IEP forms stating they decline to follow the school district's recommendation. Instead, we tell them to write a short letter clearly stating they are formally withdrawing their child from the special needs program and will pursue private assistance. The parents need to make clear they are no longer desiring to receive any further funding so as to make certain the school district knows they are no longer under the jurisdiction of the EHA.

Home schoolers should also carefully watch their legislatures in order to oppose any attempts to create excessive regulations for handicapped children being home schooled. All home schoolers need to stand together to protect special needs home schoolers from being separately and excessively regulated.

Notes

1. Charles J. O'Malley, Ph.D., Executive Assistant for Private Education, United States Department of Education, Washington D.C., Letter to Michael P. Farris, 24 June 1988, 2.

2. Arkansas Statutes Annotated section 80-1503.9.

3. 20 USCS 1401(18).

4. 268 U.S.510 (1925) [Also see *Meyer v. Nebraska*, 262 U.S.390 (1923) and *Wisconsin v. Yoder*, 406 U.S.205 (1972)]. See Chapter 17 for a full discussion of this fundamental right guaranteed by the Fourteenth Amendment.

5. The *Ehmann* brief was also expanded and filed with the secretary of education in Pennsylvania. The brief covers much precedent and other citations in this area.

A copy is available from the Home School Legal Defense Association listed in the back.

6. In *Board of Education of the City of New York v. Ambach*, 612 F.Supp. 230, (D.C.N.Y.1985), a family disagreed with the public school's placement of their handicapped child and initiated administrative proceedings. In the meantime, the child was enrolled in a private school. The court held:

> Section 1415(e)(3) *does not act to preclude parents* from removing their child from an arguably inappropriate placement, but if the parents do violate the status quo provisions of Section 1414(e)(3) and place their child in a private school without the consent of the school agency, they do so *at their own risk.* (emphasis added)

612 F.Supp. at 234. Also see *Board of Education of E. Windsor Regional School v. Diamond*, 808 F.2d 987 (3rd Cir. 1986). In the *Stemple, Ambach,* and *Diamond* cases above, nothing was even suggested that the parents had no right to unilaterally remove their handicapped children from the public school placement under EHA. In fact, the disputes only concerned whether or not the local officials had to reimburse them for this choice.

In *Springdale School District v. Grace*, 494 F.Supp. 266 (W.D.Ark. 1980), parents sued because they preferred to have their daughter placed in the State School for the Deaf, while the local school district wanted the girl to be placed in their system. The local school district prevailed when the district court held that the program for the girl was "appropriate" and thus satisfied the school's legal duties to offer appropriate special education. However, the court ended its opinion by reminding the parents that if they truly thought the other program was best for the child they could choose that on their own with their own expense. The court said:

> We also note that, upon reflection, Sherry's parents may be more desirous that their child receive the *best* instead of a mere "appropriate" scholastic exposure. (emphasis added)

494 F.Supp., at 274. [emphasis in original].

7. Charles J. O'Malley, Ph.D., Executive Assistant for Private Education, United States Department of Education, Washington D.C., Letter to Michael P. Farris, 24 June 1988, 1.

8. 34 CFR §300.403(a), the EHA-B sections immediately following, §§300.450-300.452 and EDGAR at 34 CFR §§300.651-662.

9. *Ibid.* 2.

10. *In re the Educational Assignment of George E.*, Special Education Opinion No. 353, Department of Education. of Pennsylvania, 5 June 1989, 3.

11. *Ibid.*, 3.

12. *Ibid.*

CHAPTER 16

MILITARY PURGES:
HOME SCHOOLING IN THE
ARMED FORCES

"The DoD has a specific statutory authority to operate a school for DoD dependents who are assigned overseas. Our statute, unlike the many State statutes which do not apply overseas, does not compel the attendance of any DoD dependent in DoD Dependents Schools. . . . Therefore, a dependent may choose not to enroll in our program [DoDDS] and to elect, instead, an alternative enrollment; for example, a foreign language school, a private school, or in a home schooling program."[1]

Home schooling has always been a logical choice for families in the military. Military personnel often receive training in different bases in the country and throughout the world. Many a child of a military family was subject to readjusting to a new school repeatedly, throughout his life.

For some children, the periodic transfer of their father to a new base across the country causes much insecurity and a weakening of self-esteem. Often the children's educational progress and continuity are interrupted with detrimental results to the children's levels of academic achievement.

Home schooling has provided a cure for many of these emotional and academic drawbacks of military life. Most importantly, a cohesive family unit is created, which provides a secure support system for the children.

Furthermore, the children's education rarely suffers since the continuity of instruction is not broken by the adjustment to new learning environments and new teachers. For home schoolers, the school, teachers, and curriculum remain the same, wherever the family is transferred. The home school functions as a cushion to the children, softening the pressures which occur as the result of facing dramatic change or, in some instances, culture shock.

In spite of the many advantages of home schooling in the military, some military officials have challenged the right of home schoolers to operate and, in a sense, have tried to "purge" home schoolers from their ranks by excessive restriction or intimidation. Overall, the military seems to respect home schoolers, but every year certain commanding officers take issue with home schoolers.

For instance, in Japan, I helped a home schooling private in the Army who was contacted by his commanding officer, informing him that he was not in compliance since he did not submit test results of his children to him for proof of progress. In Germany, a home schooling major was contacted by his superiors and told he must have his children's curriculum approved and submit to home visits.

In Turkey, an Air Force commander, Colonel Peter Farmer, tried to discourage home schoolers with a memo he issued:

> I've been hearing a number of sponsors here discuss bringing their school aged children back to Incirlik early and having their spouse conduct home schooling to finish out the year. The Defense Department Dependent School recommends against this and their requirements for home schooling are as follows: 1. Instructor must have passed the National Teacher Exam before any period of home school is

approved. 2. Student must pass a placement exam prior to the beginning of the next school year before that student will be passed to the next grade.

I could recount many other negative contacts in the military overseas. Of course, such requirements as described above are in excess of the military's authority. As seen below, home schooling is allowed in the military overseas, and the military, under its present regulations, really has no authority to regulate it. Military home schoolers in the United States, on the other hand, are required to follow the home school requirements of that state. Even in the States though, military social workers routinely investigate home schoolers, and I have spent much time convincing them that home schooling is legal.

One of the most blatant examples of harassment of home schoolers occurred on a military base in Germany.

Military Home Schoolers Challenged in Germany

On November 6, 1989, the commander of an Army base in Augsburg, West Germany, Commander Del Rosso, issued a memorandum condemning home schooling. He stated that according to the Status-of-Forces-Agreements, all families had to comply with the "host nation law" which involves choosing one of three options listed in his memorandum:

They can elect to enroll children in:

a. A Department of Defense Dependent School (DoDDS).

b. A locally accredited public, private, or parochial school.

c. A school accredited by an acknowledged U.S. civil or religious education association, which has applied for local accreditation.

. . . Attendance at schools not meeting the above criteria is a violation of host nation law and therefore strictly prohibited. . . . Similarly, so called "home teaching" (i.e. parent keeps child at home and personally conducts his education) is strictly prohibited.[2] (emphasis added)

As a result, home school families were warned that they had one week to enroll their children in a recognized school under one of the options listed above or face disciplinary action for misconduct. "As willful violators of host nation law, repeat offenders will be referred to the Civilian Misconduct Action Authority who can direct appropriate sanctions."[3]

Commander Del Rosso's attempt to prohibit home schooling by instituting this inaccurate policy was immediately resisted by the home schooling families in the community. Several families were planning to request transfers back to the states if they would not be allowed to home school.[4] In an interview, Michael Harris, the military head of recreational services in Augsburg, said that the policy was prompted by reports that Christian schools were operating unofficially on post and "of parents teaching their children at home."[5] He said that they needed to follow the West German mandatory attendance policy at only accredited schools, which was "designed to protect children from abuse." Harris explained further, "When I fail as a parent to educate my child, I might as well be spanking them or beating them."[6] Letters were written to the secretary of defense and the judge advocate's offices, who sent them copies of the actual policy of the military in favor of the right to home school. The commander, after being informed of the Department of Defense policy described below, quickly rescinded his memorandum which prohibited home schooling.

Policy of the Secretary of Defense and Judge Advocate

James Horn, education liaison for the Office of the Assistant Secretary of Defense stated in his reply:

> The DoD has a specific statutory authority to operate a school for DoD dependents who are assigned overseas. Our statute, unlike the many State statutes which do not apply overseas, does not compel the attendance of any DoD dependent in DoD Dependents Schools. . . . Therefore, a dependent may choose not to enroll in our program [DoDDS] and to elect, instead, an alternative enrollment; for example, a foreign language school, a private school, or in a home schooling program.[7]

While the Department of Defense does not have specific regulations to govern home schooling, it allows for it as an alternative to their Dependent Schools. It is *not* prohibited in any way.

Horn also explained the military's policy regarding military families operating within the states:

> Public education within the United States is a matter which our constitutional system leaves to the discretion of each state. These laws are binding on all persons within the State's border, including the dependents of the Department of Defense (including the Military Services). The Secretary of Defense does not have the legal authority to issue . . . regulatory exemption from State education laws.[8]

Military families in the states, as a result, have the responsibility of following the home schooling laws or regulations in that particular state.

Furthermore, regarding the issue of attendance in an accredited German school, Capt. Chris Ambrose, assistant staff judge advocate stated:

> The children of U.S. military and DoD civilian personnel assigned to Germany, however, are *not* subject to state mandatory attendance statutes of the U.S. because the children do not *reside* in any of the fifty states. The children are *not* subject to German mandatory attendance laws *either* because of NATO Status of Forces agreements which allow US forces to provide for the education of their own children.[9] (emphasis added)

Military home schoolers on foreign soil are not subject to either foreign school attendance law or any of the fifty states' attendance laws provided the NATO Status of Forces Agreement or some similar agreement applies to the specific foreign country. Capt. Ambrose emphasized, however, other non-military "U.S. citizens who reside in Germany (e.g. missionaries), *are* subject to German mandatory attendance laws."[10]

The Judge Advocate's office explained further that the federal law 20 USC 921-932 which authorizes the educational services provided by the DoDDS, does not address mandatory attendance. The implementing directive, DoD Directive 1342.13, also does not require mandatory attendance.[11] Therefore, the DoDDS presently has no authority to prohibit or regulate home schooling.

Capt. Ambrose concluded by stating:

> I have discussed the subjects of mandatory DoDDS attendance and home schooling with attorneys from the DoD General Counsel's office in Washington D.C., as well as the DoDDS administrators in Germany. They agree that it is not illegal for U.S. Military and DoD civilians to home school in Germany, regardless of whether the family lives on

or off post (base). Nevertheless, misinformed commanders occasionally attempt to initiate disciplinary action against home schoolers.[12]

In fact, in 1989, the *Stars and Stripes* newspaper reported that over two hundred military families in Europe were home schooling.[13]

In conclusion, military families are allowed to home school. However, occasionally a commander or an uninformed social worker will challenge the right of home schoolers to exist or try to excessively regulate them. HSLDA has been successful in resolving many investigations of military home schoolers by convincing through a legal letter that home schooling is legal in the specific state in which the family resides. If the family is based in a foreign country, many commanders have been convinced by the DoD and judge advocate's position that they cannot prohibit or even regulate home schooling. The only power they really have is to investigate *real* child neglect.

Home School Students Who Enlist in the Military

As the modern home school movement which began primarily in the early 1980s starts producing graduates, some children are interested in enlisting in the military. However, at present, the military is using a three-tier educational policy which favors "traditional" high school graduates who make Tier I. Tier I candidates are given as high as 95 percent of available openings.

At the printing of this book, home schoolers are relegated to Tier II, along with GED candidates. I believe that this is clear discrimination against home schoolers—to categorize them in Tier II, rather than in Tier I. Tier III is for students who dropped out of high school and do not have a high school diploma. Certain groups are classified in certain tiers, based on the attrition rate of that particular group. For instance, in 1989, the highest attrition rate of 19.4 percent was for those without any high school diploma. The second highest attrition rate is 17.5 percent for those with a GED. Public school graduates have 12.1 percent attrition rate, and those with two years or more of college is 9.2 percent.[14]

After several requests for home school statistics, in April 1990, HSLDA met with researchers for the military and found out that, for 1989, the home-schooled recruits only had an attrition rate of 9.5 percent.[15] This is the second lowest attrition rate of all the groups.

This information has marked the beginning of a closer look at home-schooled recruits by the military, which will hopefully result in abandonment of the three-tier test in favor of an "attrition predictor test," which will place all candidates in an equal evaluation mode.

Another favorable development which may contribute to easier access by home schoolers into the military is the academic failure of many public school graduates, as seen in chapter 1 of this book. All potential military recruits need to pass a three-hour Armed Services Vocational Aptitude Battery (ASVAB). This tests math, comprehension, and word knowledge. In order to pass, the person needs to read on at least an eleventh grade level, according to Sergeant Jack Gragg, manager of the Army's Bakersfield, California, recruiting station.[16] However, Gragg, in the same interview, stated that half of the graduates of the local public high schools flunk this basic test.

As seen in chapter 6, home schooling works, and continues to be one of the most successful forms of education in the United States. If the military begins to add up the academic success of home schoolers and the low attrition rate of those home-schooled students in the military, home schoolers may have an easier time enlisting. If a change does not occur soon, however, HSLDA is contemplating filing a discrimination suit against the military.

Notes

1. James G. Horn, Ph.D., Education Liaison with the Office of the Assistant Secretary of Defense, Washington, D.C., Letter to Michelle Landers, 1989.

2. Brigadier General Louis J. Del Rosso, "*Memorandum For See Distribution*; Subject: USMCA Augsburg High/Elementary School Attendance, Military Community, Policy Memorandum #31," Department of the Army, Augsburg, Germany, 6 November 1989. This policy was later rescinded.

3. *Ibid.*

4. Rosemary Sawyer, "Augsburg Community Takes Action Against Home Schooling of Children," *Stars and Stripes*, 17 November 1989, 2.

5. *Ibid.*

6. *Ibid.*

7. James , *op. cit.*

8. *Ibid.*

9. Chris E. Ambrose, Capt, United States Air Force, Assistant Staff Judge Advocate, Letter to Mrs. Gravelle, 21 July 1989.

10. *Ibid.*

11. *Ibid.*

12. *Ibid.*

13. Sawyer, *Stars and Stripes*, 2

14. The source of these statistics is Dr. Brian Waters and Janice Laurence of HumRRO in Washington, D.C. They are the researchers who provide the data by which the military establishes their recruitment policies.

15. *Ibid.*

16. Gordon Anderson, "Military Wants Literate Recruits," *The Bakersfield Californian*, 6 August 1990, A1 and A10.

Hast not thou made an
hedge about him, and
about his house?
        — Job 1:10

PART
5

A SUCCESSFUL DEFENSE: THE LEGAL ARGUMENTS

The framers of the Constitution, unfortunately, never specifically mentioned in the Constitution the right of parents to educate their children. They took it for granted that parents alone had this right and could *choose* whatever form of education they saw fit. Since biblical theism was dominant in early America, this right of parents was recognized as a God-given right derived from the Bible and codified in English common law.

In the last fifty years, however, the U.S. Constitution has been so twisted in many areas that it no longer reflects the intent of the framers. The most devastating example of the perversion of the original intent of the Constitution is the creation of the "right" to an abortion, which has resulted in the deaths of millions of babies. This has happened in spite of our Bill of Rights which clearly protects life.

Similarly, the right of parents to choose their child's education, as held sacred by the framers, has also been gradually eroded in favor of state intervention and control. The parents are no longer solely responsible for the education of their children as established in the Bible and common law. Now the courts recognize the state having an interest in education and the power to regulate that interest. As a result, prior to the 1980s, home schooling was virtually stifled by the state.

However, the tide is slowly being reversed through the application of the various Constitutional or technical defenses in the courts as described in this section or by the legislatures as seen in chapter 19. The ultimate victory will not be reached until the compulsory attendance statutes are repealed in every state. However, at his time, repeal of such laws is a long way off. Therefore, the strategy of this author and the Home School Legal Defense Association, in the meantime, is to push back the interest of the state further and further in education, limiting its power to regulate, until that interest finally evaporates. This will take time, relentless efforts, and a great deal of education of our judges, law enforcement officials, and legislators.

CHAPTER 17

PARENTS' RIGHTS
AND THE CONSTITUTION

"That some parents 'may at times be acting against
the interests of their children' . . . creates a basis for
caution, but it is hardly a reason to discard
wholesale those pages of human experience that
teach that parents generally do act in the child's best
interest. . . . The statist notion that governmental power
should supersede parental authority in *all* cases because *some*
parents abuse and neglect children is repugnant to
American tradition."[1]
—The U.S. Supreme Court

Home schooling is a right, not a privilege. This right of parents to
teach their children is guaranteed in the Fourteenth Amendment of
the United States Constitution. Parents who are home schooling for
religious reasons also have the additional protection of the First

Amendment which guarantees them the right to freely exercise their religious beliefs.

Although you will see in this chapter that parental liberty historically was held to be virtually absolute, many state courts and the passage of compulsory attendance laws in the 1900s have gradually eroded this right. These states have used the language of the United States Supreme Court which recognizes that the states have an "interest" in education. During the last seventy-five years, the power to regulate that interest of the state has steadily expanded.

However, home schools have been involved on the cutting edge in pushing back the interest of the state. In 1983, the Home School Legal Defense Association was established for the purpose of shackling the interest of the state by gradually limiting the state's power over parents. Eventually, I would like to see the interest of the state totally erased, but that may take some time while we educate the judges and legislators.

Meanwhile, it is important for us to master the history of parental rights, especially as established in the courts, so that we are better prepared for the battle for our children that is presently taking place. We need to work to reestablish the historic foundations of parental rights in our country and restore a respect of the parents' right to choose and control the education of their children.[2]

Early Recognition of Parents' Rights in the Courts

As documented in chapter 5, during the first 250 years of the United States, beginning in 1620, education was not subject to the myriads of regulations which presently conflict with the parents' right to control the *process* of their children's education. Parental liberty was held inviolate, and parents seriously heeded the rights and responsibilities of educating their children. Education was *not* a government responsibility, and it was left completely under the private control of parents and the churches.

In fact, in *Abington v. Schempp*, the U.S. Supreme Court confirmed that education historically was privately controlled and public schooling, in the modern sense, was non-existent.

> In the North American Colonies, education was almost without exception under private sponsorship and supervision, frequently under control of the dominant Protestant sects.[3]

Similarly, the modern home school movement is comprised largely of fundamental Christians who hold sacred the biblical view of the family and practically apply God's principles to each and every subject. This fact that biblical theism dominated early American education and culture[4] explains why the present states' attempt to control and secularize private, Christian education and home schooling was non-existent back then. The Court in *Schempp* further comments,

> Education, as the framers knew it, was in the main confined to *private* schools more often than not under strictly *sectarian supervision*. Only gradually did control of education pass largely to public officials.[5] (emphasis supplied) .

Until the 1900s, the Christian concept of parental liberty in education was unquestioned.

This "preferred" position of the parents' duty and right in controlling the education of their children was securely established in the foundation of America's legal system, and its roots were in English common law which was derived from the Bible.[6] One of the most influential common law sources on which the founders of our country relied was Sir William Blackstone's *Commentaries*. Blackstone recognized that the most important duty of parents to their children is that of giving them an education suitable to their station in life.[7] That duty, he admits, "was pointed out by reason."[8]

Building on this traditional liberty of parents as enunciated by Blackstone, the Oklahoma Supreme Court in *School Board Dist. No. 18 v. Thompson*[9] secured the right of parents to control the education of their children, even though the Oklahoma Constitution and Legislature had recently enacted compulsory education.

The attorney representing the school district contended that "the old common-law idea that the parent has the exclusive control over the education of the child has long since been abandoned" since the state requirement of compulsory education was enacted.[10] The Oklahoma Supreme Court, however, unanimously *disagreed* with the school district and ruled:

> Under our form of government, and at common law, *the home* is considered the keystone of the governmental structure. In this empire, *parents rule supreme* during the minority of their children.[11] (emphasis supplied)

The Court also quoted Blackstone as strong support for their decision to uphold parents' rights to control their child's education:

> Blackstone says that the greatest duty of parents to their children is that of giving them an education suitable to their station in life; a duty pointed out by reason, and of far the greatest importance of any. But this duty at common law was not compulsory; the common law presuming that the natural love and affection of the parents for their children would impel them to faithfully perform this duty, and deeming it punishment enough to leave the parent, who neglects the instruction of his family, to labor under those griefs and inconveniences which his family, so uninstructed, will be sure to bring upon him.[12]

At this time, Oklahoma is still benefiting from this 1909 decision. This decision clearly established in Oklahoma the presumption that parents act in the best interest of their children, and parents' rights are superior to the public school's authority.

This function of the parent to control the education of his children has been a constitutionally recognized right in a long line of cases beginning with Meyer v. Nebraska in 1923.[13] A U.S. Supreme Court decision to protect parents' rights in education was not necessary prior to 1923, because there were hardly any compulsory attendance laws that required children to attend public school. As soon as compulsory attendance laws were passed, however, the attack on parental liberty began. Education became a state responsibility rather than a traditional parental responsibility. As experience teaches, whenever the state takes responsibility of any private sector, controls always follow.

Parental Liberty in Education Is Derived from the Fourteenth Amendment

Even though the Constitution does not specifically mention the right of parents to educate their children, that right is derived from the Fourteenth Amendment. The Fourteenth Amendment guarantees that all citizens have the right to "liberty," which cannot be taken away without due process. The U.S. Supreme Court has determined that this guarantee of "liberty" includes "parental liberty." Based on this application of the Fourteenth Amendment, the Supreme Court has consistently held that parents have the "fundamental right" to "direct the upbringing and education of their children."[14]

The problem, however, is that the Supreme Court, in the same breath in which it reasserted the parents' right to educate their children, also created an "interest" which the state has in education. Consequently, with this "interest" in education comes government controls. The state's interest, as defined by the Supreme Court is that children must grow up to be "literate" and "self-sufficient."[15]

Since the HSLDA was founded in 1983, it has not had a single case, out of hundreds of home school cases, where the home-schooled children in question were not receiving an adequate education. In every case, the children were literate and average or above average on their standardized achievement test results. The "interest" of the state in children being educated was being "otherwise served." In fact, the public schools, as demonstrated in chapter 1, comprises the one school system where the interest of the state is *not* being met.

Of course, the state, in order to protect its "interest" in education, tries to impose restrictive requirements on parents who are home schooling, such as teacher certification requirements, curriculum approval, home visits, and countless other controls. The courts then must determine which must give way: the state's interest in regulating education or the parents' fundamental right in educating their children in the manner they choose. Since this conflict involves a "fundamental right," the "compelling interest test" must be applied, which requires that the state prove that its particular regulation imposed on home education is "necessary" and the "least restrictive means" to fulfill its interest that children be literate and self-sufficient. This test is described later in this chapter.

The states' attempts to arbitrarily regulate and limit parental control of the process of education result in the infringement of the fundamental rights of the parents as enunciated by the U.S. Supreme Court in the following three cases.

United States Supreme Court Cases Protecting Parents' Rights

In *Meyer v. Nebraska*,[16] the Court invalidated a state law that prohibited foreign language instruction to school children because the law did not "promote" education but rather "arbitrarily and unreasonably" interfered with "the natural duty of the parent to give his children education suitable to their station in life. . . ."[17] The Court chastened the legislature for attempting "materially to interfere. . . with the power of parents to control the education of their own."[18] This decision clearly affirmed that the Constitution protected the preferences of the parent in education over those of the state.[19]

In 1925, the Supreme Court decided the *Pierce v. Society of Sisters*[20] case, thereby supporting *Meyer's* recognition of the parents' right to direct the religious upbringing of their children and to control the process of their education. In *Pierce*, the Supreme Court struck down an Oregon compulsory education law which, in effect, required attendance of all children between ages eight and sixteen at *public* schools. The Court declared,

> Under the doctrine of *Meyer v. Nebraska*, we think it entirely plain that the Act of 1922 unreasonably interferes with the liberty of parents and guardians to direct the upbringing and education of children.[21]

In addition to upholding the right of parents to direct or control the education of their children, *Pierce* also asserts the parents' fundamental right to keep their children free from government standardization.

> The fundamental theory of liberty upon which all governments in this Union repose excluded any general power of the state to standardize its children by forcing them to accept instruction from public teachers only. The child is not the mere creature of the state; those who nurture him and direct his destiny have the right and the high duty, to recognize and prepare him for additional obligations.[22]

The Supreme Court uses strong language to assert that a child is not "the mere creature of the State." The holding in Pierce, therefore, preserves diversity of process of education by forbidding the state to standardize the education of children, in forcing them to accept instruction only from public schools.[23] This, of course, also prohibits the state from imposing excessive regulations on home schools, which would reduce them simply to "little public schools in the home."

Forty-eight years after *Pierce*, the U.S. Supreme Court once again upheld *Pierce* as "the charter of the rights of parents to direct the religious upbringing of their children."[24] In agreement with *Pierce*, Chief Justice Burger stated in the opinion of *Wisconsin v. Yoder* in 1972:

> This case involves the *fundamental interest* of parents, as contrasted with that of the state, to guide the religious future and education of their children.
>
> The history and culture of Western civilization reflect a strong tradition of parental concern for the nurture and upbringing of their children. This *primary* role of the parents in the upbringing of their children is now established *beyond debate* as an *enduring tradition.*[25] (emphasis supplied)

This case involved a family of the Amish religion who wanted to be exempt after eighth grade from the public schools in order to be instructed at home. Furthermore, in *Yoder* the U.S. Supreme Court emphasized:

> Thus a state's interest in universal education, however highly we rank it, is not totally free from a balancing process when it impinges on fundamental rights and interests, such as those specifically protected by the Free Exercise Clause of the First Amendment, and the traditional interest of parents with respect to the religious upbringing of their children. . . . This case involves the fundamental and religious future and education of their children.[26]

The most recent decision which upholds the right of parents is *Employment Division of Oregon v. Smith,*[27] which involved two Indians who were fired from a private drug rehabilitation organization because they ingested "peyote," a hallucinogenic drug, as part of their religious belief. When they sought unemployment compensation, they were denied because they were discharged for "misconduct."

The Indians appealed to the Oregon Court of Appeals, which reversed the earlier decision on the grounds that they had the right to freely exercise their religious beliefs by taking drugs. Of course, as expected, the U.S. Supreme Court again reversed the case and found that the First Amendment did not protect drug use. So what does this case have to do with parental rights?

After the Court ruled against the Indians, it then analyzed the application of the Free Exercise Clause generally. The Court wrongly decided to throw out the Free Exercise Clause as a defense to any "neutral" law that might violate an individual's religious convictions. In the process of destroying religious freedom, the United States Supreme Court in *Smith* miraculously reaffirmed the fact that the parents' rights to control the education of their children is still a fundamental right. The Court declared that the "compelling interest test" is still applicable, not to the Free Exercise Clause alone,

> but the Free Exercise Clause in conjunction with other *constitutional protections* such as . . . the *right of parents*, acknowledged in *Pierce v. Society of Sisters*, 268 U.S. 510 (1925), *to direct the education of their children*, see *Wisconsin v. Yoder*, 406 U.S.205 (1972) invalidating compulsory-attendance laws as applied to Amish parents who refused on religious grounds to send their children to school.[28] (emphasis supplied)

In other words, under this precedent, the fact that a family is home schooling for religious reasons is not enough to be a defense against a state requirement, such as teacher certification. However, since that religious conviction to home school is *combined* with the fundamental right of parents to control the education of their children, as guaranteed under the Fourteenth Amendment, the home school family battling the restrictive state regulation is still protected by the "compelling interest test."[29] This means that the state must prove, with evidence, that teacher certification is necessary for children to be educated and that it is the least restrictive means.

As a result, a requirement such as teacher certification, should *not* be allowed to prevail over a home school family's religious beliefs, if the state merely proves the teacher certification requirement is "reasonable." The Court in *Smith* quoted its previous case of *Wisconsin v. Yoder*:

> *Yoder* said that "The Court's holding in *Pierce* stands as a charter for the rights of parents to direct the religious upbringing of their children. And when the interests of parenthood are combined with a free exercise claim . . . *more than merely a reasonable relationship* to some purpose within the competency of the State is required to sustain the validity of the State's requirement under the First Amendment."[30] (emphasis supplied)

Instead of merely showing that teacher certification is reasonable, the state must, therefore, reach the higher standard of the "compelling interest test" which requires the state to prove that teacher certification is the least restrictive means.

Consequently, it is clear that the Constitutional right of a parent to direct the upbringing and education of his child is firmly entrenched in the U.S. Supreme Court case history.

The Free Exercise Defense: Is It Just Wishful Thinking?

Most home schoolers are home schooling for religious reasons as a result of their religious beliefs, as shown by several recent studies.[31] Many of these families believe they are commanded by God to be the primary teachers of their children. In chapter 4, these commonly held religious beliefs and supporting Scripture verses are described in detail.

Since these families have strong religious beliefs that they must home school, they are protected by the First Amendment of the United States Constitution which guarantees to all citizens the right to freely exercise their religious beliefs. This means that a home school family being prosecuted for not complying with a local restriction on their home school, such as the requirement of a college degree or teaching certificate, can use the First Amendment as a defense, as long as they prove that the particular restriction violates their religious belief.

The Four Part Compelling Interest Test

Whenever the right of parents to educate their children under either the First or Fourteenth Amendments is at issue, a specific legal test must be applied. This test is made up of four parts and is often referred to as the "compelling interest test."[32]

The U.S. Supreme Court has stated that whenever parental rights are combined with a free exercise claim, a heightened standard of review must be applied.[33] This standard of review involves the application of the "compelling interest" test, which requires the home schooler asserting a religious belief to prove two parts of the test and the State to prove the other two parts. This test was originally applied in *Sherbert v. Verner*[34] and has evolved through the years in *Wisconsin v. Yoder*,[35] *Thomas v. Review Board*,[36] *U.S. v Lee*,[37] and *Hobbie V. Unemployment Appeals Comm'n of Florida*.[38] This test involves *four* major parts.

First of all, the burden is on the home school family to prove the first two parts of the "compelling interest" test: 1) They must demonstrate that their religious belief against the particular state requirement is both "sincere" and "religious." Their belief cannot be only philosophical;[39] 2) the home school family must prove that their sincere religious belief is "burdened" *as applied* under the facts.[40]

Then the burden shifts to the state to prove, with evidence, the last two parts of the test. The two burdens that the state must prove are that its requirement is "essential" or "necessary" "to accomplish an overriding governmental [or compelling] interest" in education,[41] and that "it is the least restrictive means of achieving some compelling state interest."[42] If the state can prove that its interest in a particular regulation is necessary and the least restrictive means, then the religious belief of the home schooler must give way.

This raises the question of what is the state's legitimate interest in education. According to U.S. Supreme Court precedent, the state's interest is two-fold: *civic and economic.*[43] The state has an interest that children will acquire the necessary reading and writing skills to be able to vote and participate in our democratic system. The second interest of the state is that children will be able to eventually provide for themselves so that they will not become a burden on the state's welfare rolls. Many courts are finding that some of the present compulsory attendance laws are overly restrictive concerning home schools.

For example, a state requiring a college degree for home school parents would fail the third part of the "compelling interest test" since a college degree is not "essential" or "necessary" for a child to be educated. As seen in chapter 12, all available studies prove that there is no positive correlation between teacher qualifications and student performance.

Furthermore, a state like Michigan, which, as of September 1992, requires home schoolers to be certified or use certified teachers, is not using the least restrictive means to achieve the state's civil and economic interest. Forty-nine other states do not require such a high standard of teacher qualifications, demonstrating that teacher certification is not the least restrictive means.

Do Home Schoolers Actually Win Under the Free Exercise Clause?

The above described test is what should be applied to home schoolers whose religious beliefs are being violated by a state's education requirement. Unfortunately, few courts properly apply the "compelling interest test."

Convincing a court to actually exempt a home school family based solely on religious beliefs as guaranteed by the First Amendment is not that easy. In fact, it is very rare. Most courts try to dodge the issue or apply an improper "reasonableness" test. In other words, if a particular home school requirement is "reasonable" (virtually all restrictions on home schooling could be deemed "reasonable"), it is upheld against a family's sincerely held religious beliefs. In my upcoming book, *The Constitutional Right to Home School: A Parent's Choice*,[44] I summarize many of the cases that have gone against home schoolers or Christian schools who have used as their defense the Free Exercise clause. I also point out the key Constitutional flaw in all of those cases.

An example of the difficulty in convincing a court to grant an exemption under the Free Exercise Clause is *State v. DeJonge*.[45] I have been handling this case since 1985, and it is presently waiting for a ruling before the Michigan Supreme Court. In this case, the DeJonge family was opposed to using a certified teacher to teach their children. They proved, in court, that they had sincerely held religious convictions which made them opposed to teacher certification. However, when it came to the prosecution proving, with evidence, that teacher certification was essential for children to be educated, and that it was the least restrictive means of fulfilling the state's interest in education, the judge did not require the prosecution to carry the burden. Instead, the judge, following a whim and an earlier improper ruling against the Christian schools, found the state's interest to override the family's beliefs.

On appeal to the Michigan Court of Appeals, the Court refused to recognize the error that the prosecution never carried their burden that teacher certification is essential and the least restrictive means. The Court merely gave "lip service" to the "compelling interest test" and, instead, applied the "reasonableness test." The Court of Appeals merely ruled, without any evidence, that teacher certification is the least restrictive means of fulfilling the state's interest. The Court also ruled that "teacher certification requirement is a backbone in protection" of quality education. How could the Court of Appeals make such a ruling when we made clear to them the proper test, and informed them that the prosecution never proved that teacher certification is essential and the least restrictive means? I presented studies and facts showing that children can and are being educated better without certified teachers than the children in the public schools. I showed them the studies which indicate there is no positive correlation between teacher qualifications and student performance. I also proved that at that time, forty-eight other states did not require such an onerous requirement, disproving any claim that it is the least restrictive means. Yet, the court still ruled the way it wanted to. By God's grace, on June 10, 1992, after seven long years of litigation, the Michigan Supreme Court decided that it will review this case. Hopefully, the Court of Appeals decision will be reversed, and the Court will reestablish the free exercise of religion in Michigan.

Although many cases we have handled are won on technicalities or other Constitutional defenses, we have won some on religious grounds. For example, in Colorado, HSLDA won a case for the Main family, using local counsel Bruce Lorenzen. In *Hinsdale County School Board v. Main*, the Main family objected to seeking the "approval" of the local public school authorities because they believed that only God can approve their home schooling. The Court ruled that their religious beliefs were sincere and stated, "The state has an important interest in the education of children, but to minimize interference with sincerely held religious beliefs, it must find the least intrusive means to accomplish that interest."[46] Therefore, the Court exempted the family from the approval requirements, stating, "the Mains are complying with the purpose of the compulsory attendance law, even if they have not obtained approval of their home study program."[47]

Similarly, HSLDA has been able to use the combination of the Free Exercise defense along with other defenses, such as the vagueness defense, to win for home schoolers. For example, in HSLDA's civil rights case against school districts throughout Pennsylvania, *Jeffery v. O'Donnell*,[48] the Court ruled in favor of the home schoolers who were all opposed on religious grounds to approval by the public school authorities. The Court declared:

> . . . when First Amendment rights are affected by the enforcement of a statute, the state law will be held to a higher standard of specificity than might be the case if purely economic regulation was at issue.

> . . . the threat to sensitive First Amendment freedoms mandates judicial intrusion in the form of declaring the particular provision of the law [as applied to home schools] unconstitutional for vagueness.[49]

Since the *Jeffery* case was combined with the First Amendment Free Exercise rights of the home schoolers, the Federal Court more strictly applied the vagueness defense to find Pennsylvania's compulsory attendance law unconstitutionally void for vagueness.

Therefore, we regularly raise the Free Exercise challenge on behalf of home schoolers because we never know which courts will want to rule favorably on it.

More importantly, the Free Exercise clause has been very effective in influencing legislatures. Over and over again, I have presented the First Amendment arguments in my testimony before legislative committees who many times have either killed bad bills or passed good bills in response to wanting to protect religious freedom as guaranteed in the First Amendment.

Also, in thousands of correspondence and negotiations with school districts since 1983, the HSLDA legal staff and I have used the First Amendment to contribute to resolving the conflict in favor of home school families.

Conclusion

The First and Fourteenth Amendments are important defenses to families who are home schooling. The "compelling interest test," when properly applied by the court, can carve out an exemption for the home schooler from the particular, burdensome requirement. However, many courts try to circumvent this test by applying the wrong test.

Nonetheless, since every court is inclined differently, home schools need to continue to raise the Free Exercise defense with the hope that the Court will properly grant a religious exemption.

Notes

1. *Parham v. J.R.*, 442 U.S. 584 (1979), 602-603.

2. For a much more in-depth and thorough look at our parental and constitutional rights in regard to home schooling you may want to obtain my upcoming book, *The Constitutional Right to Home School: A Parent's Choice*, which will be due out in 1993.

3. *Abington v. Schempp*, 374 U.S. 203, at 238 Note 7.

4. Ibid, 26-29. For example, in 1647, the Massachusetts General Court passed the "Old Deluder Act" that required towns to maintain schools. The object was the defeat of "one chief project of that old deluder, satan, to keep men from the knowledge of the Scriptures." Therefore, the primary goal of education, as defined in the act, was to instruct the child so he could comprehend the Scripture. Although towns had to maintain schools, parents had the ultimate choice of how their children would be educated. [See the Laws and Liberties of Massachusetts, 1648 ed. (Cambridge, 1929), 47.]

5. *Schempp*, 374 U.S. 203, at 238. Even the public schools in existence during the early 1800s were locally controlled and nearly identical to the instruction found in private schools. Thomas Jefferson, as president of the Washington D.C. School Board, established the Bible and the Watts Hymnal as the principal books to be used for reading by the public school students. J.O. Wilson, *Public Schools of Washington* (Columbia Historical Society, 1897), 4. Attendance at these few common schools was completely voluntary.

6. Constitutional scholar, John Whitehead, in his book *Parents' Rights* (Westchester, Ill.: Crossway Books, 1985), 85, explains the Christian foundation of common law:

> Essentially, the common law is an age-old doctrine that developed by way of court decisions which applied the principles of Christianity to everyday situations. Out of these cases, rules were established that governed future cases. This principle, with its origin in Europe . . . became part of American law.

Whitehead, in the same passage, also quotes law professor John C. H. Wu who stated: ". . . There can be no denying that the common law has one advantage over the legal system of any country: it was Christian from the very beginning of its history."

7. Blackstone, *Blackstone's Commentaries*, Vol. II (New York: Augustus Kelley, 1969), 450.

8. *Ibid.*, 450.

9. *Thompson*, 103 P. 578, 24 L.R.A. 221, 24 Okla. 1. (1909).

10. *Thompson*, 24 Okla., 4.

11. *Thompson*, 9.

12. *Thompson*, 8. Lewis' Blackstone, book 1, §451.

13. *Meyer v. Nebraska*, 262 U.S. 390 (1923).

14. See *Pierce v. Society of Sisters*, 268 U.S. 510, 534-35 (1925) and *Wisconsin v. Yoder*, 406 U.S. 205, 232 (1972).

15. *Wisconsin v. Yoder*, 406 U.S. at 221 and *Plyler v. Doe*, 457 U.S. 202, 221 (1982).

16. 262 U.S. 390 (1923).

17. *Ibid.*, 402.

18. *Ibid.*, 401. Also see *Bartles v. Iowa*, 262 U.S. 404 (1923) where the Court reached a similar conclusion.

19 John Whitehead, *Journal of Christian Jurisprudence*, Oklahoma City, Oklahoma: IED Press Inc., 1982, 63.

20. *Pierce*, 268 U.S. 510 (1925).

21. *Ibid.*, 534.

22. *Pierce*, 268 U.S. 510, 535.

23. In *Windsor Park Baptist Church v. Arkansas Activities Association*, (658 F.2d 618 [1981] at 621), the U.S. Court of Appeals cautioned the State of Arkansas not to standardize its children by forcing them to accept instruction from public teachers only. The Court states: "The Fourteenth Amendment forbids the States to prohibit attendance at nonpublic schools, either secular or religious." *Windsor*, 621. In other words, the state must be careful not to overly regulate home schools and Christian

schools to the extent that they cannot operate, thereby forcing their children to attend only public schools.

24. *Yoder*, 406 U.S. 205, 233.

25. *Ibid.*, 232. Burger admonishes further, "And when the interests of parenthood are combined with a free exercise claim of the nature revealed by this record, more than merely a 'reasonable relation to some purpose within the competency of the State' is required to sustain the validity of the State's requirement under the First Amendment." (*Yoder*, 233).

26. *Ibid.*, 214.

27. *Employment Division of Oregon v. Smith*, 494 U.S.872 (1990).

28. *Ibid.*, 881.

29. The U.S. Supreme Court has regularly applied the "compelling interest test" to fundamental rights that arise out of the Liberty Clause of the Fourteenth Amendment. In *Roe v. Wade*, 410 U.S. 113, 155 (1973), the Court said:

> "Where fundamental rights are involved . . . regulation limiting these rights may be justified *only* by a *compelling state interest* . . ."

30. *Ibid.*, 881, ftn.1.

31. Dr. Brian Ray, "A Nationwide Study of Home Education," 16 November 1990, National Home Education Research Institute, Seattle, Washington. This study of over two thousand home school families found that 93.8 percent of the fathers and 96.4 percent of the mothers describe themselves as "born-again" Christians.

32. See *Wisconsin v. Yoder*, 406 U.S.205, (1972) and *Sherbert v. Verner*, 374 U.S. 398, (1963).

33. See *Wisconsin v. Yoder*, 406 U.S.205, 233(1972).

34. 374 U.S. 398 (1963).

35. 406 U.S. 205 (1972).

36. 450 U.S.707 (1981).

37. 455 U.S. 252, (1982).

38. 480 U.S. —, 94 L.Ed.2d 190, 197-198 (1987).

39. *Yoder*, 406 U.S., 216-219.

40. *Yoder*, 406 U.S., 215-219; *Thomas*, 450 U.S. at 713-716.

41. *Lee, op. cit.*, 455 U.S., 257.

42. *Thomas, op. cit.*, 450 U.S., 718.

43. *Yoder, op. cit.*, 221, *Plyler v. Doe*, 457 U.S. 202, 221 (1982) and *New Life, op. cit.*, 317-318.

44. My book, *The Constitutional Right to Home School: A Parent's Choice*, will be published in 1993.

45. *DeJonge*, 179 Mich.App. 225, 449 N.W. 2d 899 (1989).

46. Main, #86 JV 10, District Court Gunnison County, Colorado, 6 May 1987. See "Approval States Cause Trouble," *The Home School Court Report*, Vol. 3, No. 2, March/June 1987, 14.

47. *Ibid.*, 3.

48. *Jeffery*, 702 F.Supp. 516 (M.D.A 1988).

49. *Ibid.*, 519 and 521.

CHAPTER 18

OTHER WAYS TO VICTORY IN THE COURTROOM

"Education ought everywhere to be religious education . . . parents are bound to employ no instructors who will not instruct their children religiously - To commit our children to the care of irreligious persons is to commit lambs to the superintendency of wolves."

-Timothy Dwight, President of Yale, 1795-1817

There are many ways that home schoolers can win in court or avoid court altogether. In this chapter, I will summarize several major defenses of home schoolers which are either based in the rights guaranteed by the Constitution or in the rights guaranteed by state statute.

When many of the compulsory attendance laws were enacted in the early 1900's, home schooling was ignored. In other words, the laws required children between certain ages to attend either public or private school, but no exemption was provided for home schools. When home schoolers in those states tried to operate as private schools, they were prosecuted. However, some of the state courts, as discussed below, properly ruled that since a private school is a "place of learning," a home school could freely operate as a private school and, therefore, legally satisfy the law.

In several of the other states which did not have a home school alternative, the courts followed a different course. They ruled that the compulsory attendance statutes were "void for vagueness" and, subsequently struck down the laws as unconstitutional. These decisions fall into two categories: 1) the definition of the term "private school" was determined by the courts to be unconstitutionally vague, as in Wisconsin[1], Georgia[2], and California, 2) some other language in the law such as the term "equivalent instruction" or "properly qualified" was found by the courts to be vague, as in Minnesota,[3] Pennsylvania,[4] Missouri,[5] and Iowa[6].

Since there are many states which remain where there is no specific home school law, the question arises, "How can someone spot a vague law?"

Identification of a Vague Law

The simplest way to identify a vague law is: 1) after you have read the law you still do not know what you are supposed to do to be a legal home school, or 2) the local school district arbitrarily creates requirements out of "thin air."

Therefore, a vague compulsory attendance law is one in which the local school district or school official is given virtually unlimited *discretion* to define key terms in the law or generally has the freedom to "legislate" his own home school policy.

For instance, in Pennsylvania before the *Jeffery* decision, 501 different superintendents were given authority, by the law, to determine if home school instruction was "satisfactory." Nearly each of the 501 school districts had different restrictions on home schoolers covering virtually every kind of requirement imaginable. Depending on the particular superintendent in power at a given time, or what school district a family lived in, home schools were either prosecuted or left alone. Many home schoolers had to flee from one school district where home schooling was never "satisfactory" to another school district were home schooling was at least tolerated. In 1988, as the lawyer covering Pennsylvania, I was handling nearly twenty home school cases in court and negotiating on behalf of approximately thirty other families who were being threatened with prosecution. Families were completely confused, and the school districts operated as their own legislatures, regularly adopting new restrictions on home schoolers.

Other states, like Missouri prior to the *Ellis* decision, required instruction to be "equivalent." Similarly, each superintendent arbitrarily created, according to his own whim, a definition of "equivalent." In many school districts it was impossible for a home schooler to satisfy the superintendent's arbitrary definition of equivalent instruction.

Fortunately, the United States Supreme Court has dealt with this issue on numerous occasions and has set clear guidelines for determining whether a statute is unconstitutionally vague under the Due Process Clause of the Constitution.[7] The Court stated:

1. A law is vague if persons of average intelligence, such as home school parents, are not put on notice as to what is required or what is forbidden. Furthermore, "persons of common intelligence must not be left to guess at the meaning of a statute nor differ as to its application."[8] For example, in Pennsylvania prior to 1989, home schoolers were required by law to be "properly qualified," but neither the home schoolers nor the superintendents knew what that meant. Many home school families stayed "underground" (did not notify the school district) because they did not know if the superintendent would interpret "properly qualified" to mean certified, a college degree, high school diploma, or something else.

2. A law is vague if arbitrary and discriminatory enforcement is permitted. In other words, if a superintendent, under the law, is free to discriminate against home schoolers and create his own arbitrary standards for home schoolers, the law is too vague, lacking the necessary explicit standards. In addition, courts have consistently held that a law is vague if the officials charged with enforcement and application of the law are permitted to resolve questions "on an ad hoc and subjective basis." In short, the fundamental right of parents to home school cannot be denied by the enforcement of a vague law

which authorizes such a denial purely on the whim of a superintendent or other school official.

The Landmark U.S. Supreme Court Which Defined Vagueness

In a landmark case, the U.S. Supreme Court summarized its doctrine on vagueness in *Grayned v. City of Rockford*.[9] In that case the Court said:

> It is a basic principle of due process that an enactment is void for vagueness if its prohibitions are not clearly defined. Vague laws offend several important values. First, because we assume that man is free to steer between lawful and unlawful conduct, we insist that laws give the person of ordinary intelligence a reasonable opportunity to know what is prohibited, so that he may act accordingly. Vague laws may trap the innocent by not providing fair warning. Second, if arbitrary and discriminatory enforcement is to be prevented, laws must provide explicit standards for those who apply them. A vague law impermissibly delegates basic policy matters to policemen, judges and juries for resolution on an ad hoc basis, with the attendant dangers of arbitrary and discriminatory application. Third, but related, where a statute "abut[s] upon sensitive First Amendment freedoms, it 'operates to inhibit the exercise of those freedoms.' Uncertain meanings inevitably lead citizens to 'steer far wider of the unlawful zone' . . . than if the boundaries of the forbidden areas were clearly marked."[10]

Oftentimes, the problem with state compulsory attendance laws is that the "language [is] so loose as to leave those who have to apply it too wide a discretion," resulting in the arbitrary denial of parental rights in education. Many of these types of vague laws yield discriminatory results: (1) dozens of differing definitions of teacher qualifications, (2) various monitoring procedures such as home visits by school officials, (3) all types, times, and places of student testing, (4) variety of progress reports, and (5) arbitrary periodic meetings.

In many instances, these statutes allow the opinion of the superintendent to control a decision as to whether parents will be allowed to exercise the fundamental Constitutional rights of directing the upbringing of their children and the free exercise of their religion, as guaranteed by the First and Fourteenth Amendments of the U.S. Constitution.

For example, in Pennsylvania, as mentioned above, home schoolers were faced with constant harassment by their local school districts. The law gave the superintendent the power to define if a home school parent was "properly qualified" and whether or not their curriculum was "satisfactory." Since there were 501 school districts, each with its own definition of these terms, the application of this vague law often led to absurd results.

One of the most ridiculous examples involved a member family of HSLDA, the Smeltzers, whose child was designated as having various learning disabilities and in need of special education. For some reason, the superintendent allowed the family to home school for three years. At the end of the third year, the child did so well on her standardized achievement tests, that the superintendent labeled her "gifted and talented." However, he and his specialists also determined that the family could no longer handle her education because she was now gifted. He, therefore, disapproved their home school and demanded that the child be sent to the public schools. When the family refused, he filed criminal truancy charges against the family.

The family called me, and I immediately called the school district, but they would not relent. Michael Farris of HSLDA then prepared a civil rights complaint asserting the family's Constitutional rights, explaining that the superintendent was personally liable for violating their civil rights. A copy of the complaint was sent to the school board's lawyer. By the next day, the school district called and said that they had made a mistake. The Smeltzer's home school program was approved, and the charges dropped, before it was necessary to file the civil rights complaint with the court![11]

Since more and more "brush fires" started across the state with home schoolers being dragged into court, HSLDA filed a civil rights case, *Jeffery v. O'Donnell*,[12] suing school districts throughout the state for trying to enforce a vague statute. This got the attention of the school districts, and some instantly changed their policy and quickly "approved" the home schoolers. These school districts were subsequently dismissed from the suit.

By God's grace, the Federal Court finally ruled in our favor. The federal court declared:

> Disparity abounds [in Pennsylvania]. What can be satisfactory in one school district could be totally unsatisfactory in another. The ultimate conclusion one must reach concerning tutorial education in Pennsylvania is that. . . the law providing for such an education is unconstitutionally vague. . . A person of ordinary

intelligence cannot reasonably steer between the lawful and the unlawful to avoid criminal prosecution. There exists no standard for determining who is a qualified tutor or what is a satisfactory curriculum in any district. Superintendents of school districts, while exercising a legitimate and constitutional function of managing their districts according to the unique character of each district, nevertheless make their decisions on an *ad hoc* basis which can result in the dangers of arbitrary and discriminatory application. . . The threat to sensitive First Amendment freedoms mandates judicial intrusion in the form of declaring the particular provision of the law unconstitutional for vagueness.[13]

The court declared the law to be unconstitutionally vague, as applied to home schoolers, and the final result was that the legislature was forced to rewrite the law to specifically protect home schooling, eliminating the school districts' discretionary powers in approving or disapproving home schools.

In fact, the cases in Missouri, Minnesota, Georgia, and Wisconsin, mentioned above, all resulted in their respective legislatures enacting favorable laws, tremendously reducing the conflict between home schoolers and the state. Without the courts striking down the laws relating to home schooling, the new laws, which provided greater freedoms for home schoolers, would never have been passed.

Vagueness Is One of the Most Successful Defenses

Vagueness has continued to be one of the most successful defenses of home schoolers who live in states without specific home school laws. In fact, in June 1991 in Michigan, one of the most difficult states in which to home school, a home school mother had been arrested, fingerprinted, had "mug shots" taken, and was charged with criminal truancy. I, along with our local counsel Dave Kallman, filed a "motion to dismiss" in this case, *People* v. *Pebler*.[14] During oral arguments, the prosecutor admitted that he did not know what the law required for home schoolers. In fact, he said that although he did not know what the law required, he was sure this home-schooling mom was not legal. I capitalized on his statements during my time for rebuttal, and the court ruled in favor of the home schooler. The court dismissed the case and found the Michigan compulsory attendance law "vague and unclear as to what specifically constitutes a violation of that act subjecting a person to criminal prosecution and Laurel

Pebler is entitled to fair notice of what conduct is proscribed by the statute."[15] I have used this case throughout the state to get other cases dismissed or prevented altogether.

Legislation which gives any amount of arbitrary discretion over home schoolers to the public school system should be opposed to avoid this kind of discriminatory treatment. States that have vague laws at present should be carefully monitored and possibly challenged, if the law is being used to harass home schoolers.

The Private School Defense: A School Is a Place of Learning

Before home school statutes began being passed in the 1980's, most compulsory attendance laws required children to attend either public school or private school. In some states, the only other alternative was for a child to be instructed by a state-certified teacher. No specific statutory option existed for home schools. In at least twelve states, home schools can still only exist as a private school. All of these states are listed below and further discussed in chapter 19.

As a result, home school families who were home schooling based on their religious convictions as guaranteed by the First Amendment, or on their parental rights as guaranteed by the Fourteenth Amendment, were forced to qualify as a private school or, in some instances, become certified to teach as a "private tutor." Qualifying as a public school, of course, was impossible.

The rationale is simple. The right of parents to teach their children at home is a constitutional right guaranteed by the First and Fourteenth Amendments. Therefore, to outlaw home schooling altogether would be a violation of a family's constitutional rights. Since teacher certification (under the tutor option) is an overly restrictive requirement which basically prohibits families from home schooling, operating as a private school is the only option which remains. In states without specific home school laws, home schools need to be able to operate as a private schools, in order for the state to fulfill its duty to adequately protect the parents' constitutional right to teach their own children. Besides, the purpose of the compulsory attendance laws is to have children educated, and that is what home schooling, operating under the private school status, is accomplishing.

Consequently, many of these types of cases have appeared throughout the country, as home school families defend their right to exist as private schools or, in some instances, their right to exist as a "satellite" of an existing private school. I refer to this defense as the "private school defense." Much precedent has already been set, and most of that precedent favors the home schools' right to legally operate as private schools.

Home schools or groups of home schoolers are still successfully operating as private schools in many states, including Alaska, Alabama, California, Delaware, Florida, Illinois, Indiana, Kansas, Kentucky, Maine, Nebraska, and Texas. It is generally to the advantage of home schools to operate under the private school laws since private schools in these states have little to no regulations.

Home Schools Operating as Private Schools Can Face Conflict

Even though I am convinced that it is legal to home school as a private school in these states, I constantly have to deal with school districts throughout many of these states who challenge the right of home schoolers to exist as private schools. For instance, in a small Texas town, a home school family was asked to come to the office of a probation officer, just for a friendly talk on home schooling. When the home school father arrived, the local judge was in the office and proceeded to intimidate him. He flatly declared, "We don't allow home schooling in this town." He did not care if the family met all the private school requirements or not. In fact, he gave the family one week to send their children to public school.[16] After threatening a civil rights suit, I was finally able to persuade the school district to leave the family alone.

In Alabama, home schools are routinely threatened with prosecution, even though they are legally operating as church schools. On one occasion, I was called by a family who was threatened to be arrested that day by a truant officer. When I called that same day, I was told that the officer went to meet with the local judge. I called the number that was given to me, and the judge answered. He stated that when this family would be taken before him in court, he would find them guilty! He said that home schoolers were a bunch of illiterates. When I told him that they had a constitutional right to freely exercise their religious beliefs to teach their own children, he asked me, "What asylum did they escape out of!" By God's grace, the situation was resolved.

In DeKalb county in Alabama, Randy Maas, a home school father, was approached by a truant officer and told to put his children in public school. When he said that he was legally home schooling and refused to enroll his children in public school, the truant officer came back two hours later with a police officer who arrested and handcuffed the father and put him in jail overnight. Even though I explained to the prosecutor that the statute and the Alabama Supreme Court require three days written notice of truancy before he can be charged, the prosecutor and the judge ignored the statute and precedents and convicted the home school father. I appealed this blatant travesty of justice to the Alabama Criminal Court of Criminal Appeals, and on May 15, 1992, the Court reversed the decision in the *Maas* case and found that the family's statutory due process rights were violated.[17]

In Kansas, home schools operating as private schools are routinely turned over to the Social Rehabilitative Services for investigation.[18] I have talked with nearly a hundred of these SRS agents over the years, and they vary in aggressiveness. Although some insist on inspecting the homes and interrogating the children, we have refused such an invasion of privacy. Furthermore, if a home school family inquires about the legality of home schooling in Kansas, the Department of Education sends them a copy of a memorandum by the Kansas Legislative Research Department which states:

> Is home instruction permitted in Kansas as an alternative to attendance at public schools? Is home instruction, in essence, the same thing as a private, denominational, or parochial school? The answer to both of these questions is "no."[19]

In other words, as far as the state is officially concerned, home schooling is illegal. As a result, some prosecutors have told me that home schooling is illegal and have taken HSLDA families to court. One example involved the Melrose family in Kingman County in Kansas. The local principal did not like home schooling and believed that they had to be state accredited. He convinced the prosecutor to bring charges. After I negotiated with the prosecutor and wrote him a lengthy legal letter explaining the legality of a home school to operate as a nonaccredited private school, he agreed to dismiss the case.[20]

In Michigan, in the 1990-1991 school year, I was involved in representing twelve families throughout the state who were prosecuted for establishing home schools even though courts have recognized the right of home schools to operate as private schools. Although we were able to win all of these cases, the families had to put up with much harassment.[21]

Of course, the situations are nearly endless, but the majority of home schoolers in these states are still being left alone. However, it is important to be aware of your rights and to be familiar with the "private school defense."

The Meaning of the Word "School"

As can be imagined, the major contention between the home schools and the state was, and continues to be, in some states, "what is the actual definition of a private school?" Since nearly every state did not define the term "private school" in its statute, some courts, such as two courts in Florida and Arkansas, decided to exceed their bounds and do some legislating.[22] These courts argued that the "ordinary meaning" of the word "school" means an "institution" with a building and children from more than one family. However, both of these decisions were rendered moot (or of no effect) by their respective legislatures in 1984, which passed specific laws legally protecting home schools.[23]

Contrary to the above courts' claims, the ordinary meaning of the word "school" is a "place of learning." This popular definition of "school" is found in many dictionaries and recognized by many other courts around the country.

In Black's Law Dictionary, for instance, "school" is defined as "an institution *or* place of instruction or education." Funk and Wagnalls Dictionary defines "school" as "the place in which formal instruction is given." Home schooling definitely fits these descriptions because it is a "place of instruction." Many court cases involving home schoolers being charged with truancy found the home schoolers "not guilty" because their home school met all the requirements for a private school.

Cases Which Recognize Home Schools as Private Schools

In Illinois, for example, the Illinois Supreme Court found that a school in the home was a legitimate private school. In *People* v. *Levisen*,[24] the Court declared that a school is:

> a place where instruction is imparted to the young . . . *the number of persons* being taught does not determine whether a place is a school.[25] (italics added)

The Court explained further:

> Compulsory education laws are enacted to enforce the natural obligations of parents to provide an education for their young, an obligation which corresponds to the parents' right of control over the child . . . The object is that all shall be educated not that they shall be educated in any particular manner or place.[26]

Since that decision thousands of home schools, many with only one or two children, operate freely as private schools in Illinois.

In Indiana, the Indiana Appellate Court reached the same conclusions in *State* v. *Peterman*.[27] The Court defined a "school" as:

> a place where instruction is imparted to the young . . . We do not think that the *number of persons*, whether one or many, makes a place where instruction is imparted any less or any more a school.[28] (italics added)

As a result, parents in the case were vindicated, and their home school was considered to be a legal private school.

Home schools in many states do fulfill the object of the compulsory attendance law and meet all of the technical requirements of the law for private or church schools.

In California, thousands of home schools operate as private schools. Each year certain counties take families to court, challenging their right to exist as private schools and stating that their only option is to be certified tutors. However, the courts have sided with the home schoolers. For example, Michael Smith of the Home School Legal Defense Association handled the *People* v. *Darrah* and the *People* v. *Black* cases[29] in which two home school families were being denied the right to operate as private schools, even though they met all the requirements of a private school in California. The Court ruled in favor of the families, finding that the law was unconstitutionally vague and that the families could not be prosecuted for operating as private schools. Nothing in the law prohibited them from being private schools.

Although there are many more cases which could be mentioned, there is only one more which will be described. The case is *Leeper* v. *Arlington Independent School District*.[30] In Texas, thousands of home schools were operating as small private schools. When the private tutorial statute was repealed, home schools continued to operate as private schools. Then in 1981, the Texas Education Agency (TEA) issued a policy declaring that "educating a child at home is not the same as private school instruction and therefore, is not an acceptable substitute." In other words, home schools are not private schools and therefore are illegal. Over the next few years nearly 150 home school families across the state were hauled into court for criminal truancy charges. One HSLDA member family was taken to court even though both parents were certified teachers.

At this point, the home schoolers fought back. The Home School Legal Defense Association joined in with several other home school groups and brought a civil rights class action suit against the TEA and all 1060 school districts in the state for violating the civil rights of thousands of home schoolers. Attorney Shelby Sharpe of Dallas handled nearly all of the litigation. The groups representing the home schoolers sought a permanent injunction to stop the prosecution, a declaration that home schools can operate as private schools, and $4 million in damages. On April 13, 1987, the Court found that home schools who meet the minimum standards of private schools are considered to be legal private schools. He also placed a permanent injunction prohibiting prosecution of these private schools in the home throughout the entire state.

On November 27, 1991, the Court of Appeals of Texas completely affirmed the lower court in the *Leeper* case, recognizing that home schools can operate as private schools.[31] The Court of Appeals reasoned that the TEA "deprived the home school parents of equal protection under the law" since the private schools in the home were unfairly discriminated against "on the sole basis of location in the home," rather than outside the home. The Court further emphasized "that initiation of prosecution of plaintiff parents violates the parents' equal protection rights by establishing an unreasonable and arbitrary classification of parents which is not rationally related to any state interest."[32] The Court found no evidence that the home schoolers were not educating their children. The Court also held that each of the 1060 school districts were not immune from the suit because they were each liable for implementing the TEA's "unconstitutional policy" on home schooling.

This case is a tremendous victory that stands for the principle that parents have the right to be "equally protected" under the law and cannot be prohibited from operating a private school only because it is operated in the home.

How a Home School Can Operate as a Private School

In conclusion, let us apply these principles to one state, Alabama, where home schoolers have trouble being recognized as private church schools. A thorough search of the Alabama statutes and court cases does not reveal any definition of a school in which it is required to have more than one child or to meet in any type of building. The only definition of a church school which can be found in the Alabama statutes is one that offers "grades K-12 or any combination thereof" and is "operated as a ministry of a local church, group of churches, denomination, and/or association of churches..."[33] Furthermore, the statute defines a church school as being operated on a nonprofit basis and not receiving any state or federal funding.

A home school can easily meet the definition of a "church school" as defined by statute. As long as it follows the curriculum requirements, is operated as a ministry of a local church, is nonprofit, and does not receive any state or federal funding, a home school, by statute, is a private church school. In Alabama, a private church school can be a legitimate church school if it has one student taught by his parents in his home or one thousand students taught by hired teachers in a massive building complex.

The Traditional Legal Presumption That Parents Act in Their Children's Best Interest

Today many public school officials no longer hold to the tradition that parents act in the best interest of their children. Most of the public school bureaucrats and organizations that make up the educational elite have developed a statist mentality that is repulsed by the idea of individual and parental rights. They have come to believe that they, the state educators, know what is best for the children. They believe that they are the guardians of the children and act in the children's best interest. Parents are considered to be inferior and amateurs in raising and educating children, while the educators are the "professionals." I have talked to hundreds of school officials who genuinely believe this way. A quick look at the teachers' colleges will show the source of this elite and anti-parent mentality.

However, the U.S. Supreme Court still recognizes that parents' rights are supreme in *Parham* v. *J.R.*[34] This decision presented strong support of parents' rights to control the important decisions which concern their minor children. In that case, Chief Justice Burger wrote for the majority:

> Our jurisprudence historically has reflected Western civilization concepts of the family as a unit with broad parental authority over minor children. Our cases have consistently followed that course; our constitutional system long ago rejected any notion that a child is "the mere creature of the State" and, on the contrary, asserted that parents generally "have the right, coupled with the high duty, to recognize and prepare [their children] for additional obligations." *Pierce v. Society of Sisters*, 268 U.S. 510, 535 (1925) . . . [other citations omitted] . . . The law's concept of the family rests on a presumption that parents possess what a child lacks in maturity, experience, and capacity for judgment required for making life's difficult decisions. More important, historically it has been recognized that natural bonds of affection lead parents to act in the best interests of their children. 1 W. Blackstone, Commentaries 447; 2 J. Kent, Commentaries on American Law 190.
>
> As with so many other legal presumptions, experience and reality may rebut what the law accepts as a starting point; the incidence of child neglect and abuse cases attests to this. That some parents "may at times be acting against the interests of their children" . . . creates a basis for caution, but it is hardly a reason to discard wholesale those pages of human experience that teach that parents generally do act in the child's best interest . . . The statist notion that governmental power should supersede parental authority in all cases because some parents abuse and neglect children is repugnant to American tradition....
>
> We cannot assume that the result in *Meyer v. Nebraska* and *Pierce v. Society of Sisters* would have been different if the children there had announced a preference to learn only English or a preference to go to a public, rather than a church school.[35]

Therefore, school districts cannot automatically monitor home schoolers if the legislature has not specifically granted them such authority. Home schoolers are presumed to be acting in their children's best interest. In other words, they are innocent until proven guilty. This principle is particularly applicable in the "private school states" talked about in chapter 19. Also, social workers need to be reminded of this presumption, since they often try to usurp parental authority on a fabricated anonymous tip by attempting to make the parents prove that they are innocent when there is no evidence of guilt.

The Neutral Decision-Maker Defense

Every state has a compulsory attendance law, and generally the local public school officials have the exclusive authority to enforce this law. Many states give the superintendents *discretion*, in some way, over whether or not a home school will be able to operate. As a result, public school officials often treat home schooling as a privilege, not a right, which is subject to their arbitrary approval or disapproval. However, since the superintendent has a financial interest in the outcome of whether or not a home school will be allowed to operate, and has a philosophical bias against home schooling, such discretion is unconstitutional as a violation of due process.

Before 1982, most state superintendents or school boards had unlimited discretion to either approve or disapprove home schools. Since then, at least thirty states have changed their laws to specifically protect home schooling and thereby reduce or eliminate the public school officials' discretionary authority.[36]

The problem of public school officials' discretionary authority over home schoolers is most apparent in the four states which are classified as "approval states" but also in many of the "private school" states.[37] In these states, I have found that home schoolers are often subject to arbitrary requirements that change from year to year at the whim of the local school officials. Home schoolers are frequently disapproved for the flimsiest reasons, such as refusing to allow a home visit or refusing to have their children tested in the public school when they have already arranged for testing privately. Another reason for disapproval is the lack of necessary qualifications that the superintendent personally believes is necessary. Once disapproved, the families will normally face criminal truancy or "child in need of services" charges.

Even in some of the states which have passed home school laws, certain areas of the laws are still left to the discretion of the superintendent. For instance, in Florida, Virginia, Pennsylvania and South Carolina, the superintendents have the discretion to determine if a home school child's test scores or evaluation shows "adequate" progress. In Florida, at the end of the 1991-92 school year, one superintendent arbitrarily claimed an HSLDA member's test scores of his child were not adequate, even though over half of his public school students in the same grade scored lower. Virginia superintendents that I have dealt with have arbitrarily rejected a home schooler's evaluation, completed by a certified teacher, by simply saying that the progress is not satisfactory and then ordering the home school to "cease and desist."

In Tennessee, the state commissioner of education has the power to waive the college degree requirement for parents who are teaching high school children. Consistently, he abuses his discretion by denying virtually every single waiver request. He does not even take into consideration the fact that many of these high school graduate parents have been successfully teaching their children at home for the last several years prior to high school.[38]

Public School Officials Are Not Neutral Decision-Makers Regarding Home Schooling

Public school officials are not neutral when it comes to exercising their discretion and deciding whether a family should be allowed to home school. One of the most obvious reasons is that they have a *financial incentive* to disapprove a home school and thereby increase the probability that the home-schooled child will be placed in the public schools. Since a local school district receives state and federal tax dollars of between $2000 to $4000 per head count, twenty children being home schooled gives the school district a minimum net loss of $40,000 in tax money.[39] This could easily pay for another teacher's salary.

One superintendent, along with a truant officer, visited a home school family in Michigan who is a member of HSLDA and who had pulled four children out of the public schools. The home schooler called me and told me that the superintendent asked her: "How could you do this to our school district? Do you have any idea how much tax money we will be losing for that many children? You need to get them back in school." The family was soon threatened with prosecution. This is by no means an isolated incident. I have record of many superintendents who have admitted to the parents, newspapers, HSLDA lawyers, or in court, that they are concerned about the loss of tax money to their school district, a direct result of families home schooling their children.[40]

For example, in Florida, Dan Wicklund, director of finance for the Columbia County School System, explained to a reporter of the *Lake*

City Reporter that he was alarmed by the amount of families home schooling (157) in his county. He said, "The county earns $2,538 per student. The total lost revenue is $398,000 for the students enrolled in home study this year."[41]

In Texas, Pat Whelan, legal counsel to the Texas Education Association, bemoaned the fact that for each home school student not enrolled in the public schools, the public schools lose about $2,800 in tax money.[42]

In some states the financial incentive is even greater. For instance, in Pennsylvania, a superintendent is encouraged by the law to make things difficult for home schoolers. Under Chapter 24, Section 13-1333 of the Pennsylvania Statutes, he not only has the authority to commence criminal prosecutions, but also under this section all fines imposed are collected "for the benefit of the school district in which such offending person resides." The more truancy fines filed, the more fine money the local public school receives. Or the home school family can avoid prosecution by enrolling in the public schools, in which case the superintendent, on behalf of the school district, receives thousands of dollars per child in increased state aid.

For example, in one case I handled, *Pennsylvania v. Hulls*,[43] a superintendent continued to file charges on a weekly basis during the entire first half of the 1986-87 school year and resumed filing weekly charges during most of the 1987-88 school year, against a family whose mother was a former public school teacher. Over a two year period, the superintendent accumulated a very large financial interest in the prosecution of the Hulls. He only stopped his harassment when the compulsory attendance statute was ruled unconstitutional in regards to home schooling, in HSLDA's successful federal right suit, *Jeffery v. O'Donnell.*[44]

Another reason that public school officials are not neutral when making a discretionary decision concerning a home school is that many of them really believe that they are the guardians of the children within the boundaries of their school district. They sincerely believe that they know what is best for the children, especially since they have seven years of higher education, and the home school mother, half of the time, only has a high school diploma.[45] With this type of bias, it is hard for many public school officials to approve home schoolers and allow them to operate freely.

The home schools are competitors with the public schools. In North Dakota, the year after the home school law was passed, the number of home-schooled children doubled. The more lenient the local home school policy or state law, the more families will home school their children. This is a monetary loss to the public schools, and a threat to the teacher's unions.

This situation in which public school officials have arbitrary discretionary authority over whether or not home schools can freely operate is synonymous with the following hypothetical illustration. Let us say that the legislature in a particular state is concerned over the quality of new cars. As a result, the legislature passes a law requiring all car dealers to be licensed. It then delegates the licensing power to the Ford dealership. Ford is not only given the discretion to decide which car dealers should be licensed but is also given the discretion to draft its own "rules." One of the first rules Ford naturally adopts is that all car dealers, Toyota, Chrysler, etc., can only sell cars built with Ford parts. Is the Ford dealership neutral in determining who should be licensed? Certainly it is no more neutral than public school officials, with a vested interest in public school survival, determining who should be allowed to home school.

The U.S. Supreme Court Condemns Non-Neutral Decision-Makers

The Fourteenth Amendment guarantees that life, liberty, and property cannot be taken away from an individual unless he receives "due process." This means that an individual will receive certain procedural safeguards that will ensure that he will be treated fairly. One of the elements of due process is that if an individual's liberty is at stake, in this instance, parental liberty, he has a right to be heard by a *neutral decision-maker*, at the first level. The first level for a home schooler who is being challenged is usually the biased superintendent or school board.

The Supreme Court of the United States has definitively ruled that a decision-maker with a financial stake in the outcome is not a "neutral magistrate" and, therefore, is in violation of the Fourteenth Amendment Due Process Clause. In *Tumey v.Ohio*,[46] a mayor was the decision-maker in a process concerning a liquor law. If the mayor decided in favor of the individual, the city would receive no money. But if the mayor decided against the individual appearing before him, the mayor received a nominal sum of money, while the city received a substantial sum of money.

The Supreme Court held that *both* types of financial incentives violate the due process clause. It makes no difference if the monetary gain goes exclusively to the governmental entity (the public school) and not to the state official (superintendent). *Tumey* clearly stands for the principle that a local government official, such as a superintendent, who has a financial stake in the outcome on behalf of his local governmental unit or public school is not a neutral decision-maker for the purpose of the due process clause.

In another case, *Ward v.Monroeville*, the United States Supreme Court reaffirmed *Tumey* and made even more clear that the financial incentive need not be personal to the decision-maker.[47]

Only two home school cases, at this point, have dealt with this issue of the right to a neutral decision-maker. Both of these cases were ruled on by the Supreme Court in North Dakota. In *State v. Toman*,[48] the North Dakota Supreme Court upheld a truancy conviction of a home school family and avoided the challenge that the superintendent was not neutral. The principle to learn from the *Toman* case is that the non-neutral decision-maker defense may be only applicable if the home school family specifically requested the home school exemption and was denied *before* they were charged with criminal truancy.

In addition, this same Court also considered this due process argument in another case, *State v. Anderson*.[49] The principle to learn from this case is that the function of the decision-maker, which in this case was the local superintendent, must be discretionary and not merely ministerial. In other words, if the legislature enacts a law that requires a home school parent to have a "high school diploma," the superintendent performs a ministerial function in determining whether the parent has a high school diploma. However, if a statute requires a home school parent to be "qualified," the superintendent performs a discretionary function in defining "qualified" and applying his whim to his decision. The latter would violate the due process clause.

School officials cannot be given the authority to decide whether or not families can teach their children at home. They have both a financial incentive and a natural partisanship or bias which precludes them from serving as a neutral decision-maker, as required by the due process clause. The ultimate goal of HSLDA is to repeal compulsory attendance statutes in all the states, which would definitely end this problem because no educational authorities would be needed. However, in the meantime, HSLDA is working with home schoolers and legislatures to remove all discretionary authority of public school officials and reduce their duty to merely gathering information.

Technical Defenses of Home Schoolers

Many times we have found that the most successful cases for home schoolers have involved technicalities. For instance, in North Dakota there were a number of occasions where we were able to win cases on behalf of home schoolers who were charged with criminal truancy because the prosecution was not able to prove a very important element of the crime—that the child involved was actually of school age. The Nelson family of Sargent County was charged with criminal truancy since they did not use a cerified teacher during the 1988-89 school year. Although the prosecutor made several attempts to introduce evidence to prove the age of the child, I objected to these on procedural grounds. The Court sustained the objections and granted my motion to dismiss the case since the prosecution wasn't able to prove the child was of actual school age![50]

In another situation, God enabled us to successfully win a major victory before the Iowa Supreme Court, based on a mere technicality. In Iowa in 1987, home schoolers had to be certified in order to teach their children at home. The Trucke family was charged in September with criminal truancy. We appealed the case to the Iowa Supreme Court, arguing that teacher certification was unconstitutional. After we submitted our briefs, the Iowa Supreme Court contacted our office. They requested that we submit a supplemental brief concerning the issue that possibly the criminal charges were brought prematurely. In Iowa, children only needed to attend school 120 days, so the court was hinting that a family could have hired a certified teacher later in the school year and still have completed 120 days in compliance with the law. Mike Farris from our office prepared the brief, arguing this point, explaining that the charges were brought prematurely since the family could conceivably have secured a certified teacher in May of that school year and crammed in 120 days of instruction until the end of August when the school year officially ends. The Iowa Supreme Court, as a result, reversed the criminal conviction of the Trucke family and held that the criminal charges were in fact premature. After that decision, for the next several years, school districts did not have any idea of when to file criminal charges against home schoolers, thereby protecting numerous families from prosecution.[51]

I will recount one more instance in which a technicality won the day. In the state of Alabama, some school districts periodically attempt to require home schoolers to be certified tutors in order to operate legally. In Fort Payne City, the Johnson family was taken to court since they were not using a certified teacher. In preparing for the case, I discovered that the family lived 1,000 feet outside the city limits of Fort Payne City. I immediately filed a motion to dismiss the Johnson case with the DeKalb County court, based on "lack of jurisdiction." One of the elements of the "crime of home schooling" is that the child has to reside within the boundaries of the school district. The school board attorney was frustrated and hired a surveying team to determine if the family was in fact outside the school district. The surveying team confirmed what we already knew, that the family lived outside the school district. As a result, the motion to dismiss was granted, based on the "One Thousand Foot Rule" in Alabama![52]

In conclusion, there are many ways for home schoolers to win their cases. Each case must be dealt with in a thorough manner with all potential defenses thoroughly checked. Oftentimes courts will be very favorable towards arguments that raise technicalities.

Notes

1. *Wisconsin v. Popanz*, 112 Wis.2d 166, 332 N.W.2d 750 (1983).

2. *Roemhild v. Georgia*, 251 Ga.569, 308 S.E.2d 154 (1983).

3. *Minnesota v. Newstrom*, 371 N.W.2d 533 (Minn. 1985).

4. Two separate and favorable decisions resulted: *Jeffery*, 702 F.Supp. 513 (M.D. PA 1988) and *Jeffery*, 702 F.Supp. 516 (M.D. PA 1988).

5. *Ellis v. O'Hara*, 612 F.Supp 379 (E.D. Mo. 1985). *Ellis*, was "reversed" by an order of the Eighth Circuit. 802 F.2d 462 (8th Cir. 1986). The published decision gives only the word "reversed" as a docket entry. From reviewing the actual opinion of the Eighth Circuit, it is obvious that the decision was reversed to permit the district court to make an inquiry into the issue of mootness, in light of a newly enacted Missouri statute which eliminated the vagueness of the compulsory attendance statute.

6. *Fellowship Baptist Church* v. *Benton*, 620 F.Supp. 308 (S.D. Iowa 1985); aff'd 815 F.2d 486 (8th Cir. 1986).

7. When parents are home schooling for religious reasons under the First Amendment, "special scrutiny" must be applied whenever a vague compulsory attendance statute imposes criminal penalties which tend to operate to inhibit the exercise of those freedoms. See *Kolender v. Lawson*, 461 U.S. 352, 358 n. 8 (1983).

8. *Connally v. General Construction Co.*, 269 U.S. 385, 391, 46 S.Ct. 126, 127, 70 L.Ed. 322 (1925).

9. 408 U.S. 104 (1972).

10. 408 U.S., 108-109.

11. *Home School Court Report*, "Pennsylvania Under Fire," Jan.-Feb. 1987 edition, Vol. 3 No. 1, Paeonian Springs, Virginia. This article also documents many other cases pending in Pennsylvania during that time.

12. Two separate and favorable decisions resulted: *Jeffery*, 702 F.Supp. 513 (M.D. PA 1988) and *Jeffery*, 702 F.Supp. 516 (M.D. PA 1988).

13. *Jeffery*, 702 F.Supp. 516, 521.

14. *Pebler*, No. 91-0840-SM, St. Joseph County District Court, July 2, 1991.

15. *People v. Pebler*, No. 91-0848-SM, St. Joseph County 3-B District Court, Judge William McManus, Order of Dismissal, 2 July 1991.

16. "*Leeper* Decision Challenged in Texas," *The Home School Court Report*, Vol. 4, No. 4, Fall 1988, 10.

17. *Maas v. Alabama*, 601 So. 2d 209, Alabama Court of Criminal Appeals, 15 May, 1992. Also see "Alabama: Court Ignores Statute," *The Home School Court Report*, Vol. 7, No. 6, November-December 1991, 8.

18. For example see "Kansas School Districts Challenge Parents," *The Home School Court Report*, Vol. 6, No. 4, Fall 1990, 9.

19. The Memorandum is entitled "Kansas Compulsory School Attendance Laws and the Nonpublic Schools," Revised 1 June 1988.

20. "Kansas Tremors," *Home School Court Report*, Vol. 6, No. 1, Fall-Winter 1992, 2.

21. "Michigan: Litigation Proliferates," *The Home School Court Report*, Vol. 7, No. 4, July-August 1991, 15 and "Michigan: More Cases Dismissed," *The Home School Court Report*, Vol 7, No. 5, September-October 1991, 8-9.

22. For instance, in Florida and Arkansas, two state court decisions ruled that the definition of school did not include a home school. *Burrow v. State*, 282 Ark. 479, 669 S.W.2d 441 (1984), and *State of Florida v. Buckner*, 472 So. 2d 1228, (Fla. Dist. Ct. App. 1985). In both of these decisions, the courts created definitions of private school out of thin air. Since the Arkansas and Florida statutes did not define the term "private school," these courts decided to "legislate" and create a definition that would exclude home schooling. The home school families were convicted even though their home schools satisfied all the statutory requirements for private schools.

23. See Florida Statutes Annotated sections 228.041(34) and 232.02(4) and Arkansas Statutes Annotated section 80-1503.

24. 90 N.E.2d 213 (1950).

25. *Levisen*, 215.

26. *Ibid.*

27. 70 NE 550 (1904).

28. *Peterman,* 551.

29. *Darrah,* No. 853104 and *Black,* No. 853105, Santa Maria Mun. Ct., 10 March 1986.

30. No 17-88761-85, Tarrant County, 17th Judicial Ct., 13 April 1987.

31. *Texas Education Agency et al. v. Leeper, et al,* (No. 2-87-216-CV), 27 November 1991. Also see "Texas Home Schoolers Welcome Victory at Last," *The Home School Court Report,* Vol. 8, No. 1, January/February 1992.

32. *Ibid.*

33. Alabama Code §16-28-1(2).

34. 442 U.S. 584 (1979).

35. *Ibid.* 402 U.S., at 602-604.

36. See Chapter 19 for a list of these states. For a more detailed summary of the requirements for home schoolers in all fifty states see: Christopher J. Klicka, *Home Education in the United States: A Legal Analysis,* February 1992, Home School Legal Defense Association.

37. The four remaining "approval" states are Massachusetts, Rhode Island, South Dakota, and Utah. For more details on the "approval" states, the "private school" states, and those states with "home school" laws, see Christopher J. Klicka, *Home Schooling in the United States: A Legal Analysis,* August 1992, Home School Legal Defense Association.

38. *Home School Court Report,* Vol. 6 No. 3, Summer edition 1990, HSLDA, Paeonian Springs, Virginia.

39. Theodore Wade, Jr., editor, *The Home School Manual,* chapter 5, "The Battle for the Right to Teach," by Christopher Klicka (Auburn, CA: Gazelle Publications, 1988), 68. Also see *The Home School Court Report,* "Denying Constitutional Rights For Money," Vol. 3 No.1, Jan.-Feb. 1987.

40. Home School Legal Defense Association, P.O Box 159, Paeonian Springs, Virginia 22159. The court records where school officials admit the loss of money include cases in North Dakota, Michigan, Pennsylvania, New York, and Minnesota.

41. "Teach Me Mom," *Lake City Reporter,* 14 September 1989, 1-B.

42. Mark Schlachtenhaufen, "Home Schooling Under Fire," Baytown Sun, Houston, 7 August 1991.

43. See "PA Victory May Come in Legislature," *The Home School Court Report,* Vol 4, No.3, Summer 1988, 13.

44. 702 F.Supp. 516 (M.D. PA 1988).

45. This description of the public school officials' mind set is based on over five-hundred conversations Chris Klicka has had with school officials, while negotiating on behalf of home schoolers since 1983.

46. 273 U.S.510 (1927).

47. *Ward,* 409 U.S. 57, 60 (1972).

48. *Toman,* Criminal Nos. 880186 and 880187, Slip. Op. 1-2, 10 February 1989.

49. *Anderson,* 427 N.W.2d 316, 320 (N.D.) *cert. denied,* ____U.S.___, 109 S.Ct. 491 (1988).

50. "Governor Signs North Dakota Home Schooling Law," *The Home School Court Report*, Vol. 5, No. 3, Summer 1989, 2.

51. *Iowa v. Trucke*, 410 NW2d 242 (1987). Also see "Supreme Court Victory in Iowa," *The Home School Court Report*, Vol. 3, No. 3, September/November Edition 1987, 5.

52. "Case Won in Alabama Due to the Thousand Foot Rule," *The Home School Court Report*, Vol. 6, No. 2, Spring 1990, 9.

PART
6

AN UNEASY PEACE:
CONSERVING OUR FREEDOMS

As stated earlier, home schoolers will not be free from conflict
until the compulsory attendance laws are repealed. This will
remove the public school's legal authority over home schoolers.
However, there is much we can do to gain more freedom for
home schoolers in the meantime.

This section will describe how you can make a difference by
influencing the media, educating the legislature, and having legal
solidarity with home schoolers throughout the country by joining
with the Home School Legal Defense Association.

And all thy children shall be
taught of the LORD; and great
shall be the peace of thy children.
　　　　　　— Isaiah 54.13

CHAPTER 19

THE GOOD, THE BAD
AND THE UGLY STATE LAWS

"The competitions of the state for the educating power have been so engrossing that we have almost forgotten the parent as the rightful competitor. And now many look at its claim almost contemptuously. It is vital to a true theory for human rights, that the real independence of the parent be respected."

—Dr. Robert Dabney

As demonstrated in chapter 5, home schooling has been operating in the United States since its inception. However, with the advent of the public schools and subsequent compulsory attendance laws primarily in the 1900s, home schooling nearly died out.

In the 1980s, however, home schooling experienced a rebirth in popularity as hundreds of thousands of families diligently began teaching their own children at home. This rekindling of a historical system of education continues to grow at a tremendous pace in the 1990's, with no sign of slowing down.

The legal road to home school, however, has not been easy since most states did not formally recognize the right of parents to home school their own children. In 1980, only three states in the entire country, Utah, Ohio, and Nevada, officially recognized the right to home school in their state statutes. In most states, it was "open season" on families teaching their children at home, and they were often prosecuted under criminal truancy laws and educational neglect charges.

The Home School Legal Defense Association, from the beginning, realized that litigation was only a "necessary evil" which would yield unpredictable results. Since most courts no longer merely apply the law, but make law, the results would depend on which particular court the case was heard in. Litigation and legal defense has been necessary "to hold back the tide" of legal harassment until the legislatures start changing laws to specifically protect the rights of home schools. Since 1983, HSLDA has been able to help over fourteen thousand families who were negatively contacted by legal authorities. HSLDA has also provided expert testimony before legislatures to help defeat bad bills or to help pass good bills.

God blessed the efforts of home schoolers with tremendous success in the legislatures across the country in spite of great odds. It is clear that these victories were not the result of families merely home schooling for the sake of home schooling, but rather because families were and are home schooling their children in order to train them up so that they love and obey God, all for His glory. God has honored those thousands of families who have honored Him in the godly training of their children. HSLDA, too, dedicates its work to God's glory. The home school movement, meanwhile, continues to expand.

A Summary of the Home School Laws

A short summary of the home school legislation and case precedent will reveal the national trend to limit state controls over private education in favor of expanding parental liberty. Since 1982, thirty-two states have changed their compulsory attendance laws, and four State Boards of Education have amended their regulations to specifically allow for home schooling, with certain minimal requirements. In addition, two more states, Alaska and Nebraska, amended their private school statutes in 1984 allowing for any private schools to opt out of accreditation and certification requirements by asserting sincerely-held religious beliefs.[1] Home schoolers in these two states can now freely operate under these religious exemptions. It is important to notice that many of these states mentioned above abandoned prior statutory requirements that all teachers, including home schooling parents, be certified, because it infringed on parental rights and offered no guarantee as to the quality of education.[2] A close review of these new home school laws reveals a trend across the nation to lessen state control over private forms of education.

As of September 1992, there are thirty-four states that *by statute or regulation* specifically allow "home instruction" or "home schooling," provided certain requirements are met. These states are Arkansas, Arizona, Connecticut, Colorado, Georgia, Hawaii, Florida, Iowa, Louisiana, Maine, Maryland, Minnesota, Missouri, Mississippi, Montana, New Hampshire, New Mexico, New York, Nevada, North Carolina, North Dakota, Ohio, Oregon, Pennsylvania, Rhode Island, South Carolina, Tennessee, Utah, Virginia, Vermont, Washington, Wisconsin, West Virginia, and Wyoming.[3]

At least five of these thirty-four compulsory attendance statutes merely require home schoolers to submit an annual notice of intent, verifying that instruction will be given in certain core subjects for the same amount of days as the public schools. These states are Montana, Wyoming, Mississippi, Wisconsin, and Missouri. In fact, in Missouri, home schoolers even have an option not to notify at all. These states' laws tend to be "model" laws since they are properly based on the "honor system" which protects parental liberty and takes all monitoring power from the state authorities.

Colorado and Georgia have laws similar to the five mentioned above, but the parents are required to have the children tested every other year. The best part of these laws is that the test scores do not have to be submitted to the public schools.

The rest of these home school statutes have an additional requirement that home schoolers administer an annual standardized achievement test or have an evaluation performed which shows that the child has made adequate progress. Tennessee, for example, requires that home-schooled children be tested in grades 2, 3, 6, 8, and 10. West Virginia mandates that students be tested annually and achieve above the 40th percentile. Oregon requires that home schoolers score in at least the 15th percentile, while Minnesota requires the 30th percentile and Virginia the 23rd percentile. Colorado requires only the 13th percentile. Arkansas requires that children score no lower than eight months below grade level.

All of these thirty-four home school states allow parents with only high school diplomas or less to teach their children at home. However, Arizona requires all home school teachers to take a minimum competency test geared for the eighth grade level. New Mexico requires that parents have a bachelor's degree, but allows parents to get a waiver which is routinely granted. North Dakota allows parents to take a teacher exam which exempts them from supervision by a certified teacher, which nearly 100 percent of home school parents have passed. Tennessee requires a college degree for parents teaching high school children at home. South Carolina had required home schoolers without a college degree to take a test designed for education majors in college. HSLDA attorney Mike Farris challenged the law in the *Lawrence, et al v. S.C. State Board of Education*[4] case, and won. The South Carolina Supreme Court found teacher exams to be invalid and prohibited them from being required for home schoolers. Chapter 12 of this book exposes the fact that, according to numerous studies and experts, such qualification requirements are completely unnecessary for educating children.

For the most part, these states with home school laws have less conflict than before. However, no matter how good the law, some school districts will always add to the law. Many school officials have told me they actually believe the law is the minimum amount of authority to which they can add. Of course, the opposite is true: the law represents the maximum of their authority. In fact, one important case in Michigan, *Clonlara v. State Board of Education*,[5] struck down the Michigan Department of Education's onerous "Home School Compliance Procedures," because it is illegal for the Department of Education to create or enforce requirements *which are not in the law.*

Therefore, every year I have to deal with hundreds of school districts in these states which create "out of thin air" some new policy which illegally restricts the rights of home schoolers. The bi-monthly

Home School Court Report, published by the HSLDA, documents this common abuse in certain school districts throughout the country.

States Where Home Schools Can Operate as Private Schools

The rest of the sixteen states have no specific statutes referring to home instruction, although *all states allow home schooling* under certain conditions. For example, in at least twelve states, home schools may presently operate as private schools.[6] In all of these states except Michigan (which requires teacher certification), home schoolers need only provide instruction in certain core subjects for the same time as public schools. Although each year certain school districts challenge the right of home schools to exist as private schools in these states, home schoolers have thus far been successful.

States Where Home Schools Are Subject to Discretionary State Approval

The remaining four states require that home schools be approved by the local school superintendent or school board in order to legally operate. A couple of the "home school" states cited above should also be included as approval states.[7]

These "approval states," however, have somewhat vague requirements for home schoolers. Of course, each school district in these states creates its own arbitrary definition of these terms, resulting in great disparity between school districts. In Massachusetts, for example, in one school district a home schooler may be completely legal, but when he moves into the neighboring school district with different standards, that same home schooler is prosecuted. Other home school families have legally and successfully home schooled in one district for several years, but a new superintendent comes to office, changes the rules, and criminally prosecutes the family. In fact, the vagueness in these "approval state" statutes has caused several states to abandon their approval requirements altogether, in favor of having home schoolers file notices of intent and take standardized tests.

To illustrate the abuse that often occurs in these "approval states," let me recount one incident which happened in Massachusetts. The Searles family was beginning to home school for the first year and they notified the local school district with the proper information.

The school district official responded with a call demanding that they place their child in public school immediately. He said it might be weeks before he could get to "approve" their material. I contacted the school official, telling him that it would violate the family's religious beliefs to put their child in public school, and that they had submitted everything they needed to in order to be legal.

The next day the principal contacted the family, reiterating the demand to put their child in school. This was followed a little later by a visit from a police officer who told them that the child would be "forcibly removed" from the home if the child was not in public school the next day! The mother, badly shaken, called me. While we were on the phone, another knock came on her door. This time a probation officer was there, repeating the threats. She handed the phone to him and he proceeded to tell me that it was in "the child's best interest to go to public school." Although I persuaded him to abandon trying to take the child, he expedited the filing of charges so that the family had to appear in court in just two days, giving us barely enough time to secure a local attorney, Dave Chamberlain. At that hearing, God miraculously brought a substitute judge there who was sympathetic to the Searles, and she ruled that the family did not have to put their child in public school.[8] She told the parties of the case to try to settle the dispute.

The school district, however, did not believe the mother's high school diploma was adequate, and they also required regular home visits, testing at least twice a year in the public schools, and meetings eight times a year with a public school official to determine if the family could continue to home school. Of course, none of these restrictive requirements were in the law. The family refused to agree to such terms, and the school district "disapproved." In a subsequent hearing, the court gave us two weeks to prepare, and during the course of that time I was able to convince the opposing attorney (who knew nothing about home schoolers' constitutional rights) that they would not win. By God's grace, the case was settled without the family having to comply with the ridiculous requirements.[9] Obviously, "approval states" do not protect the right to home school but leave it to the arbitrary discretion of biased public school officials.

The "Vagueness Defense" and the "Neutral Decision-Maker Defense" which are discussed in chapter 18, directly apply to these types of "approval states" and are used frequently by HSLDA to defend the rights of parents to teach their children at home.

Trend Toward Lesser State Control of Home Schooling

Finally, all the cases and amended statutes mentioned above and many dozens more, point to a trend in the courts and legislatures for less state control of home education. Although this author objects to the state having any interest in controlling the education of our children, a long line of U.S. Supreme Court cases does recognize that the state has an interest in education. However, at present, the state only has an interest in the *product* of education, not the *process*. Whenever the state attempts to control the *process* of education, such as dictating teacher qualifications, approving curricula, or requiring home visits, it is in clear opposition with parental liberty.

On the other hand, if the states pass laws concerning the *product* of education, such as various notification requirements or, perhaps, standardized testing or evaluations, the parents' rights and the state's interests can be more peacefully balanced. Of course, this is basically a short-term solution. Ultimately, the long-term goal is to eradicate the state's interest by repealing all of the compulsory attendance laws. But this will not be easily achieved until home schoolers are able to influence legislatures and have their biblically trained home-schooled students become judges, legislators, reporters, teachers, and college professors.

Notes

1. See Alaska Statutes §§14.45.100 through 14.45.140 (1984) and Revised Statutes of Nebraska* §79-1701(2). Prior to 1984, Nebraska had been prosecuting private schools and home schools across the state who refused to use certified teachers. Pastor Sileven of Faith Baptist Church Academy was jailed and his school padlocked. An appointed Governor's Commission investigated the problem and recommended that the legislature pass an exemption for these religious schools to protect the parents' constitutional rights. The legislature adopted the recommendation into law.

2. Some of these states include Colorado, Florida, Nebraska, North Dakota, Iowa, New Mexico, Virginia, and Washington.

3. See, generally, Christopher Klicka, *Home Schooling in the United States: A Legal Analysis* (Paeonian Springs, Vir.: Home School Legal Defense Association, 1992), for further specific statute citations. This publication is updated every August and is available from HSLDA.

4. *Lawrence*, Opinion #23526, 9 December 1991. See "Home Schoolers Win EEE Case," *The Home School Court Report*, Vol 8, No. 1, January/February 1992, 1.

5. *Clonlara*, 496 N.W. 2d 66(Mi App. Ct. 1991).

6. Those states are Alabama, Alaska, California, Delaware, Illinois, Indiana, Kansas, Kentucky, Michigan, Nebraska, and Texas. See Klicka, *Home Schooling In the United States: A Legal Analysis*, published by the Home School Legal Defense Association for an annually updated summary of the cases and statutes in these states which allow for home schools to operate as private schools. Individual state summaries are also available from HSLDA.

7. See *Ibid.* for a complete description of these state laws.

8. *In the Matter of Johnna M. Searles*, No. 9037CH0017, District Court of the Amesbury Division, 4 September 1989.

9. "Major Courtroom Victory in Massachusetts," *The Home School Court Report*, Vol. 6, No. 4, Fall 1990, 2.

CHAPTER **20**

WE CAN'T AFFORD NOT TO BE INVOLVED: TIPS FOR INFLUENCING LEGISLATION

S ince 1982, thirty-two states have passed laws or regulations recognizing and defining home schooling. Some of these new laws passed according to the plans of home schoolers, and others passed leaving home schoolers in disarray.

The enemies of home schooling are just beginning to wake up. From 1982 to 1988, home schoolers, for the most part, surprised the National Education Association and the other public school lobbying groups. In the 1990s, however, the legislative road has not been as smooth.

In fact, in 1991 alone, negative bills were introduced: 1) in Kansas, to require home schools to be certified teachers; 2) in Maine, to require home schools to submit to monthly home visits in order to determine if they can continue to home school; 3) in Montana, to require home schools to be tested by the public school authorities; 4) in Illinois, to prohibit spanking in all private schools (which includes home schools); 5) in Connecticut, to require two meetings with schools each year, quarterly progress reports, and to limit the number of home school students per household to five; 6) in Georgia and Colorado, to require an expansion of ages over which children would be required to attend school; 7) and in Wisconsin and Mississippi legislative study committees were formed to draft more restrictive legislation for home schoolers.[1] In addition to these negative bills, several positive bills were introduced in Iowa (to repeal the teacher certification requirements), in New Mexico (to repeal the college degree requirement), and in Oregon (to put the home school regulations into law).

By God's grace, all of the negative legislation was defeated, and the study committees were disassembled with no recommendations for change to the present favorable laws! The home school organizations worked hard, and HSLDA provided research, gave expert testimony at committee hearings, and sent out legislative alerts to HSLDA members in many of the various states. Concerning the positive bills, teacher certification was knocked out by the Iowa Legislature, but the two favorable bills in Oregon and New Mexico were defeated.[2]

However, the point is that, more than ever, it is important for the average home school family to stay informed of the latest legislation affecting parents' rights and to be prepared to participate in the political process. The onslaught of negative bills from State School Board Associations, School Administrator Associations, and State Teacher Associations is just beginning.

The importance of everyone joining together and being involved in legislative activity has been grounded in me for a long time. In fact, for sixteen years my father was a state representative in the Wisconsin Legislature, so I received much experience and valuable insight from him concerning what is the most effective lobbying techniques.

Since I started working for HSLDA in 1985, I have been directly involved in the passage of six new home school laws or regulations. In addition, in conjunction with local home school leaders, I have drafted various amendments to legislation to protect home schoolers and have fought bills that would have restricted home schools. I have given expert testimony before numerous legislative committees and administrative hearings. I also regularly review newly introduced bills and send out legislative alerts to state home school leaders concerning legislation that may affect home schoolers in their state.

As a result, I have gathered some ideas on how to lobby effectively. Below are some tips and suggestions which the reader may find useful.

The Need for a Vision

First of all, each home schooler and each home school organization needs to decide what the goal is for their state law concerning home schooling. Ultimately, my goal is to see states repeal their compulsory attendance laws, but as I have stated elsewhere in this book, the timing is not right. Much more education of the legislators needs to take place, which may take at least a generation.

In the meantime, you must first ask the question: Are we, as a body of home schoolers in a given state, satisfied with the status quo? In many states without home school laws, home schoolers, as a whole, are doing pretty well. Although each year some families are harassed, most families enjoy much freedom. Many of the "private school states" fit into this category.

Also several of the states with home school laws already allow maximum freedom and are, therefore, worth protecting. Missouri's home school law, which requires no monitoring of any kind nor any registration, would definitely fit into this category. If it is your position to be content with the status quo, your lobbying strategy should be defensive—keeping the law the way it is. Sometimes it is better to work to contain a few legal brush fires each year, than to open all home schoolers to scrutiny and possibly greater regulation by introducing a bill.

However, if you decide that you are not satisfied with the present law, you need to develop an offensive strategy. This, of course, will involve much planning and coordinating. The most important consideration will be the timing of the legislative bill. Is the legislature ready to deal favorably with home schooling? Or will they make the legal atmosphere worse for home schooling? The bottom-line which we must realize is that not every state needs home school legislation.

The Need for Organization

However, home schoolers need to be organized. They should make a determination as to who will spearhead the offensive strategy or who will monitor the legislature for defensive purposes. Most state home school organizations can work together with local support groups to accomplish this task.

Home school organizations in each state should work together on legislative action in order to present a united front and, as a result, be the most effective. This does not mean, of course, that each state must limit themselves to establishing only one home school organization in order to appear united. Rather, there can be several independent state home school organizations which each meet the needs of the type of home schoolers they represent. Each of these independent home school organizations, however, should be prepared to work together whenever there is a need for legislative action.

An excellent example of "separate but united" home school organizations working together is in Illinois. There, at least four different home school organizations, representing both Christian and secular home schoolers, have formed the "Ad Hoc Committee." The sole purpose of this committee is to facilitate communication and planning strategy for legislative action. Each home schooling group sends a representative to the periodic meetings in order to participate in setting strategy. Then each representative, in turn, communicates the plan of action to their mailing lists in order to activate the grassroots. In short, each home school organization retains its autonomy and independence but, at the same time, the home school organizations present a united front when battling the legislature. Their effectiveness is demonstrated in the fact that they have killed, in committee, all harmful legislation introduced since the Add Hoc Committee came together.

The Need for Education

The best investment for a home schooler to make in the legislature is to take time to educate his or her legislative representatives. Most legislators have never met a home school family personally and probably know very little about it.

I recommend that home schoolers write to their state representatives and state senators, even when there is no particular legislation at stake. Even more beneficial is to visit the legislators' office at the capitol (which, incidentally, will be an excellent field trip for your children) or to invite him to speak to a local gathering of home school constituents in his district. Some families I know have invited their legislator over to their house for dinner or for a "coffee" involving local home school parents.

It is a good idea to have information to leave with him that will introduce him to the concept of home schooling and document the fact that home schooling really works. The HSLDA has various concise resources available to its members, which have been frequently used to educate legislators and state officials. Also your state organization may want to consider printing an educational brochure that would summarize what home schooling is, its academic successes, and its legal rights.

One very effective activity is to organize an annual "Capitol Day." One of the home school organizations in Oklahoma, OCHEC, has organized "Capitol Days" for the last several years with good success.[3] This involves advance planning since home schoolers throughout the state must be notified of the date in order to prepare a trip. It is also a good idea for families to contact their legislator in advance and arrange a meeting with him to extol the virtues of home schooling and let him see real live home-schooled children. If the legislator is not available, it is important to still stop by his office and leave a message and information on home schooling.

Usually a rally is planned on "Capitol Day," where a few people speak to the crowd of home schoolers and where display tables are set up with free information. These rallies and visits to the legislators' offices tend to draw their attention to the benefits of home schooling. In the future when a bill is introduced involving home schooling, the legislator will remember the home school families and children he has met. It is much easier to vote against the faceless issue of home schooling than it is to vote against people he has met personally. Education of the legislature is something that must take place all year—not just when the home school bill is already introduced.

I might make mention that another effective way of winning a legislator to your side is to work on his campaign, especially when he is a first-time candidate. This past year my wife and I worked for and came to know a local candidate for the Virginia Legislature. Many other home schoolers also became involved in his campaign. He won and now is completely supportive of home schooling, although prior to his candidacy he was unfamiliar with the subject.

Lobbying workshops are also a suggestion. Home school support groups or state organizations can organize workshops in which individuals familiar with the political process can train home school leaders and families on effective ways to lobby. Sometimes these lobbying workshops can take place at the annual state home school conference.

The Need for Preparation

Monitoring legislation and the ability to communicate that information to the "grassroots" home schoolers are key elements to successfully defeating negative legislation and passing beneficial legislation. Some of the ways to do this are: 1) hire an actual lobbyist to monitor legislation (who preferably is a home schooler himself or is related to one); 2) start a relationship with an existing lobbying group that is supportive of home schooling and who is willing to watch out for harmful legislation to home schoolers; 3) and/or utilize home schoolers who live in the capitol city who can visit legislators, pick up copies of bills, or "camp out" for a few days in the capitol, monitoring a bill progressing through various amendments.

As an additional support for the states, the HSLDA subscribes to a computer service called "state net," enabling it to monitor legislation affecting home schoolers in all fifty states. During legislative sessions, HSLDA does a "search" every other day, and all the bills which are found are reviewed by the HSLDA lawyers who cover the particular states. The lawyers, in turn, notify the state home school leaders and normally send out "legislative alerts" to the HSLDA members in the state.

It is also useful to develop a good relationship with a couple of legislators and senators who will keep you informed on bills being introduced, their progress, and chance of passage. If you keep them supplied with favorable documentation on home schooling, they can "lobby" on your behalf and set up key meetings for you to talk with other legislators. One home school mom in Colorado works one day a week for a senator, and her home school son works as a page. That is one way to stay on top of legislation!

State home school organizations also must be able to communicate the information quickly to their members, in order to have them pray, write letters, make phone calls, or attend legislative hearings. Establishing a phone tree can be very effective. In Oklahoma, the Christian Home Educators Fellowship (CHEF) has developed an inexpensive computerized phone system on which they can record a legislative action item. Then the computer program will automatically call approximately two hundred home schoolers and support group leaders, giving them all the same message. The support group leaders can, in turn, contact their local families. In this way news is spread quickly and accurately.

What Needs to Be Considered When Dealing with Actual Legislation?

When introducing a home school bill or amending an existing bill, always decide how far you will compromise or if you will compromise at all. Concerning most harmful legislation, such as the negative bills introduced in 1991 and listed above, "no compromise" is usually the best policy.

If introducing a bill to improve a law for the benefit of home schoolers, it is suggested that three versions of the bill be drafted, but only submit the "ideal" bill at first. If this bill begins to pass "as is," no need to use any of the other versions. If the "ideal" bill, however, begins to be vigorously challenged by the home-schooling opponents, either submit one of your other versions of the bill or, if the risk is too great, abandon the bill altogether. For example, in Alabama a few years ago, I testified in favor of a bill that the home schoolers had introduced. Due to some strings pulled by the Alabama teachers union and some political maneuvering, the good law died altogether, and a substitute bill was introduced in the same committee that had been considering the home schoolers' bill. The new bill was so restrictive that the home schoolers quickly withdrew all support, and the restrictive bill died.

If a hearing is set for a piece of legislation that will either help or harm home schooling, it is often wise strategy to alert as many home schoolers as possible to attend the hearing. This usually impresses the legislators and gets their attention. Some of the witnesses to have testify are: 1) one or two articulate home school students who will convince the legislators of the excellent product of home schooling; 2) at least one educational expert who can testify to the academic benefits of home schooling, rebuff the lack of socialization claims, and recite various statistics on the success of home schoolers; 3) a legal expert who will testify as to the constitutionality of the bill, the legal conflict it will cure or cause (telling some true accounts of harassment), and the national trend to deregulate home schooling; 4) and several home school mothers and fathers of various educational levels, races, religious backgrounds, and jobs. I have found it beneficial to submit all testimony in writing in case you are cut short, and it also provides the legislators with something to review and pass around as the bill progresses.

Some of the home school leaders may want to target key legislators on the committee before and after the hearing in order to try to influence them favorably. Of course, a rally could also be organized right before the hearing, and the media could be invited to publicize the large crowds.

An Example of the Passage of a Home School Bill

Below is an example of how a bill was passed against great odds. Some of the strategy used may prove helpful in your state.

In the spring of 1988, home schoolers in Colorado were still faced with difficult restrictions. Home schooling had to be "approved" by local school districts which were often quite arbitrary. Families who were disapproved could appeal to the Department of Education which generally affirmed the denial. I was involved in intervening on behalf of dozens of families in various school districts who were having difficulty. Some of the families were already in court.

Bill Moritz, a lawyer and home school father, sent me a draft of an "ideal" home school law which would simply give home schools the same status as private schools, which were not regulated in Colorado. Home schoolers would merely have to notify the school district, and there would be no approval by the school district. The passage of such a bill in Colorado was virtually hopeless, considering the strength of the public school lobbying organizations and the makeup of the legislature at that time. Yet, we talked with the home school leaders and the bill was submitted to the legislature.

Two legislators agreed to sponsor the bill. The House sponsor was very liberal. The Senate sponsor was conservative. The bill was never promoted as a Republican or Democratic bill. I talked at length with the House sponsor and referred to the home schoolers as a "minority" which was getting muscled by the state. He loved the idea of helping a "minority." I then wrote up a letter for him which supported the bill and demonstrated that home schoolers were a minority who were protected by the First and Fourteenth Amendments of the Constitution. He gave a copy of the letter to all the legislators in the House. As you will see, he carried the banner so well for the home schoolers that he was able to get the final version of the bill passed unanimously in the House!

Meanwhile, Rory Schneeberger, a home school mother and home school leader, "camped out" at the capitol for about a week. Many home schoolers wrote in support of the bill and others testified at various hearings.

Rory constantly kept up with the various committees and with the amendments which legislators were trying to get attached. The two sponsors of the bill regularly called me over a two-week period to get my view on various language changes and my suggestions on counter-language.

First, the opposing side wanted some sort of record-keeping which could be inspected by the local superintendent. We added the language that he could only inspect records "if he had probable cause that the family was not in compliance." This language applied a constitutional standard of probable cause which can only be used if the superintendent has actual evidence that the family is not educating their children. The language was adopted. (Ever since this law was passed, HSLDA has not heard of a single family who has ever had to have their records inspected!).

Second, the opposing side wanted accountability in the form of annual testing. The home school advocates explained that they only wanted to allow it if it started in the third grade and was administered every three years thereafter. It was finally settled that home schoolers would be tested beginning in third grade and every other year thereafter. The home school advocates also felt that there needed to be a standard, so that families could not be arbitrarily shut down. We suggested the same standard as the public schools, which was the 13th percentile, and the opposing side agreed!

Finally, we explained that many home schooling families were opposed to sending the scores to the public schools and suggested sending them to a private school of their choice. It was agreed. We also made sure that the option was still available for home schoolers who did not want anything to do with the school district to be able to enroll in a private school but to do their teaching at home.

By the end of all this, a very short "ideal" bill became a very long and wordy bill. In fact, the *Denver Post*, which had been against the original bill and wanted excessive restrictions on home schoolers, came out in support of the final, lengthy bill believing it was restrictive.

However, in the final analysis, the bill was mostly unenforceable and hardly restrictive at all. In effect, home schoolers only have to communicate once a year with the public schools in the form of a short notice of intent. This is comparable to some of the better home school laws, such as in Wisconsin, Montana, Wyoming, and Mississippi. The inspection of records never happens because of the "probable cause" protection, and the test results can be sent to a private school. Also the option for home schoolers to enroll in a private school but teach at home was left intact.[4]

Many prayers were offered during this time, and God truly worked a miracle against all odds. Also many valuable lessons in legislative strategy were learned throughout the process.

Conclusion

The information in this chapter is only suggestions, ideas, and recounted experiences. Each home schooler and home school organization will have to weigh their situation in their state, and act accordingly. Hopefully, one important message will have penetrated the reader: the price of freedom is eternal vigilance.

Notes

1. See, generally, two editions of the *Home School Court Report*, Vol 7, No. 2, March/April 1991, and Vol 7, No. 2, May/June 1991.

2. *Ibid.*

3. OCHEC newsletter, Vol. IX, No. 1, February-March 1992, p. 1-2, OK Central Home Educators' Consociation, Oklahoma City.

4. For more details on the home school bill which was passed in Colorado see "Legislative Victory in Colorado," *The Home School Court Report*, Vol. 4, No. 2, Spring 1988, 10-11.

CHAPTER 21

IT IS NEWS TO ME:
HOW TO RECRUIT YOUR LOCAL MEDIA'S
SUPPORT FOR HOME SCHOOLING

"Home schooling" is considered different, or unusual, to most Americans when they initially hear the term. As stated earlier, most people are only used to institutional schools because that is where they, their parents, and maybe even their grandparents, were educated. However, most people, once they are confronted with the benefits of home schooling, as discussed in chapter 6, are inclined to recognize its legitimacy. Therefore, a process of education must continue to take place so that an accurate picture of home schooling is presented.

This is why recruiting the local media is so important. It can serve as a useful means of not only educating others on home schooling, but also helping to protect home schooling. Let us consider several questions that home schoolers have concerning dealing with the media.

Will the Media Twist the Information on Home Schooling?

This is always a possibility but it rarely happens. In fact, in my experience in dealing with hundreds of newspaper and radio reporters and various talk show hosts, nearly 90 percent of the coverage has been favorable.

I have repeatedly told member home school families that they should participate in media interviews for one simple reason: if home schoolers do not speak out on home schooling, no one is going to do it for them. In fact, only those critical of home schooling will probably be interviewed if home schoolers refuse to participate.

Of course, dealing with the media is not always positive. A few years ago, a couple of home schoolers and I were interviewed in Florida. The resulting article began with something to this effect: "What do ax murderers, rapists, and other parents have in common? They all can home school in the state of Florida." The reporter obviously was very biased and wanted more restrictions on home schoolers. Fortunately, such articles are very rare, and I believe that the benefits of much positive publicity by the media outweighs the risks.

How Should Home Schooling Be Presented to the Media?

Three major points to get across to the reporter is that home schoolers are a *minority*, home schooling *works*, and it is a *right*. The media certainly favors minorities, and since home schoolers are a true "minority," it is very beneficial to represent it as such. It is helpful to portray the home school parent as the "little guy" who is being picked on by the "bully" of the state, school district, or the teachers' union. More often then not, the media loves to defend the underdog.

Secondly, be sure to demonstrate that home schooling works. This is the most powerful argument that convinces most reporters and the public. Describe the average school day at home. Extol the success of your own home school and supply the reporter with statistics and studies which show the academic success of home schoolers in general. By using the information in chapter 6, the academic excellence of home schooling can be easily proved. Lawyers at HSLDA regularly talk with the media and will send the reporter summaries of the academic statistics, so be certain to refer the reporter to HSLDA for further information. The fact that home schooling works, silences most critics and embarrasses the public schools. Reporters are generally impressed.

A common question raised by reporters is: "But what about the child's socialization?" One way to be prepared for this question is to study the section on socialization in chapter 6. Summarize many of the activities of your child and emphasize how your child is protected from negative socialization.

Thirdly, try to mention that home schooling is a right. In other words, it is legal. It is a constitutional right, as guaranteed by the First and Fourteenth Amendments, and generally is a right according to the individual state's cases or statutes. You may want to refer the reporter to HSLDA for further information on the legalities of home schooling and what is happening legally around the state.

Could a Home Schooler Get in Legal Trouble by Interviewing with the Media?

In some states, where home schoolers are regularly harassed or legally challenged, a home school family is taking a risk by interviewing with the media. In fact, some families ask the media to only use their first names and thus protect their identity from the school district.

However, HSLDA has found that home schoolers who are more public through the media and who are members of HSLDA will be more likely to be left alone by the school district. The school district figures that it is much easier to try to pick on a lonely home school family without media contacts or legal counsel because they can quietly close them down without public embarrassment.

Therefore, a family who is being legally harassed may want to contact the press if legal negotiations behind the scenes fail. This type of coverage is not what the public schools want. Many times I have seen the media indirectly contribute to the resolution of a case and turn public opinion in favor of home schooling.

Conclusion

Developing good relations with the media is important in many ways. The media can both help home schoolers educate the public on the legitimacy of home schooling and indirectly protect home schoolers from harassment. The more the public is aware of the positive aspects, the less likely it is that neighbors will turn families in to truant officers and social workers for home schooling and "educational neglect."

CHAPTER 22

DON'T STAY HOME WITHOUT IT:
JOIN HSLDA

A truant officer is at the door. He pushes his way in. He will not leave until he can take your children to the public school. What can you do?

A police officer is at your door with an arrest warrant to take your six-year-old child. Who can you call?

A social worker demands entry to your home and insists on interrogating your children. What are your rights?

The local public school official insists that your home school arrangement is not legal and threatens you with criminal charges. Where can you get help fast?

The Home School Legal Defense Association (HSLDA) is the answer. The above accounts all actually happened to HSLDA members in Maine, Michigan, Alabama, and Indiana, respectively. In each situation, the family called me, and I was able to resolve the conflict on behalf of our members by telephone, fax, or Federal Express. This typifies the work of each of HSLDA's lawyers and legal staff on nearly a daily basis.

HSLDA is a nonprofit organization established in 1983 expressly for the purpose of defending the right of parents who choose to home school their children. It was founded by three home-schooling fathers, two of which, Michael Farris and J. Michael Smith, presently comprise the HSLDA Board along with home schooling fathers Jeff Ethell of Virginia and George Stroh of Arizona. HSLDA is based in the Washington D.C. area in Paeonian Springs, Virginia.

Membership in HSLDA Is an Investment

The establishment of HSLDA has enabled home school parents throughout the country to pool their resources together in order to defend in court those home school families who were being legally challenged. Each year HSLDA handles nearly three thousand negative legal contacts on behalf of member-families who are faced with public school officials who attempt to exceed the law. HSLDA also handles hundreds of court cases on behalf of member families each year. HSLDA also gives legal information to thousands or more home schoolers annually. This book, in fact, summarizes many of the cases and legal threats which HSLDA has handled on behalf of home schoolers. In many ways, HSLDA has become the major barrier stopping many legal attempts to infringe on the freedoms of home schoolers.

Membership in HSLDA costs $100 annually per family. If you do not use your $100 in receiving legal representation, another family will. In fact, in one case alone involving a member home school family, HSLDA expended over $50,000 in legal services and representation. You are making an investment in protecting home schoolers throughout the nation and Canada. It is a way of having "solidarity" with home schoolers in every state, to work together to protect our commonly shared freedoms.

Although home schooling is "legal" in every state, each state varies as to the manner in which it restricts the right to home school.

Each year many parents face criminal prosecution for teaching their children at home. Generally, only a few home schoolers in any community are selected for prosecution. When this happens, the family faces enormous legal expense, mostly for attorneys' fees. Families who are not prosecuted are often intimidated into giving up or moving, by the mere threat of prosecution.

HSLDA brings together a large number of those families in order to enable each family to have a low-cost method of obtaining quality legal defense, should the need arise. HSLDA *guarantees* experienced legal counsel and representation by qualified attorneys to every member family who is challenged in the area of home schooling. The attorneys' fees, court costs, transcript charges, expert witnesses, and attorney transportation will be paid in full by the Association.

HSLDA guarantees legal representation to all our members which as of December 1992 numbers 28,000 families. HSLDA's legal team is presently comprised of six attorneys—all of whom home school their children: Michael Farris, Michael Smith, Jordan Lorence, Dee Black, Scott Somerville, and myself. Defending home schoolers is not just a job for us—it is our very way of life and our heartfelt conviction.

We are supported by six legal assistants. HSLDA has also established a network of Christian attorneys throughout the fifty states and Canada who serve as our local counsel whenever we have to defend our families in court. Normally, one of our attorneys from the national office will travel to the particular court and serve as lead counsel in the case.

Not only will you help protect your own rights, your membership will help others establish their right to home school in difficult states. You can join HSLDA by writing or calling us at:

Home School Legal Defense Association
P.O. Box 159
Paeonian Springs, VA 22129
(703) 338-5600

Since 1983, after thousands of legal battles, HSLDA has never had a member home school family who was forced to stop home schooling by the state. If a case was lost, HSLDA has been able to win the case on appeal, find an alternate legal way or change the law through legislation.

HSLDA reserves the right to refuse membership to anyone who is already in trouble with their school district—so join before you have any problems. We depend on most of our member families not to be in trouble at a given time, in order for there to be adequate finances to represent all the families who are threatened or criminally charged.

Offensive Litigation

In addition to legally *defending* home school families, HSLDA is prepared to go on the *offensive* and sue local school districts or departments of education which blatantly violate our member's constitutional rights. Your annual fees enable us to take the offensive as needed, thereby sending a message to the public school authorities that we are serious in preserving the rights and freedoms of home school families.

For example, in Pennsylvania, after dozens of home-schooling families were in criminal court and many more were threatened, we went on the offensive and filed a civil rights action, suing the school districts for violating the home schoolers' civil rights. We won the case, *Jeffery v. O'Donnell,* and the Federal Court declared the law unconstitutionally vague.[1]

In Texas, many member home school families were being criminally charged for home schooling, so we decided to go on the offensive by joining as plaintiffs in the *Leeper* case. The main attorney handling the case was Shelby Sharpe of Ft. Worth. The case involved suing every school district in the state of Texas for violating the civil rights of the home school families. The trial court and the Texas Court of Appeals ruled favorably, making home schooling clearly legal in Texas.[2]

Another example in which we chose to proceed on the offensive occurred in St. Joseph County, Michigan. Four HSLDA families were visited by a local principal and a police officer and threatened with arrest, and in one instance, with having their children removed. These four families and a few others also received intimidating letters from the county school district giving them one day in which to enroll their children in public school.

Later, the local newspaper printed an article based on an interview with the prosecutor announcing that approximately seven home school families would be criminally prosecuted. I contacted the prosecutor to try to convince him not to prosecute, but he would not budge.

As a result, in January, attorney Michael Farris and I filed a Civil Rights suit, *Arnett v. Middleton,* in the St. Joseph County Circuit

Court, suing the prosecutor, superintendent, and school district for $200,000 for violating the civil rights of these home school families. We cited five "causes of action" against the prosecutor and school district. They violated the civil rights of the home schoolers by: 1) threatening to prosecute the families under an unconstitutionally vague law; 2) denying the families equal protection under the law; 3) attempting to require an illegal reporting procedure; 4) threatening to prosecute while intentionally disregarding the law requiring the families to first have a due process hearing with the Department of Education; and 5) for making an unconstitutional demand that the children had to attend public school under the penalty of law.

Within weeks, HSLDA was contacted by the school district and prosecutor wanting to settle the suit. Both promised, in writing, that they would not pursue or prosecute home schoolers in the county unless the law changed. They agreed that the law was vague. As a result, we dismissed the suit, since we achieved the protection of our families.[3]

Other Benefits of HSLDA

There are several other functions of HSLDA which your membership dues help to support.

First, HSLDA regularly assists home school organizations to promote good legislation or fight restrictive legislation. Oftentimes, HSLDA will send attorneys to testify at legislative hearings. For example, during the 1990-91 legislation session, Mike Farris testified in Connecticut and Montana, Michael Smith testified in Arizona, Maryland, and Oregon, and I testified in Maine and North Dakota.[4] Regularly, we are also involved in the drafting of favorable amendments to legislation affecting home schooling. In many instances, HSLDA sends out special mailings to members, urging them to write to their legislators about a specific bills.

Sometimes we will meet with departments of education in order to change their policies to be more favorable to home schoolers' rights. For example, the District of Columbia had adopted one of the most restrictive sets of home school requirements, which included teacher certification and unannounced home visits. I arranged a meeting with the D.C. school administration and presented two memoranda proving the unconstitutionality of home visits and teacher certification requirements. By the end of the meeting, one of the officials ripped in half the D.C. home school guidelines and said,

"I guess we won't be needing these anymore!" As a result, all requirements for home schoolers were suspended, and they asked me to help draft new guidelines.[5]

In addition to monitoring state legislation in all fifty states that would impact home schooling, HSLDA monitors federal legislation and alerts state home school leaders and its members to legislation that will hurt or promote parental rights.

Secondly, at least six times per week, the HSLDA legal staff is contacted by newspaper, radio, or TV reporters. As a result, we have the opportunity to "get the word out" on the rights of home schoolers and their tremendous academic success.

Thirdly, HSLDA provides a bimonthly magazine, *The Home School Court Report*, for member families at no extra charge. This magazine covers legal issues and other matters of concern to home-schooling parents. It is usually twenty-four pages long and it is filled with valuable information.

Fourthly, each month, HSLDA attorneys speak at home school conferences throughout the country, sharing legal information on the rights of home schoolers, encouraging home school families, and often strategizing with state home school leaders.

Fifthly, HSLDA attorneys routinely help counsel home school parents who are involved in custody disputes where home schooling is an issue. Although HSLDA will not represent the families in Domestic Relations Court, we do provide legal counsel to their lawyers and statistics and research on home schooling.

Sixthly, HSLDA also has a division, the National Center for Home Education, which serves state leaders by providing information on the current legal bills and developments, on both the state and federal levels, of concern to home schoolers. Founded in February 1990, NCHE also works on special public relations projects related to home schooling. It serves as a "clearing house" of major home school research and other news and resources regarding home schooling.

For instance, the NCHE arranged with the Psychological Corporation to voluntarily test 10,750 home school children throughout the country and report their scores. This was the largest survey of the academic achievement of home schools' performance. The results of these 10,750 children showed that the home schoolers scored in the top third of the nation. The composite scores on the basic battery of tests ranked 15 to 32 percentile points above public school averages.[6]

NCHE also prepares and mails monthly "packets" of key information, as a free service, to hundreds of home school leaders throughout the country. This information is usually then distributed to home schoolers in each state by state newsletters or home school support groups. In addition, NCHE hosts an annual leadership seminar with special speakers, which is attended by many state home school leaders, in order to exchange ideas, learn strategies, fellowship with other state leaders, and provide training. NCHE also hosts several regional conferences for home school support leaders each year throughout the country. These workshops are effective in training support group leaders on the latest legal and legislative developments.

In short, HSLDA is committed to the overall success and advancement of home education in the arenas of education, the media, Congress, state legislatures, churches, families, and neighborhoods.

Conclusion: HSLDA's Goal Is to Serve the Home School Community

HSLDA's only goal is to serve the home school community. We are willing to defend any member home school family who is diligently home schooling their children, regardless of their religious affiliation. An investment in HSLDA of $100 not only guarantees legal defense for your family but also makes it possible for us to wage legal and legislative battles throughout the country on behalf on home schoolers.

However, as an organization and as individuals, we are committed to promote the cause of Christ and His kingdom. We believe that God alone is making it possible for home schoolers to gain greater freedoms and to be successful in the courts and legislatures and in the area of academics and family life. God honors those who honor Him and seek first His kingdom and righteousness. If we have anything to boast in, we boast in the Lord, who deserves all the glory.

Notes

1. "Pennsylvania Law Declared Unconstitutional," *The Home School Court Report*, Volume 4, No. 4, Fall 1988, 1. Also see chapter 18 for more information on the court's decision.

2. "Texas Home Schoolers Welcome Victory at Last!" *The Home School Court Report*, January/February 1992, 1.

3. "Michigan Home Schoolers Protected by Civil Rights Suit," *The Home School Court Report*, Vol. 8, No. 2, March/April 1992, 3.

4. "The 1990-91 School Year in Review," *The Home School Court Report*, Vol. 7, No. 4, July/August 1991, 7.

5. "District of Columbia: School Board Agrees to Revise Restrictive Policy," *The Home School Court Report*, Vol. 7, No. 5, September/October 1991, 5.

6. This study was released 9 August 1992 and is available from the Home School Legal Defense Association, P.O. Box 159 Paeonian Springs, Virginia 22129.

PART
7

A NOBLE ALLIANCE:
RESOURCES AND APPENDICES

In conclusion, home schooling has proven to be a revival of a time-tested method of individualized education. It reflects a deep concern by parents to be involved in the education of their children. The home school movement is also profoundly religious, for the most part, making the revival more than educational. It is a Christian revival and restoration of the family, with a focus on God's absolute moral values and principles.

Home schoolers can be proud of their great heritage. Many renowned statesman, presidents, economists, pastors, generals, scientists, lawyers, jurists, and accomplished men and women from almost every field were taught at home by their parents. Most of these home-schooled leaders of the past were trained in biblical principles by their parents, and they actively applied those principles throughout their lives.

Home schoolers have realized God's commands to parents demand they give their children a comprehensive, biblical education, and that these commands are impossible to fulfill by sending children to the public schools. The home schoolers are not only training the hearts of their children to believe in Jesus, but they are training their children's minds in God's principles, as applied to every subject. The home school children, as a result, will become men and women of godly character who will be able to lead.

Home school parents have become aware of the failure of the public school system, academically, morally, and philosophically. They do not want to take the risk that their children will become functionally illiterate or simply a crime statistic. They want to protect their children from the "vain philosophies" of this world (Colossians 2:8), which are destroying America's youth. The public school children are regularly being indoctrinated in value-free humanism and mind-controlling cultism, all in the name of neutrality. As the public schools continue to slide into chaos, home schooling is steadily achieving success. It is a fast-growing trend and has already proven that it can academically compete with, and nearly always surpass, the present results from conventional schooling.

Furthermore, it is a movement to restore the right of all parents, both Christian and secular, to control and direct the education of their children, with minimal state interference. The home schoolers are informing the state that they do not want "Big Brother" indoctrinating their children anymore. Home schoolers are on the front lines of the battle for freedom, as they counter the attempts of the state to control the minds of our children and to replace the family with "government nannies." Home schoolers are standing up to the monopolistic public schools, the out-of-control and abusive child welfare system, and the agenda of the educational elite. These battles are being fought from house to house, in the legislatures, and in the courts.

Home schooling is working—and it here to stay. Parents are getting serious as they die to themselves and dedicate their lives to training and loving their children in the Lord. Let us all work to save our children!

The following appendices will provide more information on the academic success of home schooling; how to recognize humanistic education from Christian education; and why you should home school all the way through high school; and numerous resources for home school families.

APPENDIX A

THE DIFFERENCE BETWEEN CHRISTIAN EDUCATION AND HUMANISTIC EDUCATION

This simple chart summarizes the basic differences between a biblically based education and humanistic education. Christians should check their public schools, private schools, and even home school curricula to determine on which side of the chart below it best fits. God honors those who honor Him. Let us give our children the best biblical education possible.

Christianity	Humanism
1. The sovereignty of the triune God is the starting point, and this God speaks through His infallible word.	1. The sovereignty of man and the state is the starting point, and it is the word of scientific, elite man which we must heed.
2. We must accept God as God. He is alone Lord.	2. Man is his own god, choosing or determining for himself what constitutes good and evil (Genesis 3:5).
3. God's Word and Person is the Truth.	3. Truth is pragmatic and existential: it is what we find works and is helpful to us.
4. Education is into God's truth in every realm.	4. Education is the self-realization and self-development of the child.
5. Education is discipline under a body of truth. This body of truth grows with research and study, but truth is objective and God-given. We begin by presupposing God and His Word.	5. Education is freedom from restraint and from any idea of truth outside us. We are the standard, not something outside us.

6. Godly standards grade us. We must measure up to them. The teacher grades the pupil.

6. The school and the world must measure up to the pupil's needs. The pupil grades the teacher.

7. Man's will, and the child's will, must be broken to God's purpose. Man must be remade, reborn by God's grace.

7. Society must be broken and remade to man's will, and the child's will is sacred.

8. Man's problem is sin. Man must be recreated by God.

8. Man's problem is society. Society must be recreated by man

9. The family is God's basic institution.

9. The family is obsolete. The individual or the state is basic.

The comparison above was written by R. J. Rushdoony in his book *The Philosophy of the Christian Curriculum* (Vallecito, Calif.: Ross House Books, 1981), 172-73. Chalcedon, P.O. Box 158, Vallecito, California 95251. Reprinted by permission.

APPENDIX B

COLLEGES AND UNIVERSITIES
THAT HAVE ACCEPTED HOME SCHOOLERS
(Compiled by HSLDA from 1989 through December 1992)

The list below is by no means a comprehensive list of colleges and universities that have accepted home school students. Rather, this covers only those colleges for which HSLDA has documentation, which was supplied by home schoolers who happened to notify them.

Adrian College, MI
American River Community Junior College, CA
Amherst College, MA
Antelope Valley College, CA
Antioch College, OH
Arkansas State University
Austin College, TX
Barber College, OH
Baylor College, TX
Belhaven College, MS
Belmont College, TN
Bethany College of Missions, MN
Bethany Lutheran College, MN
Biola University, CA
Blackburn College, IL
Bob Jones University, SC
Boston University, MA
Brigham Young University, UT
Broome Community College, NY
Brown University, RI
Bryan College, TN
Buffalo State, NY
Calvin College, MI
Carleton College, MN
Casper College, WY
Cedarville College, OH
Central Piedmont Community College, NC
Christendom College, VA
Christian Heritage College, CA
Christian Liberty College, VA
The Citadel, SC
Clearwater Christian College, FL
College of Lake County, IL

Colorado Baptist University,CO
Columbus College, GA
Concordia College, MN
Cooke County College, TX
Covenant College, TN
Criswell College, TX
Cumberland County College, NJ
Dallas Christian College, TX
DeKalb Community College, GA
Delta College, MI
Diablo Valley College, CA
East Central College, MO
Eastern Hillsdale College, MI
Evergreen Valley Community College, CA
Faith Baptist Bible College, IA
Fresno Pacific College, CA
Garden City College, KS
Geneva College, PA
George Fox College, OR
George Mason University, VA
G.M.I. School of Engineering, MI
Grand Rapids Baptist College, MI
Grand Valley State University, MI
Grove City College, PA
Harvard University, MA
Heritage Baptist University, IN
Hillsdale College, MI
Hope College, MI
Houghten College, NY
John Brown University, TX
Joliet Junior College, IL
Kalamazoo Valley Community College, MI
Kenyon College, OH
Keystone Community College, PA
King College, TN
Kings College, NY
Lansing Community College, MI
Lawrence Technological University, MI
LeTourneau College, TX
Liberty University, VA
Loyola College, MD
Maranatha Baptist Bible College, WI
The Master's College, CA
Messiah College, PA
Middlebury College, VT
Mississippi State University

Mississippi College
Modesto Junior College, CA
Montreat Anderson, NC
Moody Bible Institute, IL
Morrisville College, NY
Mt. Vernon Nazarene College, OH
Nebraska School of Technical Agriculture, NE
New Mexico State University, NM
Niagra University, NY
Northampton Community College, PA
Oakland University, MI
Oberlin College, OH
Ohio State University, Agricultural, Technical Institute, Wooster, OH
Oklahoma Baptist University, OK
Oklahoma City Community College, OK
Oklahoma State University, OK
Oklahoma University of Science & Arts, OK
Onondago Community College, NY
Oral Roberts University, OK
Owens Technical College, OH
Oxford University, England
Pennsylvania State University - York, PA
Pensacola Christian College, FL
Pepperdine University, CA
Princeton University, NH
Rensselaer Polytechnic Institute, NY
Rice University, TX
Ricks College, ID
St. Joseph's School of Nursing, NY
St. Phillips College, TX
Salem College, WV
Sam Houston State University, TX
Shimer College, IL
Simpson College, CA
Stanislaus State University, CA
Stockton State College, NJ
Southwest Baptist University, MO
Southwest Texas State University
Taylor University, IN
Texas A&M, TX
Texas Christian University
Texas Woman's University
Thomas Aquinas College, CA
Towson State University, MD
Tyler Junior College, TX
U.S. Air Force Academy, CO

Union University, TN
University of Akron, OH
University of Alabama in Hunstville, AL
University of California, Berkley
University of California, Los Angeles
University of California, Santa Cruz
University of Colorado, Colorado Springs
University of Dallas, TX
University of Delaware
University of Evansville, IN
University of Michigan
University of Minnesota
University of Mississippi
University of Missouri-Rolla
University of New York
University of North Carolina, Chapel Hill
University of South Carolina
University of the South, TN
University of Tennessee
University of Texas, Austin
University of Texas, Denton
University of Texas, El Paso
University of North Texas
University of Virginia, Charlottesville
University of Wisconsin, Madison
U.S. Naval Academy, Annapolis, MD
Victoria College, TX
Virginia Polytechnic Institute & State University, VA
Washington Univ. Medical Center, MO
Western Baptist College, OR
Wheaton College, IL
Whitman College, WA
Whitworth College, WA
Wisconsin Lutheran College, WI
Yale University, CT
York College of Pennsylvania

APPENDIX C

SELECTED RESOURCES
FOR HOME SCHOOLING FAMILIES

STATE HOME SCHOOLING ORGANIZATIONS

ALABAMA - Christian Home Education Fellowship of Alabama, 3423 19th Street, Tuscaloosa, AL 35401 (205) 237-2976

ALASKA - Alaska Private & Home Educators Association, Box 141764, Anchorage, AK 99504 (907) 753-3018

ARIZONA - Arizona Families for Home Education, P.O. Box 4661, Scottsdale, AZ 85261-4661 (602) 276-8548

Christian Home Educators of Arizona, 14401 N. 51st Street, Scottsdale, AZ 85254-2806

Northern Arizona Home Educators, P.O. Box 30082, Flagstaff, AZ 86003-0082

ARKANSAS - Arkansas Christian Home Education Association, Box 501, Little Rock, AR 72203 (501) 758-9099

CALIFORNIA - Christian Home Educators Association, P.O. Box 2009, Norwalk, CA 90651-2009 (310) 864-2432

Family Protection Ministries, 910 Sunrise Avenue Suite A-1, Roseville, CA 95661

COLORADO - Christian Home Educators of Colorado, 1015 South Gaylord Street, #226, Denver, CO 80209 (303) 777-1022

Concerned Parents for Colorado, P.O. Box 62062, Colorado Springs, CO 80902 (719) 598-8444

CONNECTICUT - The Education Association of Christian Homeschoolers, P.O. Box 91, Bloomfield, CT 06002 (203) 234-3830

Connecticut Home Education Association, 63 Spindrift Lane, Gulford, CT 06437 (203) 457-1642

DELAWARE - Delaware Home Education Association, 2272 St. James Drive, Wilmington, DE 19808 (302) 998-6194

Tri-State Home School Network, P.O. Box 7193, Newark, DE 19714 (302) 368-4217

FLORIDA - Florida at Home, 7615 Clubhouse Estates Drive, Orlando, FL 32819 (407) 740-8877

Christian Home Education News, 11801-5A 28th Street North, St. Petersburg, FL 33716 (813) 572-4579

GEORGIA - Georgia Home Education Association, P.O. Box 88775, Dunwoody, GA 30356 (404) 461-3657

North Georgia Home Education Association, 200 West Crest Road, Rossville, GA 30741 (404) 861-1795

Georgia for Freedom in Education, 209 Cobb Street, Palmetto, GA 30268 (404) 463-3719

HAWAII - Christian Homeschoolers of Hawaii, 91-824 Oama Street, Ewa Beach, HI 96706 (808) 689-6398

IDAHO - Idaho Home Educators, Box 4022, Boise, ID 83711

ILLINOIS - Illinois Christian Home Educators, Box 261, Zion, IL 60099 (708) 662-1909

Christian Home Educators Coalition, P.O. Box 470322, Chicago, IL 60647 (312) 278-0673

INDIANA - Indiana Association of Home Educators, Box 17135, Indianapolis, IN 46217 (317) 865-3013

IOWA - Network of Iowa Christian Home Educators, Box 158, Dexter, IA 50070

Iowa Home Educators Association, Box 213, Des Moines, IA 50301 (319) 323-3735

KANSAS - Christian Home Education Confederation of Kansas, P.O. Box 3564, Shawnee Mission, KS 66203 (316) 945-0810

KENTUCKY - Christian Home Educators of Kentucky, 691 Howardstown Road, Hodgensville, KY 42748 (502) 358-9270

Kentucky Home Education Association, P.O. Box 81, Winchester, KY 40392-0081

LOUISIANA - Christian Home Educators Fellowship, P.O. Box 14421, Baton Rouge, LA 70898 (504) 642-2059

MAINE - Homeschoolers of Maine, P.O. Box 124, Hope, ME 04847 (207) 763-4251

MARYLAND - Maryland Association of Christian Home Education, Box 1041, Emmitsburg, MD 21727 (301) 662-0022

Christian Home Educators Network, 304 North Beechwood Avenue, Catonsville, MD 21228

MASSACHUSETTS - Massachusetts Home Schooler's Organization of Parent Educators, 15 Ohio Street, Wilmington, MA 01887 (508) 658-8970

MICHIGAN - Information Network for Christian Homes, 4150 Ambrose N. E., Grand Rapids, MI 49505 (616) 364-4438

MINNESOTA - Minnesota Association of Christian Home Educators, P.O. Box 188, Anoka, MN 55303 (612) 753-2370

MISSISSIPPI - Mississippi Home Educators Association, P.O. Box 177, Meadville, MS 39653 (601) 384-3042

Home Educators of Central Mississippi, 109 West Willow Court, Ridgeland, MS 39157 (601) 856-2176

MISSOURI - Families for Home Education, 4400 Woods Road, Sibley, MO 64088 (816) 826-9302

MONTANA - Montana Coalition of Home Schools, P.O. Box 654, Helena, MT 59624 (406) 443-5826

NEBRASKA - Nebraska Home Education Association, P.O. Box 57041, Lincoln, NE 68505-7041 (402) 423-4297

NEVADA - Christian Home Educators of Nevada, 1001 Sagerock Way, N. Las Vegas, NV 89031-1402 (702) 593-7661

Nevada Home Schools, P.O. Box 21323, Reno, NV 89515 (702) 323-0566

Silver-State Education Association, P.O. Box 5479, Sparks, NV 89432

NEW HAMPSHIRE - Christian Home Educators of New Hampshire, P.O. Box 961, Manchester, NH 03105 (603) 432-9510

Parents for Unalienable Rights in Education, 9 Blueberry Lane, Nashua, NH 03062 (603) 881-8323

NEW JERSEY - Education Network of Christian Homeschoolers, 65 Middlesex Road, Matawan, NJ 07747 (908) 583-7128

NEW MEXICO - New Mexico Christian Home Educators, 5749 Paradise Blvd., N.W., Albuquerque, NM 87114 (505) 897-1772

New Mexico Family Educators, P.O. Box 92276, Albuquerque, NM 87199-2276

NEW YORK - Loving Education At Home, Box 12846, Albany, NY 12212-2846, (518) 377-6019

NORTH CAROLINA - North Carolinians for Home Education, 204 North Person Street, Raleigh, NC 27601 (919) 834-6243

NORTH DAKOTA - North Dakota Home School Association, P.O. Box 486, Mandan, ND 58554 (701) 663-2868

OHIO - Christian Home Educators of Ohio, P.O. Box 262, Columbus, OH 43216 (800) 274-CHEO

Home Education Action Council of Ohio, P.O. Box 24133, Huber Heights, OH 45424 (513) 845-8428

OKLAHOMA - Christian Home Educators Fellowship of Oklahoma, P.O. Box 471363 Tulsa, OK 74147-1363 (918) 583-7323

Oklahoma Central Home Educators, P.O. Box 270601, Oklahoma City, OK 73137

OREGON - Oregon Christian Home Education Association Network, 2515 N.E. 37th, Portland, OR 97212 (503) 288-1285

PENNSYLVANIA - Christian Homeschool Association of Pennsylvania, 1464 Old Line Road, Manheim, PA 17545 (717) 665-7091

Pennsylvania Home Educators Association, R.D. 2 Box 117, Kittaning, PA 16201-9311, (412) 783-6512

Lancaster County Home Education Association, 2200 Huber Drive, Manheim, PA 17545-9130

RHODE ISLAND - Rhode Island Guild of Home Teachers, 272 Pequot Avenue, Warwick, RI 02886 (401) 737-2265

SOUTH CAROLINA - South Carolina Home Educators Association, P.O. Box 612, Lexington, SC 29071-0612 (803) 356-0798

South Carolina Association of Independent Home Schools, P.O. Box 2104, Irmo, SC 29063-2104, (803) 732-8680

SOUTH DAKOTA - Western Dakota Christian Home Schools, Box 528, Black Hawk, SD 57718 (605) 787-4153

TENNESSEE - Tennessee Home Education Association, 3677 Richbriar Court, Nashville, TN 37211 (615) 834-3529

TEXAS - Home-Oriented Private Education for Texas, P.O. Box 17755, Austin, TX 78760-7755 (512) 280-4673

Texas Home School Coalition, P.O. Box 6982, Lubbock, TX 79493 (806) 797-4927

Family Educators Alliance of South Texas, 8122 Data Point Dr., Suite 210, San Antonio, TX 78299 (512) 692-7214

South East Texas Home School Association, 4950 S.M. 1960 W., Suite C-387, Houston, TX 77069 (713) 370-8787

UTAH - Utah Christian Home Schoolers, P.O. Box 3942, Salt Lake City, UT 84110 (801) 394-4156

VERMONT - Vermont Home Schoolers Association, P.O. Box 161, Pittsford, VT 05763 (802) 483-6296

VIRGINIA - Home Educators Association of Virginia, P.O. Box 1810, Front Royal, VA 22630 (703) 635-9322

WASHINGTON - Washington Association of Teaching Christian
    Homes, P.O. Box 980, Airway Heights, WA 99001
    (509) 299-3766

WASHINGTON, D.C. - Bolling Area Home Schoolers of D.C.,
    1516 E Carswell Circle, Bolling AFB, D.C. 20336
    (202) 563-6210

WEST VIRGINIA - Christian Home Educators of West Virginia,
    P.O. Box 8770, South Charleston, WV 25303
    (304) 776-4664

WISCONSIN - Wisconsin Christian Home Educators, 2307 Carmel
    Avenue, Racine, WI 53405 (414) 637-5127

WYOMING - Homeschoolers of Wyoming, P.O. Box 926,
    Evansville, WY 82636 (307) 745-3536

FOREIGN HOME SCHOOL ORGANIZATIONS

ENGLAND - Education Otherwise, 36 Kinross Road, Leamington
    SPA, Warks, England, CV32 7EF Tel. 0926 886828

CANADA - Alberta Home Education Association, Box 3451, Leduc,
    Alberta, T9E 6M2, (403) 986-4264

   Round-Up (newsletter), R.R. 6, Calgary, Alberta, T2M 4L5
    (403) 285-9855

MILITARY HOME SCHOOL ORGANIZATIONS

   On the Move (newsletter), 1435 N.W. 9 Court, Homestead, FL
    33030

   The Military Homeschooler (newsletter), Paul Rodgers, 849
    Leehigh Drive, Merced, CA 95348

   Christian Home Educators on Foreign Soil (CHEFS), Jan Inman,
    HHB V Corps Arty, Unite 25212, APO AE 09079

   European edition of *The Military Homeschooler* (newsletter), Dan
    Smith, HHC 160th Sig Bde, A.P.O., NY 09164

NATIONAL ORGANIZATIONS

General Mail Order of Home School Curriculum & Resources
Christian Life Workshops, P.O. Box 2250, Gresham, OR 97030
• Phone 1-800-225-5259 • FAX (503)-665-6637

CLW offers *Our Family Favorites* Magazine/Catalog free of charge. All purchases carry a full 30 day money-back guarantee of satisfaction. Phone or FAX orders may be made with VISA or Master Card.

Handicapped Resources
National Handicapped Home School Associated Network,
5383 Alpine Rd. S. E., Olalla, WA 98359 (206) 857-4257

Legal Defense
Home School Legal Defense Association, P.O. Box 159, Paeonian Springs, VA 22129
• Phone (703) 338-5600

Home School Research
The National Home Education Research Institute, Dr. Brian Ray, c/o Western Baptist College, 500 Deer Park Drive, S.E. Salem, OR 97301-9392
• Phone 503-581-8600

The National Center for Home Education, P.O. Box 125, Paeonian Springs, VA 22129
• Phone (703) 338-7600

Magazines
The Teaching Home Magazine, P.O. Box 20219, Portland, OR 97220-0219
• Phone 503-253-9633 • FAX 503-253-7345

H.E.L.P. Magazine, Mary & Bill Pride, Home Life, P.O. Box 1250, Fenton, MO 63026
• Phone (FAX Only) 314-225-0743

Nature Friend Magazine, 22777 State Road, 119, Goshen, IN 46526
• Phone 219-534-2245

World Magazine, God's World Publications, P.O. Box 2330, Asheville, NC 28802
• Phone 800-951-5437

CURRICULUM PUBLISHERS

The following curriculum publishers have proven to be a valuable part of the home schooling movement throughout the U.S. and Canada. Our recommendation does not necessarrily imply that we endorse all of their various materials.

A Beka Books, Pensacola, FL 32523-1960
 • Phone 800-874-BEKA

ACE School of Tomorrow, P.O. Box 14380, Lewisville, TX 75067-1438
 • Phone 214-315-1776

Alpha Omega Publications, P.O. Box 3153, Tempe, AZ 85280
 • Phone 800-821-4443,

Bob Jones University Press, Greenville, SC 29614
 • Phone 803-242-5100

Christian Liberty Academy, 502 W. Euclid Avenue, Arlington Heights, IL 60004
 • Phone 708-259-8736

Christian Light Education, H.C. 01, Box 26, Kingston, ID 83839
 • Phone 208-682-4363

KONOS, P.O. Box 1534, Richardson, TX 75083
 • Phone 214-669-8337

Master Books (Creation Science Materials), P.O. Box 1606, El Cajon, CA 92022
 • Phone 800-999-3777

Mortensen Math, P.O. Box 98, Hayden, ID 83835-0098
 • Phone 208-667-1580

Rod and Staff Publishers, Hwy. 172, Crockett, KY 41413
 • Phone 606-522-4348,

Weaver Curriculum Series, 2752 Scarborough, Riverside, CA 92503
 • Phone 714-688-3126

APPENDIX D

FIFTEEN REASONS TO HOME SCHOOL DURING THE TEEN YEARS

1. You get to see the completion of your efforts. Something is lost when you turn over your home discipling to others.

2. You can customize your children's education to provide motivation for their gifts and abilities. No one else will be able to provide the consistent and loving support that you can in weak areas.

3. You can direct them to early college entrance. Even public high schools realize many students are ready for college level courses and have cooperating programs with junior colleges.

4. You can continue the family building process. The teen years continue to be impressionable and formative. This is an invaluable time to cement family relationships.

5. You can be sure that your teens are learning, if they are at home. Studies have revealed that public high school students average 2 hours and 13 minutes of academic work a day.

6. You can continue to have influence over their peer relationships. Teen rebellion is not in God's plan for the family, but it is the humanist agenda for the public schools.

7. You can protect them from pressure to conform to what the other kids are doing. This pressure is so strong in the public high school. You won't need to spend time de-programming.

8. If you send your teens to high school, there will be a diversion away from the academic focus, as well as spiritual priorities. Be aware of the many distractions that won't parallel the home life you have maintained.

9. Your young people will be thrown into things like boy/girl preoccupation, focus on clothes, and pressure to conform in appearance and music.

10. Vast amounts of time separated from the family will affect their relationship with you. We have all put great amounts of our heart and time into our home-schooling years, and we want those efforts preserved.

11.   Home school is the best preparation for college studies. The home education "style" is closer to college-type instruction.

12.   There is greater flexibility for work/study opportunities.

13.   The institutional method of public education is designed around "crowd control," not learning. If and when they learn, it will be a by-product of other priorities to maintain class room order.

14.   Home educators have the best available curriculum and greater selection. Public schools offer revisionist history and science that promotes their humanist perspective. The godly commitment of many great Americans has been deleted from public text books.

15.   Age/grade isolation or segregation inhibits socialization. Public school children are behind their home school counterparts in maturity, socialization, and vocabulary development, as demonstrated by available research.

Compiled by Elizabeth Smith, 1992 Home School Legal Defense Association, reprinted by permission.

AUTHOR INFORMATION

Christopher J. Klicka is Senior Counsel of the Home School Legal Defense Association (HSLDA), a nonprofit legal organization dedicated to protecting the rights of parents to home school in all fifty states, the U.S. territories, and Canada. HSLDA is based near Washington, D.C., in Paeonian Springs, Virginia and has twenty-eight thousand member families as of December 1992.

Klicka earned his BA from Grove City College in Grove City, Pennsylvania, and his Juris Doctorate from O.W. Coburn School of Law, Tulsa, Oklahoma (renamed School of Law, Regent University and relocated to Virginia Beach, Virginia).

Since 1985, he has worked at HSLDA handling scores of court cases and administrative appeals on behalf of home school families throughout the country. He has argued before four state supreme courts and argued before or submitted briefs to appellate courts in Michigan, Alabama, Maine, Colorado, Virginia, Massachusetts, Pennsylvania, and North Dakota on behalf of home schoolers.

Also for the last eight years, he has successfully represented over two thousand home school families with legal conflicts requiring him to deal with thousands of public school officials, truant officers, school board members, social workers, prosecutors, and police officers.

He has provided expert testimony before numerous legislatures (including South Dakota, Virginia, Maine, Pennsylvania, Alabama, North Dakota, South Carolina, Maryland, and Colorado) and state boards of education (including Maryland, Iowa, and Maine) on behalf of home schoolers.

He is a member of the bars of the Virginia Supreme Court, the United States Supreme Court, the Fourth Circuit Court of Appeals, and the U.S. District Court of Virginia (Eastern Division).

He has spoken at over one hundred home school conferences throughout the country and has been interviewed by hundreds of newspapers including the *Washington Times, Chicago Tribune, Washington Post, Insight,* and *USA Today* where he was featured as a guest editorial "Face Off." He has been interviewed on many radio shows on the legal and academic aspects of home schooling including "Family News In Focus," Marlin Maddoux's "Point of View," and James Kennedy's "Truths That Transform."

Mr. Klicka is the author of *Home Schooling in the United States: A Legal Analysis* published by HSLDA and updated each year since 1985. It describes in detail the legal atmosphere of home schooling in each state. He also authored *The Case For Home Schooling* and has published articles in the *Religion and Public Education* journal and in the *Ohio Northern Law Review*.

He is married to Tracy and has three children, Bethany, Megan, and Jesse who are being home schooled.

Gregg Harris is a home-schooling father of four sons and one daughter, instructor for *The Home Schooling Workshop*, and author of, *The Christian Home School*. Gregg is also Director of *Christian Life Workshops* and Chairman of the Board for the *National Home Education Research Institute*. He serves as a member of the Governor's Advisory Committee on Private Education in Oregon. He and his wife, Sono, reside in Gresham, Oregon.

CASE INDEX

NAME INDEX